MW01103384

Family
and
Peers

FAMILY
AND
PEERS

Linking Two Social Worlds

Edited by
Kathryn A. Kerns, Josefina M. Contreras,
and Angela M. Neal-Barnett

Praeger Series in Applied Psychology
Stevan E. Hobfoll, Series Adviser

Westport, Connecticut
London

Library of Congress Cataloging-in-Publication Data

Family and peers : linking two social worlds / edited by Kathryn A.
   Kerns, Josefina M. Contreras, and Angela M. Neal-Barnett.
        p.   cm.—(Praeger series in applied psychology)
     Includes bibliographical references and index.
     ISBN 0–275–96506–6 (alk. paper)
     1. Parent and child.   2. Child rearing.   3. Interpersonal
   relations in children.   4. Interpersonal relations in adolescence.
   5. Social interaction in children.   6. Social interaction in
   adolescence.   I. Kerns, Kathryn A., 1961–   . II. Contreras,
   Josefina M., 1960–   . III. Neal-Barnett, Angela M., 1960–
   IV. Series.
   HQ755.85.F365   2000
   306.874—dc21   99–16059

British Library Cataloguing in Publication Data is available.

Library of Congress Catalog Card Number: 99–16059
ISBN: 0–275–96506–6

First published in 2000

Praeger Publishers, 88 Post Road West, Westport, CT 06881
An imprint of Greenwood Publishing Group, Inc.
www.praeger.com

Printed in the United States of America

The paper used in this book complies with the
Permanent Paper Standard issued by the National
Information Standards Organization (Z39.48–1984).

10 9 8 7 6 5 4 3 2

Contents

Introduction   vii
Kathryn A. Kerns, Jeffery E. Aspelmeier, and Patricia L. Tomich

1. Emotion Regulation Processes: Explaining Links between
   Parent-Child Attachment and Peer Relationships   1
   Josefina M. Contreras and Kathryn A. Kerns

2. The Ecology of Premature Autonomy in Adolescence:
   Biological and Social Influences   27
   Thomas J. Dishion, François Poulin, and Nani Medici Skaggs

3. Russian Parenting Styles and Family Processes: Linkages with
   Subtypes of Victimization and Aggression   47
   Craig H. Hart, David A. Nelson, Clyde C. Robinson,
   Susanne F. Olsen, Mary Kay McNeilly-Choque,
   Christin L. Porter, and Trevor R. McKee

4. Links between Adult and Peer Relations across Four
   Developmental Periods   85
   Carollee Howes and Holli Tonyan

5. Living in a Hostile World: Toward an Integrated Model of
   Family, Peer, and Physiological Processes in Aggressive
   Preschoolers   115
   Lynn Fainsilber Katz

6. Explaining the Link between Parenting Behavior and
   Children's Peer Competence: A Critical Examination of the
   "Mediating-Process" Hypothesis   137
   Jacquelyn Mize, Gregory S. Pettit, and Darrell Meece

7. Parental Management of Adolescent Peer Relationships:
   What Are Its Effects on Friend Selection?   169
   Nina S. Mounts

8. Family-Peer Relationships: The Role of Emotion Regulation,
   Cognitive Understanding, and Attentional Processes as
   Mediating Processes   195
   Robin O'Neil and Ross D. Parke

9. Intimacy in Preadolescence and Adolescence: Issues in
   Linking Parents and Peers, Theory, Culture, and Findings   227
   Ruth Sharabany

10. Family and Peer Relationships and the Real-World
    Practitioner: A Commentary   251
    Angela M. Neal-Barnett

Index   257

About the Editors and Contributors   263

Introduction

*Kathryn A. Kerns, Jeffery E. Aspelmeier, and
Patricia L. Tomich*

This volume is designed to advance the understanding of the connections between two of the social worlds of childhood: the family and the peer domain. As Baumrind (1967; 1973) first showed in the late 1960s, there are predictable linkages between parent-child interaction and how children relate to peers. The contributors to this volume confirm and extend evidence for family and peer linkages in a number of important ways. For example, the chapters illustrate that parent childrearing practices, the quality of the parent-child relationship, and the functioning of the marital dyad are all associated with the quality of children's peer relationships. At this point, there can be no doubt that connections between the family and peers exist.

Despite evidence of these linkages, much less progress has been made on the question of why there is predictability in children's functioning across the two social contexts of family and peers. After finding family-peer links, researchers often suggest but only rarely test specific mechanisms that may account for these effects. Identifying the mechanisms accounting for the linkages is necessary for both development of theories of social development as well as interventions designed to improve children's interpersonal relationships. One of the key contributions of this volume is that almost all of the contributors to it explore the question of mediating mechanisms.

Several of the contributors take this question as the focus of their chapters (Contreras & Kerns, Chapter 1; Dishion, Poulin, & Skaggs, Chapter 2; Katz, Chapter 5; Mize, Pettit, & Meece, Chapter 6; and O'Neil & Parke, Chapter 8). Mize et al. review published evidence testing the mediation hypothesis. Their review examines a number of potential mediators (e.g., information-processing mechanisms, emotion regulation). They draw the provocative and challenging conclusion that there is currently relatively little evidence for mediation in the literature. They also provide an analysis of the factors that may affect the conditions under which evidence of mediation will be found.

In the other chapters that explicitly examine mediation, a common theme is that a child's emotion regulation capacities may account for relationship continuities. Both Chapters 1 and 8 present models and evidence suggesting that children develop emotion regulation skills within parent-child relationships that can account for variation in children's competence with peers. In her chapter, Katz extends this analysis by considering how parents' own beliefs about emotion socialization both are affected by the marital relationship and in turn influence children's emotion regulation capacities. All of the chapters consider learning mechanisms that might account for family-peer linkages. Chapters 2 and 5 consider biological mechanisms as well.

Contributors also were asked to address developmental and cultural issues when relevant to their work. These two areas were chosen because of their relative neglect in the literature. Developmental issues receive comment in almost all of the chapters. They are particularly prominent in the three chapters reporting data from longitudinal studies of family and peer relationships (Dishion et al., Chapter 2; Howes & Tonyan, Chapter 4; and O'Neil & Parke, Chapter 8). The longitudinal approach allows these contributors to understand how family and peer relationships play out across time. For example, Dishion et al. ask how family relationships serve as a setting condition that may promote premature autonomy and identification with the peer group.

Chapter 4 is unique in exploring peer, teacher-child, and parent-child relationships as antecedents to current peer functioning. This chapter also raises two important issues. First, adults outside the family, in this case teachers, are important figures who can have an impact on children's peer relationships. Additionally, Howes and Tonyan note that there is substantial continuity within relationship domains (i.e., within family, peer, and teacher-child relationships). This within domain continuity is important because it suggests that peer relationships are influenced not only by family relationships but by prior peer relationships, a point that is often overlooked.

One other way in which developmental issues are considered is by focusing on the unique developmental challenges that arise in particular developmental periods. Howes and Tonyan argue that the importance of teacher-child relationships and children's friendships change across development. Three chapters address issues unique to adolescence. In Chapter 7, Mounts highlights the fact that parents need to adapt their efforts to influence peer relationships to take account of adolescents' desire for greater independence. Dishion et al. (Chapter 2) identify how changes in physical maturation around puberty alter the nature of peer relationships in adolescence. O'Neil and Parke (Chapter 8) also discuss how puberty and entrance into adolescence may alter parent-child relationships and linkages between parent-child and peer relationships.

Cultural issues receive some comment from most contributors but are an explicit focus in the two chapters that examine family and peers in non-U.S. cultures. In Chapter 3, Hart et al. studied families in Russia. Despite some differences between Russian and Western cultures, Hart et al. find that many of the findings on linkages between family and peers replicate in this particular culture. Sharabany (Chapter 9) studied several samples in Israel. By recruiting different types of samples (e.g., children raised on a kibbutz versus family-reared), she was able to examine how the ecological context may change the degree to which there is continuity in the intimacy of parent-child and peer relationships. Sharabany also compares her findings with U.S. results, and she points to cultural factors that may explain the different pattern of results found in the two countries.

In addressing these three broad themes (i.e., mechanisms, developmental issues, culture), contributors have used a variety of theoretical approaches to describe variations in both parent–child and peer relationships. On the family side, several chapters (1, 4, 8, and 9) focus on the quality of parent–child relationships, using an attachment or relationship perspective. Other chapters (2, 3, 5, and 7) focus on general or specific parenting practices. On the peer side, there is also breadth in the areas considered. Attention is given to friendship (Chapters 4, 7, and 9), competent or aggressive behavior patterns (Chapters 1, 3, 4, and 8), and peer group processes (Chapter 2).

The final chapter, a commentary by Neal-Barnett, raises questions regarding how the findings can benefit practitioners. Those doing basic research often do not make clear the public policy and clinical implications of their findings. Neal-Barnett's chapter provides a reminder that the concerns of the ultimate consumers of research are often quite different from the concerns of researchers.

What is missing from this volume? Only some family members are studied. Fathers as well as mothers are represented in several chapters. Nevertheless, only Katz and Hart et al. consider the marital dyad as well as the parent-child dyad. Close-age relatives, including siblings and cousins, also may play a special role in socializing skills and attitudes that affect a child's interactions with peers. Although there are a few studies on siblings and peer relationships (see Dunn, 1993), to our knowledge connections between cousins and other extended family and children's peer relationships have been ignored in the literature.

Family-peer research could also benefit from having investigators in the area reach agreement on the use of terms and from specifying more precisely how seemingly related concepts differ. Researchers may believe they are studying different concepts, and refer to them with different terms, but are they investigating different concepts? For example, are working models the same as social–information-processing styles? If they are not, how do the two constructs overlap? Similarly, the field could benefit by reaching agreement on terms used to describe degrees of mediation, such as full, partial, direct, or indirect mediation. Consistency in use of terms would facilitate integration of findings in this area.

One area in particular could benefit from a refinement in definition, which may also lead to subsequent refinements in methodology. As noted by Mize et al. (Chapter 6), there are several studies of cognitive processing mechanisms in the literature that make use of the concept of mental representations. Most investigations of mental representations have focused on self-reports, projective measures, and analyses of discourse to infer the content and organization of mental representations. Recently, researchers have begun to direct attention toward identifying the information-processing consequences of mental representations of relationships (Baldwin, 1992; Crick & Dodge, 1994). This work suggests several methods that could assess the outputs of information processing more directly. For example, some researchers have employed psychophysical tasks borrowed from cognitive and social cognitive psychology and found that representations of attachment may guide attention and influence memory for relationship information (Baldwin, Fehr, Keedian, Seidel, & Thomson, 1993; Kirsh & Cassidy, 1997). Thus, it would seem that family-peer research could benefit from incorporating an array of methods to analyze the role cognitive mechanisms play in accounting for family-peer linkages.

NOTE

This book is published in connection with the Tenth Kent State Psychology Forum. The Kent Forum is an annual think tank sponsored by the Applied Psychology Center of Kent State's Psychology Department. The goal of the forum is to bring together researchers investigating a topic in psychology that has clear applied implications. The 10th forum was devoted to explaining the linkages between family and peer relationships. The 13 invited scholars met in April 1998 to present their findings and discuss new directions in this area. The support of the Applied Psychology Center, for the conference and this volume, is gratefully acknowledged.

REFERENCES

Baldwin, M. W. (1992). Relational schemas and the processing of social information. *Psychological Bulletin, 112*(3), 461–684.
Baldwin, M. W., Fehr, B., Keedian, E., Seidel, M., & Thomson, D. W. (1993). An exploration of the relational schema underlying attachment styles: Self-report and lexical decision approaches. *Personality and Social Psychology Bulletin, 19*(6), 746–754.
Baumrind, D. (1967). Child care practices anteceding three patterns of preschool behavior. *Genetic Psychology Monographs, 4* (no. 1, part 2).
Baumrind, D. (1973). The development of instrumental competence through social-

ization. In A. D. Pick (Ed.), *Minnesota symposia on child psychology* (Vol. 7, pp. 3–46). Minneapolis: University of Minnesota Press.

Crick, N. R., & Dodge, K. A. (1994). A review and reformulation of social information–processing mechanisms in children's social adjustment. *Psychological Bulletin, 115*(1) 74–101.

Dunn, J. (1993). *Young children's close relationships*. Newbury Park, CA: Sage.

Kirsh, S. J., & Cassidy, J. (1997). Preschoolers' attention to and memory for attachment-relevant information. *Child Development, 68*(6), 1143–1153.

1

Emotion Regulation Processes: Explaining Links between Parent-Child Attachment and Peer Relationships

Josefina M. Contreras and Kathryn A. Kerns

Why is it that children who form secure attachments to mothers or fathers have less difficulty forming relationships and behaving competently with peers? Although numerous studies have documented a link between parent-child attachment and the quality of peer relationships, the mechanisms that account for this association have rarely been tested. The goal of this chapter is to argue that emotion regulation, or the processes by which children monitor, evaluate, and modify emotional reactions in order to accomplish social goals (Thompson, 1994), is one of the important mechanisms. Children develop emotion regulation styles largely within parent-child relationships. These modes of dealing with emotions in interpersonal relationships are thought to generalize to other interpersonal contexts, such as relationships with peers, and therefore influence the quality of children's relationships outside the family. Thus, we propose that emotion regulation processes are one of the causal links explaining the observed associations between parent-child relationships and children's social functioning in the peer context. In this chapter, we first review the literature linking parent-child attachment and peer relationships. We then provide the conceptual bases and empirical evidence for conceptualizing emotion regulation as a mediator of these links. Finally, we present findings from an empirical study that tests the proposed model.

PARENT-CHILD ATTACHMENT AND SOCIAL
BEHAVIOR WITH PEERS

Bowlby (1973; 1982) proposed attachment theory to explain both the normative event of child to parent bonding and individual differences in the quality of child-parent bonds. According to Bowlby, all children form attachments to primary caregivers, with variations in the quality of attachment bonds due primarily to differences in caregivers' behavior. In particular, Bowlby (1982) highlighted the need for caregivers to be responsive to a child's signals and to be available and accessible to the child when needed. Sensitive and responsive caregiving is thought to contribute to a child forming a secure attachment relationship with the parent, and available data confirm the maternal sensitivity hypothesis (De Wolff & van Ijzendoorn, 1997). In a secure relationship, a parent comes to serve as a safe haven for his or her child, meaning that a parent provides comfort and acceptance when a child is distressed; the parent also functions as a secure base, supporting the child's bids for exploration (Bowlby, 1973; 1982). Quality of care, and to a lesser extent child temperament, also affect how insecure attachments are manifested. Children who experience rejection from caregivers are thought to form avoidant attachment relationships in which they minimize contact with the attachment figure, especially when distressed (Cassidy, 1994). Children who experience parenting that is inconsistent or interfering are thought to form resistant or ambivalent relationships in which they are chronically uncertain about the availability of the attachment figure (Cassidy, 1994; Cassidy & Berlin, 1994). A difficult temperament may predispose a child to form ambivalent rather than avoidant relationships (Belsky & Rovine, 1987; Goldsmith & Harman, 1994).

Children in secure attachment relationships are confident in the responsiveness, availability, and trustworthiness of their attachment figures (Bowlby, 1973; 1982). In older children, open communication around emotionally laden content is a hallmark of secure attachment (Bowlby, 1987, cited in Ainsworth, 1990; Bretherton, 1987). Children are thought to internalize the affect and behavior patterns learned within attachment relationships and to recreate these patterns with others. Therefore, the quality of attachments to parents has implications for the nature of a child's interactions and relationships with people outside the family (Bowlby, 1973; Sroufe & Fleeson, 1986). For example, a child who has been rejected by his or her parents may subsequently behave in a rejecting and hostile manner to peers, and may also expect other children to behave in a rejecting or hostile way toward him or her. The implication of this perspective, discussed in more detail later, is that cognitive models of relationships and affect-regulation skills mediate the link between parent-child attachment and behavior with peers.

It should be noted that most studies testing attachment-peer links examine mother-child and not father-child relationships. Although children have attachment relationships with multiple caregivers, they are arranged in a hierarchy, with the relationship with the primary caregiver at the top (Bowlby, 1982). In U.S. culture, mothers usually serve the role of primary caregiver. This has led some researchers to argue that mother-child attachment may have a greater impact than father-child attachment on children's competence (e.g., Suess, Grossman, & Sroufe, 1992).

Because there is a large literature on mother-child attachment and peer relationships, our discussion emphasizes reviews of the literature and recent studies. Some work suggests that attachment security in mother-child relationships is related to traitlike patterns of behavior around peers such as tendencies to be aggressive or sociable (Belsky & Cassidy, 1994; Lamb & Nash, 1989; Lyons-Ruth, 1996), although these effects are not always evident in low-risk samples (Lyons-Ruth, 1996). Additionally, effects are sometimes stronger for boys than for girls (e.g., Renken, Egeland, Marvinney, Mangelsdorf, & Sroufe, 1989). A second set of studies indicates that children securely attached to their mothers are more socially competent and popular with peers. For example, Kerns, Klepac, and Cole (1996) found that fifth- and sixth-grade securely attached children were better liked by classmates, and Sroufe, Carlson, and Shulman (1993) found that 10- to 11-year-old securely attached children were rated as more competent with peers by teachers at school and by counselors at a summer camp. Associations between attachment and peer competence have also been shown with younger children (e.g., Sroufe et al., 1993).

A third way of testing the hypothesis is to examine links between mother-child attachment and friendship. Attachment theory is a theory of relationships, and attachment might therefore have the strongest implications for the quality of close relationships (i.e., friendships) children form with peers (Belsky & Cassidy, 1994; Park & Waters, 1989). Several studies demonstrate a link between attachment and friendship (Kerns, 1996). For example, in both early and middle childhood friend pairs with both children securely attached to their mothers are more responsive than pairs containing one securely and one insecurely attached child (Kerns et al., 1996; Park & Waters, 1989).

Four studies have assessed both mother-child and father-child attachment and their links to peer relationships, and provide a test of the hypothesis for the central role of mother-child attachments. Results from these studies have not consistently supported the hypothesis. One study (Freitag, Belsky, Grossmann, Grossman, & Schuerer-Englisch, 1996) found that friendship competence at age 10 was related to earlier mother-child attachment but not father-child attachment. Youngblade, Park, and Belsky (1993) found the opposite pattern with 5-year-olds, in that earlier secure attachment to fathers, but not secure attachment to mothers, was linked with positive interactions with friends. Kerns and Barth (1995) found some effects for mother-child and father-child attachment in a sample of preschoolers; secure attachment to mothers was linked to peer popularity for boys, whereas secure attachment to fathers was linked with children's cooperative and friendly behavior with peers. Finally, Suess et al. (1992) found that early attachments to both mothers and fathers were related to behavior around peers in preschool, with effects being stronger for mothers.

In summary, although not every study has found effects, for the most part mother-child and father-child attachment have been related to several aspects of peer relationships. Evidence is available for both early and middle childhood, and from studies examining both concurrent and longitudinal links between attachment and peer relationships. Thus, at this point there is no great need for additional studies to document an association between attachment and peer relationships in childhood. Instead, what is needed are studies that will explain these associations.

EMOTION REGULATION AS A MEDIATOR OF ATTACHMENT-PEER RELATIONSHIPS LINKS

Despite the large literature showing attachment and peer relationship associations, there is less attention to mechanisms that may account for these effects. Most commonly, researchers argue for the concept of working models as the mechanism. Working models are relationship rules (Main, Kaplan, & Cassidy, 1985) or schemas (Baldwin, 1992; Bretherton, 1987) that are based on past experiences in attachment relationships, and that guide the processing of information in social interaction and in relationships. They influence how individuals interpret others' actions as well as guiding their own actions. Because working models operate largely outside conscious awareness they are difficult to revise.

Three studies have tested the hypothesis that beliefs and expectations about self and others mediate the link between attachment and peer relationships. Cassidy, Kirsch, Scolton, and Parke (1996) found that attachment was linked with peer representations (e.g., feelings with peers, attributions of intent), which were in turn linked to measures of friendship. There was some evidence that peer representations were serving as a mediator between attachment and friendship. Tomich (1998) found that mother-child attachment was related to fourth graders' working models of self and others, which in turn were related to children's behavior with peers. Mother-child attachment was not, however, related to peer relationships. Father-child attachment was related to peer competence, but effects were not mediated by working models of self or others. Sroufe et al. (1993) found that links between infant attachment and peer competence in middle childhood were mediated by children's working models of self and of relationships. Thus, there is some evidence that working models are one of the mechanisms explaining associations between parent-child attachment and peer relationships.

In this chapter, we argue for the importance of emotion regulation processes in explaining associations between attachment and peer relationships. Emotion regulation is a critical component of attachment in that children who are securely attached are able to use the parent effectively to help them regulate their emotions (Bowlby, 1982; Sroufe & Waters, 1977). Moreover, assessment of attachment organization in the strange situation (Ainsworth, Blehar, Waters, & Wall, 1978) has been conceptualized as assessment of regulation (Sroufe, Schork, Motti, Lawroski, & LaFreniere, 1984). Securely attached children will seek out the parent when upset or scared, thereby using the parent as a safe haven. When securely attached children's fears and concerns are successfully addressed, they will use the parent as a secure base from which to explore the environment. The patterns of emotion regulation that operate within the parent-child dyad are thought to be internalized by the child, and in turn, displayed in other interpersonal contexts (Cassidy, 1994; Sroufe & Fleeson, 1986). As discussed below, empirical studies also show that emotion regulation is related to the quality of children's interpersonal behaviors with peers. Thus, emotion regulation processes appear to be linked both to parent-child attachment and to peer relationships, and as such, emotion regulation is an excellent candidate for explaining the observed associations between the two. The proposed model specifying links among attachment, processes involved in emotion regulation, and children's social behaviors with peers is presented in Figure 1.1. The conceptual bases and empirical evidence for the proposed links are then examined. We start with a description of emotion regulation processes and examine their links to the other constructs in the model.

EMOTION REGULATION

The importance of emotions, and their regulation, has been widely recognized (Campos, Campos, & Barrett, 1989; Thompson, 1994). However, empirical research on emotion regulation has only recently begun to emerge. Thompson (1994) proposed a definition of *emotion regulation* that captures the components of emotion regulation most researchers consider central. According to Thompson, emotion regulation includes both "extrinsic and intrinsic processes responsible for monitoring, evaluating, and modifying emotional reactions, especially their intensive and temporal features, to accomplish one's goals" (p. 27). This definition is consistent with a functionalist perspective on emotional development in that it highlights the importance of considering the individual's goals for specific emotion-eliciting situations that are meaningful for the individual (Campos, Mumme, Kermoian, & Campos, 1994).

Figure 1.1
Model of Links between Attachment, Emotion, Regulation, and Social Interaction with Peers

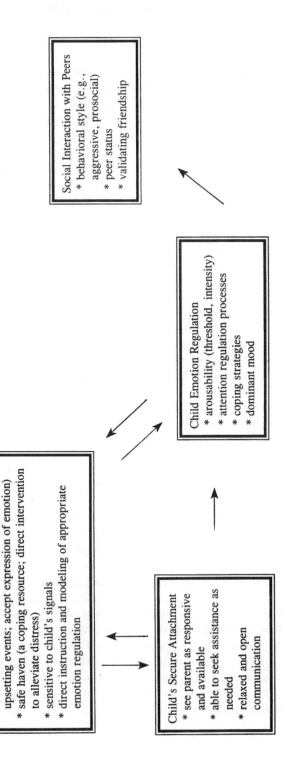

Within Thompson's conceptualization, regulation processes have both dispositional and acquired origins, and refer not only to the control or suppression of the emotional arousal but more generally to the attunement or modulation of the emotional experience. As noted in Figure 1.1, intrinsic processes include child dispositional influences such as emotional arousability and regulatory mechanisms. Emotional arousability refers both to the threshold for the arousal of an emotional response, and the intensity of the emotional response to the evocative stimulation. Neurophysiological regulatory mechanisms, including attentional control processes, are thought to modulate the arousal. Attention management abilities allow the child to regulate the intake of emotionally arousing information (Rothbart, Posner, & Boylan, 1990). Emotional arousal may be elicited or maintained through shifting or focusing attention toward positive stimuli or reduced through shifting attention away from negative stimuli. These two temperamentally based aspects, level of arousability and attentional processes, are interdependent and interact to influence a person's emotional response (Rothbart & Derryberry, 1981). For example, attention shifting and attention focusing have been found to be associated with negative emotions (Rothbart & Derryberry, 1981). Recently, researchers have begun to use physiological indicators to assess emotional regulation (e.g., vagal tone, cortisol levels). Some of this research is described by Katz (Chapter 5, this volume). In this review, we focus only on behavioral and affective indices of emotion regulation processes.

Parental socialization practices are considered to be the primary extrinsic processes influencing the development of emotion regulation. In fact, several researchers have argued that parents begin to mold children's regulatory styles early in infancy and continue throughout childhood (Campos et al., 1989; Casey & Fuller, 1994; Cassidy, 1994; Thompson, 1994). At the same time, there is some evidence that children's temperamental characteristics influence the kinds of strategies parents use to help children regulate their emotional experiences (Casey & Fuller, 1994). Thus, intrinsic and extrinsic processes are thought to influence emotion regulation in a transactional way.

Children's use of strategies to cope with emotion-eliciting events are also a crucial component of emotion regulation (see Figure 1.1). *Coping* has been defined as efforts to manage external and internal demands that are appraised as taxing or exceeding the resources of the individual (Lazarus & Folkman, 1984). Within the emotion regulation literature, this component has been conceptualized as the behavioral outcome of the emotion regulation process, and empirical studies of individual differences have used coping as an index of the adequacy of the emotion regulation process. Mood state can be thought of as the emotional outcome of emotion regulation processes. Consequently, traitlike measures of mood (e.g., negative affectivity) can also be used as an index of the adequacy of emotion regulation processes.

In the coping literature, coping strategies vary along four dimensions. Most broadly, coping strategies can be divided into those that are aimed at altering the person-environment situation (problem-focused coping) and those that are primarily aimed at regulating the emotional state elicited by the stressful event (emotion-focused coping) (Folkman & Lazarus, 1980). They can also be grouped according to whether they are undertaken alone by the child or whether they involve the use of others, as in seeking social support. Because younger children have relatively limited internal resources as well as limited access to external resources, they are more likely to rely on seeking support coping than do older children and adults (Maccoby, 1983; Rossman, 1992). Coping strategies can also be grouped into those that are aimed at addressing the situation and those that attempt to avoid it (approach/avoidance) (Endler & Parker, 1990). Although the use of avoidant strategies can diminish distress in the short run, excessive reliance on avoidance coping is assumed to have negative long-term repercussions for the individual's adaptation. Finally, coping can be categorized according to whether strategies are intrapsychic/cognitive or external/situationally focused. Cognitive strategies include reframing, where the meaning of the event is altered, and distraction, where attention is shifted away from the distressing situation. These strategies are used to render a negative emotional experience less distressing, and can be considered adaptive when the individual has limited control over the emotion-eliciting event. Intrapsychic strategies appear to become more common as children make cognitive developmental advances (Band & Weisz, 1988; Compas, Phares, & Ledoux, 1989).

The extent to which specific coping strategies are considered adaptive to some extent depends on both the developmental level of the child (Band & Weisz, 1988) and the level of control the child perceives over the event (Skinner & Wellborn, 1994). Nonetheless, strategies such as problem solving and support seeking can be considered constructive ways of coping, whereas other strategies such as avoidance and venting that address the evoked emotion but not the eliciting event, are thought to be less adaptive. The quality of planning and the type of coping strategy that is used to some degree depends on dispositional aspects of emotion regulation such as the intensity with which emotions are felt (Eisenberg, et al., 1993; Stein & Levine, 1990). At the same time, perceptions of the efficacy of one's coping strategies are also likely to influence the intensity of the emotional arousal, especially in situations eliciting negative emotionality. Thus, the different components of emotion regulation are not independent, but interact to influence both the behavioral and affective outcomes of the emotion regulation process.

EMOTION REGULATION AND SOCIAL BEHAVIOR WITH PEERS

For emotion regulation to be a plausible mechanism linking attachment and peer relationships, it would have to be related to the latter. Emotion regulation skills are crucial for managing the various demands present in interpersonal situations, such as being able to resolve conflicts (Gottman & Mettetal, 1986). The ability to manage demands then influences the extent to which children are able to achieve social goals in a socially appropriate and effective way. Therefore, the ability to regulate emotions should be linked to peer success.

The literature has demonstrated several associations between the two. In this review, a few examples are presented to illustrate the range of findings. For example, emotional competence is related to peer status. J. Hubbard and Coie's (1994) review of the emotional correlates of peer liking revealed that better liked children are better at reading and interpreting others' emotions. Additionally, higher status boys use more constructive coping strategies. By contrast, rejected children are more moody and emotionally negative around peers (J. Hubbard & Coie, 1994).

Emotion regulation is linked also to children's behavior patterns around peers. For example, children who are negative and dependent with peers show a bias in that they tend to erroneously attribute angry feelings to peers (Barth & Bastiani, 1997). Additionally, internalizing behavior problems are linked with wary or fearful temperament, whereas externalizing behavior problems are linked with an overactive and fussy temperament (Rubin, Bukowski, & Parker, 1998). Eisenberg and colleagues (Eisenberg, et al., 1995; Eisenberg, et al., 1997) also demonstrated that measures of emotionality and emotion regulation are related to children's socially appropriate behavior. For example, children high on negative emotionality (i.e., tendency to experience negative emotion states) showed less appropriate social behavior at home and at school. The use of destructive coping (e.g., use of aggression or venting) and difficulty regulating attention are also associated with less competent social behavior. Links between emotion regulation and socially appropriate behavior are sometimes stronger for boys than for girls, especially at younger ages (Eisenberg et al., 1995; Eisenberg et al., 1997). Additionally, effects are also weaker when examined across different sources or contexts.

In summary, there is substantial evidence that traitlike measures of negative emotions and an inability to regulate emotion are related to the quality of children's interactions with peers in early and middle childhood.

ATTACHMENT AND THE SOCIALIZATION OF EMOTION
REGULATION

Although there is agreement among researchers from both the coping and emotion regulation traditions about the importance of parents in the development of coping and emotion regulation, the specific ways in which parents influence their children's emotion regulation have not been well researched (Hardy, Power, & Jaedicke, 1993; Saarni, Mumme, & Campos, 1998). We have grouped parental socialization efforts into four modes of influence. First, parents are thought to directly influence children's emotion regulation through their interventions to alleviate their children's distress or to enhance positive emotional arousal (Lamb & Malkin, 1986; Thompson, 1990). Additionally, parents are likely to play a role in molding children's regulatory styles by providing coping resources to their children. Third, parents also directly instruct their children regarding coping strategies and consequences of specific responses to particular emotionally arousing situations (Dunn & Brown, 1991; Miller, Kliewer, Hepworth, & Sandler, 1994). A fourth mode is the parents' own responses to emotion-eliciting situations that can function as models for their children (Dunn, 1988). Children are thought to internalize their parents' typical emotional reactions and coping strategies and to use these same strategies in their own coping efforts. Through these modes of socialization, parents project whether they are accepting of emotional expression. The parents' acceptance of emotion in turn affects both the general affective climate maintained and accepted within the family context (Thompson, 1990), and the specific types of emotions that are differentially reinforced by parents (Izard & Malatesta, 1987).

As noted in Figure 1.1, a parent's role as the attachment figure has clear implications for how a parent will enact the modes of emotion socialization just outlined. Affect management within the parent-child dyad is thought to have a central role in the formation of the attachment organization (Sroufe & Waters, 1977). Additionally, from a functionalist approach to understanding emotions and their development, the affective bond present in parent-child attachment relationships and the primacy of these relationships during infancy and childhood make them an especially salient interpersonal context in which children learn and exercise their emotion regulation skills (Thompson, 1994). Moreover, some parental characteristics and behaviors that are relevant for the formation of a secure attachment are also relevant to the socialization of more adaptive emotion regulation in children. In what follows, we review each of the modes in which parents socialize children's emotions and discuss, in turn, ways in which parental characteristics and behaviors associated with the formation of secure attachments influence the socialization process and children's emotion regulation outcomes.

The most direct mode of influence, and the one most common early in development, is parents' interventions to alleviate distress. Direct intervention is likely to have different effects on regulation depending on the parents' sensitivity to the infant's or child's distress signals and their flexibility in responding. For example, parents who intervene promptly when the infant is severely distressed but delay their response when the infant is only mildly distressed appear to facilitate regulation in that their infants tend to display shorter bouts of crying or distress at later ages (Bell & Ainsworth, 1972; F. Hubbard & van Ijzendoorn, 1991). Similarly, the way in which parents manage the "interactive errors" or mismatches that often occur in the face-to-face interactions of infant-parent dyads also has an impact on the development of emotion regulation. Sensitivity to the child's signals facilitates parents' effectiveness in "repairing" these mismatches. These reparative experiences, where distress is alleviated through regaining synchrony, allow the child to remain engaged in stressful interactions and contribute to the development of affective communicative and self-regulatory skills (Gianino & Tronick, 1988; Tronick, 1989). Experiences of effective dyadic emotional regulation lead, in turn, to an increased sense of self-efficacy in regulating emotional arousal (Bell & Ainsworth, 1972). Thus, parents of securely attached children, who are high on sensitivity (De Wolff & van Ijzendoorn, 1997), may intervene to alleviate distress in ways that lead to the development of more optimal emotion regulation; they may take into account the limits of their children's internal resources vis-à-vis the level of their arousal and distress, and more readily help a child transition from emotional upset to a positive and mutually coordinated state.

A second and less direct way parents influence their children's emotion regulation styles is through their availability to provide emotional support and resources for children's emotion regulation and coping efforts. This mode of influence is likely to be most relevant during childhood and, although parents remain crucial sources of support for the more severe distressing events children encounter, they gradually diminish in importance as children develop close relationships with peers and adults outside of the family. One of the markers of a secure attachment relationship is parents' willingness to serve as a safe haven for their children. Children who enjoy secure attachment relationships with their parents have a history of interactions in which their requests for support have been met with responsive parental interventions that successfully addressed their emotional and coping needs. Children's perceptions of parents' availability to provide support are also likely to influence their appraisals of stressful events. A child who perceives his or her parent as a safe haven is likely to become less distressed when confronted with a stressful situation because he or she perceives help and resources will be available if needed. This lower level of negative arousal, in turn, facilitates reflective appraisal processes (Clore, Schwarz, & Conway, 1994) that lead to the selection of more adaptive coping strategies. In contrast, a child who is uncertain about the availability of his or her parents is likely to experience elevated levels of negative arousal in situations where his or her own coping resources are perceived as insufficient. These elevated levels of arousal are thought to constrain reflective appraisal processes (Crick, & Dodge, 1994; Zillmann, Bryant, Cantor, & Day, 1975) and lead to the use of more impulsive and less adaptive coping strategies.

Two parental characteristics important for the formation of secure attachment relationships, sensitivity and preference for open communication around affectively laden content, appear especially relevant for influencing how the next two socialization modes (i.e., direct instruction, modeling) are carried out. A central tenant of attachment theory is that parents of securely attached children accept and encourage open and flexible expression of a range of both positive and negative emotions. Additionally, they themselves are comfortable and open regarding their own feelings, especially negative ones. Given this, parents who function as secure attachment figures for their children are likely to instruct them more effectively regarding strategies for emotion regulation. They are also more likely to advocate for the use of constructive strategies for coping with negative emotions (Cassidy, 1994). Given that parents who function as secure attachment figures for their children are likely to more adaptively regulate their own emotions and verbally discuss their own coping efforts with their child, they are more likely to provide the child both behavioral and verbal models of effective regulation that do not inappropriately dismiss or overemphasize certain families of emotions (Cassidy, 1994).

Note that parental acceptance of emotion expression involves both the general openness with which emotions are expressed within the family and the types of emotions that are differentially reinforced. Several studies have demonstrated a positive relation between the degree to which emotions are freely expressed by family members and children's skills in recognizing and understanding emotions (Cassidy, Parke, Butkovsky, & Braungart, 1992; Dunn & Brown, 1994; Roberts & Strayer, 1987), suggesting that levels of affective expression within the family are likely to influence children's emotion regulation capacity. In fact, preschool children have been found to better regulate negative emotions when their parents talk to them more frequently and in a more sophisticated way about emotions (Denham, Cook, & Zoller, 1992). However, the relation between emotional expression and emotion regulation competence does not appear to be a simple or direct one. For example, the expression of high levels of negative emotions in families where there is intense marital conflict has been associated with lower socioemotional functioning in children (Cummings & Davies, 1994). Thus, moderate rather than extreme levels of expressed negative affect are more likely to be related to optimal regulation (Roberts & Strayer, 1987). Additionally, what parents do when family members are expressing negative emotions is critical for the development of children's emotion regulation abilities. Specifically, parents who talk about feelings with their children in these situations have children who later develop better emotion recognition skills

(Dunn & Brown, 1994). Thus, it appears that what may be most helpful for the development of emotion regulation competence is the opportunities that are provided for open expression and discussion of emotions in an accepting environment, and not simple exposure to unmodulated, impulsive expression of negative emotion where the disruptive effects of high arousal may interfere with attentional and reflective processes (Cummings, Iannotti, & Zahn-Waxler, 1985).

ATTACHMENT AND EMOTION REGULATION

Because children use the attachment figure to aid in regulating their own emotions, emotion displays and emotion regulation assessed during parent-child interaction may index the quality of the parent-child relationship rather than more general emotion regulation skills. For emotion regulation to mediate links between attachment and peer relationships, one would need to show that attachment is related to emotion regulation outside of the parent-child dyad. Thus, in our review of studies examining attachment and emotion regulation, we exclude studies that only examine emotion regulation during the mother-child interaction.

One set of studies has examined how attachment is related to the expression of affect toward peers. Children securely attached to their mothers are able to use positive affect to initiate, respond to, and sustain interaction with acquainted peers (Sroufe, 1983). Additionally, secure-secure friend pairs show more positive affect during play than do secure-insecure friend pairs (Park & Waters, 1989). Securely attached children also display less negative affect and whining than do insecurely attached children when playing with familiar peers (Sroufe, 1983).

A second set of studies has linked attachment patterns to the expression of specific emotions such as anxiety or hostility. Lutkenhaus, Grossmann, and Grossmann (1985) found that securely attached children were more open about expressing sadness after failure in a competitive task than were avoidantly attached children. In some cases, only certain insecure subgroups differ from securely attached individuals. For example, Warren, Huston, Egeland, and Sroufe (1997) found that resistant attachment at age 1 predicted the development of anxiety disorders in late adolescence. Kobak and Sceery (1988) showed that secure college students were rated as less anxious than those who were dismissing or preoccupied, with preoccupied individuals showing the highest levels of anxiety. By contrast, secures differed only from the dismissing on measures of hostility, with secures rated lower (Kobak & Sceery, 1988).

There is some evidence that security of attachment is related to the allocation of attention. Olson, Bates, and Bayles (1990) found that boys who were securely attached at age 1 showed better inhibitory control and were more patient on various laboratory tasks of attention. These effects were not, however, found for girls. Kirsch and Cassidy (1997) found that children secure at age 1 spent more time than insecurely attached children looking at attachment relevant pictures. However, Belsky, Spritz, and Crnic (1996) did not find relations between attachment and attention to affectively laden information in stories. Thus, although there is some evidence for a link between attachment and attention, effects are only found for some types of tasks.

We were unable to locate any published studies that link attachment to coping. Here, we present results from one of our studies in which we found some evidence that coping style serves as a mediator between attachment and peer relationships. Our study is also the first to test explicitly whether emotion regulation serves as a mediator between attachment and peer relationships.

EMOTION REGULATION AS MEDIATOR OF ATTACHMENT-PEER LINKS: SOME EMPIRICAL EVIDENCE

In this section, we provide preliminary findings of an investigation designed to examine emotion regulation processes as mediators of associations between mother-child and father-child attachment and social behavior with peers. Our approach has been to develop attachment-based assessments of parent-child relationships that tap both the child's and parent's perspective. We chose this approach because it explicitly recognizes there are two participants in the attachment relationship, and allows for the two members to have different perspectives. One would, of course, expect some convergence between the two, in that children who are securely attached to a parent should have a parent who is functioning as an adequate attachment figure. We have also used a combination of self-report, observational, and projective techniques to provide different windows on the attachment construct.

The study included multiple indices of each construct. For example, attachment is indexed with child report, parent report, and observations of parent acceptance of emotions. Emotion regulation is assessed with parent and child reports of child emotionality and coping strategies, as well as with observer ratings of child emotional openness during mother-child and father-child conversations regarding emotionally laden topics. From this larger data set, we have selected one example that illustrates the links between the constructs in our model. Specifically, we tested whether coping strategies mediated the association between attachment and social behavior with peers in a sample of preadolescents. To obtain independent assessments of the constructs in our model, we used child reports of attachment, mother and father reports of child coping with upsetting events, and teacher reports of behavioral and peer competence.

Subjects were 77 fifth graders (53% boys, 47% girls) who were participating with their parents in a study of parent-child relationships and peer competence. All parents residing with the child were invited to participate. Sixty-five percent of the participating families were intact; 26 percent were mother-headed single parent families; and 9 percent were stepparent families. Families were predominantly middle class and 92.2 percent were white. The data were gathered during a laboratory visit in which children were videotaped interacting with each parent during a series of conversational tasks. Parents and children also completed questionnaire measures of, among other constructs, attachment and emotion regulation. The primary teacher of the children provided reports of behavioral and peer competence in the school context. Teacher data were available for 75 percent of the sample. Thus, mother, child, and teacher data were available for 58 subjects. Given the number of mother-headed single parent families in the sample, 36 subjects had data from all sources including fathers. Only questionnaire measures and teacher reports were used in the current analyses.

Children's perceptions of mother-child and father-child attachment security were assessed with the Security Scale (Kerns et al., 1996), a 15-item self-report questionnaire. Items on this scale are scored on a continuous dimension of security (range = 1 to 4) and assess openness of communication, accessibility, and responsivity with regard to a specific attachment figure. Children completed this measure twice to report on their relationship with each parent (once for children in single-parent households). One security score for each relationship was obtained by averaging responses across the 15 items. The internal consistency was adequate for both security with mother (α = .81) and father (α = .87).

An adaptation of the Children's Coping Strategies Checklist (Eisenberg et al., 1996) was used to obtain an index of children's predominant coping strategies. Using a 5-point scale, mothers and fathers were asked to respond how often their child does various types of behaviors when he or she is upset or is confronted with a problem. Types of coping strategies were grouped into avoidant coping; emotion-focused and problem-focused support seeking; use of verbal and physical aggression; cognitive decision making and problem solving. One score was computed for each of the four types of coping strategies by averaging responses across items. Alphas for mother reports ranged from .74 to .92; the range for father reports was .72 to .91. To create a composite variable reflecting the extent to which the child tended to engage in more constructive coping strategies, we subjected these four variables to a Principal Components Analysis and extracted the resulting factor score (all variables loaded into one component as they were intercorrelated; r range = .23 − .64). Higher scores indicate greater reliance on constructive coping (support seeking and cognitive decision making and problem solving) and less reliance on avoidant or aggressive strategies. The factor score for mother and father reports was highly correlated (r = .72; p < .0001) indicating substantial agreement between parents. Given this, and the fact that father reports were not available for all subjects, we used mother reports of child coping in the analyses reported here.

Three subscales of the Teacher-Child Rating Scale (TCRS) (Hightower et al., 1986), a 38-item paper-and-pencil measure, were used to obtain indices of behavior regulation and competence with peers as reported by teachers. Additionally, teachers ranked the child relative to his or her classmates on peer competence (Sroufe, Egeland, & Kreutzer, 1990). Two subscales of the TCRS, Frustration Tolerance ($\alpha = .89$) and Acting-out Behaviors (reverse coded; $\alpha = .88$), were standardized and averaged to create a composite variable reflecting behavioral regulation with peers ($r = .75$; $p < .0001$). The Peer Skills subscale ($\alpha = .93$) was combined with the peer competence ranking to obtain an overall competence with peers variable ($r = .72$; $p < .0001$).

To test the proposed mediational model, we followed Baron and Kenny's (1986) criteria for establishing a mediational relation. These criteria indicate that the predictor variable (i.e., attachment), the criterion variable (i.e., behavioral and peer competence), and the proposed mediator (i.e., child coping) should be intercorrelated, and that the association between the predictor and criterion variables should be substantially reduced when the effects of the mediator variable on the criterion variable are controlled.

Figure 1.2 shows the bivariate correlations among child report of mother-child security, mother report of the child's coping, and teacher report of both the child's behavioral regulation with peers and competence with peers. Child security was strongly associated with child coping, with more securely attached children displaying greater reliance on constructive coping strategies. Child coping was also significantly correlated with both behavioral and peer competence variables. Child security was significantly correlated with behavioral competence and marginally correlated with peer competence.

To test whether the mediator reduced the association between attachment and peer outcomes, we ran two hierarchical regression models, one to predict behavioral regulation and another to predict peer competence. In both models, child coping was entered in the first step of the model and security in the second step. Security did not contribute to the prediction of either of the two peer outcome variables when coping was controlled. The partial correlation between security and behavioral regulation, after controlling for coping, was .04 ($\beta = .05$; $p =$ n.s.), substantially lower than its zero-order correlation ($r = .30$; $p < .05$). In contrast, coping was significantly associated with behavioral regulation even when security was included in the model ($\beta = .41$; $p < .01$). Analyses for peer competence were similar: The partial correlation between security and peer competence, controlling for coping, was .04 ($\beta = .05$; $p =$ n.s.), again substantially lower than its zero-order correlation ($r = .24$, $p < .10$). In this model, coping was marginally significant at the $p < .06$ level ($\beta = .31$) after controlling for security.

The parallel analyses for child report of father-child security (Figure 1.2) indicated that security with father was significantly correlated with child cop-

Figure 1.2
Associations between Attachment, Coping, and Behavior with Peers for Child Report of Security with Mothers and with Fathers

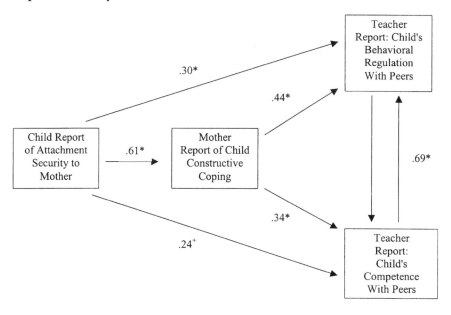

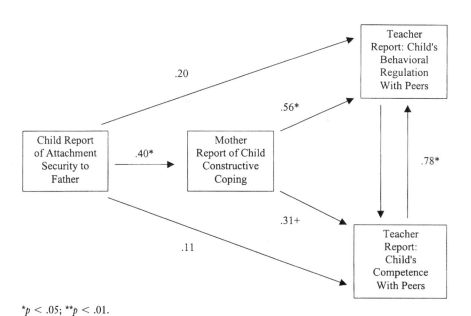

*p < .05; **p < .01.

ing, and coping was significantly correlated with behavior regulation with peers and marginally correlated with competence with peers. However, child report of security with fathers was not associated with the peer outcome variables. Given that security with father did not show direct associations with peer outcomes, we did not test the mediational model for father-child security. Nonetheless, these data show an indirect association between security with fathers and behavior regulation in the peer context, in that security was significantly correlated with coping, and coping was, in turn, associated with behavior regulation with peers.

Overall, our results suggest that coping strategies mediate mother-child attachment and peer behavior links. A strength of our findings is that these effects were shown with independent assessments of the three constructs. Father-child attachment was not related to behavior with peers. Thus, father-child attachment appears to affect peer behavior in an indirect way, in that it has an influence on the types of coping strategies children use, which in turn is related to children's behavior with peers.

CONCLUSIONS

The goal of this chapter was to discuss a model that proposes linkages between attachment, emotion regulation, and peer relationships. A review of the literature indicated that there is evidence for each of the bivariate links specified in the model. Furthermore, we presented results from one of our recent studies that tested mediation. The findings showed that emotion regulation mediates links between mother-child attachment and peer relationships. Contrary to our hypotheses, this effect was not shown for father-child attachment, where there was no direct link between attachment and peer relationships.

We also wish to introduce some caveats regarding our model. We chose to focus on emotion regulation in this chapter. This is not to suggest that emotion regulation is the only mediator of attachment-peer links. Other variables, such as social information processing, deserve attention. Each mediator is likely to account for a portion of the variance. There may also be cases where effects are not mediated by cognitive or affective processes (see also Mize, Pettit, & Meece, Chapter 6, this volume).

The model includes directional arrows, and we used attachment theory as the basis for proposing direction of influence. Other models are plausible. For example, emotion regulation might not be a mediator, but instead it may be an outcome influenced jointly or independently by attachment and peer relationships.

We also note that the development of the proposed model was guided by conceptual and empirical evidence primarily based on mainstream U.S. culture, and as such, its applicability to other cultural contexts must be examined. Certain aspects of parents' behaviors (e.g., overall level of sensitivity to the child's emotional signals) may function similarly across cultural contexts to promote emotional competence. But, the meaning of emotion-eliciting events and the adaptiveness of responses to these events are to a large extent culturally determined. For example, cultures vary in the extent to which certain emotions are seen as needing to be brought under control. They also vary in terms of the specific social contexts in which expression of certain emotions are acceptable or encouraged, and in terms of the appropriateness of different coping strategies for dealing with specific affectively laden situations. Thus, emotion regulation competence must be examined in light of the particular sociocultural context in which the child in embedded.

Similarly, cultural factors are likely to also play a role in the ways in which socialization of emotion regulation takes place. The model proposes that open communication regarding a wide range of emotions within the parent-child dyad provide children with experiences that lead to the development of greater competence in emotion regulation. Cultural values regarding parent-child relationships, however, may to some extent limit the types of emotions that are openly expressed within parent-child dyads. For example, Latino cultural values and socialization goals for children include the development of "respect" for authority figures (especially parents) and obedience and acceptance of parents' directives. In this family context, direct expression of negative emotions (i.e., anger, disapproval) toward parents is actively discouraged, and is more likely to be present in conflicted than in well functioning parent-child relationships. Therefore, the absence of open communication regarding some negative emotions may not be associated with emotion regulation in the same way as in mainstream U.S. culture. However, this should not be taken as an indication that the development of emotion regulation will be hampered, as other socialization mechanisms may be in place that allow children in this cultural context to fully develop their ability to modulate and cope with emotions. For instance, in cultures such as the Latino culture, where children are raised within an extended family system, adults other than the parents as well as children of different ages function as important socialization agents. The ways in which children's relationships with these agents influence the development of emotion regulation skills must also be considered. In this context, it would be interesting to examine whether the role of these agents complements or supplements that of the primary attachment figures (e.g., they influence the development of different aspects of emotion regulation or influence competence in regulating different types of emotions).

NOTE

Preparation of this chapter and the research reported here were supported by a Challenge Grant awarded to both authors by the Kent State University Psychology

Department and by a grant from National Institutes of Child Health and Human Development awarded to the second author (HD 32377). We thank Barbara Weimer, Patricia Tomich, and Amy Gentzler for their assistance with data collection. We also express our appreciation to the families and teachers who participated in the study. Address correspondence to Josefina M. Contreras at Department of Psychology, Kent State University, Kent, OH 44242; jcontrer@kent.edu

REFERENCES

Ainsworth, M.D.S. (1990). Epilogue: Some considerations regarding theory and assessment relevant to attachments beyond infancy. In Greenberg, M.T., Cicchetti, D., & Cummings, E.M. (Eds.), *Attachment in the preschool years* (pp. 463–488). Chicago: University of Chicago Press.

Ainsworth, M.D.S., Blehar, M., Waters, E., & Wall, S. (1978). *Patterns of attachment*. Hillsdale, NJ: Erlbaum.

Baldwin, M. (1992). Relational schemas and the processing of social information. *Psychological Bulletin, 112*, 461–484.

Band, E., & Weisz, J. (1988). How to feel better when it feels bad: Children's perspectives on coping with everyday stress. *Developmental Psychology, 24*, 247–253.

Baron, R.M., & Kenny, D.A. (1986). The moderator-mediator variable distinction in social psychological research: Conceptual, strategic, and statistical considerations. *Journal of Personality and Social Psychology, 25*, 23–33.

Barth, J.M., & Bastiani, A. (1997). A longitudinal study of emotion recognition and preschool children's social behavior. *Merrill-Palmer Quarterly, 43*, 107–128.

Bell, R.A., & Ainsworth, M.D. (1972). Infant crying and maternal responsiveness. *Child Development, 43*, 1171–1190.

Belsky, J., & Cassidy, J. (1994). Attachment: Theory and evidence. In Rutter, M.L., Hay, D.F., & Baron-Cogen, S. (Eds.), *Development through life: A handbook for clinicians* (pp. 373–402). Oxford: Blackwell.

Belsky, J., & Rovine, M. (1987). Temperament and attachment security in the Strange Situation: An empirical rapprochement. *Child Development, 58*, 787–795.

Belsky, J., Spritz, B., & Crnic, K. (1996). Infant attachment security and affective-cognitive information processing at age 3. *Psychological Science, 7*, 111–114.

Bowlby, J. (1973). *Attachment and Loss: Vol. 2. Separation: Anxiety and Anger*. New York: Basic Books.

Bowlby, J. (1982). *Attachment and Loss: Vol. 1. Attachment* (2nd ed.). New York: Basic Books.

Bretherton, I. (1987). New perspectives on attachment relations: Security, communication, and internal working models. In Osofsky, J.D. (Ed.), *Handbook of infant development* (2nd ed., pp. 1061–1100). New York: Wiley.

Campos, J., Campos, R., & Barrett, K. (1989). Emergent themes in the study of emotional development and emotion regulation. *Developmental Psychology, 25*, 394–402.

Campos, J., Mumme, D., Kermoian, R., & Campos, R. (1994). A functionalist perspective on the nature of emotion. In N.A. Fox (Ed.), The development of emotion regulation: Biological and behavioral considerations (pp. 228–249). *Monographs of the Society for Research in Child Development, 58* (2–3, Serial No. 240).

Casey, R., & Fuller, L. (1994). Maternal regulation of children's emotions. *Journal of Nonverbal Behavior, 18*, 57–89.

Cassidy, J. (1994). Emotion regulation: Influences of attachment relationships. In Fox, N.A. (Ed.), The development of emotion regulation: Biological and behavioral considerations. *Monographs of the Society for Research in Child Development, 59* (Serial No. 240).

Cassidy, J., & Berlin, L.J. (1994). The insecure/ambivalent pattern of attachment: Theory and research. *Child Development, 65*, 971–991.

Cassidy, J., Kirsh, S.J., Scolton, K.L., & Parke, R.D. (1996). Attachment and representations of peer relationships. *Developmental Psychology, 32*, 892–904.

Cassidy, J., Parke, R., Butkovsky, L., & Braungart, J. (1992). Family-peer connections: The roles of emotional expressiveness within the family and children's understanding of emotions. *Child Development, 63*, 603–618.

Clore, G., Schwarz, N., & Conway, M. (1994). Affective causes and consequences of social information processing. In Wyer, R.S. & Srull, T. (Eds.), *Handbook of social cognition* (Vol. 2, pp. 323–417). Hillsdale, NJ: Erlbaum.

Compas, B., Phares, V., & Ledoux, N. (1989). Stress and coping preventive interventions for children and adolescents. In Bond, L. & Compas, B. (Eds.), *Primary prevention and promotion in the schools* (pp. 319–340). London: Sage.

Crick, N., & Dodge, K. (1994). A review and reformulation of social information-processing mechanisms in children's social adjustment. *Psychological Bulletin, 115*, 74–101.

Cummings, E., & Davies, P. (1994). *Children and marital conflict*. New York: Guilford Press.

Cummings, E., Iannotti, R., & Zahn-Waxler, C. (1985). The influence of conflict between adults on the emotions and aggression of young children. *Developmental Psychology, 21*, 495–507.

Denham, S., Cook, M., & Zoller, D. (1992). Baby looks very sad: Discussions about emotions between mother and preschooler. *British Journal of Developmental Psychology, 10*, 301–315.

De Wolff, M.S., & van Ijzendoorn, M.H. (1997). Sensitivity and attachment: A meta-analysis of parental antecedents of infant attachment. *Child Development, 68*, 571–591.

Dunn, J. (1988). *The beginnings of social understanding*. Cambridge, MA: Harvard University Press.

Dunn, J., & Brown, J. (1991). Becoming American or English? Talking about the social world in England and the United States. In Bornstein, M.H. (Ed.), *Cultural approaches to parenting: Crosscurrents in contemporary psychology* (pp. 155–172). Hillsdale, NJ: Erlbaum.

Dunn, J., & Brown, J. (1994). Affect expression in the family, children's understanding of emotions, and their interactions with others. *Merrill-Palmer Quarterly, 40*, 138–156.

Eisenberg, N., Fabes, R.A., Bernzweig, J., Karbon, M., Poulin, R., & Hanish, L. (1993). The relations of emotionality and regulation to preschoolers' social skills and sociometric status. *Child Development, 64*, 1418–1438.

Eisenberg, N., Fabes, R.A., Karbon, M., Murphy, B., Wosinski, M., Polazzi, L., Carlo, G., & Juhnke, C. (1996). The relations of children's dispositional pro-social behavior to emotionality, regulation, and social functioning, *Child Development, 67*, 974–992.

Eisenberg, N., Fabes, R.A., Murphy, B., Maszk, P., Smith, M., & Karbon, M. (1995). The role of emotionality and regulation in children's social functioning: A longitudinal study. *Child Development, 66*, 1360–1384.

Eisenberg, N., Fabes, R.A., Shepard, S.A., Murphy, B.C., Guthrie, I.K., Jones, S., Friedman, J., Poulin, R., & Maszk, P. (1997). Contemporaneous and longitudinal prediction of children's social functioning from regulation and emotionality. *Child Development, 68*, 642–664.

Endler, N., & Parker, J. (1990). Multidimensional assessment of coping: A critical evaluation. *Journal of Personality and Social Psychology, 58*, 844–854.

Folkman, S., & Lazarus, R. (1980). An analysis of coping in a middle aged community sample. *Journal of Health and Social Behavior, 2*, 219–239.

Freitag, M. K., Belsky, J., Grossmann, K., Grossmann, K. E., & Scheuerer-Englisch, H. (1996). Continuity in parent-child relationships from infancy to middle childhood and relations with friendship competence. *Child Development, 67*, 1437–1454.

Gianino, A., & Tronick, E. Z. (1988). The mutual regulation model: The infant's self and interactive regulation and coping and defensive capacities. In Field, T. M., McCabe, P. M., & Schneiderman, N. (Eds.), *Stress and coping across development* (pp. 47–68). Hillsdale, NJ: Erlbaum.

Goldsmith, H. H., & Harman, C. (1994). Temperament and attachment: Individuals and relationships. *Current Directions in Psychological Science, 3*, 53–57.

Gottman, J. M., & Mettetal, G. (1986). Speculations about social and affective development: Friendship and acquaintanceship through adolescence. In Gottman, J. M. & Parker, J. G. (Eds.), *Conversations of friends* (pp. 192–237). New York: Cambridge University Press.

Hardy, D., Power, T., & Jaedicke, S. (1993). Examining the relation of parenting to children's coping with everyday stress. *Child Development, 64*, 1829–1841.

Hightower, A., Work, W., Cowen, E., Lotyczewski, B., Spinell, A., Guare, J., & Rohrbeck, C. (1986). The Teacher-Child Rating Scale: A brief objective measure of elementary children's school problem behaviors and competencies. *School Psychology Review, 15*, 393–409.

Hubbard, F., & van Ijzendoorn, M. (1991). Maternal unresponsiveness and infant crying across the first 9 months: A naturalistic longitudinal study. *Infant Behavior and Development, 14*, 299–312.

Hubbard, J. A., & Coie, J. D. (1994). Emotional correlates of social competence in children's peer relationships. *Merrill-Palmer Quarterly, 40*, 1–20.

Izard, C., & Malatesta, C. (1987). Perspectives in emotional development I: Differential emotions theory of early emotional development. In Osofsky, J. D. (Ed.), *Handbook of infant development* (2nd ed., pp. 494–554). New York: Wiley.

Kerns, K. A. (1996). Individual differences in friendship quality: Links to child-mother attachment. In Bukowski, W. M., Newcomb, A. F., & Hartup, W. W. (Eds.), *The company they keep: Friendship in childhood and adolescence* (pp. 137–157). New York: Cambridge University Press.

Kerns, K. A., & Barth, J. (1995). Parent-child attachment and physical play: Convergence across components of parent-child relationships and their relations to peer competence. *Journal of Social and Personal Relationships, 12,* 243–260.

Kerns, K. A., Klepac, L., & Cole, A. (1996). Peer relationships and preadolescents' perceptions of security in the child-mother relationship. *Developmental Psychology, 32,* 457–466.

Kirsch, S. J., & Cassidy, C. (1997). Preschoolers' attention to and memory for attachment-relevant information. *Child Development, 68,* 1143–1153.

Kobak, R. R., & Sceery, A. (1988). Attachment in late adolescence: Working models, affect regulation, and representations of self and others. *Child Development, 59,* 135–146.

Lamb, M. E., & Malkin, C. M. (1986). The development of social expectations in distress-relief sequences: A longitudinal study. *International Journal of Behavioral Development, 9,* 235–249.

Lamb, M. E., & Nash, A. (1989). Infant-mother attachment, sociability, and peer competence. In Berndt, T. J. & Ladd, G. W. (Eds.), *Peer relationships in child development* (pp. 219–245). New York: Wiley.

Lazarus, R. S., & Folkman, S. (1984). *Stress, appraisal, and coping.* New York: Springer.

Lutkenhaus, P., Grossmann, K. E., & Grossmann, K. (1985). Infant-mother attachment at 12 months and style of interaction with a stranger at the age of three years. *Child Development, 56,* 1538–1542.

Lyons-Ruth, K. (1996). Attachment relationships among children with aggressive behavior problems: The role of disorganized early attachment patterns. *Journal of Consulting and Clinical Psychology, 64,* 64–73.

Maccoby, E. (1983). Social-emotional development and response to stressors. In Garmezy, N. & Rutter, M. (Eds.), *Stress, coping, and development in children* (pp. 217–234). New York: McGraw-Hill.

Main, M., Kaplan, N., & Cassidy, J. (1985). Security in infancy, childhood, and adulthood: A move to the level of representation. In Bretherton, I. & Waters, E. (Eds.), *Monographs of the SRCD, 50* (Serial No. 209).

Miller, P., Kliewer, W., Hepworth, J., & Sandler, I. (1994). Maternal socialization of children's post divorce coping: Development of a measurement model. *Journal of Applied Development Psychology, 15,* 457–487.

Olson, S. L., Bates, J. E., & Bayles, K. (1990). Early antecedents of childhood impulsivity: The role of parent–child interaction, cognitive competence, and temperament. *Journal of Abnormal Child Psychology, 18,* 317–334.

Park, K. A., & Waters, E. (1989). Security of attachment and preschool friendships. *Child Development, 60,* 1076–1081.

Renken, B., Egeland, B., Marvinney, D., Mangelsdorf, S., & Sroufe, L. A. (1989). Early childhood antecedents of aggression and passive-withdrawal in early elementary school. *Journal of Personality, 57,* 257–281.

Roberts, W., & Strayer, J. (1987). Parents' responses to the emotional distress of their children: Relations with children's competence. *Developmental Psychology, 23,* 415–422.

Rossman, B. (1992). School-age children's perceptions of coping with distress: Strategies for emotion regulation and the moderation of adjustment. *Journal of Child Psychology and Psychiatry, 33,* 1373–1397.

Rothbart, M. K., & Derryberry, D. (1981). Development of individual differences in temperament. In Lamb, M. E. & Brown, A. L. (Eds.), *Advances in developmental psychology* (Vol. 1, pp. 37–86). Hillsdale, NJ: Erlbaum.

Rothbart, M. K., Posner, M. I., & Boylan, A. (1990). Regulatory mechanisms in infant development. In Enns, J. T. (Ed.) *The development of attention: Research and theory* (pp. 47–66). Dordrecht: Elsevier North-Holland.

Rubin, K. H., Bukowski, W., & Parker, J. G. (1998). Peer interactions, relationships, and groups. In Damon, W. (Ed.), *Handbook of child psychology* (5th ed., pp. 619–700). New York: Wiley.

Saarni, C., Mumme, D., & Campos, J. (1998). Emotional development: Action, communication, and understanding. In Damon, W. & Eisenberg, N. (Eds.), *Social, emotional, and personality development, Vol. 3, Handbook of child psychology* (pp. 237–309). New York: Wiley.

Skinner, E., & Wellborn, J. (1994). Coping during childhood and adolescence: A motivational perspective. In Lerner, R. (Ed.), *Life-span development and behavior* (pp. 91–133). Hillsdale, NJ: Erlbaum.

Sroufe, L. A. (1983). Infant-caregiver attachment and patterns of adaptation in preschool: The roots of maladaptation and competence. In Perlmutter, M. (Ed.), *Minnesota symposium in child psychology* (Vol. 16, pp. 41–81). Hillsdale, NJ: Erlbaum.

Sroufe, L. A., Carlson, E., & Shulman, S. (1993). Individuals in relationships: Development from infancy through adolescence. In Funder, D. C., Parke, R. D., Tomalinson-Keasey, C., & Widaman, K. (Eds.), *Studying lives through time* (pp. 315–342). Washington, D.C.: American Psychological Association.

Sroufe, L. A., Egeland, B., & Kreutzer, T. (1990). The fate of early experience following developmental change: Longitudinal approaches to individual adaptation in childhood. *Child Development, 61,* 1363–1373.

Sroufe, L. A., & Fleeson, J. (1986). Attachment and the construction of relationships. In Hartup, W. W. & Rubin, Z. (Eds.), *Relationships and development* (pp. 51–71). Hillsdale, NJ: Erlbaum.

Sroufe, L. A., Schork, E., Motti, F., Lawroski, N., & LaFreniere, P. (1984). The role of affect in social competence. In Izard, C., Kagan, J., & Zajonc, R. (Eds.), *Emotions, cognition and behavior* (pp. 289–319). Cambridge, England: Cambridge University Press.

Sroufe, L. A., & Waters, E. (1977). Attachment as an organizational construct. *Child Development, 48,* 1184–1199.

Stein, N., & Levine, L. (1990). Making sense of emotion: The representation and use of goal structure knowledge. In Stein, N., Leventhal, B., & Trabasso, T. (Eds.), *Psychological and biological approaches to emotion* (pp. 45–73). Hillsdale, NJ: Erlbaum.

Suess, G. J., Grossman, K. E., & Sroufe, L. A. (1992). Effects of infant attachment to mother and father on quality of adaptation in preschool: From dyadic to individual organization of self. *International Journal of Behavioral Development, 15,* 43–65.

Thompson, R. A. (1990). Emotion and self-regulation. In Thompson, R. A. (Ed.), *Nebraska Symposium on Motivation, Vol. 36, Socioemotional development* (pp. 367–467). Lincoln: University of Nebraska Press.

Thompson, R. A. (1994). Emotion regulation: A theme in search of definition. In

Fox, N. A. (Ed.), The development of emotion regulation (pp. 25–32). *Monographs of the Society for Research in Child Development, 59* (Serial No. 240).

Tomich, P. L. (1998). *Parent-child relationships and children's peer competence in middle childhood.* Paper presented at the Kent Psychology Forum, Millersburg, Ohio.

Tronick, E. Z. (1989). Emotions and emotional communication in infants. Children and their development: Knowledge base, research agenda, and social application [Special issue]. *American Psychologist, 44,* 112–119.

Warren, S. L., Huston, L., Egeland, B., & Sroufe, L. A. (1997). Child and adolescent anxiety disorders and early attachment. *Journal of the American Academy of Child and Adolescent Psychiatry, 36,* 637–644.

Youngblade, L. M., Park, K. A., & Belsky, J. (1993). Measurement of young children's close friendship: A comparison of two independent assessment systems and their associations with attachment security. *International Journal of Behavioral Development, 16,* 563–587.

Zillmann, D., Bryant, J., Cantor, J., & Day, K. (1975). Irrelevance of mitigating circumstances in retaliation behavior at high levels of excitation. *Journal of Research in Personality, 9,* 282–293.

2

The Ecology of Premature Autonomy in Adolescence: Biological and Social Influences

Thomas J. Dishion, François Poulin, and Nani Medici Skaggs

Involvement in adolescent problem behavior is often seen as a syndrome reflective of disorder at the individual level. A social interaction model of problem behavior, however, focuses on the function of such problem behavior within close relationships (Dishion & Patterson, 1997; Patterson, 1982; Patterson & Reid, 1984). Studies guided by a social interaction perspective focus on functional outcomes at the microsocial level, that is, how behavior is embedded within action-reaction sequences. For example, analyses of friendship interactions reveal that deviant talk functions to organize the positive affective exchanges for antisocial boys, a process referred to as *deviancy training*. In the long run, deviancy training within adolescent friendships is associated with escalation in delinquency, violence, and substance use (Dishion, Capaldi, Spracklen, & Li, 1995; Dishion, Eddy, Haas, Li, & Spracklen, 1997; Dishion, Spracklen, Andrews, & Patterson, 1996).

Several research programs identify association with deviant peers as the strongest proximal correlate of adolescent problem behavior (Elliott, Huizinga, & Ageton, 1985). Less research, however, focuses on the function of the deviant peer group in understanding adolescent adaptations (Dishion, 1990). In this chapter, we explore the role of the deviant peer group in adolescents' premature realization of normative adolescent milestones: autonomy and sexual activity. Why are young adolescents apparently so interested in establishing peer networks? Why is there a pattern, across cultures, for problem behavior to peak in middle adolescence (Gottfredson & Hirshi, 1990)?

Questions such as these call for the integration of microsocial and bio-

Figure 2.1
An Ecological Overview of Social Development

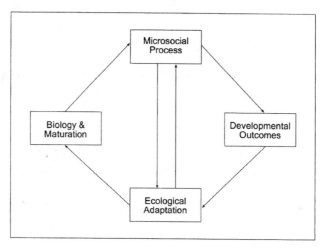

logical influences on development (Lickliter & Berry, 1990). Biologically based preferences and predisposition could result from natural selection processes that unfold over generations (Hinde, 1989). For example, evolutionary theory has been invoked in making specific predictions about male and female preferences in forming close relationships (Buss & Schmitt, 1993). On the role of poor parenting, Belsky, Steinberg, and Draper (1991) proposed an evolutionary perspective to adolescent sexual activity and teenage pregnancy. The key concept of an evolutionary viewpoint is that biology and social outcomes are intertwined vis-à-vis the natural selection process. Learning occurs through the natural selection of behaviors and evolution occurs through natural selection of species-specific biological potential. By integrating these macro and micro natural selection processes, the potential is increased for understanding parameters and dynamics of human development throughout the life cycle.

An ecological framework is particularly useful as an integrative framework for understanding variations in developmental outcomes (Bronfenbrenner, 1989; Dishion, French, & Patterson, 1995). This framework promotes systemic thinking concerning the interaction between personal characteristics (e.g., biological maturation) and social processes (e.g., deviant peer involvement) in accounting for development. A key idea within this framework is that of "ecological adaptation" (see Figure 2.1). Ecological adaptations refer to the settings within which development occurs and communicates the concept that the individual is active in the selection of context. The formation of a deviant peer group, for example, could be considered an ecological adaptation. Children at risk for forming a deviant peer group have a history of peer rejection, academic failure, antisocial behavior, and poor parenting (Dishion, Patterson, Stoolmiller, & Skinner, 1991). The adaptation process is relatively simple: Antisocial children select others with whom to spend time (Cairns, Cairns, Neckerman, Gest, & Gariepy, 1988; Dishion, Andrews, & Crosby, 1995). Microsocial interactions within the deviant peer group support more problem behavior and continued membership in a deviant peer group (Dishion et al., 1997; Patterson, Dishion, & Yoerger, 1998).

Most of the research on friendship selection focuses on social processes. Unfortunately, the biological underpinnings of learning and development are often overlooked. Individual differences in abilities, maturation, temperament, and gender may impact the individual's ecology and concomitant social learning. For example, puberty maturation can set the stage for change in relationship networks, and therefore, the kinds of microsocial processes that define the fabric of an interpersonal life. The work by Magnusson, Stattin, and Allen (1985) reveals the impact of early puberty maturation on females. Early maturation in girls leads to increases in association with older male peers; simultaneously, increases occur in adolescent problem behavior. Clearly, early maturation confers both motivational change within the individual and a change in ecology (e.g., cars driven by teenagers) and social reactions (interest by older males).

Although adolescent problem behavior is often conceptualized as the "developmental outcome" and deviant peer associations as the "cause," an ecological model suggests a more complex system of interrelations. Within the web of mutual causal influences, the key is to understand how a pattern of behavior is "functional" (Dishion & Patterson, 1997). Adolescent problem behavior can be seen, not only as an outcome of extended developmental processes (Patterson, Reid, & Dishion, 1992), but also as functional in the daily life of adolescents, or perhaps, the species.

In this chapter, we suggest that adolescent problem behavior functions to link teenagers with peers who are alike in attitude and behavior (Kandel, 1986), including and facilitating access to potential sexual interactions. Hence, the deviant peer group may be critical in disengaging from the family and establishing autonomy within the peer group. As in the world of primates (Sameroff & Suomi, 1996), the formation of an autonomous peer network is seen as a critical step toward mating and establishment in the adult world, primarily in the context of heterosexual relationships.

Peer groups in adolescence facilitate interactions with the opposite gender. Dunphy (1963), for example, used a participant observation method in a naturalistic setting to study the role of adolescent peer groups in achievement of heterosexuality. Dunphy identified stages of group development between early adolescence and late adolescence. During that period, same-gender cliques start to form heterosexual cliques, especially in the case of higher status members. The function of these heterosexual cliques is to provide youths opportunities for establishing a heterosexual role through dating situations. In late adolescence, these cliques tend to disintegrate as individuals become more involved in couples. A key element in that model is that leaders play the most advanced heterosexual roles. In the deviant peer group, the higher status members are likely to be the more antisocial youths.

Peer groups also function to distance youth from parental influences and control (Elder, 1980). In particular, deviant peer groups seem to accelerate the autonomy process by virtue of rendering the young adolescent virtually impossible to supervise (Stoolmiller, 1990) and by increasing parent-child conflict (Patterson et al., 1992). Patterson's (1993) analysis of changes in wandering, deviant peer associations, and problem behavior revealed that all three constructs were changing in unison during adolescence. Apparently, autonomy in the peer group is necessary in order to provide adolescents with ample unsupervised time for informal interactions to grow into close relationships, and eventually, intimacy.

There are two components in adolescent autonomy: disengagement from parental ties and greater unsupervised involvement in the peer group (Steinberg & Silverberg, 1986). Developing friendships with older peers seems especially instrumental for the autonomy process for young adolescents. Older adolescents have cars, access to drugs and alcohol, and party situations in which heterosexual relationships evolve. Indeed, Maccoby (1998) reported that in adolescence, social contact with the other gender occurs mainly in mixed gender groups in places like shopping malls (i.e., unsupervised setting). Parties, malls, and other community settings are the playground for young adolescents to meet and interact with the opposite gender.

In this sense, a broader view can be taken of the function of the peer group and problem behavior in adolescence. Biological change, developmental history, and social contexts interplay to redefine trajectories during critical periods and perhaps define patterns that reoccur across generations. For example, adolescent problem behavior peaks shortly after puberty (around ages 15 and 16), across cultures and generations (Gottfredson & Hirshi, 1990). Warr (1993) found that the age-crime curve could be explained by changes in association with deviant peers. Reduction in delinquency in late adolescence is often associated with establishment of long-term close relationships and change in peer social networks (e.g., Osborne & West, 1979, 1980; West & Farrington, 1977).

From a functional perspective, involvement in a deviant peer group and problem behavior may increase the likelihood of autonomous peer network and sexual relations. This view differs considerably from problem behavior theory (Jessor & Jessor, 1977), where adolescent sexual activity is seen as one symptom within a general syndrome. Sexual interest has strong biological underpinnings, and sexual behavior has important implications for subsequent individual development and the evolution of the species. Aside from psychodynamic theory, sexual impulse and behavior is often neglected in constructing models of development and behavior.

Sexual strategy theory is an exception (Buss & Schmitt, 1993). This model uses evolutionary theory to construct a set of compelling predictions about individual and gender-specific preferences for close relationships. Similar to social interactional models of development (Patterson et al., 1992), sexual "strategies" are not consciously driven, but biologically based preferences derived from a natural selection process. Gender-specific sexual preferences emerge with pubertal maturation and may well encompass a set of social and sexual strategies, including the need to become autonomous within a peer group.

Capaldi, Crosby, and Stoolmiller (1996) found that membership in a deviant peer group was one of the key predictors of adolescent sexual intercourse for the Oregon Youth Study (OYS) males, along with substance use and other problem behaviors. Similarly, French, Dishion, and Medici Skaggs (1998) found deviant peer involvement to predict the age of first sex for both males and females. In both studies, low parental monitoring was an indirect predictor of adolescent sexual activity, mediated primarily by deviant peer involvement. These findings suggest that adolescent "partying" may have a function as simple as the history of the species—to bring sexually mature individuals in contact for mate selection.

Much of adolescent problem behavior, then, can be seen as a form of social commerce that promotes three developmentally significant outcomes: (a) disengagement from adult supervision and intervention, (b) involvement in an autonomous peer group, and (c) increased contact with the opposite gender. For many adolescents, minor delinquent behavior is normative, referred to as *adolescent onset* (Moffitt, 1993) and associated with a less disruptive impact on adult development (Stattin & Magnusson, 1991). For example, in the OYS sample, nearly 50 percent of the boys had a police contact for misbehavior by age 18. Children with a history of antisocial behavior, however, are more likely to be prematurely autonomous and to engage in unsafe or indiscreet sexual practices (Capaldi et al., 1996). The developmental history for these youngsters has been well established: Their antisocial behavior leads to peer and academic failure and attenuated family systems. The biological pull of pubertal maturation induces further motivation for ecological adaptations that provide access to multiple reinforcers. As discussed in the volume *Antisocial Boys* (Patterson et al., 1992), the pattern is one of maximizing short-term gains at the expense of long-term outcomes.

The early emergence of sexual and social autonomy could be referred to as the *premature autonomy model*. The basic hypothesis is that children's maladaptation within the school, and lack of parental monitoring, influences children's tendency to cluster into deviant peer groups. The deviancy training process occurring in these deviant peer groups is also hypothesized to be functional at the macrolevel, by providing peer resources to facilitate adolescent social and sexual autonomy. Autonomy within a peer group provides the opportunity for sexual activity in adolescence. Biological maturation is quite powerful to the autonomy process, by virtue of changes in the adolescent's motivations, as well as by eliciting changes in the reactions of the social environment.

The premature autonomy model is examined within this chapter using a sample (n = 224) of high-risk young adolescent boys and girls from the Adolescent Transitions Program (ATP); they were originally assessed at age 12 and followed for 3 years into middle adolescence. Correlational and structural equation modeling analyses were used to evaluate the zero-order and multivariate relations between pubertal maturation, school maladaptation, parent monitoring, and deviant peer clustering at age 12, to autonomous peer network and sexual activity at age 15.

METHOD

Participants

The 224 participants of this longitudinal study included 111 boys and 113 girls. Participants were recruited in seven cohorts over a 4-year period, from 1988 to 1992.[1] All participants in the study were considered at risk. Cohorts 1 through 5, in Grades 6, 7, and 8, were referred by parents. Cohorts 6 and 7, recruited through the schools, were all in Grade 7. At the beginning of this study they ranged in age from 10 to 14 years, with an average age of 12.2 years. In this chapter, we used data collected at the first phase of the study, 4 months later, and finally 3 years later, when participants were an average 15.2 years of age. At this last phase, 81 percent of the original participants remained part of the study.

The family status of the participants included 42.9 percent from single-family households (mostly single mothers), 36.2 percent from two-parent families (where one of the parents was a stepparent), and 21 percent from intact, two-parent families. The families tended to be economically disadvantaged, with 48.2 percent receiving some sort of financial assistance; 60 percent of the families had a gross annual income under $20,000. Eighty percent of the mothers and 74 percent of the fathers had completed high school; for both mothers and fathers, 17 percent had graduated from college. The participants were predominantly (90 percent) Euro-American.

The assessment strategy was multiagent, multimethod, and included data from teachers, parents, youths, and interviews. Data types included interviews, questionnaires, brief telephone interviews, and staff impressions.

Procedures

Interviews and Questionnaires

At each phase of the study, the teens and their parents were interviewed separately. The interviews lasted approximately 45 minutes. The content of the interviews consisted of family management, peer adjustment, and youth problem behavior. At yearly follow-up interviews, the focus was primarily on the youth problem behavior, including involvement in deviant peer groups and sexual activity.

Prior to the interviews, the parent (or parents) and youths were asked to complete several questionnaires. These forms, including the Peer Involvement and Social Skill Questionnaire (Walker & McConnell, 1988), were also sent to the teachers, along with the teacher Child Behavior Checklist (CBCL; Achenbach, 1991).

Telephone Interviews

At each assessment phase, the parents and teens were contacted for a series of six brief telephone interviews, conducted at 3-day intervals. An attempt was made to conduct both the parent and the youth telephone interviews on the same day whenever possible. The telephone interview included an assessment of youth involvement in deviant peer groups, time spent with friends, hours unsupervised, and problem behaviors.

Friendship Network Report

In the follow-up phase of the study, the youths were asked to identify the members of their friendship network and describe them, including their gender, age, and the kinds of activities in which they engaged.

Construct Scores

The development of constructs was hypothesis driven. Variables were selected, based largely on previous research with the OYS (Capaldi & Patterson, 1989; Patterson et al., 1992), as indicators of each construct. The constituency of these constructs, as well as psychometric properties, are presented in Table 2.1.

Early Adolescence Constructs

In early adolescence, four constructs were created: school maladaptation, deviant peer associations, biological maturation, and parent monitoring. The school maladaptation construct is based on the teachers' ratings on the CBCL externalizing scale, academic grades (as coded from youth grade point averages during the academic year and corresponding to the first two phases of the study), and the teachers' ratings of youth peer relationships in the

Table 2.1
Measurement Strategy and Reliability of the Instruments

Construct and Measure	Number of Items				Sample Item	Reliability			
	P	Y	T	O		P	Y	T	O
School Maladaptation									
1. CBCL externalizing	*				Bullies, mean to others.			*	
2. Social preference			2		What proportion of this student's peers dislike or reject (like and accept) him or her?			r = -.19	
3. Academic grades			1					n/a	
Parent Monitoring									
1. Child report									
a. Child interview		8			Do your parents let you go anywhere without asking?		a = .68		
b. Child phone		4			How much time have you spent with your parents in the previous 24 hours?		a = .55		
2. Parent report									
a. Parent interview	13				How difficult is it to know where your child is?	a = .84			
b. Parent phone	5				Was your child away from home after 7 p.m. without an adult?	a = .38			
3. Staff impression				1	How well did the parent(s) seem to monitor the child?		n/a		
Biological Maturation									
1. Chronological age		1					n/a		
2. Pubertal maturation		5			Have your breasts begun to grow?		a = .76		
Deviant Peer Association									
1. Child report									
a. Child interview		32			During the past year, how many of your friends stole something less than $5?		a = .82		
b. Describing friends		6			Do your school friends get into trouble a lot?		a = .62		
2. Parent report									
a. Peer	7				He or she hangs out with kids who fight.	a = .79			
3. Teacher report									
a. Peer involvement and social skills			4		How often is he or she with misbehaving kids?			a = .88	
Autonomous Friendship Network									
1. Child report									
a. Friendship network questionnaire		1			Age of your friends.		n/a		
b. Phone interview		1			In the last 24 hours, how much of your free time did you spend with friends?		n/a		
2. Parent report									
a. Phone interview	1				Within the last 24 hours, how many hours was he or she involved in activities outside your home without adult supervision?	n/a			
Adolescent Sexual Activity									
1. Intercourse frequency		1			How many times in the last year have you had sex with someone?		n/a		
2. Number of partners		1			How many different people have you had as sexual partners?		n/a		

Note: P = Parents; Y = Youth; T = Teacher; O = Observer. *See Achenbach (1992).

classroom. The latter score is derived in a manner analogous to the social preference score of Coie, Dodge, and Coppotelli (1982). Teachers rated how each youth was accepted by his or her classmates and rejected by his or her classmates on a 1- to 5-point Likert scale. These scores were then standardized (z scores). Social preference was obtained by the subtraction of the rejection score from the acceptance score.

The deviant peer associations construct was based on the OYS work. The youths, teachers, and parents were asked independently to report on the extent to which each youth's peers were involved in deviant activities, including both substance use and delinquent behavior. The deviant peer associations construct was derived from aggregating Phase 1 and Phase 2 data (4 months of interval). Because there was substantial variability in the age of these participants, ranging from 11 to 14 years (average age 12), we employed two indicators for biological maturation, using both the chronological age of the youth at the first phase of this study and a self-report of physical maturation in adolescence (Petersen, 1984).

The parent monitoring construct was derived using a multiagent and multi-method strategy, including the youth, parent, and staff impressions (Dishion, Li, Spracklen, Brown, & Haas, in press). In the youth interview, questions were asked about parents' practices. Parent report consisted of questions asked in a structured face-to-face interview, as well as in the telephone interview. Finally, the families were involved in a structured, videotaped problem-solving task. In this task, issues were discussed that often provided a sense of the parents' monitoring practices. Coders were asked to give impressions of how well the parent (or parents) seemed to monitor the child. A correlation of .55 was observed between coders on their ratings of parent monitoring. The parent monitoring construct was derived from aggregating Phase 1 and Phase 2 data.

Middle Adolescence Constructs

The scores for each indicator used to create the middle adolescence constructs were derived from data collected while the youths were 15 years of age, on average. Two constructs were scored: autonomous peer network and adolescent sexual activity. One indicator of the autonomous peer network construct was derived from the youth report on their friendship network (age of friends), one from the child telephone interview (time spent with friends), and one from the parent telephone interview (hours without adult supervision). At this last phase of the study, the youth were also asked about their sexual activity during the previous year. Their reports of frequency and variety of partners were used as the two indicators for the sexual activity construct. The convergent and discriminant correlations among the constructs' indicators are presented in Table 2.2.

Table 2.2
Convergent/Discriminant Correlation Matrix for Constructs Indicators

	1	2	3	4	5	6	7	8	9	10	11	12	13	14	15	16
School Maladaptation																
1. Externalizing	1.00															
2. Social preference	-.36	1.00														
3. Academic grades	-.39	.38	1.00													
Parent Monitoring																
4. Child report	-.09	.18	.18	1.00												
5. Parent report	-.24	.12	.30	.38	1.00											
6. Staff impressions	-.04	.10	.19	.32	.38	1.00										
Biological Maturation																
7. Chronological age	.06	.08	.07	-.10	-.17	-.09	1.00									
8. Pubertal maturation	.07	.18	.14	.06	-.13	-.15	.28	1.00								
Deviant Peer Associations																
9. Child report	.36	-.02	-.17	-.25	-.31	-.17	.23	.28	1.00							
10. Parent report	.36	-.07	-.33	-.14	-.45	-.21	.18	.14	.58	1.00						
11. Teacher report	.58	-.18	-.42	-.15	-.40	-.13	.12	.16	.47	.54	1.00					
Autonomous Friendship Network																
12. Age of friends	.05	.06	-.04	.04	-.22	-.04	.46	.30	.21	.20	.21	1.00				
13. Time with friends	.04	.10	.02	.02	-.11	-.03	.19	.17	.14	.19	.07	.31	1.00			
14. Time without adult supervision	.00	-.01	-.03	-.28	-.34	-.26	.22	.18	.28	.23	.19	.35	.27	1.00		
Adolescent Sexual Activity																
15. Intercourse frequency	.28	-.07	-.06	-.15	-.26	-.25	.25	.32	.38	.39	.41	.34	.24	.29	1.00	
16. Number of partners	.22	-.03	-.01	-.13	-.28	-.11	.16	.24	.31	.41	.35	.32	.21	.29	.76	1.00

Analysis Strategy

First, gender differences on each indicator were examined by way of a series of multivariate analysis of variance (MANOVAs) conducted within constructs. Second, the predictive relationships between the early adolescent adjustment and premature adolescent autonomy were examined through correlational analyses. Finally, the complete structural model was tested using the AMOS program (Arbuckle, 1997) for structural equation modeling. In this model, we hypothesized that deviant peer clustering would mediate the relation between early adolescent family, school, and biological risk to middle adolescent autonomy.

RESULTS

Gender Differences

The means and standard deviations of each indicator for boys and girls, as well as multivariate and univariate effects, are presented in Table 2.3.

As would be expected, boys showed higher levels of school maladaptation than girls. More specifically, they showed more behavior problems, were perceived by the teacher as less liked by their peers, and earned lower grades than girls at school. Interestingly, as observed by the staff during the problem-solving task and as reported by the youths themselves, parents seem to monitor the whereabouts of their girls more than they do with their boys. With respect to biological maturation, girls were more physically mature than boys at age 12. No gender difference was observed for youth levels of associations with deviant peers. Finally, in adolescence, boys and girls presented similar levels of autonomy in both their friendship network and levels of sexual activity.

Predicting Adolescent Autonomy

Correlations among early adolescent adjustment constructs and premature adolescent autonomy constructs were computed separately for boys and girls. These correlations are reported in Table 2.4.

Correlations among school maladaptation, parent monitoring, and biological maturation were relatively low, suggesting that these constructs represent independent risk factors. Consistent with previous studies, these three constructs were significantly associated with deviant peer associations. All early adolescent adjustment constructs are significantly correlated with the two adolescence constructs except school maladaptation, which was not associated with autonomous friendship network. Finally, the sexual activity and autonomous peer network constructs were moderately correlated, supporting the idea that youth who become more autonomous from the family are also

Table 2.3
Mean and Standard Deviation for Each Indicator by Gender

Constructs/Indicators		Male	Female	Univariate *F*s
School Maladaptation				
Externalizing	M	57.31	54.44	4.16*
	SD	10.93	9.37	
Social preference	M	-0.36	0.41	10.04**
	SD	1.94	1.56	
Academic grades	M	2.14	2.5	6.28*
	SD	0.90	0.86	
			Wilk's lambda = .95**	
Parent Monitoring				
Child report	M	-0.16	0.16	11.81**
	SD	0.69	0.72	
Parent report	M	-0.07	0.02	0.84
	SD	0.77	0.71	
Staff impressions	M	0.89	1.10	4.01*
	SD	0.79	0.76	
			Wilk's lambda = .94**	
Biological Maturation				
Chronological age	M	12.49	12.32	1.96
	SD	0.87	0.90	
Pubertal maturation	M	10.98	13.85	42.12**
	SD	2.98	3.54	
			Wilk's lambda = .79**	
Deviant Peer Associations				
Child report	M	0.02	-0.01	0.08
	SD	0.71	0.79	
Parent report	M	0.10	-0.08	2.54
	SD	0.87	0.78	
Teacher report	M	2.44	2.28	1.85
	SD	0.88	0.86	
			Wilk's lambda = .98	
Autonomous Friendship Network				
Age of friends	M	16.10	16.55	2.51
	SD	1.71	1.60	
Time with friends	M	1.61	1.75	0.63
	SD	1.13	1.01	
Hours without adult	M	1.87	1.36	1.95
supervision	SD	2.28	2.02	
			Wilk's lambda = .95	
Adolescent Sexual Activity				
Intercourse frequency	M	0.94	1.13	1.26
	SD	1.09	1.17	
Number of partners	M	0.82	0.80	0.03
	SD	0.98	0.81	
			Wilk's lambda = .98	

*$p < .05$; **$p < .01$.

Table 2.4
Intercorrelations between Constructs for Boys and Girls

Construct	1	2	3	4	5	6
			Boys			
1. School maladaptation	1.00					
2. Parent monitoring	-.12	1.00				
3. Biological maturation	.07	-.21	1.00			
4. Deviant peer associations	.41	-.37	.23	1.00		
5. Autonomous friendship network	.17	-.25	.35	.25	1.00	
6. Adolescent sexual activity	.33	-.27	.33	.48	.37	1.00
			Girls			
1. School maladaptation	1.00					
2. Parent monitoring	.07	1.00				
3. Biological maturation	.05	-.22	1.00			
4. Deviant peer associations	.35	-.37	.38	1.00		
5. Autonomous friendship network	.06	-.25	.33	.32	1.00	
6. Adolescent sexual activity	.23	-.30	.33	.50	.37	1.00

more likely to be sexually active. Because the pattern of intercorrelations among the constructs did not vary as a function of youth gender, the sample was aggregated to conduct the structural equation modeling analysis described in the next section.

Model Testing

We hypothesized that deviant peer clustering would mediate the relation between early adolescent family, school, and biological risk to middle adolescent autonomy (see Figure 2.2). First, we evaluated the measurement model for the constructs included in this analysis. The factor loadings for indicators for these three constructs are provided in Table 2.5.

The modeling analyses were conducted in two phases to address potential inferential problems associated with missing data. The hypotheses were tested using the AMOS program model for structural equation modeling. Initially, the model was run with the listwise deletion sample of participants, yielding a sample of 83. Using independent t tests, the model for participants with partial data was compared with those with all data, and no significant differences were found. Finally, the standardized path coefficients were generated using all participants (provided in Fig. 2.2).

The model shown in Fig. 2.2 suggests some support for the premature autonomy process described. Indeed, biological maturation was found to be important in accounting for initial peer clustering ($\beta = .32$; $p < .001$) and the development of an autonomous peer network ($\beta = .50$; $p < .001$), controlling for other social influences on these variables. The impact of pubertal maturation on later sexual activity was mediated by deviant peer clustering

Table 2.5
Factor Loadings on Early Adolescent Constructs

	Factor Loadings
School Maladaptation	
Teacher: externalizing	.62
Teacher: social preference	.52
School records: grades	.53
Parental Monitoring	
Parent report	.60
Child report	.57
Teacher report	.48
Physical Maturity	
Self-report: puberty	.64
Age	.64

and establishing an autonomous peer network. Parent monitoring and school maladaptation also contributed to peer clustering. Deviant peer clustering and having an autonomous peer network jointly accounted for 66 percent of the variance in sexual activity in middle adolescence.

In contrast to expectations, the influence of deviant peer clustering was not entirely mediated through peer autonomy in middle adolescence. The value orientation and the problem behavior of peers makes an independent contribution to the propensity to be sexually active. This finding is basically consistent with other findings on sexual behavior in adolescence (Capaldi et al., 1996).

Discussion

These data confirm what has been found in many other studies on adolescent problem behavior—that such behavior is highly embedded within a deviant peer group. Additionally, these data suggest that deviant peer involvement may predict other outcomes (e.g., the adolescents' accelerated sexual and social autonomy).

The paradox presented by these data is that a variable previously considered an index of maladaptation has been shown to be important in predicting a normative developmental milestone. The majority of adolescents will eventually develop a social niche within which they function autonomously. Moreover, most adolescents will become sexually active—the issue is one of timing. From a psychopathological stance, accelerated development in adolescence is seen as a sign of individual dysfunction. From an ethological perspective, however, early achievement of the autonomy and sexual adolescent milestones serve a rather primary evolutionary goal.

There are two important implications to understanding this developmen-

Figure 2.2
A Structural Equation Model for the Development of Adolescent Sexual Precocity

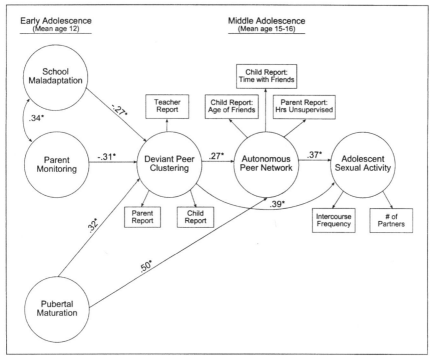

χ^2 (28) = 31.00, p = .32, CFI = .98, GFI = 93, listwise N = 83, $^*p < .05$ standardized coefficients based on full sample.

tal pattern. First, problem behavior may have a powerful function in adolescence, and therefore, is expected to peak during this period; consequently, it may be quite difficult to change using individually oriented strategies. In fact, aggregating high-risk youth for the purpose of reducing problem behavior may increase the problem, as shown in two studies reported by Dishion, McCord, and Poulin (1998). Second, the dynamics of niche-finding in adolescence (e.g., Scarr & McCartney, 1983) may inadvertently provide setting conditions that facilitate deviant peer groups.

The social interactional and ethological perspectives share features. The role of conscious processing is minimized in both accounts of human development, and social contingencies can shape individuals in ways that the participants may not imagine. A "story" about why or how an individual ends up at various life stations may not actually reflect the full range of forces affecting that person's development. In this respect, evolutionary and learning processes can provide complementary insights regarding the joint influence of peers and family on children's social development.

For a small subset of U.S. adolescents who are college bound, well-established institutions exist that provide autonomy transitions, such as dorms, fraternities, sororities, and so forth. In the same vein, many youngsters are not college bound, and may not matriculate through high school. The lack of social and occupational planning for this relatively large segment of the adolescent population creates a vacuum within which biologically driven adaptations can readily unfold. A reasonable solution seems to be for communities to provide alternative contexts, rituals, or customs for adolescents, as a means to establish autonomy that does not comprise adult development.

The resultant understanding may have very important implications for the design of interventions intended to promote health and well-being in young people. Because the formation of peer coalitions is so critical to adolescent development, it is quite natural that children who fail in school, and whose families are disengaged and/or disrupted, will naturally form clusters with others who have similar sets of experiences. This ecological adaptation has an enormous impact in shaping the severity and duration of problem behavior.

NOTES

This project was supported by grant DA 07031 from the National Institute on Drug Abuse at the National Institutes of Health to the senior author, by grant MH 37940 from the National Institute of Mental Health to Gerald R. Patterson, and by grant MH 46690 from the National Institute of Mental Health to John B. Reid. Correspondence regarding this research may be addressed to Thomas J. Dishion, Oregon Social Learning Center, 160 East 4th Avenue, Eugene, Oregon 97401–2426; tomd@tigger.oslc.org; www.oslc.org

1. The participants were recruited for a series of studies underlying the development of the Adolescent Transitions Program (ATP), designed to prevent adolescent drug and alcohol use (see Dishion & Andrews, 1995; Dishion, Andrews, Kavanagh, & Soberman, 1996).

REFERENCES

Achenbach, T. M. (1991). *Manual for the Teacher's Report Form and 1991 profile*. Burlington: University of Vermont. Department of Psychology.

Arbuckle, J. L. (1997). *AMOS Users' Guide (version 3.6)* [computer software]. SmallWaters Corporation, Chicago, IL.

Belsky, J., Steinberg, L., & Draper, P. (1991). Childhood experience, interpersonal development, and reproductive strategy: An evolutionary theory of socialization. *Child Development, 62*, 647–670.

Bronfenbrenner, U. (1989). Ecological systems theory. In Vasta, R. (Ed.), *Annals of child development, Vol. 6. Six theories of child development: Revised formulations and current issues* (pp. 187–249). London: JAI Press.

Buss, D. M., & Schmitt, D. P. (1993) Sexual strategies theory: An evolutionary perspective on human mating. *Psychological Review, 100,* 204–232.

Cairns, R. B., Cairns, B. D., Neckerman, H. J., Gest, S., & Gariepy, J. L. (1988). Social networks and aggressive behavior: Peer support or peer rejection? *Developmental Psychology, 24,* 815–823.

Capaldi, D. M., Crosby, L., & Stoolmiller, M. (1996). Predicting the timing of first sexual intercourse for adolescent males. *Child Development, 67,* 344–359.

Capaldi, D. M., & Patterson, G. R. (1989). *Psychometric properties of fourteen latent constructs from the Oregon Youth Study.* New York: Springer-Verlag.

Coie, J. D., Dodge, K. A., & Coppotelli, H. (1982). Dimensions and types of social status: A cross-age perspective. *Developmental Psychology, 18,* 557–570.

Dishion, T. J. (1990). Peer context of troublesome behavior in children and adolescents. In Leone, P. (Ed.), *Understanding troubled and troublesome youth* (pp. 128–153). Beverly Hills, CA: Sage.

Dishion, T. J., & Andrews, D. W. (1995). Preventing escalation in problem behaviors with high-risk young adolescents: Immediate and 1-year outcomes. *Journal of Consulting and Clinical Psychology, 63,* 538–548.

Dishion, T. J., Andrews, D. W., & Crosby, L. (1995). Antisocial boys and their friends in early adolescence: Relationship characteristics, quality, and interactional process. *Child Development, 66,* 139–151.

Dishion, T. J., Andrews, D. W., Kavanagh, K., & Soberman, L. H. (1996). Preventive interventions for high-risk youth: The Adolescent Transitions Program. In Peters, R. D. & McMahon, R. J. (Eds.), *Preventing childhood disorders, substance abuse, and delinquency* (pp. 184–212). Thousand Oaks, CA: Sage.

Dishion, T. J., Capaldi, D., Spracklen, K. M., & Li, F. (1995). Peer ecology of male adolescent drug use. *Development and Psychopathology, 7,* 803–824.

Dishion, T. J., Eddy, J. M., Haas, E., Li, F., & Spracklen, K. (1997). Friendships and violent behavior during adolescence. *Social Development, 6,* 207–223.

Dishion, T. J., French, D. C., & Patterson, G. R. (1995). The development and ecology of antisocial behavior. In Cicchetti, D. & Cohen, D. (Eds.), *Manual of developmental psychopathology* (pp. 421–471). New York: Wiley.

Dishion, T. J., Li, F., Spracklen, K. M., Brown, G., & Haas, E. (in press). The measurement of parenting practices in research on adolescent problem behavior: A multimethod and multitrait analysis. In Ashery, R. S. (Ed.), *Research meeting on drug abuse prevention through family interventions* (NIDA Research Monograph). Washington, DC: U.S. Government Printing Office.

Dishion, T. J., McCord, J., & Poulin, F. (1998). *Iatrogenic effects in interventions that aggregate high-risk youth.* Manuscript submitted for publication.

Dishion, T. J., & Patterson, G. R. (1997). The timing and severity of antisocial behavior: Three hypotheses within an ecological framework. In Stoff, D., Brieling, J., & Maser, J. (Eds.), *Handbook of antisocial behavior* (pp. 205–217). New York: Wiley.

Dishion, T. J., Patterson, G. R., Stoolmiller, M., & Skinner, M. (1991). Family, school, and behavioral antecedents to early adolescent involvement with antisocial peers. *Developmental Psychology, 27,* 172–180.

Dishion, T. J., Spracklen, K. M., Andrews, D. W., & Patterson, G. R. (1996). De-
    viancy training in male adolescent friendships. *Behavior Therapy, 27*, 373–390.
Dunphy, D. C. (1963). The social structure of urban adolescent peer groups. *Soci-
    ometry, 26*, 230–246.
Elder, G. (1980). *Family structure and socialization.* New York: Arno.
Elliott, D. S., Huizinga, D., & Ageton, S. S. (1985). *Explaining delinquency and drug
    use.* Thousand Oaks, CA: Sage.
French, D. C., Dishion, T. J., & Medici Skaggs, N. (1998). *Predicting early onset of
    sexuality among high risk adolescents.* Manuscript submitted for publication.
Gottfredson, M. R., & Hirschi, T. (1990). *A general theory of crime.* Stanford, CA:
    Stanford University Press.
Hinde, R. A. (1989). Ethological and relationship approaches. In Vasta, R. (Ed.),
    *Annals of child development, Vol. 6. Six theories of child development: Revised for-
    mulations and current issues* (pp. 251–285). London: JAI Press.
Jessor, R., & Jessor, S. L. (1977). *Problem behavior and psychosocial development.* New
    York: Academic Press.
Kandel, D. B. (1986). Process of peer influence on adolescence. In Silbereisen, R. K.
    (Ed.), *Development as action in context* (pp. 33–52). Berlin, Germany: Springer-
    Verlag.
Lickliter, R., & Berry, T. D. (1990). The phylogony fallacy: Developmental psy-
    chology's misapplication of evolutionary theory. *Developmental Review, 10*,
    348–364.
Maccoby, E. E. (1998). *The two sexes: Growing up apart, coming together.* Cambridge,
    MA: Harvard University Press.
Magnusson, D., Stattin, H., & Allen, D. L. (1985). Biological maturation and social
    development: A longitudinal study of some adjustment processes from mid-
    adolescence to adulthood. *Journal of Youth and Adolescence, 14*, 267–283.
Moffitt, T. E. (1993). Adolescence-limited and life course persistent antisocial be-
    havior: Developmental taxonomy. *Psychological Review, 100*, 674–701.
Osborne, S. G., & West, D. J. (1979). Marriage and delinquency: A postscript. *British
    Journal of Criminology, 18*, 254–256.
Patterson, G. R. (1982). *A social learning approach: III. Coercive family process.* Eugene,
    OR: Castalia.
Patterson, G. R. (1993). Orderly change in a stable world: The antisocial trait as a
    chimera. *Journal of Consulting and Clinical Psychology, 61*, 911–919.
Patterson, G. R., Dishion, T. J., & Yoerger, K. (1998). *Adolescent growth in new forms
    of problem behavior: Macro- and micro-peer dynamics* (Manuscript submitted for
    publication).
Patterson, G. R., & Reid, J. B. (1984). Social interactional processes within the family:
    The study of moment-by-moment family transactions in which human social
    development is imbedded. *Journal of Applied Developmental Psychology, 5*, 237–
    262.
Patterson, G. R., Reid, J. B., & Dishion, T. J. (1992). *A social learning approach: IV.
    Antisocial boys.* Eugene, OR: Castalia.
Petersen, A. C. (1984). A self-image questionnaire for young adolescents (SIQYA):
    Reliability and validity studies. *Journal of Youth & Adolescence, 13*(2), 93–111.
Sameroff, A. J., & Suomi, S. J. (1996). Primates and persons: A comparative devel-
    opmental understanding of social organization. In Cairns, R. B. & Elder,

G. H. Jr. (Eds.), *Developmental science. Cambridge studies in social and emotional development* (pp. 97–120). New York: Cambridge University Press.

Scarr, S., & McCartney, K. (1983). How people make their own environments: A theory of genotype to environment effects. *Child Development, 54*, 424–435.

Stattin, H., & Magnusson, D. (1991). Stability and change in criminal behaviour up to age 30. *British Journal of Criminology, 31*, 327–346.

Steinberg, L., & Silverberg, S. B. (1986). The vicissitude of autonomy in early adolescence. *Child Development, 57*, 841–851.

Stoolmiller, M. S. (1990). *Parent supervision, child unsupervised wandering, and child antisocial behavior: A latent growth curve analysis.* Unpublished doctoral dissertation, University of Oregon, Eugene.

Walker, H. M., & McConnell, S. R. (1988). *Walker-McConnell scale of social competence and school adjustment.* Austin, TX: Pro-Ed.

Warr, M. (1993). Age, peers, and delinquency. *Criminology, 31*, 17–40.

West, D. J., & Farrington, D. P. (1977). *The delinquent way of life.* London: Heinemann Educational Books, Ltd.

3

Russian Parenting Styles and Family Processes: Linkages with Subtypes of Victimization and Aggression

Craig H. Hart, David A. Nelson,
Clyde C. Robinson, Susanne F. Olsen,
Mary Kay McNeilly-Choque, Christin L. Porter,
and Trevor R. McKee

Political changes in the former Soviet Union have allowed social scientists to explore a variety of family and child development issues that were closed to systematic investigation for many decades (Maddock, Hogan, Antonov, & Matskovsky, 1994). Prior Soviet psychological research focused on cognitive rather than socioemotional processes for political reasons (Kerig, 1996). Therefore, Western researchers had little opportunity to conduct research on children's social development in the context of the family in the former Soviet Union.

During 1995, we gathered extensive parenting, marital, family interaction, and child behavioral data from 207 ethnic Russian families residing in Voronezh, Russia. Portions of this project explored cross-cultural parenting practices and peer contact patterns in China, Russia, and the United States (e.g., Hart, Yang et al., 1998; Hart et al., in press). We also investigated ways that responsive, coercive, and psychologically controlling Russian parenting styles and marital conflict are mutually associated with children's overt and relational aggression in the peer group (Hart, Nelson, Robinson, Olsen, & McNeilly-Choque, 1998).

To further explore our Russian data set in a more comprehensive manner than can usually be done in a more tightly focused journal article format, we identified three aims for this chapter. First, we sought to determine whether broader parenting styles (e.g., authoritative, authoritarian, overprotective) could be reliably measured in the Russian culture. A similar goal was pursued for measuring marital relationships, and patterns of family cohesion and conflict. Second, we made conceptual and empirical distinctions between proactive and reactive overt and relational aggression, as well as between subtypes of overt and relational victimization, and responses to provocation (e.g., assertive and submissive reactions to aggression). Third, using the Western literature as a backdrop, we investigated whether these behavioral subtypes were linked to parenting styles and patterns of marital and family interaction in the Russian culture.

We first provide a brief overview of the social and historical context in which this investigation occurred. To begin, we explore whether parenting styles and patterns of family-marital interaction can be identified in prior writings about Russian family life (cf. Hart, Nelson et al., 1998). This is followed by a synthesis of the Western literature describing subtypes of children's aggression and victimization in the peer group as related to parenting styles and patterns of marital and family interaction. In accordance with the aims of this volume, we highlight child social cognitive and emotional mechanisms that may account for linkages between parenting-family processes and children's aggression and victimization. The measurement of the parenting, marital, and family interaction constructs, as well as different forms of aggression, victimization, and responses to provocation in our Russian data set is then described. The concluding section centers on our findings regarding Russian parenting-family process linkages with different forms of children's aggression and victimization in the peer group.

SOCIAL AND HISTORICAL CONTEXT

In the mid- to late-1980s, prior to *glasnost* and *perestroika*, traditional Soviet pedagogy promoted childrearing methods designed to foster values supportive of citizenship in a totalitarian socialist society. Conformity, loyalty, group-mindedness, and unquestioning acceptance of and obedience to authority were values deemed to be important (Ispa, 1994; Shipler, 1983). The government did not consider the family to be primarily responsible for the upbringing of children. Rather, a collective-centered system of childrearing was developed (Bronfenbrenner, 1970; Maddock et al., 1994; H. Smith, 1990).

Despite these collectivist ideologies, Soviet data suggests that by 1988, only 58 percent of all children ages 1 to 7 were enrolled in early childhood programs. However, significantly more (71 percent) were attending in the Russian republic than in most of the other former Soviet republics (Maddock et al., 1994). By 1993, this appears to have increased to 86 percent for Russian children ages 2 to 7 (Ispa, 1994). A combination of relatives (e.g., grandparents) or both parents working different shifts were caring for the balance of young children. Recent economic instability may have resulted in less availability of preschool or child care, leaving more responsibilities to families, particularly mothers (Maddock et al., 1994).

Traditionally, child-care personnel and other sources (e.g., medical practitioners, media) conveyed philosophies endorsed by the Central Ministry of Education to parents. Thus, Soviet parents were exposed to little diversity in childrearing opinions from government sources (Ispa, 1993, 1995). The set of expectations and goals for childrearing was quite different for home and school. In accordance with traditions persisting from czarist Russia, restrictiveness, structure, sternness, and emotional distance were the rule in nursery school and other school settings, whereas permissiveness, indulgence, and warmth were used at home (Ispa, 1993; Raeff, 1966).

In this context, parents' use of corporal punishment as a means of fostering conformity to Soviet values was discouraged by the Soviet government for many decades (Ispa, 1994) and authoritarian parenting (i.e., spanking) is viewed as uniformly negative by Russian parents, although it does occur (Ispa, 1995). From the work of Makarenko (1937/1967), a highly influential Soviet educator, to more recent authors (e.g., Azarov, 1983), teachers and parents were counseled to be warm, responsive, and nurturing (withdrawing such only in instances of child disobedience), to use reasoning and persuasion, and to avoid corporal punishment (cf. Bronfenbrenner, 1970). Thus, by the early 1990s the major theme in Soviet/Russian educational writing appeared to endorse democratic childrearing strategies that encouraged initiative and independent problem solving in children (Ispa, 1994; Tudge, 1991).

Despite relative uniformity in childrearing advice, observations and descriptions of Russian parenting styles gathered by Hart, McKee, Nelson, and Robinson during our initial informal interviews with educators, parents, and grandparents in Russia (prior to conducting this study) suggested considerable diversity. This corroborated Bronfenbrenner's anecdotal observations in the 1960s of authoritative and authoritarian parenting patterns that corresponded to Baumrind's conceptualizations of U.S. parenting during the same time period (e.g., Baumrind, 1967). References to permissive parenting (Raeff, 1966) are also available, and these three parenting styles were measured in the Russian culture during the mid-1980s (Subbotskii, 1992).

Another style reportedly used by both parents and teachers was "close watchfulness" over Soviet children (Shipler, 1983). This seems akin to "overprotectiveness" in the Western literature (Rubin, Stewart, & Coplan, 1995). Many parents smothered their children with affectionate, bossy attention or anxious affection. Teachers engaged in "more calculated effort(s) at manipulation" (Shipler, 1983, p. 56) and were taught to actively guide play (Ipsa, 1994).

Additionally, Bronfenbrenner (1970), in his description of "love-oriented" discipline, suggested that guilt induction (telling a child he or she is not as good as other children) and love withdrawal (avoiding a child when he or she does not meet parents' expectations) are two other patterns of Soviet childrearing. Such stylistic patterns of parenting have been referred to as *psychological control* and may be used by parents to manipulate the love and

attachment relationship with a child (Barber, 1996). Such parenting patterns
constrain, invalidate, and manipulate children's psychological and emotional
experience and expression and have also been reported to have been empirically measured in the Russian culture (Subbotskii, 1992).

Unlike writings on parenting, literature concerning specific aspects of family life does not provide much insight concerning the historical Russian past;
instead, it is more recent and focuses on contemporary family relationships.
For example, some Russian studies indicate that although families are valued,
40 percent of marriages end in divorce (Maddock et al., 1994). The emotional quality of many marriages is reported as being quite low, and drinking
and family violence are noted as major sources of marital conflict leading to
divorce in families (Maddock et al., 1994). Thus, although little empirical
research has examined marital and family relationships in Russian families,
it can be assumed that varying levels of conflict and cohesion exist.

Although brief, this historical overview of former Soviet childrearing ide-
ology provides a starting point for our investigation. To our knowledge, no
empirical studies have explored children's peer relations or child aggressive
behavioral linkages to parenting styles and family interactions in the former
Soviet Union. Prior to identifying ways that patterns of parenting and family
interaction just noted have been associated with children's aggression and
victimization in the Western literature, we synthesize recent research that
has been conducted on subtypes of aggression, victimization, and reactions
to provocation. Understanding subtypes of these behaviors, particularly relational forms, is a relatively new area of empirical inquiry.

Proactive Forms of Overt and Relational Aggression

The nature of childhood aggression has been greatly clarified in recent
years with the identification of various styles, or forms, of aggression. One
form, proactive aggression, is defined as nonprovoked, coercive behavior that
is used to obtain something desirable or to intimidate others in ways that
meet self-serving goals (Coie & Dodge, 1998; Crick & Dodge, 1996; Olweus, 1993b). Further clarification of this form can be made according to
the intent of the aggressor. For example, *proactive instrumental aggression* is
typically defined as hitting, pushing, grabbing, or otherwise using physical
force to obtain a desired object, territory, or privilege (Hartup, 1974). In
contrast, *proactive bullying aggression* is used to intimidate or harass, and may
include name calling, teasing, taunting, and threatening for the sake of just
being mean (e.g., Blatchford, 1998; Bowers, Smith, & Binney, 1994; Olweus,
1993a; Slee & Rigby, 1993). Proactive bullying can also include physical
aggression such as hitting, pushing, and kicking for the sake of dominating
peers or just being mean (see McNeilly-Choque, Hart, Robinson, Nelson,
& Olsen, 1996) and may also subsume proactive instrumental forms of aggression as well (Olweus, 1993b). For the purposes of our research in Russia,

proactive instrumental and bullying aggression were conceptualized as a single construct called *proactive overt aggression* (McNeilly-Choque et al., 1996; Price & Dodge, 1989). Accordingly, proactive overt aggression is goal-oriented and self-serving (e.g., for object acquisition or intimidation for subduing others), and harms others through damage (or threat of damage) to another's physical or psychological well-being (Crick, Werner et al., in press). It may often be manifested by children who display high levels of prosocial behavior (Pepler, Craig, & Roberts, 1998), thus highlighting the possibility that some socially capable children utilize aggression to manipulate peers.

In contrast with overt aggression, relational aggression harms others through damage (or threat of damage) to relationships and is more typical of girls (Crick, Werner et al., in press). It has also been referred to as "indirect bullying" (Olweus, 1993a), and "indirect aggression" (Lagerspetz, Bjorkqvist, & Peltonen, 1988). Relational aggression consists of exclusionary tactics such as ostracism, purposeful withdrawal of friendship or acceptance, or spreading of malicious rumors to damage the peer's relationship with others, and is often included in a broader construct of social aggression (cf. Galen & Underwood, 1997).[1]

Like overt aggression, some forms of relational aggression may be proactive in nature (cf. McNeilly-Choque et al., 1996). Crick (1995) postulated that manipulative forms of relational aggression may be used for gaining control of peers (cf. Crick, Bigbee, & Howes, 1996). For school-age and preschool-age children, proactive aggression is driven by the expectation of achieving desired outcomes or by feelings of confidence about being able to manipulate others through aggressive means (e.g., Crick & Dodge, 1996; Hart, DeWolf, & Burts, 1992; Hart, Ladd, & Burleson, 1990; Perry, Williard, & Perry, 1990). Similar motivations are associated with school-age boys who are relationally aggressive (Crick & Werner, 1998). For our purposes, manipulative forms of relational aggression are referred to as *proactive relational aggression*.

Overt and Relational Victimization

Prior studies have established that victims of childhood aggression are at considerable risk for maladaptive sociopsychological outcomes, particularly if they associate with other children who are also at risk for victimization (Hodges, Malone, & Perry, 1997), and if they have low self-regard (Egan & Perry, 1998). As noted by Crick and Bigbee (1998), being mistreated by peers provides relatively clear feedback that one does not fit into the peer group. Specifically, children who are victimized typically are more depressed, lonely, anxious, rejected by peers, have lower perceived competence, and experience greater school adjustment problems and behavioral difficulties (e.g., Crick, Casas, & Ku, 1999; Kochenderfer & Ladd, 1997; Schwartz, McFadyen-

Ketcham, Dodge, Pettit, & Bates, 1998). The majority of studies regarding peer maltreatment have focused on overt forms of victimization, particularly physical maltreatment, and suggests this is more commonly experienced by boys than girls (e.g., Boulton, 1999; Boulton & Underwood, 1992; Schwartz, Dodge, Pettit, & Bates, 1997). However, recent studies indicate no gender differences in physical victimization for extreme groups of victimized children (e.g., Kochenderfer & Ladd, 1997).

Additional research on older and younger children indicates that girls are more often the target of relational aggression (Crick, Werner et al., in press), although boys are often victimized by girls in relationally aggressive ways (Boulton, 1996). In direct correspondence to overt and relational aggression, these studies have identified overt and relational victimization in school-age and preschool-age children (Crick & Bigbee, 1998; Crick, Casas, & Ku, 1999). *Overt victimization* represents children being harmed and controlled through harassment, physical harm, or threats (cf. Schwartz et al., 1997). Most children singled out by aggressors respond to this type of provocation in a submissive manner due to their shy and inhibited nature. However, there is a smaller group who react to such provocation in a hostile and aggressive manner.

Relational victimization refers to children being harmed by peers who attempt to control or damage their relationships with others through exclusionary means. Children who are aggressed against relationally are typically excluded from peer interaction when a request is not obeyed or are the target of a hostile rumor. Relationally victimized children have also been shown to exhibit adjustment problems (Crick & Bigbee, 1998; Crick, Casas, & Ku, 1999).

Overt and Relational Reactions to Provocation

A number of studies also have focused on ways that children respond to aggressive provocations. Overtly aggressive reactions are the most studied form of this behavior. Children, particularly boys (Kochenderfer & Ladd, 1997), who display overt reactions are prone to hit, push, yell, or fight back when provoked and are referred to as *provocative victims, aggressive victims,* or *bully victims* (e.g., Bowers et al., 1994; Olweus, 1993a; Schwartz et al., 1997). They typically display a highly affectively charged response to a perceived threat or blocking of a goal (Coie & Dodge, 1998; Dodge & Coie, 1989). Unlike nonprovoked overt aggression, which is motivated by self-serving outcomes (e.g., object possession or intimidation), reactive aggression stems from anger and arousal associated with hostile attributional biases about the ambiguous intent of a peer, such as perceiving maliciousness when none is intended (Crick & Dodge, 1996; Dodge & Coie, 1989; Price & Dodge, 1989).

Specifically, it has been hypothesized that children who are aggressive reactive may have difficulty in early stages of social information processing (Dodge, 1991). This includes failure to attend to relevant social cues (due to hypervigilance to hostile cues), thereby interpreting peers' intentions as hostile (Burks et al., 1999). They are also more likely to access aggressive responses to hypothetical provocations. In contrast, proactive overt aggression is thought to be associated with later stages of outcome-related processing as reflected in positive evaluations of likely consequences for aggressive behavior. General support for these assumptions has been obtained in empirical studies, although not always for every component process (see Dodge, Harnish, Lochman, Bates, & Pettit, 1997).

Furthermore, Olweus (1993b) described provocative victims as being hot-tempered (although ineffective in retaliating), anxious, hyperactive or restless, generally clumsy, offensive, vengefully hostile, and immature with irritating habits. Such children typically constitute a smaller proportion of victimized children (cf. Kupersmidt, Patterson, & Eickholt, 1989; Rigby, 1994; P. Smith & Boulton, 1991), and are more likely to be recurrently victimized (Kochenderfer & Ladd, 1997). This behavior pattern is also more likely to be linked to peer rejection than proactive overt aggression in young children (e.g., Dodge et al., 1997; Price & Dodge, 1989).

For this research, such reactions to provocation are referred to as *reactive overt aggression*, in contrast to overt aggression that is proactive and goal-oriented (Waschbusch et al., 1998). Reactive overt aggression has typically been measured as the degree to which children (as rated by teachers) display hostile reactions to provocation (cf. Crick & Dodge, 1996; Dodge et al., 1997). This construct has also been conceptualized as describing children who are both highly aggressive and highly victimized by peers (e.g., Schwartz et al., 1997; 1998).

Recent conceptualizations of relational aggression focus not only on proactive, manipulative forms, but on ways that relational aggression can be used as a form of retaliation (e.g., Crick et al., 1996; McNeilly-Choque et al., 1996). It is not always clear whether spreading rumors or excluding peers from interaction represents retaliation, a dislike of someone because of physical appearance or "strange" mannerisms, a preference for other company, or a proactive and manipulative form of aggression. However, some relationally aggressive acts could be viewed as reactive, particularly when accompanied by visible anger in the face of provocation, implying further contact is not desired (e.g., walking away or turning one's back when angry, pouting or sulking when mad, or not listening when upset). For example, girls are more likely than boys to walk away from provocation when upset (Kochenderfer & Ladd, 1997). Child perceptions of provocation may or may not always be accurate. However, the angry attributional pattern exhibited by relationally reactive children appears similar to that of overtly reactive children. Relationally reactive children tend to not give peers the "benefit of the doubt" and perceive overt hostility or exclusion by peers even when none is intended and react accordingly (Crick, 1995). For this research, such reactions to provocation are called *reactive relational aggression* (Crick & Werner, 1998).

Assertive and Submissive Reactions to Provocation

Finally, other responses to provocation include assertion and submission. For example, Schwartz (1995) identified differences in the degree of assertiveness and submissiveness children display in the face of provocation. Assertive children who stand up assertively but not aggressively to a bully (e.g., saying something in a strong voice like, "that's mine, give it back)" tend to dissuade bullying behavior (Olweus, 1993b).

Most chronically victimized children display submissive characteristics, including anxiety and fearfulness, poor self-esteem, cautiousness, sensitivity, withdrawn behavior, and difficulty in asserting themselves, both physically and verbally in the peer group. They are more frequently found playing alone (Boulton, 1995) and are not aggressive or provoking (Olweus, 1993b; Schwartz et al., 1997). *Submissive reactions* to aggression could include cowering or withdrawing from provocation, appearing worried, sad, or afraid, exhibiting emotional distress such as crying, and engaging in avoidant behaviors. Such anxious vulnerability may signal to aggressors that they are an easy mark, rewarding attackers by submission or the relinquishing of resources (Olweus, 1993a; Troy & Sroufe, 1987). Children displaying these characteristics are referred to as *passive victims* or *nonaggressive victims* (e.g., Olweus, 1993b; Schwartz et al., 1997).

Family and Parenting Variables Associated with Aggression and Victimization

As noted by Schwartz et al. (1997), past research does not provide a strong foundation for specificity in hypothesis formulation regarding the distinct socialization experiences associated with different aggression and victimization profiles (e.g., aggressive victims, submissive victims). This problem is compounded when overt and relational aggression and victimization are considered (Crick, Werner, et al., in press), particularly when couched in the framework of reactions to provocation. Most of the literature also centers on older, but not younger preschool-age children.

Accordingly, our goal was to identify sociocognitive and emotional mechanisms that may link family processes to subtypes of overt and relational aggression, victimization, and reactions to provocation in young children. Research on subtypes of aggression has focused on sociocognitive processes and are emphasized in our synthesis. In prelude to a description of the Russian data, a general overview of parenting styles and patterns of family and marital interaction associated with subtypes of aggression and victimization (in Western samples) is presented.

Parenting Styles and Proactive/Reactive Overt and Relational Aggression

Research exploring linkages involving patterns of family interaction, parenting styles, and children's aggression has focused primarily on overt aggression (see Hart, Olsen, Robinson, & Mandleco, 1997), although proactive and reactive forms of overt aggression have not usually been delineated. Parenting style dimensions associated with overt aggression include lack of responsiveness, less warmth and involvement, nonreasoning coercion, permissiveness or condoning of aggression, and coercive discipline reflected in physical punishment, verbal hostility, and psychological control (see Hart, Nelson et al., 1998; MacKinnon-Lewis et al., 1994; Olweus, 1993a, for reviews).

In prior analyses of our Russian data (Hart, Nelson et al., 1998), similar correlational patterns for overt aggression involving less responsiveness and more coercive parenting appeared to hold true for both mothers and fathers. However, when entered into the same statistical model, lower levels of paternal responsiveness accompanied by higher levels of maternal coercion appeared to work in combination to predict overt aggression. These findings are supportive of research in Western samples highlighting the importance of positive, playful, sensitive, and engaging interactions with children for fathers and less punitive parenting for mothers in the development of socially competent behavior (see Carson & Parke, 1996).

Research also suggests that children reared in a power-assertive manner are more likely to expect to get their way by being mean and aggressive with peers (Hart, DeWolf, & Burts, 1992; Hart et al., 1990). Thus, expectations of positive outcomes associated with coercion is one of a variety of mechanisms described in social information-processing models that may link parenting styles to proactive overt aggression, particularly as parents model coercion as an efficacious means of resolving interpersonal conflict (see Coie & Dodge, 1998; Crick, Werner et al., in press; Crick & Dodge, 1994; Parke, Burks, Carson, Neville, & Boyum, 1994; Pettit, Polaha, & Mize, in press).

In contrast, extremely harsh and abusive treatment by adults may serve to disregulate and handicap children by altering their ability to successfully encode social cues and correctly interpret ambiguous peer provocations (Dodge, Bates, & Pettit, 1990; Dodge, Pettit, Bates, & Valente, 1995), lending itself to reactive aggression. Rather than being goal-oriented toward self-serving gains, reactive overt aggression is characterized by hostile attributional biases toward the aggressor and an angry and hypervigilant style of personal interaction (e.g., viewing others as out to get them, easily taking offense). Supporting research indicates that overtly aggressive reactive

school-aged boys experienced more extreme abusive family backgrounds
during their preschool years when compared with proactive aggressive boys
(Schwartz et al., 1997).

What emerges from this line of research is the view that young children
who are victimized by adults may come to expect hostile intentions from
others, become hypervigilant to these cues, and are less able to control their
anger responses to perceptions of danger. Coie and Dodge (1998) speculated
that this orientation toward defending self and attacking others may limit
alternative thinking about ways social cues could be perceived as not reflecting danger to oneself. How this applies to younger nursery school-age children such as those studied in our Russian sample is uncertain (see Crick &
Dodge, 1994; Pettit et al., in press). For example, evidence for hostile attributional biases in reactive aggressive children is mixed across different samples of children, depending on the methodology used and the age group
studied (see Crick & Dodge, 1996; Dodge et al., 1997; Pettit et al., in press).
Although evidence is far from conclusive (cf. Katsurada & Sugawara, 1998),
recent studies suggest that hostile attributional biases may not be very reliable predictors of behavioral adjustment for preschool-age children (see Pettit et al., in press).

It appears that associations between parenting and overt aggression may
also operate with relational aggression (see Crick, Werner et al., in press).
In prior analyses of our Russian data, and similar to findings for overt aggression, less responsiveness for fathers and more coercion for mothers were
found to be the most important contributors to relational aggression (Hart,
Nelson, et al., 1998). Additionally, psychological control (e.g., love withdrawal) has also been associated with more overt and relational aggression
in school-age children (Grotpeter & Crick, 1997). For this study, we attempted to approximate child sociocognitive and emotional processes in
proactive and reactive relational and overt aggression by embedding attributional biases, positive outcome expectations, and anger reactions in the
teacher-rated items delineating these forms of aggression. Because we did
not measure extreme forms of maltreatment in Russia, we expected associations for proactive rather than reactive aggression (cf. Dodge et al., 1997;
Schwartz et al., 1997). We also expected psychological control (i.e., love
withdrawal and guilt induction implying less acceptance) to be associated
with proactive aggression (Chen & Rubin, 1994; Hart, Nelson et al., 1998).

Linkages between authoritative dimensions of Russian parenting and children's proactive but not reactive forms of overt and relational aggression
were also anticipated. However, these expectations were confined to responsive parenting (particularly for fathers) and parental warmth and involvement
(see Russell & Russell, 1996). There is little support in the Western literature connecting reasoning-oriented control and democratic parenting dimensions with less aggression in young children. These stylistic dimensions
are typically associated with enhancing prosocial and empathetic forms of

behavior as well as more friendly and assertive consequential thinking skills (e.g., Hart, DeWolf, Wozniak, & Burts, 1992; Krevans & Gibbs, 1996).

Marital Relationships and Proactive/Reactive Overt and Relational Aggression

Relative to the parenting literature, little is understood concerning how childhood aggressive subtypes may be related to interparental conflict and harmony (Fincham, 1994; Fincham, Grych, & Osborne, 1994). With few exceptions (Harrist & Ainslie, in press; Schwartz et al., 1997), the marital interaction literature has focused on global categories of child maladjustment (e.g., externalizing, internalizing) to the exclusion of delineating specific aggressive subtypes (e.g., Katz & Gottman, 1993).

Because marital conflict typically does not exist in isolation from other aspects of family interaction (e.g., Hayden et al., 1998), a number of studies have investigated how parenting variables and marital conflict are linked to children's adjustment (e.g., Davies & Cummings, 1994). One line of studies has explored how marital relationships work through the parent-child relationship to predict children's behavioral adjustment (e.g., Fauber & Long, 1991; Harrist & Ainslie, in press). Alternatively, and in accordance with other research traditions in this area (Fincham, 1994), we examined how parent-child interactions and marital conflict were each associated with Russian childhood aggression on an independent basis.

In terms of explanatory mechanisms for how marital conflict is related to children's behavior problems, research conducted by Davies and Cummings (1998) focused on children's emotional security as a mediating link. Their findings suggest that child adjustment problems associated with marital conflict (including internalizing and externalizing symptoms) are mediated, in part, by children's emotional reactivity (e.g., distress reactions including anxiety, tension, fearfulness, vigilance, as well as suppressed anger and hostility). Although child emotional reactivity was not directly measured in our Russian sample, these recent findings can help explain at a conceptual level how emotional arousal associated with marital conflict might stimulate distressful affect that may be manifest in overt and/or relationally aggressive peer group behavior. Cummings and Zahn-Waxler (1992) postulated that exposure to adult anger may lower thresholds for emotional regulation that can, in turn, be translated into aggressive coping responses.

Extrapolating from gender-based findings derived from the marital relations research (see Cummings, 1994), we anticipated that marital conflict would be associated with higher levels of proactive overt aggression in boys but not girls. As postulated by Crick, Werner et al. (in press) and assuming that similar conflictive family processes might contribute to both overt and relational aggression, we anticipated similar findings for proactive relational aggression as well. Whether this expectation applies to both boys and girls is explored in our Russian data. Findings reported by Schwartz et al. (1997)

also suggest that extreme forms of marital violence may contribute to reactive forms of aggression in school-age children (i.e., victimized aggressors).
However, proactive aggressors (i.e., nonvictimized aggressors) appeared to
have more exposure to marital conflict that was not extremely violent. Rather
than being seen as emotion evoking, moderate levels of conflict were interpreted as providing vicarious learning experiences for children by demonstrating how aggression could be used to achieve desired outcomes in the
marital relationship. Because extreme forms of marital violence were not
captured in our analysis of the Russian data, we anticipated that marital
conflict would be linked to proactive forms of overt and relational aggression
and not with reactive forms of these aggressive subtypes. Alternatively, in
accordance with findings from the Western literature, we anticipated that
marital harmony would not be associated with aggression in any form (see
Cummings, 1994).

Global Family Processes and Proactive/Reactive Overt and Relational Aggression

Because marital conflict and individual parent–child interactions represent
smaller subsystems that are interlinked within the larger family system (see
Davies & Cummings, 1998; Hart et al., 1997; Hayden et al., 1998), we also
sought to describe Russian family interactions at a broader level. In so doing,
we focused on family conflict and cohesion, two constructs that have been
associated with childhood aggression in prior research. Specifically, less cohesive and more disengaged family relationships have been associated with
overt forms of aggression (Berdondini & Smith, 1996; Bowers et al., 1994).
Similarly, overt family hostility displayed in the home may form a basis for
exclusionary tactics that are used with peers (Bryant & De Morris, 1992).

These conclusions might be interpreted in light of a stressor model that
may undermine children's emotional security (Davies & Cummings, 1994;
Mann & MacKenzie, 1996). Extremely conflictive or less cohesive patterns
of family interaction may upset children and subsequently precipitate aggression (cf. Davies & Cummings, 1998; Parke et al., 1994). In support of
this perspective, Gottman and Fainsilber-Katz (1989) noted that cold, un-
responsive and angry parenting associated with conflictive interparental relationships is related to higher levels of childhood anger, noncompliance,
and higher levels of stress-related hormones.

Less extreme exposure to aggressive, violent, and exclusionary role models
might only be associated with proactive rather than reactive overt and relational aggression. Instead of emotional security deficits being the driving
mechanism, it is presumed that proactive aggression develops through early
vicarious learning experiences in the family where aggression is used instru-
mentally to achieve desired outcomes (cf. Bandura, 1973; Schwartz, et al.,
1997). This could include manipulating other family members through anger

expressions, coercive behavior and/or ostracizing tactics in order to focus on self-oriented rather than family goals.

Parenting and Family Processes Associated with Victimization

As noted earlier, children who display reactive aggression are also more victimized by peers, likely because their behavior makes them targets for anger and rebuff by peers (e.g., Olweus, 1993b; Schwartz et al., 1997). However, the majority of children who are overtly victimized do not respond to aggression in overtly or relationally reactive ways. Children who are overtly victimized are often characterized by a pervasively submissive behavior pattern and are frequently found playing by themselves (Boulton, 1995; Olweus, 1978; Schwartz, Dodge, & Coie, 1993). The familial correlates of such behavior include overprotective and restrictive parenting (Bowers et al., 1994; Finnegan, Hodges, & Perry, 1998; Ladd & Ladd, 1998; Olweus, 1993b). As noted by Rubin et al. (1995), anxiously overinvolved and overprotective parents encourage dependency by restricting children's behavior to low risk-taking activities. This may limit spontaneous interaction with peers, thus inhibiting opportunities to explore the social milieu and develop social skills (LaFreniere & Dumas, 1992).

In accordance with overprotective and restrictive parenting correlates obtained with older victimized children in the Western literature, we sought to explore whether such parenting was related to overt and relational victimization as well as to submissive reactions to victimization in younger Russian children. Given that there is little research from which to draw for establishing hypotheses regarding ways that marital and family relationships might be associated with victimization, we also explored whether there were any linkages in this regard in our Russian data. As discussed earlier, emotional insecurity or positive outcome expectations associated with marital and family conflict could result in reactive or proactive child aggression. It is not inconceivable that negative family interactions could also make children more prone to being victimized by peers, particularly if their anxiety and emotional insecurities associated with punitive parenting, marital or family conflict, or family disengagement are displayed in pervasively submissive or aggressive reactive ways (see Siqueland, Kendall, & Steinberg, 1996).

In summary, findings from the Western research literature indicate that a variety of parenting style dimensions and patterns of family interaction may be linked to different forms of childhood aggression and victimization. However, we would not expect all parenting and family variables to be associated with all types of these childhood outcomes. Our literature review indicates that there may be specificity in many of these linkages (e.g., overprotective parenting and child victimization). The data gathered in our Russian sample included all the parenting, marital, and family interaction variables just discussed, as well as all the forms of aggression and victimization outlined earlier. This gave us a unique opportunity to explore on a variable-by-variable basis that Russian parenting and family variables were (or were not) related to aggression and victimization subtypes as compared with Western findings.

As noted earlier, analyses describing how a select few parenting dimensions (e.g., responsiveness) and patterns of marital hostility (e.g., marital exclusion) may mutually operate to be associated with Russian children's overt and relational aggression are presented in Hart, Nelson et al. (1998). This chapter extends this work by highlighting all the Russian parenting styles and family variables measured (e.g., broader authoritative, authoritarian, permissive, and family interaction styles) and examining the specific linkages with subtypes of proactive and reactive aggression and forms of victimization and reactions to provocation.

METHOD

Setting

The parents and their preschool-age children involved in this study resided in Voronezh, Russia. Voronezh is a city of approximately 1 million inhabitants and is located approximately 250 miles southeast of Moscow. The vast majority of inhabitants of Voronezh are ethnic Russians, reflecting the relative homogeneity of the sample (100 percent ethnic Russian).

Sample

Subjects for the study were parents (207 mothers and 167 fathers) and their preschool-age children (207 children out of a potential 255 eligible children). The children attended 1 of 15 classrooms in three nursery schools. The discrepancy between mother and father participation was due to 32 single-parent families and 8 fathers declining to participate. Russian nursery schools act *in loco parentis*, and thus we were not allowed to obtain written parental permission. However, the three nursery school administrators helped arrange group meetings with parents to explain procedures of the study in their own language. Parents were assured of confidentiality concerning data that they or the teachers provided and were informed that they could withdraw themselves or their child from voluntary participation at any time.

Parents were administered a family information questionnaire. Education level ranged from 9 years (high school beginning) to 17 years (college education) for both mothers and fathers. Mothers averaged 14.95 years ($SD = 2.34$) and fathers averaged 14.53 years ($SD = 2.42$), representing a generally well-educated sample. The sample was comprised of 101 boys and 106 girls, ages ranging from 3.6 to 6.6 years ($M = 5.1$; $SD = .72$) upon participation during May and June 1995 (roughly preschool and kindergarten age in the United States). Sixty-nine percent of the families in the study had one child, 30 percent had two children, and 1 percent had more than two children.

Measuring Russian Parenting, Family Interactions, and Marital Relationships

Paper-and-pencil measures, most with demonstrated psychometric qualities in North American samples, were selected and/or modified for our study of Russian family, marital, and parenting variables. All measures were successfully forward- and back-translated by Russian linguists who were fluent in both Russian and English, with input from the investigators for difficult-to-translate items. Back-translated items were comparable to the English versions. With only minor exceptions, all items were judged to be culturally appropriate by two Russian linguists (see Hart, Nelson et al., 1998). Parenting style and family process measures were administered in conjunction with other instruments addressing different research questions (e.g., Hart, Yang et al., 1998) and were distributed in three packets on three different occasions, each approximately 1 week apart. Mothers and fathers were asked to rate their behaviors as well as their perceptions of marital and family interactions on Likert-scaled items representing the dimensions outlined here. Due to space limitations, full descriptions of measure development and psychometric analyses are not included here but are available from the authors.

Parenting Styles, Marital, and Family Interactions

Parenting styles are currently defined in the Western literature as "aggregates or constellations of behaviors that describe parent-child interactions over a wide range of situations and that are presumed to create a pervasive interactional climate" (Mize & Pettit, 1997, p. 291). A taxonomy of parenting styles measured is presented in Table 3.1 and includes measurements of stylistic dimensions that exist within overall parenting typologies (Russell et al., 1998; Smetana, 1995), which were derived using factor-analytic procedures outlined in Robinson, Mandleco, Olsen, and Hart (1995). Also measured were psychological controlling styles (Barber 1996; Hart, Nelson et al., 1998) and parental overprotectiveness (our own derivation). The same factors shown in Tables 3.1 and 3.2 were obtained for mothers and fathers. Maternal and paternal psychological control and overprotectiveness were generally uncorrelated with other parenting dimensions, except for maternal psychological control being correlated with the authoritarian style ($r = .37$; $p < .001$).

Family interaction variables were measured using items from the family cohesion and family conflict subscales from Bloom and Naar (1994). Marital interactions observed by the child were assessed using eight items from the O'Leary-Porter Scale (OPS) for hostility (Porter & O'Leary (1980) and four

Table 3.1
Russian Parenting Style[a,b] and Dimension Measure (Sample Items)

Authoritative Style (26 items; Eigenvalue = 7.58; α = .87)

    Dimension 1 (Reasoning/Reinforcing) ([c]10 items; Load = .36-.77; α = .80; [d]r = .36*)
        Explains the consequences of the child's behavior
        Gives child reasons for why rules should be obeyed
        Tells child what he or she tries or accomplishes is appreciated

    Dimension 2 (Responsive/Easy Going) ([c]4 items; Load = .41-.75; α = .76; [d]r = .34*)
        Shows patience with child
        Is easy going and relaxed with child
        Jokes and plays with child
        Responsive to child's feelings or needs

    Dimension 3 (Democratic Participation) ([c]5 items; Load = .45-.71; α = .71; [d]r = .38*)
        Allows child to give input into family rules
        Encourages child to freely express him or herself even when disagreeing with parents
        Shows respect for child's opinions by encouraging child to express them

    Dimension 4 (Warmth and Involvement) ([c]8 items; Load = .35-.74; α = .70; [d]r = .33*)
        Expresses affection by hugging, kissing, and holding child
        Knows the names of child's friends
        Gives comfort and understanding when child is upset

Authoritarian Style (17 items; Eigenvalue = 4.72; α = .82)

    Dimension 1 (Corporal Punishment/Verbal Hostility) ([c]9 items; Load = .49-.70; α = .80; [d]r =.23*)
        Slaps child when child misbehaves
        Uses physical punishment as a way of disciplining child
        Yells or shouts when child misbehaves

    Dimension 2 (Nonreasoning/coercion) ([c]6 items; Load = .39-.75; α = .61; [d]r=.24*)
        Punishes by taking privileges away from child with little, if any explanations
        Uses threats as punishment with little or no justification
        When child asks why he or she has to conform, states: "Because I said so."

Permissive Style[e] (9 items; Eigenvalue = 2.59; Load = .35-.80; α = .60; [d]r = .25*)
        Gives into child when he or she causes a commotion about something
        Ignores child's misbehaviors
        States punishments to child and does not actually do them

[a]A three-factor, parenting style solution was derived first, followed by varimax rotation.
[b]Authoritative/authoritarian ($r = -.21$*); Authoritative/permissive ($r = .09$); Authoritarian/permissive ($r = .28$*)
[c]Eigenvalues for dimensions extracted from each of the three styles (using oblique rotation) were all > 1.
[d]Correlations between mother and factor scores *$p < .001$.
[e]Three dimensions emerged (i.e., lack of follow through, ignoring, self-confidence) but were unreliable.

Table 3.2

Russian Psychological Control, Overprotectiveness, Family, and Marital Interaction Measures (Sample Items)[a]

Psychological Control and Overprotectiveness Measure[b]

Psychological Control (7 items; Eigenvalue = 3.12; Load = .47 to .65; α = .72; [c]r = .40[c])
    I tell our child he or she is not as good as other children
    I stop talking to my child until he or she pleases me
    I am less friendly when my child doesn't see things my way

Overprotectiveness (6 items; Eigenvalue = 2.50; Load = .53 -.73; α = .74; [c]r = .35[c])
    I readily step in when my child is having difficulties
    I worry that my child will get hurt
    I am overly involved in my child's activities

Family Interaction Measure[c]

Family Cohesion (10 items; Eigenvalue = 4.72; Load = .48 to .71; α = .82; [c]r = .64[c])
    Family members spend time together
    Family members help and support each other
    Family members do not avoid contact with each other

Family Conflict (6 items; Eigenvalue = 1.44; Load = .50-.67; α = .70; [c]r = .60[c])
    Family members criticize each other
    Family members yell and scream at each other
    Family members hit and fight with each other

Marital Relationships Measure[d]

Marital/Conflict (8 items; Eigenvalue = 3.18; Load = .48-.77; α = .78; [c]r = .57[c])
    Argue with one another in front of child
    Verbally hostile with one another in front of child
    Physically hostile with one another in front of child

Marital Harmony (4 items; Eigenvalue = 2.00; Load = .62 to .76; α = .67; [c]r = .36[c])
    Display affection with one another in front of child
    Laugh together in front of child
    Calmly discuss matters in front of child

[a]Principle components with varimax rotation was used in all these measure analyses.
[b]These two scales were correlated at $r = .13$.
[c]These two scales were correlated at $r = -.44$.
[d]These two scales were correlated at $r = -.09$.
[e]Correlation between mother and father factor scores.
*$p < .001$.

items we developed for marital harmony. Although the same factor structures were obtained for both mothers and fathers, only mother scores were used in subsequent analyses due to incomplete data on all the fathers in the sample for the family interaction measures.

Correlations Among Family-Marital Measures and Parenting Measures

Although family conflict correlated with marital conflict at .60, correlations among the other family-marital scales were low to moderate in magnitude and in expected directions (*r*s ranging from −.43 to .37). These correlations suggested a moderate degree of construct specificity (i.e., nonoverlap) in the areas of marital and family functioning assessed, which allowed them to be analyzed as separate scales in subsequent analyses (cf. Hayden et al., 1998; Jouriles et al., 1991). Family and marital measures were generally uncorrelated with parenting style and dimension measures with no significant correlations exceeding .24. Tables with all correlations are available from the authors.

Measuring Russian Children's Aggressive and Victimization Subtypes

Teacher ratings were used to assess the various forms of proactive aggression, victimization, and reactions to provocation. Observations and teacher and peer reports indicate that overt and relational forms of aggression occur on a relatively frequent basis in North American samples across the age span of children in this study (Crick, Casas, & Mosher, 1997; McNeilly-Choque et al., 1996). Crick, Werner et al. (in press) concluded that teacher reports are more valid than peer reports for this age group, particularly because they have been shown to correlate significantly with naturalistic observations for preschool-age populations (e.g., McNeilly-Choque et al., 1996). Again, all items on the teacher measures were both forward and backtranslated by Russian linguists. Teachers rated the frequency of proactive aggressive, victimization, and aggressive, assertive, and submissive reactions to provocation for each child whose parent was participating in the study on a 3-point scale (*never, sometimes, often*) across items representing each of the domains. Items were derived from pilot work with teachers who rated the behaviors of approximately 600 U.S. children, ages 4 to 5 (McNeilly-Choque et al., 1996).

The results of factor analyses on the Russian measure versions are presented in Table 3.3. Intercorrelations for these measures are presented in Table 3.4. Interestingly, the correlations between teacher measures of proactive overt and proactive relational aggression, overt and relational victimization, and proactive and reactive overt aggression are almost identical to those found in North American samples (see Crick, Casas, & Ku, 1999;

Table 3.3
Teacher Measures (Sample Items)*

Proactive Aggression Measure

    Overt (8 items; Eigenvalue = 7.74; Load = .58-.85; α = .90)
        Threatens or intimidates to be mean
        Enjoys picking on others
        Hits, kicks, or pushes to get something he or she wants
    Relational (8 items; Eigenvalue = 1.92; Load = .61-.94; α = .91)
        Tells a peer that he or she won't play with them if don't do as asked
        Tells other children not to play with or be a peer's friend
        Tells a peer that they won't be invited to a party unless they do what is wanted

Victimization Measure

    Overt (3 items; Eigenvalue = 1.08; Load = .48-.89; α = .72)
        Is pushed around by others
        Is picked on by mean kids
        Is made fun of by mean kids
    Relational (4 items; Eigenvalue = 3.69; Load = .77-.86; α = .85)
        Is told to go away by other children
        Is often excluded by other children
        Others tell him or her that he or she can't play with them
        Is ignored by others

Reactions to Provocation Measure

    Overt (9 items; Eigenvalue = 7.07; Load = .68-.84; α = .92)
        Lashes out even when peer did not intend to hurt
        Misinterprets friendly intent of others
        Retaliates with force when intimidated
    Relational (3 items; Eigenvalue = 1.11; Load = .44-.76; α = .73)
        Does not listen or covers ears when mad
        Pouts or sulks when mad
        Walks away when mad
    Submissive (5 items, Eigenvalue = 3.70; Load = .58-.91; α = .83)
        Cowers or slinks away when confronted by a bully
        Cries when picked on
        Withdraws when provoked
    Assertive (3 items; Eigenvalue = 1.91; Load = .44-.76; α = .68)
        Stands up assertively but not aggressively to bullies
        Says assertively "that is mine" or "give it back"
        Is assertive rather than aggressive when something is taken away

*The three measures were the result of principle components factor analysis with oblique rotations.

Table 3.4

Intercorrelations between Subscales of Children's Aggression, Victimization, and Reactions to Provocation

	Proact. Overt Aggres.	Proact. Relat. Aggres.	Overt Victim.	Relat. Victim.	React. Overt Aggres.	React. Relat. Aggres.	Submis. Reactive	Assert. Reactive
Proactive Overt Aggres.		.62***	.42***	.52***	.83***	.39***	.01	.21**
Proactive Relat. Aggres.			.35***	.38***	.63***	.62***	.25***	.29***
Overt Victimization				.53***	.46***	.39***	.48***	.14
Relational Victimization					.53***	.42***	.38***	.02
Reactive Overt Aggres.						.49***	.03	.31***
Reactive Relat. Aggres.							.47***	.15*
Submissive Reactive								-.05

$* = p < .05$; $** = p < .05$; $*** = p < .001$.

Crick, Werner et al., in press; Dodge & Coie, 1989; Price & Dodge, 1989; Vitaro, Gendreau, Tremblay, & Oligny, 1998).

ANALYSIS STRATEGY

In this research, the subscale means for each parenting, marital, and family measure as well as for each teacher measure of aggression and victimization were used in analyses. Pettit and Bates (1989) as well as others (e.g., Belsky, 1984) noted that alternate courses of socialization can often be better appreciated when extremes in parenting and family interaction can be compared and contrasted. However, conclusions about the nature and source of observed differences between extreme groups constituting only a very small proportion of a sample can be problematic (see Pettit & Bates, 1989). Therefore, we chose to create larger "extreme" groups of family, marital, and parenting style differences that were more typical and representative of our sample, but still distinct enough to highlight important family interaction and parenting effects associated with theoretically central differences in aggression and victimization.

We reasoned that this approach would not only allow us to capture a large enough sample from our Russian data to maintain statistical power due to adequate cell sizes, but would also reduce the possibility of generalizing findings from Russian family groupings that are too extreme and therefore atypical. In accordance with this aim, families were classified into higher and lower groupings for family cohesion, family conflict, marital harmony, and marital conflict by selecting families that fell .5 standard deviations above and below the mean on each of these variables. The same approach was used to classify mothers and fathers on parenting stylistic dimensions.

Typically, we would be interested in aggregating across a number of variables and finding ways to present findings in a more parsimonious manner. However, for this chapter, our goal was simply to highlight specific relations between each family-parenting variable and each aggression-victimization subtype outcome. Although our approach increased the possibility of Type 1 error due to the number of analyses run, it allowed for more specificity in illustrating how results from our Russian data compare with those reported in the Western literature on a variable-by-variable basis. Thus, analyses were not designed to illuminate ways that parenting style and family interaction variables might singly or mutually be related to subtypes of aggressive and victimized behavior in the context of one another, or whether there are mediating paths involving a variety of variables that link up with these outcomes in young children.

RESULTS

With these limitations in mind, a series of 2 (sex) $\times$ 2 (high-low parenting or family-marital variables) multivariate analyses of variance (MANOVA) was used to investigate the individual and interactive contributions of gender as well as parenting, family, and marital variables to preschoolers' subtypes of aggression and victimization. Gender was included due to findings in the Western literature suggesting that boys are typically more overtly aggressive and victimized, whereas girls are more relationally aggressive and victimized (see Crick, Casas, & Ku, 1999; Crick, Werner et al., in press; McNeilly-Choque et al., 1996). However, this has not always been found in all cultural contexts (e.g., Tomada & Schneider, 1997).

All results are summarized in Table 3.5. The left side of the table highlights findings associated with MANOVAs that included all four of the overt and relational aggression and overt and relational victimization variables together in each analysis (as seen across the top of the table on the left-hand side). A parallel set of analyses for reactions to provocation are presented on the right side of the table. In all analyses, child gender was included as an independent variable, with higher and lower groupings of family cohesion, family conflict, marital conflict, or marital harmony scores alternately serving as independent variables in each separate analysis (as seen going down the left-hand side of the table). A similar procedure was followed for higher and

Table 3.5
Summary of Russian Analyses[a]

	Overt/Relational Aggression and Victimization					Reactions to Provocation				
	Mult. F	Overt Proactive	Relational Proactive	Overt Victim	Relational Victim	Mult. F	Overt Reactive	Relational Reactive	Submissive Reactive	Assertive Reactive
Family /Marital (IVs)										
Family conflict	2.64*	H 2.48* / L 2.19	--	--	--	0.67	--	--	--	--
Family cohesion	2.52*	H 2.18*** / L 2.47	2.36** / 2.52	--	1.37* / 1.52	2.58*	H 1.38** / L 1.63	--	--	--
Marital harmony	0.29	--	--	--	--	1.60	--	--	--	--
Marital conflict x gender (boys)	2.49*	H 2.38* / L 2.11	2.55** / 2.35	1.75* / 1.43	1.53* / 1.27	2.71*	H 1.70* / L 1.48	2.11*** / 1.81	--	--
Parenting Styles (IVs)										
M Authoritative	0.80	--	--	--	--	0.20	--	--	--	--
P Authoritative	2.17	--	--	--	--	0.52	--	--	--	--
M Authoritarian	5.58***	H 2.33*** / L 2.12	2.44** / 2.27	--	--	3.21***	H 1.60*** / L 1.32	1.94* / 1.76	--	--
P Authoritarian	3.42**	H 2.38*** / L 2.16	2.51*** / 2.32	--	--	3.88***	H 1.71*** / L 1.39	--	--	--
M Permissive	0.35	--	--	--	--	0.90	--	--	--	--
P Permissive	1.16	--	--	--	--	0.98	--	--	--	--
Authoritarian Style Dimensions (IVs)										
M Corporal/Hostile	5.13***	H 2.34*** / L 2.13	2.49*** / 2.30	1.58* / 1.45	--	3.70***	H 1.63*** / L 1.28	1.98* / 1.69	--	--
P Corporal/Hostile	5.43***	H 2.55*** / L 2.15	2.56*** / 2.31	--	--	5.82***	H 1.82*** / L 1.42	--	--	--

	Mult. F	Overt Proactive	Relational Proactive	Overt Victim	Relational Victim	Mult. F	Overt Reactive	Relational Reactive	Submissive Reactive	Assertive Reactive
M Nonreasoning	3.08**	H 2.31** L 2.16	--	--	--	0.93	--	--	--	--
P Nonreasoning	2.72*	H 2.35*** L 2.18	--	--	--	3.70***	H 1.66*** L 1.39	--	1.63* 1.79	--
Authoritative Style Dimensions (IVs)										
M Reasoning	1.00	--	--	--	--	1.27	--	--	--	--
P Reasoning	0.47	--	--	--	--	1.17	--	--	--	--
M Responsiveness	1.84	--	--	--	--	0.31	--	--	--	--
P Responsiveness	6.11***	H 2.18*** L 2.43	2.32*** 2.57	--	--	2.82*	H 1.44*** L 1.71	1.84* 2.03	--	--
M Democracy	3.12*	--	2.31** 2.47	--	--	1.14	--	--	--	--
P Democracy	3.03*	--	2.31* 2.49	--	--	1.94	--	--	--	--
M Warmth/involve x gender (boys)	1.00	--	--	--	--	2.73*	--	1.75* 2.00	1.59* 1.82	--
P Warmth/involve	1.27	--	--	--	--	0.73	--	--	--	--
Psych. Control/ Overprotective (IVs)										
M Psych. control	2.52*	H 2.33* L 2.19	--	--	--	1.83	--	--	--	--
P Psych. control	1.12	--	--	--	--	0.58	--	--	--	--
M Overprotective	2.36*	--	--	1.61* 1.51	1.41* 1.26	0.73	--	--	--	--
P Overprotective	0.64	--	--	--	--	1.11	--	--	--	--

Note. IV= Independent variable; M= Maternal; P= Paternal; H= Higher group mean; L= Lower group mean
[a] See text for table explanation; -- nonsignificant mean differences
* $p < 0.05$; ** $p < 0.01$; *** $p < 0.001$; multivariate df ranged from 4,98 to 4,140; univariate df ranged from 1,116 to 1,143

69

lower groupings of parenting style and stylistic dimension constructs that
were alternately used as independent variables in subsequent MANOVAs
that continue down the left side of the table.

Small cell sizes precluded the possibility of testing maternal and paternal
effects simultaneously. Interactions of child gender with each of the family-
marital and parenting style independent variables were also tested in each
analysis. For all analyses, Wilks lambda was used to test for multivariate
effects. Multivariate main effect F values for each of the analyses are shown
on the left side of Table 3.5 for overt and relational aggression and victimization findings and on the right side of Table 3.5 for reactions to provocation. For brevity, gender main effects are not shown as none were
significant. Also, only significant interaction effects are shown.

Univariate effects were not examined unless the corresponding multivariate effect was significant. Only significant mean differences in aggression-
victimization as a function of high (H) and low (L) groupings of
family-parenting variables are shown in Table 3.5 for each subsequent univariate analysis. The superscripts to the right of the means denote the level
of significance for the univariate Fs. Complete tables showing univariate F
values, degrees of freedom, and standard deviations accompanying the means
are available from the authors. Results are discussed next.

DISCUSSION

Russian findings shown in Table 3.5 corroborated and extended our understanding of linkages between family processes and children's aggression
and victimization as described in the Western literature. Most of the Western literature has focused on overt forms of these constructs. Our research
extends this inquiry not only to the Russian culture, but to examining family
process linkages with relational aggression and victimization as well. Unlike
most prior victimization research that focuses on older children, the sample
for this study consisted of younger nursery school-age children. The analysis
explored ways that Russian parenting styles, marital interactions, and family
interactions were associated with overt and relational forms of childhood
aggression and victimization as well as with ways that children react to provocation. Our discussion is organized around each group of these distinct
child behaviors.

Proactive and Reactive Overt and Relational Aggression

Proactive Overt Aggression

Corroborating findings obtained in other samples focusing on overt aggression, Russian children who were more proactive overtly aggressive had

mothers and fathers who were not only more authoritarian, but who specifically directed corporal punishment and verbal hostility toward them. Russian mothers and fathers also perceived themselves as engaging in more nonreasoning and coercive interactional styles with children who were more proactive overtly aggressive. More proactive overtly aggressive children also had mothers who were more psychologically controlling and fathers who were less responsive in terms of being patient, playful, easy going, and sensitive to their needs (cf. Hart, Nelson et al., 1998).

Findings from this investigation also provided new insights into the specificity of linkages between certain dimensions of authoritative parenting styles and children's aggressive behavior. In light of Darling and Steinberg's (1993) assertion that only certain aspects of overall parenting typologies might be specifically linked with certain child behavioral outcomes, we noted that only high levels of paternal responsiveness were significantly associated with less proactive overt aggression. The paucity of findings for the reasoning, democratic parenting, and warmth-involvement dimensions suggests that it may only be the absence of paternal responsiveness in the authoritative style that contributes to proactive overt aggression in children.

In terms of interparental interactions and family relationships, proactively aggressive children were more likely to come from families whose members were more conflictive in their interactions with one another, and who were less cohesive and more disengaged. Mirroring findings from the Western literature, only boys (and not girls) who were more proactively overt aggressive had been exposed to more marital conflict (e.g., Cummings, 1994).

Proactive Relational Aggression

We also obtained partial support for the assumption that processes and associations with parenting and family interactions for overt aggression operate similarly for relational aggression, as well (see Crick, Werner et al., in press). As with overt aggression, higher levels of marital conflict were associated with more proactive relational aggression in boys only. Similarly, less family cohesion was related to more proactive relational aggression. Maternal and paternal authoritarian parenting, particularly corporal punishment and verbal hostility directed toward the child, was associated with proactive relational aggression. Proactive relational aggression was also linked to less responsive parenting on the part of fathers.

Less democratic parenting associated with the authoritative style on the part of mothers and fathers was related to higher levels of relational aggression. From a social learning perspective, not allowing input into family decision making and discouraging child expression may model a form of exclusion that parents use to maintain control of their own agenda in presiding over their children. Such parental manipulation may be perceived by children to be an efficacious means of maintaining control over others (e.g., peers). These tendencies may be exacerbated by less cohesive family inter-actions, which may also model exclusionary behaviors.

Similar to findings for proactive overt aggression, reasoning and warmth-involvement dimensions as well as marital harmony were not associated with proactive relational aggression. Psychological control was also not associated with proactive relational aggression. These findings suggest that corporal punishment and verbal hostility directed toward children, less paternal re-sponsiveness, more marital conflict, less family cohesion, and more exclu-sionary tactics are the operative family process variables that may facilitate greater proactive relational aggression. Whether these variables act singly or in combination needs further exploration.

Overt and Relational Victimization

The majority of victimized children are characterized by a pervasively sub-missive behavior pattern and are more often found playing alone (e.g., Ol-weus, 1993b; Schwartz et al., 1993), and overprotective and restrictive parenting are the known family correlates (e.g., Bowers et al., 1994; Finne-gan et al., 1998; Ladd & Ladd, 1998). This appears true for Russian children as well. Children of more overprotective mothers were found to be more overtly and relationally victimized. As suggested by Rubin et al. (1995), anxiously overinvolved and overprotective parents may deprive children of opportunities to interact spontaneously with peers, thus inhibiting oppor-tunities to become more socially skilled. Their children consequently be-come targets for peer maltreatment.

Little is known about ways that marital and family relationships might be associated with victimization. Earlier, we postulated that anxiety and emo-tional insecurity associated with hostile parenting, marital or family conflict, and family disengagement could also contribute to children being more prone to victimization by peers (see Siqueland et al., 1996). Some support was obtained for this hypothesis. Mothers who directed more corporal pun-ishment and verbal hostility toward their children were more overtly victim-ized by peers. Likewise, Russian boys who were exposed to more marital conflict were found to be more overtly and relationally victimized by peers. Children from less cohesive families were also more relationally victimized. Similar to Western findings, other parenting styles and family dimensions were unrelated to victimization.

Reactions to Provocation

Reactive Overt Aggression

A similar pattern of findings for proactive overt aggression emerged for reactive overt aggression. More authoritarian mothering and fathering was associated with children's reactive overt aggression. This was particularly true for the corporal punishment and verbal hostility dimension, although fathers (but not mothers) who engaged in nonreasoning coercion also had children who were more reactive overtly aggressive. Likewise, children of fathers who were less responsive were perceived by teachers to exhibit more reactive overtly aggressive behavior. Children from less cohesive and more disengaged families were also more prone to be overtly aggressive reactive. Reactive overt aggression was also more characteristic of boys (but not girls) who were exposed to higher levels of marital conflict (cf. Cummings, 1994).

Less extreme forms of negative parenting, marital, and family interactions as measured here were associated with reactive overt aggression. This contradicts literature reviewed earlier suggesting that it is only extreme forms of abusive parenting and violent family interactions that are associated with child aggressive reactive tendencies (e.g., Schwartz et al., 1997; Shields & Cicchetti, 1998). At first glance, these findings could suggest that moderate levels of family conflict and hostile parenting might also result in some degree of social cognitive, emotional, and behavioral impairment. However, these results should be cautiously regarded because teacher ratings of proactive and reactive forms of aggression were highly correlated ($r = .82$) similar to magnitudes reported in past research utilizing teacher measures of proactive and reactive aggression (Dodge & Coie, 1987; Price & Dodge, 1989; Vitaro et al., 1998). Thus, similar findings obtained for proactive and reactive overt aggression were not surprising. It may be difficult for teachers to distinguish these two forms of aggression. In practice, many aggressive children display both types of behavior in a pervasive aggressive behavior pattern (Dodge et al., 1997; Vitaro et al., 1998).

Reactive Relational Aggression

Similar to teacher perceptions of proactive and reactive aggression, proactive and reactive relational aggression were correlated, but were not quite as redundant ($r = .62$). Results for reactive relational aggression did not always directly correspond with those obtained for proactive relational aggression. As with proactive relational aggression, more marital conflict was associated with more reactive relational aggression for boys. Less paternal responsiveness and more maternal corporal punishment and verbal hostility were also linked to reactive relational aggression. Reflecting specific child behaviors associated with authoritative style dimensions (Darling & Steinberg, 1993), boys of mothers who were more warm and involved were less relationally reactive to perceived provocation. Thus, in addition to more responsiveness on the part of fathers, more maternal warmth and involvement in the lives of boys could lend itself to less angry, relationally reactive responses to perceived provocation.

Submissive and Assertive Reactions

The only finding for submissive reactions suggested that boys of more warm and involved mothers were less submissive in the face of perceived provocation. This might be interpreted in the context of other findings for Russian boys which suggest that more paternal responsiveness and maternal warmth and involvement lends itself to less angry, relationally aggressive reactive responses to perceived peer provocation.

Although speculative, findings in this chapter might suggest that children (particularly boys) who are raised in emotionally secure home environments where parents are warm and responsive may be more likely to correctly read emotional signals from others (e.g., Boyum & Parke, 1995; Eisenberg, Fabes, & Murphy, 1996), making them less likely to perceive others as threatening (Gordis, Margolin, & John, 1997). This may diminish the felt need to respond in submissive or overt and relationally aggressive ways. From an attachment theory perspective, this could be due to "secure" models of self that may give rise to more positive attributions of intent on the part of others and to less likelihood of making hostile attributions (Kerns, Klepac, & Cole, 1996; Pettit et al., in press). In essence, more emotionally secure children may be more likely to give others the benefit of the doubt because they may perceive and remember others in a positive light (e.g., Kerns, 1996). Emotionally secure children may also be more sociable, have greater social confidence, and be better able to handle rebuffs from peers, not needing to be submissive because they are more likely to view others as being nonthreatening (Kerns, 1996). They may be less likely to be victimized because their behavior does not evoke anger from others or make them targets of aggression due to a timid and solitary play style.

Alternatively, from a cognitive social psychology view, children raised in emotionally secure environments may be less likely to develop maladaptive mental representations (i.e., scripts) reflective of repeated exposure to family conflict and parental hostility (e.g., Rogers & Holmbeck, 1997). Rather than behavior being guided by scripts reflecting negative perceptions and expectations of more malicious intentions in others, more positive perceptions of others associated with warm and responsive caregiving may result in less likelihood of hypervigilant submissive or aggressive reactive behavior occurring. Such negative behavior (including reactive aggression or submissive behavior) could stem from maladaptive scripts that are chronically triggered in social situations by emotional anger or wariness in response to ambiguous behavior by others being misperceived as threatening or malicious. However, little research has assessed how emotional arousal and cognitive processing *work together* to facilitate submissive or aggressive reactive behavior (Crick & Werner, 1998; Pettit et al., in press).

Limitations and Conclusions

As with most findings derived from Western samples, our analyses did not address whether all family and parenting variables act singly or in combination to facilitate aggressive and victimized behavior. Future research with larger samples using more sophisticated analytic techniques will be needed to ascertain whether parenting style and family interaction variables are singly or mutually related to subtypes of aggressive and victimized behavior, or whether there are mediating paths that link up with these outcomes in young children. We also did not assess dispositional and psychobiological influences important for studying the direction of effects and transactional processes (e.g., Coie & Dodge, 1998; Katz, Chapter 5, this volume), or attempt to address how aversive interaction patterns may be maintained and strengthened through coercive family processes and coercive peer interactions (e.g., Dishion, Andrews, & Crosby, 1995).

Based on the existing Russian parenting-family literature, it appears that our results were more likely to have arisen from the Russian culture than from an imposition of our conceptual and metric biases (see Hart, Nelson et al., 1998). Findings paralleled what has been found in Western cultures with regard to aggression and victimization (e.g., Australia, Norway, Sweden, United Kingdom, North America), thus lending support for what Berry (1989) referred to as "derived etics" or "cultural universals" as pertaining only to Russian and some Western cultures. This does imply, however, that some theoretical and empirically based concepts derived in Western cultures may not reflect some unique conditions in the Russian culture ("imposed etics"). In essence, this research suggests that there might be similarities between Russian and Western cultures in ways that parenting and family processes are linked to different forms of early childhood aggression and victimization. However, this investigation only represents a starting point for cross-cultural comparisons. Replication studies, particularly those using qualitative methods, may prove useful in further understanding possible "emics" (arising from the culture) when studying Russian parenting and family life as related to child peer group outcomes.

NOTES

We are grateful to Dr. Nina Bazarskaya, head of the Foreign Language Department, Voronezh Forestry Institute, Voronezh, Russia, for her assistance in providing access to this sample. Appreciation is also extended to the Kennedy Center for International Studies for primary grant support, and to the College of Family, Home, and Social Sciences, the Camilla Eyring Kimball Endowment, and the Center for Family Studies at Brigham Young University for additional support of this work. Dr. Joseph Olsen of Brigham Young University is also gratefully acknowledged for his statistical consultation. All correspondence concerning this chapter should be directed to Dr. Craig H. Hart, School of Family Life, Brigham Young University, Provo, Utah, 84602.

1. As the aggression literature has progressed since conceptualizing our measures for data collection in Russia, it is becoming increasingly apparent that describing aggressive subtypes in terms of "social," "indirect," and "overt" has limitations, particularly in the context of the relational aggression construct. *Social aggression* is de-

fined by some as behaviors that damage another's self-esteem or social standing (Galen & Underwood, 1997), and by others as representing physically aggressive acts (Patterson, 1982). Galen and Underwood's construct subsumes verbal disparagements (e.g., yelling or arguing, teasing, making fun of, or calling peers names), and non-verbal hostilities such as negative facial expressions or body movements (e.g., rolling one's eyes). Social aggression also includes some relationally aggressive behaviors such as rumor spreading and social exclusion. As noted by Crick, Werner et al. (in press), social aggression is a broader construct than relational aggression, which focuses only on hostile acts in which intentional damage to relationships or social standing is the vehicle of harm (e.g., rumor spreading, gossiping, divulging peer's personal secrets, talking behind one's back, verbally or nonverbally excluding others from play).

Relational aggression is typically contrasted with overt aggression and is oftentimes referred to as indirect aggression. Relational aggression does subsume indirect, covert, hostile behaviors where the target child is not directly confronted (e.g., gossiping, talking behind one's back). However, relational aggression can also be direct in the dictionary sense of the term (i.e., straightforward, frank, with nothing or no one in between). For example, telling another child that he or she cannot play with a group unless the child does what is wanted involves direct confrontation. Relational aggression can also be overt (i.e., not hidden, open, observable, apparent, with evident intent, without attempt to conceal). For example, intentional covert behaviors such as gossiping, telling secrets, and talking behind one's back can be open and observable to the target child on occasion. Likewise, being told that "I won't be your friend if you don't do things my way" is direct and overt. Thus, acts of relational aggression may be indirect and covert, as well as direct and overt.

In order to avoid pitfalls associated with the social, indirect, and overt aggression terminologies, future researchers may do well to conceptualize aggression in terms of physical, verbal, nonverbal, and relational subtypes, with the understanding that some of these subtypes can co-occur (Galen & Underwood, 1997). Because relational aggression may be overt in nature (e.g., children directly and openly telling other children they won't play with them), Crick, Werner et al. (in press) recently discarded the term *overt* and have instead focused on *physical* aggression (which also includes verbal threats to another's physical well-being for intimidation or instrumental gains). This is distinct from *verbal* aggression or verbal intimidation that includes direct, disparaging, or contemptuous verbal insults and derogation designed to damage self-esteem (e.g., calling a peer mean names, making sarcastic comments, teasing or making fun of peers).

Another category of *nonverbal* aggression could also be contrived (e.g., negative facial expressions or body movements such as rolling one's eyes, or tossing one's hair to convey contempt and damage self esteem). *Relational aggression* encompasses only hostile acts where relationships are used as the vehicle of harm, be it verbal or nonverbal, direct or indirect, overt or covert in nature (e.g., threatening not to invite another child to a birthday party unless the child does what is wanted, excluding others to manipulate or to enact revenge, walking away when angry, revealing a peer's secrets to others, gossiping, talking behind one's back, rumor spreading). Damage to relationships and social standing (reputation) may also occur as a byproduct of physical, verbal, and nonverbal aggression as previously defined, even when the primary motives of these hostile acts is to dominate, intimidate, or harass. Relational aggression may also serve to carry out these motives, but uses relationally exclusive or slanderous means to accomplish these ends.

As seen in this chapter, there are likely proactive and reactive forms as well as bullying (i.e., intimidating, harassing) and/or instrumental (i.e., meeting self-serving goals) delineations of these four behavioral categories. Because of the way our measures were initially conceptualized, implied verbal and manifest physical forms of aggression were called *overt* in light of the recent mainstream usage of the term (e.g., Crick & Bigbee, 1998; Crick et al., 1997). Although cumbersome, *physical/verbal* could be substituted for *overt* throughout this chapter.

REFERENCES

Azarov, Y. (1983). *A book about bringing up children.* Moscow: Progress Publishers.
Bandura, A. (1973). *Aggression: A social learning analysis.* Englewood NJ: Prentice-Hall.
Barber, B. K. (1996). Parental psychological control: Revisiting a neglected construct. *Child Development, 67,* 3296–3319.
Baumrind, D. (1967). Child care practices anteceding three patterns of preschool behavior. *Genetic Psychology Monographs, 75,* 43–88.
Belsky, J. (1984). The determinants of parenting: A process model. *Child Development, 55,* 83–96.
Berdondini, L., & Smith, P. K. (1996). Cohesion and power in the families of children involved in bully/victim problems at school: An Italian replication. *Journal of Family Therapy, 18,* 99–102.
Berry, J. W. (1989). Imposed etics-emics-derived etics: The operationalization of a compelling idea. *International Journal of Psychology, 24,* 721–735.
Blatchford, P. (1998). *Social life in school.* London: Falmer Press.
Bloom, B. L., & Naar, S. (1994). Self-report measures of family functioning: Extensions of a factorial analysis. *Family Process, 33,* 203–216.
Boulton, M. J. (1995). Playground behavior and peer interaction patterns of primary school boys classified as bullies, victims, and not involved. *British Journal of Educational Psychology, 65,* 165–177.
Boulton, M. J. (1996). Bullying in mixed sex groups. *Educational Psychology, 16,* 439–443.
Boulton, M. J. (1999). Concurrent and longitudinal relations between children's playground behavior and social preference, victimization, and bullying. *Child Development, 70,* 944–954.
Boulton, M. J. & Underwood, K. (1992). Bully/victim problems among middle school children. *British Journal of Educational Psychology, 62,* 73–87.
Bowers, L., Smith, P. K., & Binney, V. (1994). Perceived family relationships of bullies, victims, and bully/victims. *Journal of Personal and Social Relationships, 11,* 215–232.
Boyum, L. A., & Parke, R. D. (1995). The role of family emotional expressiveness in the development of children's social competence. *Journal of Marriage and the Family, 57,* 593–608.
Bronfenbrenner, U. (1970). *Two worlds of childhood: U.S. and U.S.S.R.* New York: Russell Sage Foundation.

Bryant, B. K., & DeMorris, K. A. (1992). Beyond parent-child relationships: Potential links between family environments and peer relations. In Parke, R. D. & Ladd, G. W. (Eds.), *Family–peer relationships: Modes of linkage* (pp. 159–189). Hillsdale, NJ: Erlbaum.

Burks, V. S., Laird, R. D., Dodge, K. A., Pettit, G. S., & Bates, J. E. (1999). Knowledge structures, social information processing, and children's aggressive behavior. *Social Development, 8,* 220–236.

Carson, L., & Parke, R. (1996). Reciprocal negative affect in parent-child interactions and children's peer competency. *Child Development, 67,* 2217–2226.

Chen, X., & Rubin, K. H. (1994). Family conditions, parental acceptance, and social competence and aggression in Chinese children. *Social Development, 3,* 269–290.

Coie, J. D., & Dodge, K. A. (1998). Aggression and antisocial behavior. In N. Eisenberg (Ed.), *Handbook of child psychology: Vol. 3. Social, emotional, and personality development* (pp. 779–862). New York: Wiley.

Crick, N. R. (1995). Relational aggression: The role of intent attributions, feelings of distress and provocation type. *Developmental Psychology and Psychopathology, 66,* 313–322.

Crick, N. R., & Bigbee, M. A. (1998). Relational and overt forms of peer victimization: A multi-informant approach. *Journal of Consulting and Clinical Psychology, 66,* 337–347.

Crick, N. R., Bigbee, M. A., & Howes, C. (1996). Gender differences in children's normative beliefs about aggression: How do I hurt thee? Let me count the ways. *Child Development, 67,* 1003–1014.

Crick, N. R., Casas, J. F., & Ku, H. (1999). Relational and physical forms of peer victimization in preschool. *Developmental Psychology, 35,* 376–385.

Crick, N. R., Casas, J. F., & Mosher, M. (1997). Relational and overt aggression in preschool. *Developmental Psychology, 33,* 579–588.

Crick, N. R., & Dodge, K. A. (1994). A review and reformulation of social information-processing mechanisms in children's social adjustment. *Psychological Bulletin, 115,* 74–101.

Crick, N. R., & Dodge, K. A. (1996). Social information-processing mechanisms in reactive and proactive aggression. *Child Development, 67,* 993–1002.

Crick, N. R., & Werner, N. E. (1998). Response decision processes in relational and overt aggression. *Child Development, 69,* 1630–1639.

Crick, N. R., Werner, N. E., Casas, J. F., O'Brien, K. M., Nelson, D. A., Grotpeter, J. K., & Markon, K. (in press). Childhood aggression and gender: A new look at an old problem. In Bernstein, D. (Ed.), *The Nebraska Symposium on Motivation* (Vol. 45). Lincoln: University of Nebraska Press.

Cummings, E. M. (1994). Marital conflict and children's functioning. *Social Development, 3,* 16–36.

Cummings, E. M., & Zahn-Waxler, C. (1992). Emotions and the socialization of aggression: Adults' angry behavior and children's arousal and aggression. In Fraczek, A., & Zumkley, H. (Eds.), *Socialization and aggression* (pp. 61–84). New York: Springer-Verlag.

Darling, N., & Steinberg, L. (1993). Parenting style as context: An integrative model. *Psychological Bulletin, 113,* 487–496.

Davies, P. T., & Cummings, E. M. (1994). Marital conflict and child adjustment: An emotional security hypothesis. *Psychological Bulletin, 116,* 387–411.

Davies, P. T., & Cummings, E. M. (1998). Exploring children's emotional security as a mediator between marital relations and child adjustment. *Child Development, 69*, 124–139.

Dishion, T. J., Andrews, D. W., & Crosby, L. (1995). Antisocial boys and their friends in early adolescence: Relationship characteristics, quality, and interactional process. *Child Development, 66*, 139–151.

Dodge, K. A. (1991). The structure and function of reactive and proactive aggression. In Pepler, D. J., & Rubin, K. H. (Eds.), *The development and treatment of childhood aggression* (pp. 201–218). Hillsdale, NJ: Erlbaum.

Dodge, K. A., Bates, J. E., & Pettit, G. S. (1990). Mechanisms in the cycle of violence. *Science, 250*, 1678–1683.

Dodge, K. A., & Coie, J. D. (1987). Social information-processing factors in reactive and proactive aggression. *Journal of Personality and Social Psychology, 53*, 1146–1158.

Dodge, K. A. & Coie, J. D. (1989, April). *Bully-victim relationships in boys' play groups.* Paper presented at the biennial conference of the Society for Research in Child Development, Kansas City, MO.

Dodge, K. A., Harnish, J. D., Lochman, J. E., Bates, J. E., & Pettit, G. S. (1997). Reactive and proactive aggression in school children and psychiatrically impaired chronically assaultive youth. *Journal of Abnormal Psychology, 106*, 37–51.

Dodge, K. A., Pettit, G. S., Bates, J. E., & Valente, E. (1995). Social information-processing patterns partially mediate the effect of early physical abuse on later conduct problems. *Journal of Abnormal Psychology, 104*, 632–643.

Egan, S. K., & Perry, D. G. (1998). Does low self-regard invite victimization? *Developmental Psychology, 34*, 299–309.

Eisenberg, N., Fabes, R. A., & Murphy, B. C. (1996). Parents' reactions to children's negative emotions: Relations to children's social competence and comforting behavior. *Child Development, 67*, 2227–2247.

Fauber, R. L., & Long, N. (1991). Children in context: The role of the family in child psychotherapy. *Journal of Consulting and Clinical Psychology, 59*, 813–820.

Fincham, F. D. (1994). Understanding the association between marital conflict and child adjustment. *Journal of Family Psychology, 8*, 123–127.

Fincham, F. D., Grych, J. H., & Osborne, L. N. (1994). Does marital conflict cause child maladjustment? Directions and challenges. *Journal of Family Psychology, 8*, 128–140.

Finnegan, R. A., Hodges, E. V. E., & Perry, D. G. (1998). Victimization by peers: Associations with children's reports of mother-child interaction. *Journal of Personality & Social Psychology, 75*, 1076–1086.

Galen, B. R., & Underwood, M. K. (1997). A developmental investigation of social aggression among children. *Developmental Psychology, 33*, 589–600.

Gordis, E. B., Margolin, G., & John, R. S. (1997). Marital aggression, observed parental hostility, and child behavior during triadic family interaction. *Journal of Family Psychology, 11*, 76–89.

Gottman, J. M., & Fainsilber-Katz, L. (1989). Effects of marital discord on young children's peer interaction and health. *Developmental Psychology, 25*, 373–381.

Grotpeter, J. K., & Crick, N. R. (1997). *Relational aggression, physical aggression, and family relationships.* Manuscript submitted for publication.

Harrist, A. W., & Ainslie, R. C. (in press). Marital discord and child behavior problems: Parent-child relationship quality and child interpersonal awareness as mediators. *Journal of Family Issues.*

Hart, C. H., DeWolf, M. D., & Burts, D. C. (1992). Linkages among preschoolers' playground behavior, outcome expectations, and parental disciplinary strategies. *Early Education and Development, 3,* 265–283.

Hart, C. H., DeWolf, M. D., Wozniak, P., & Burts, D. C. (1992). Maternal and paternal disciplinary styles: Relations with preschoolers' playground behavioral orientations and peer status. *Child Development, 63,* 879–892.

Hart, C. H., Ladd, G. W., & Burleson, B. R. (1990). Children's expectations of the outcomes of social strategies: Relations with sociometric status and maternal disciplinary styles. *Child Development, 61,* 127–137.

Hart, C. H., Nelson, D. A., Robinson, C. C., Olsen, S. F., & McNeilly-Choque, M. K. (1998). Overt and relational aggression in Russian nursery-school-age children: Parenting style and marital linkages. *Developmental Psychology, 34,* 687–697.

Hart, C. H., Olsen, S. F., Robinson, C., & Mandleco, B. L. (1997). The development of social and communicative competence in childhood: Review and a model of personal, familial, and extra familial processes. In Burleson, B. R. (Ed.), *Communication yearbook* (Vol. 20, pp. 305–373). Thousand Oaks, CA: Sage.

Hart, C. H., Yang, C., Nelson, D. A., Jin, S., Bazarshaya, N., Nelson, L. J., Wu, X., & Wu, P. (1998) Peer contact patterns, parenting practices, and preschoolers' social competence in China, Russia, and the United States. In Slee, P., & Rigby, K. (Eds.), *Peer relations amongst children: Current issues and future directions* (pp. 3–30). London: Routledge.

Hart, C. H., Yang, C., Nelson, L. J., Robinson, C. C., Olsen, J. A., Nelson, D. A., Porter, C. L., Jin, S., Olsen, S. F., & Wu, P. (in press). Peer acceptance and subtypes of socially withdrawn behavioral in China, Russia, and the United States. *International Journal of Behavioral Development.*

Hartup, W. W. (1974). Aggression in childhood: Developmental perspectives. *American Psychologist, 29,* 336–341.

Hayden, L. C., Schiller, M., Dickstein, S., Seifer, R., Sameroff, A. J., Miller, I., Keitner, G., & Rasmussen, S. (1998). Levels of family assessment: Family, marital, and parent-child interaction. *Journal of Family Psychology, 12,* 7–22.

Hodges, E. V. E., Malone, M. J., & Perry, D. G. (1997). Individual risk and social risk as interacting determinants of victimization. *Developmental Psychology, 33,* 1032–1039.

Ispa, J. M. (1993, March). *A comparison of the child-rearing ideas of Russian mothers and child care center teachers.* Paper presented at the Society for Research in Child Development meetings, New Orleans, LA.

Ispa, J. M. (1994). *Child care in Russia: In transition.* Westport, CT: Greenwood Press.

Ispa, J. M. (1995). Ideas about infant and toddler care among Russian child care teachers, mothers, and university students. *Early Childhood Research Quarterly, 10,* 359–379.

Jouriles, E. N., Murphy, C. M., Farris, A. M., Smith, D. A., Richters, J. E., & Waters, E. (1991). Marital adjustment, parental disagreements about child rearing, and behavior problems in boys: Increasing the specificity of the marital assessment. *Child Development, 62,* 1424–1433.

Katsurada, E., & Sugawara, A. I. (1998). The relationship between hostile attributional bias and aggressive behavior in preschoolers. *Early Childhood Research Quarterly, 13*, 623–636.

Katz, L. F., & Gottman, J. M. (1993). Patterns of marital conflict predict children's internalizing and externalizing behaviors. *Developmental Psychology, 29*, 940–950.

Kerig, P. K. (1996, Fall). More than six volumes of Vygotsky: Lessons from Russian psychology. *SRCD Newsletter.*

Kerns, K. A. (1996). Individual differences in friendship quality: Links to child-mother attachment. In Bukowski, W. M., Newcomb, A. F., & Hartup, W. W. (Eds.), *The company they keep: Friendship in childhood and adolescence* (pp. 137–157). Cambridge: Cambridge University Press.

Kerns, K. A., Klepac, L., & Cole, A. (1996). Peer relationships and perceptions of security in the child-mother relationship. *Developmental Psychology, 32*, 457–466.

Kochenderfer, B., & Ladd, G. W. (1997). Victimized children's responses to peers' aggression: Behaviors associated with reduced versus continued victimization. *Development and Psychopathology, 9,* 59–73.

Krevans, J., & Gibbs, J. C. (1996). Parents' use of inductive discipline: Relations to children's empathy and prosocial behavior. *Child Development, 67*, 3263–3277.

Kupersmidt, J. B., Patterson, C., & Eickholt, C. (1989). Socially rejected children: Bullies, victims, or both? *Aggressors, victims, and peer relationships.* Paper presented at the Society for Research in Child Development, Kansas, MO.

Ladd, G. W., & Ladd, B. K. (1998). Parenting behaviors & parent-child relationships: Correlates of peer victimization in kindergarten? *Developmental Psychology, 34*, 1450–1458.

LaFreniere, P. J., & Dumas, J. E. (1992). A transactional analysis of early childhood anxiety and social withdrawal. *Development and Psychopathology, 4*, 385–402.

Lagerspetz, K., Bjorkqvist, K., & Peltonen, T. (1988). Is indirect aggression typical of females? Gender differences in aggressiveness in 11- to 12-year-old children. *Aggressive Behavior, 14*, 403–414.

MacKinnon-Lewis, C., Volling, B. L., Lamb, M. E., Dechman, K., Rabiner, D., Curtner, M. E. (1994). A cross-contextual analysis of boys' social competence: From family to school. *Developmental Psychology, 30*, 325–333.

Maddock, J. W., Hogan, M. J., Antonov, A. I., & Matskovsky, M. S. (1994). *Families before and after Perestroika: Russian and U.S. perspectives.* New York: Guilford Press.

Makarenko, A. S. (1967). *The collective family: A handbook for Russian parents* (R. Daglish, Trans.). New York: Anchor Books (original work published 1937).

Mann, B. J., & MacKenzie, E. P. (1996). Pathways among marital functioning, parental behaviors, and child behavior problems. *Journal of Clinical Child Psychology, 25*, 183–191.

McNeilly-Choque, M. K., Hart, C. H., Robinson, C. C., Nelson, L. J., & Olsen, S. F. (1996). Overt and relational aggression on the playground: Correspondence among different informants. *Journal of Research in Childhood Education, 11*, 47–67.

Mize, J., & Pettit, G. S. (1997). Mothers' social coaching, mother-child relationship style, and children's peer competence: Is the medium the message? *Child Development, 68*, 291–311.

Olweus, D. (1978). *Aggression in the schools: Bullies and their whipping boys*. Washington, DC: Hemisphere.

Olweus, D. (1993a). Bullies on the playground: The role of victimization. In Hart, C. H. (Ed.), *Children on playgrounds: Research perspectives and applications* (pp. 85–128). Albany: State University of New York Press.

Olweus, D. (1993b). *Bullying at school: What we know and what we can do*. Oxford: Blackwell.

Parke, R. D., Burks, V. M., Carson, J. L., Neville, B., & Boyum, L. A. (1994). Family-peer relationships: A tripartite model. In Parke, R. D., & Kellan, S. (Eds.), *Exploring family relationships with other social context* (pp. 115–145). Hillsdale, NJ: Erlbaum.

Patterson, G. R. (1982). *Coercive family process*. Eugene, OR: Castalia.

Pepler, D. J., Craig, W. M., & Roberts, W. L. (1998). Observations of aggressive and nonaggressive children. *Merrill-Palmer Quarterly, 44*, 55–76.

Perry, D. G., Williard, J. C., & Perry, L. C. (1990). Peers' perceptions of the consequences that victimized children provide aggressors. *Child Development, 61*, 1310–1325.

Pettit, G. S., & Bates, J. E. (1989). Family interaction patterns and children's behavior problems from infancy to 4 years. *Developmental Psychology, 25*, 413–420.

Pettit, G. S., Polaha, J. A., & Mize, J. (in press). Perceptual and attributional processes in aggression and conduct problems. In Hill, J., & Maughan, B. (Eds.), *Cambridge monographs in child and adolescent psychiatry: Conduct disorders in childhood*. Cambridge, UK: Cambridge University Press.

Porter, B., & O'Leary, K. D. (1980). Marital discord and childhood behavior problems. *Journal of Abnormal Child Psychology, 8*, 287–295.

Price, J. M., & Dodge, K. A. (1989). Reactive and proactive aggression in childhood: Relations to peer status and social context dimensions. *Journal of Abnormal Child Psychology, 17*, 455–471.

Raeff, M. (1966). *Origins of the Russian intelligentsia: The eighteenth century nobility* (pp. 122–129). New York: Harcourt, Brace, & World.

Rigby, K. (1994). Psychosocial functioning in families of Australian adolescent schoolchildren involved in bully-victim problems. *Journal of Family Therapy, 16*, 173–187.

Robinson, C. C., Mandleco, B., Olsen, S. F., & Hart, C. (1995). Authoritative, authoritarian, and permissive parenting practices: Development of a new measure. *Psychological Reports, 77*, 819–830.

Rogers, M. J., & Holmbeck, G. N. (1997). Effects of interparental aggression on children's adjustment: The moderating role of cognitive appraisal and coping. *Journal of Family Psychology, 11*, 125–130.

Rubin, K. H., Stewart, S. L., & Coplan, R. J. (1995). Social withdrawal in childhood. In Ollendick, T. H., & Prinz, R. J. (Eds.), *Advances in clinical child psychology* (Vol. 17, pp. 157–196). New York: Plenum Press.

Russell, A., Aloa, V., Feder, T., Glover, A., Miller, H., & Palmer, G. (1998). Sex based differences in parenting styles in a sample with preschool children. *Australian Journal of Psychology*, 1–11.

Russell, A., & Russell, G. (1996). Positive parenting and boys' and girls' misbehavior during a home observation. *International Journal of Behavioral Development, 19,* 291–307.

Schwartz, D. (March, 1995). *The behavioral correlates of peer victimization.* Paper presented at the biennial meetings of the Society for Research in Child Development, Indianapolis, IN.

Schwartz, D., Dodge, K. A., & Coie, J. D. (1993). The emergence of chronic peer victimization in boys' play groups. *Child Development, 64,* 1755–1772.

Schwartz, D., Dodge, K. A., Coie, J. D., Hubbard, J. A., Cillessen, A. H., Lemerise, E. A., & Bateman, H. (1998). Social-cognitive and behavioral correlates of aggression and victimization in boys' play groups. *Journal of Abnormal Child Psychology, 26,* 431–440.

Schwartz, D., Dodge, K. A., Pettit, G. S., & Bates, J. E. (1997). The early socialization of aggressive victims of bullying. *Child Development, 68,* 665–675.

Schwartz, D., McFadyen-Ketchum, S. A., Dodge, K. A., Pettit, G. S., & Bates, J. E. (1998). Peer group victimization as a predictor of children's behavior problems at home and in school. *Development and Psychopathology, 10,* 87–99.

Shields, A., & Cicchetti, D. (1998). Reactive aggression among maltreated children: The contributions of attention & emotion dysregulation. *Journal of Clinical Child Psychology, 27,* 381–395.

Shipler, D. K. (1983). *Russia: Broken idols, solemn dreams.* New York: Times Books.

Siqueland, L., Kendall, P. C., & Steinberg, L. (1996). Anxiety in children: Perceived family environments and observed family interaction. *Journal of Clinical Child Psychology, 25,* 225–237.

Slee, P. T., & Rigby, K. (1993). Australian school children's self appraisal of interpersonal relations: The bullying experience. *Child Psychiatry and Human Development, 23,* 273–281.

Smetana, J. G. (1995). Parenting styles and conceptions of parental authority during adolescence. *Child Development, 66,* 299–316.

Smith, H. (1990). *The new Russians.* New York: Random House.

Smith, P. K., & Boulton, M. J. (July, 1991). *Self-esteem, sociometric status and peer-perceived behavioral characteristics in middle school children in the United Kingdom.* Paper presented at the XI meeting of the International Society for the Study of Behavioral Development, Minneapolis, MN.

Subbotskii, E. V. (1992). Moral socialization of the child in the Soviet Union from birth to age seven. In Roopnarine, J. L., & Carter, D. B. (Eds.), *Parent-child socialization in diverse cultures* (pp. 89–105). Norwood, NJ: Ablex.

Tomada, G., & Schneider, B. H. (1997). Relational aggression, gender, and peer acceptance: Invariance across culture, stability over time, and concordance among informants. *Developmental Psychology, 33,* 601–609.

Troy, M., & Sroufe, L. A. (1987). Victimization among preschoolers: Role of attachment history. *Journal of the American Academy of Child and Adolescent Psychiatry, 26,* 166–172.

Tudge, J. (1991). Education of young children in the Soviet Union: Current practice in historical perspective. *The Elementary School Journal, 92,* 121–133.

Vitaro, F., Gendreau, P. L., Tremblay, R. E., & Oligny, P. (1998). Reactive and proactive aggression differentially predict later conduct problems. *Journal of Child Psychology and Psychiatry, 39,* 377–385.

Waschbusch, D. A., Willoughby, M. T., & Pelham, W. E. (1998). Criterion validity

and the utility of reactive and proactive aggression: Comparisons with attention deficit hyperactivity disorder, oppositional defiant disorder, conduct disorder, and other measures of functioning. *Journal of Clinical Child Psychology*,
27, 396–405.

4

Links between Adult and Peer Relations across Four Developmental Periods

Carollee Howes and Holli Tonyan

This chapter explores developmental changes in links between adult-child relationships and peer relations. Social development occurs within a network of social relationships, thus it is expected that the quality of these relationships would be interrelated. Past research in this area has focused primarily on the ways in which the quality of the mother-child relationship is related to later peer relations, although there is a growing body of literature that shows the importance of teacher-child relationships on peer relations as well (for a review, see Howes, in press). We hope to broaden the understanding gained from studies of links between mother-child relationships and peer relations in two ways: to include teacher-child relationships as well as mother-child relationships and to examine friendships and generalized social skills as somewhat independent dimensions of peer relations.

We examine developmental changes by focusing on a single sample of children. Because this sample is somewhat unique, it is important to specifically address the ways in which this particular sample shaped the analyses we can present and the conclusions we can hope to draw. At the time of this analysis, these children had just entered early adolescence. We have been following them since their first birthdays. The children have grown up under relatively privileged circumstances. They are white, affluent, and live in stable families in a suburban area. All of the children in this longitudinal sample were enrolled in child care during their preschool years and they experienced remarkably few changes in caregiving arrangements. This means that for most of the children, their first encounters with peers outside of their families were within small organized groups of same-age peers who were closely monitored by an adult. These contextual features limit our work in that we can only speak to a particular set of developmental experiences. Pathways toward developing competent peer relations might be quite different for children within an alternative context (e.g., grandmothers, aunts, and cousins as the primary social partners).

It is not just the families that are unique in the present study. As mentioned previously, unlike more traditional studies of parents, children, and their peers, we have included teachers as well as mothers in our observations of attachment relationships. When the children were toddlers and preschoolers we studied their child-care settings as the context for constructing peer relations. When the children were in elementary school, we again considered teachers as potential attachment figures. Our longitudinal approach, which included observations in similar locations (i.e., child care and school), allows us to examine the role of teacher-child relationships over time even though different teachers fill the teacher role at each time point. This allows examination of the relative importance of both early and contemporary relationships with mothers and teachers for the long-term development of peer relations.

We have placed this work within an attachment theory framework. In our earlier work, we provided a rationale for considering other-than-mothers as attachment figures (Howes, in press; Howes, Hamilton, & Althusen, in press). Although there are important differences that would be expected in examining these two classes of people as attachment figures, teachers can be central figures in the social contexts of young children's lives and therefore are important to include in an analysis of children's social development. We return to this topic later. First, however, we use attachment theory to describe potential mechanisms accounting for links between social relationships with adults and relations with peers. These mechanisms are often formulated with regard to mothers as attachment figures, but could theoretically be more generally applied to all adults within children's networks of caregiving adults. Early in development, the construct of the attachment figure as a secure base may best describe links between adults and peers. The construct of internal representations of relationships may be a better explanation when predicting from earlier relationships to later developmental periods.

Similarly, we have focused on two aspects of peer relations: friendships and social interaction with peers. By *friendship* we mean an affective, reciprocated dyadic relationship built on trust and companionship (Howes, 1988; 1996). By *social interaction* we mean behaviors that promote positive or prosocial interaction so that children can achieve their own social goals without constraining the social goals of peers (Howes, 1988; Waters & Sroufe, 1983). These two aspects of social relations with peers are semi-independent (Asher, Parker, & Walker, 1996; Howes, 1988). In subsequent sections of this chapter, we identify these aspects and explore whether the mechanisms described in attachment theory for explaining links between adults and peers are equally applicable to both aspects of peer relations. Because we are concerned with several developmental periods, we make this question more complex by asking if the mechanisms described in attachment theory are equally applicable to both aspects of peer relations within different periods.

In examining these issues, we (a) present a more detailed account of relevant aspects of attachment theory, peer relations, and the ways that these literatures relate to one another; (b) present several possible pathways of connections between adult-child and peer relations based on previous research and attachment theory; and (c) describe the longitudinal study from which we draw our conclusions. The approach we have taken allows us to model how relationships are interrelated from early childhood through adolescence.

USING ATTACHMENT THEORY TO LINK ADULT-CHILD AND PEER RELATIONS

The Adult as a Secure Base from Which to Explore Peers

Bowlby (1982) and Ainsworth, Blehar, Waters, and Wall (1978) proposed that infants and toddlers who have constructed a secure attachment relationship with an adult caregiver use that caregiver as "secure base" for the exploration of their worlds. Because in our work we are focusing on children who first encounter peers in the context of stable peer groups within child care, we consider the peer group as part of this world to be explored. We expect that children who construct secure attachment relationships with the adult in that world, the child-care teacher, will be the children who use that adult as a base and a resource for entering the peer group.

There is ample evidence, primarily based on studies of young children who are observed with their mothers and with peers who are strangers, that in this context children who have secure mother-child attachment relationships engage in more positive peer interactions than children with insecure mother-child attachment relationships (Booth, Rose-Krasnor, & Rubin, 1991; Waters, Wippman, & Sroufe, 1979). This suggests that indeed children with secure maternal attachment relationships use their mothers as a base to explore the strange peers and thus begin the process of constructing social relationships.

We observed children in this sample when they were between 18 and 30 months old, but when they had only been in child care from 2 to 6 months. The observations occurred within child care. At that point, children who had constructed secure teacher-child attachment relationships were more socially competent with peers than the children who were insecure with their teachers (Howes, Rodning, Galluzzo, & Meyers, 1988). This link between teacher-child attachment security has been replicated in several other studies

(Howes, 1997; Howes, Hamilton, & Matheson, 1994; Howes, Phillips, & Whitebook, 1992). The results from these studies of the impact of secure teacher-child relationships indicate that when children are young, and newly exposed to peers, a secure relationship with an attachment figure facilitates the beginning development of social interaction with peers.

Internal Representation of Adult-Child Relationships Used to Guide Children's Encounters with Peers

Attachment theory also proposes that through many iterative experiences with an attachment figure, children form an internal representation of their relationship with that caregiver (Bowlby, 1982). This mental-affective structure guides perceptions, expectations, and behaviors relevant to children's concept of the generalized other (Bretherton, 1985; Bost, Vaughn, Washington, Cielinski, & Bradbard, 1998; Rudolph, Hammen, & Burge, 1995). Specifically, children's internalized representations of attachment relationships guide their encounters with others throughout development, even when the attachment figure is not physically present (Bowlby, 1982). Both the Strange Situation and Attachment Q-Set measures are designed to measure internal working models by observing the children's use of the attachment figure when experimentally stressed (Strange Situation) or experiencing everyday stress (Attachment Q-Set).

There is a large body of literature that supports the expectation that children's internal representations of felt security with significant adult caregivers influence peer relations. Children with secure mother-child attachment relationships are concurrently more socially competent and have more positive friendship relationships (Booth, Rose-Krasnor, MacKinnon, & Rubin, 1994; Cohn, 1990; LaFreniere & Sroufe, 1985; Park & Waters, 1989; Rudolph et al., 1995; Turner, 1991). Furthermore, the quality of early mother-child attachment relationships is predictive of social competence with peers over time (Elicker, Egland, & Sroufe, 1992). This literature supports the assumption that children form internal representations of their mother-child relationship, which they then use as a guide for peer relations.

There is not a corresponding body of literature making links between child-care teacher attachment and peer relations. All of the literature linking teacher-child relationships and peer relations has been conducted contemporaneously. That is, the child-care teacher is part of children's social world and peers and can be considered a secure base. In this analysis, we examine the predictability of early mother-child and teacher-child attachment security for later social interaction and friendships with peers. We assume, with attachment theory, that early attachment relationships are internalized as working models of relationships and that these internal models influence future peer relations.

ALTERNATIVE PATHWAYS BETWEEN ADULT AND PEER RELATIONSHIPS

There are at least four plausible pathways between adult and peer relations, which are examined here: (a) attachment relationships may predict friendship but not social interaction, (b) individual differences in social interaction may not be explained by attachment relationship quality, (c) attachment relationship quality may predict friendship quality and friendship quality may predict social interaction competence, and (d) it may not be the mother who serves as the attachment relationship representation. In the following section the evidence for each of these plausible pathways is discussed.

Attachment Relationships May Predict Friendship But Not Social Interaction

Attachment theorists have argued that internal representations of relationships derived from adult-child attachment relationships are particularly influential in the development of positive peer friendships rather than social interaction (Park & Waters, 1989). Children with secure adult-child attachment relationships can use these relationships as templates for the construction of positive peer friendships. This is a particularly compelling argument when peer friendships are considered to be a form of an attachment relationship (Howes, 1996). That is, friendships between peers, especially between peers in early adolescence, are based on trust, intimacy, and self disclosure, all attributes of a close and intimate relationship.

Individual Differences in Social Interaction May Not Be Explained By Attachment Relationship Quality

An alternative theoretical framework to the attachment framework suggests that the development of children's peer relations is largely independent of their relationships with adults (Hay, 1985). This argument is based in part on the premise that the construction of play sequences with a peer is different than with an adult. Peers, unlike adults, are not particularly more knowledgeable or skillful in social interaction than the infant or toddler. But, to their advantage, peers share interests in activities that adults generally do not. Most adults quickly tire of games like run and chase or jump off a step. Howes (1988) outlined a sequence of competent social interaction that serves as a marker of social interaction with peers and has designed an assessment of increasing complexity in peer social interaction called the peer play scale (Howes, 1988; Howes & Matheson, 1992). Early work with this scale suggested that it was experience with peers, particularly the rich experience provided by intensive and early child care, that supported development of competent play with peers (Howes, 1988). Therefore, attachment relationships may not directly influence the construction of social interaction with peers.

The perspective that peer relations are primarily constructed within peer groups is not necessarily at odds with an attachment theory perspective. It is possible that early adult-child attachment relationships serve to orient children toward or away from the peer group. Children with secure adult-child attachment relationships would perceive peers as potentially fun and interesting social partners, enter into peer play, and with experience become socially skilled. Children with insecure adult-child attachment would perceive peers as hostile or threatening and withdraw from or aggress towards peers. Once a child has withdrawn from peers or has constructed antagonistic patterns of interaction and relationships, it may be especially difficult to develop alternative behaviors with peers. Unlike some sensitive adults who can understand that what appear to be maladaptive behaviors are instead based on mistrust, peers may perceive the potential peer partner as unpleasant and to be avoided. A skillful adult can work to disconfirm a child's hostile or withdrawing behavior. A peer is more likely to react in ways that maintain the maladaptive sequences. Once these patterns of engaging with peers are established, they are resistant to change (Coie, 1990). Following this reasoning, we would expect the earliest adult-child attachment relationship quality to be more influential for peer social interaction than later adult-child attachment relationship quality. Early adult-child interactions would set the stage for patterns of interaction with peers, but once the stage is set, peer interaction itself would be a more powerful influence than adult-child attachment relationships.

Attachment Relationship Quality May Predict Friendship Quality and Friendship Quality May Predict Social Interaction Competence

It is also possible that the two aspects of peer relations are interrelated: friendship quality may predict later social interaction with peers. In this case adult attachment relationships would predict friendship quality, which in turn would predict social interaction with peers. There is some evidence that toddler and preschool-age children's social interaction skill development occurs within the context of specific friendships as opposed to general peer interactions (Howes, 1992). The construction of complex interactive play sequences appears first within toddler friendship pairs (Howes, 1983). Preschool friends appear to explore themes of trust and intimacy within increasingly complex social pretend play (Howes, 1992). It is plausible that in the course of changing peer groups (i.e., preschool to kindergarten; elementary school to middle school), children may construct more positive friendships and subsequently engage in more positive social behaviors with peers.

Therefore, secure attachment may initially predict friendship quality, which then predicts social interaction competence and further ability to make friends.

It May Not Be the Mother Who Serves as the Attachment Relationship Representation

Teachers Are Caregivers and Organizers of Children's Experiences

In this work, we have been concerned with both mothers and teachers as attachment figures. Child-care teachers serve as attachment figures in part because they fill in for the mother in her absence (Howes, in press; Howes & Hamilton, 1992a, 1992b). When mothers leave children with child-care teachers, all of the social participants—mothers, teachers, and children—understand that the teacher is responsible for keeping the child safe during the mother's absence. The teacher also fulfills basic caregiving functions, by feeding the children, supervising their toileting, and helping them with their naps. A growing body of literature suggests that the antecedent and predictive links between attachment security with child-care teachers and children's outcomes are similar to links between attachment security with mother and children's outcomes (Gossen & van Ijzendoorn, 1990; Howes, in press; Howes & Hamilton, 1992a; Howes et al., in press; Sagi et al., 1985; van Ijzendoorn, Sagi, & Lamberman, 1992).

Less is known about links between elementary school teachers and children's peer relations. Much in the same way that child-care teachers are the adults who are present as children construct their early relations with peers in child care, elementary school teachers are the adults who monitor peer relations in middle childhood. Recently, several researchers extended the attachment paradigm to include elementary school teachers (Birch & Ladd, 1996; Howes, Phillipsen, & Piesner-Feinberg, 1997; Pianta, Steinberg, & Rollins, 1995). Several assumptions are made in this work. First, we assume that the cognitive and social development that promotes learning in school occurs in an interactive context (Pianta & Walsh, 1996). Second, we assume that teachers act as organizers and resources for children's learning in much the same way that mothers and teachers provide very young children with a literal secure base for exploration. Third, we assume that if children are preoccupied with their teacher-child relationships they will be less likely to positively adjust to school. Instead, if children can trust the teacher, they can use the teacher to organize and structure their learning and their relationships with the other children in the class (Birch & Ladd, 1996; Howes & Smith, 1995a; Pianta & Walsh, 1996). The children who do not trust but are instead preoccupied with the teacher-child relationship use their time in school resisting, attempting to control, or avoiding the teacher. Their focus on the teacher rather than on the content of school takes away from their ability to learn, may interfere with the learning of other children in the class, and makes it difficult for them to establish socially competent relationships with the other children. Following in this line of reasoning we examine the contemporary and predictive links between teacher-child relationships in middle childhood and social interaction and friendships with peers.

Mothers as Supportive Figures

In our earlier work with this sample, mother-child attachment relationship quality was not a good predictor of social relations with peers through pre-school (Howes, Matheson, & Hamilton, 1994). We have argued that the physical presence of the child-care teacher as relations with peers were con-structed in the peer group may account for this lack of predictability from mother-child attachment quality to peer relations. These links may shift over development. Mothers in this sample were attachment figures who remained in their children's daily lives after preschool when the child-care teachers were only directly involved for a limited amount of time. Once children are in middle childhood, mothers may not have a direct influence: They prob-ably do not arrange their children's peer contacts and they are less likely to be present when their children are engaged with peers. However, moth-ers of older children may very well be the social support and consultant for their children around peer relations even though their children have more freedom to choose friends and interact as they wish. Many affluent, well-educated mothers describe "car talk" during these middle childhood developmental periods. That is, while providing transportation to school or sports events, children talk about their issues with peers. Children who have more positive contemporary mother-child relationships may be more likely to use their mothers as resources in this manner.

Relative Importance of Mothers and Teachers in Predicting Peer Relations

With recent advances in broadening traditional attachment theory to in-clude a network of adult caregivers (Howes, in press) comes increasing in-terest in understanding the various influences of alternative attachment figures. One hypothesis is that the mother-child attachment relationship is the most dominant one (Bretherton, 1985). However, two recent studies in addition to the preschool analysis of this sample suggest that early child-care experience may alter or dilute the dominance of the mother-child attachment relationship in predicting relations with peers. Egeland and Hiester (1995) reported that within a high-risk disadvantaged sample, infant-mother attach-ment quality was a stronger predictor of social development in middle child-hood when children had not attended infant child care. If children had attended infant child care, early mother-child attachment quality did not predict children's outcomes. Similarly, Pierrehumbert, Ramstein, Karmaniola, and Halfon (1994), reporting on a Swiss sample of children, found links between early insecure mother-child attachment quality and aggression with peers in middle childhood only for those children without child-care experience. Because all the children in the current sample had child-care experience during the preschool period, our work further extends this line of research examining the influence of child care on links between mother-child attachment and peer relations.

LONGITUDINAL DESIGN

Figure 4.1 presents in schematic form the design of this longitudinal analysis. Mother-child attachment quality was assessed at four different points in development: toddler, preschool, middle childhood, and adolescence. Teacher-child attachment quality was assessed at three different points in development: toddler, preschool, and middle childhood. In previous work, we found mother-child and teacher-child relationship quality to be independent of each other and to be stable across development (Howes & Hamilton, 1992a; Howes, Hamilton, & Phillipsen, 1998; Howes & Rosenblatt, 1996). Friendship quality was assessed at three different points in development: preschool, middle childhood, and adolescence. Peer social interaction also was assessed at three points in development: toddler, preschool, and middle childhood. Previous work also found continuity in friendship quality and peer social interaction across development (Howes et al., 1998; Howes & Phillipsen, 1998). In the current analysis, we examine the independence of friendship quality and social interaction and links between attachment quality and peer relations within middle childhood and adolescence and across toddler to adolescent developmental periods.

METHODS

Participants

Fifty-four (27 girls) 12-year-olds and their mothers participated in the study. At earlier periods in the longitudinal study, child-care and elementary school teachers also participated in the study. The families were primarily Euro-American (90 percent), two parents in the home (87 percent), and upper middle class.

Child care in this study was defined as any arrangement in which a non-parental caregiver provided care for the child for at least 10 hours a week. Child-care history was collected from the families from the time the children were 12 months old until they entered elementary school. The children who participated in the study as 9- or 12-year-olds entered child care between the time they were 2 months and 50 months old ($M = 24.7$ months; $SD =$

Figure 4.1
Links between Family and Peer Relationships across Developmental Periods

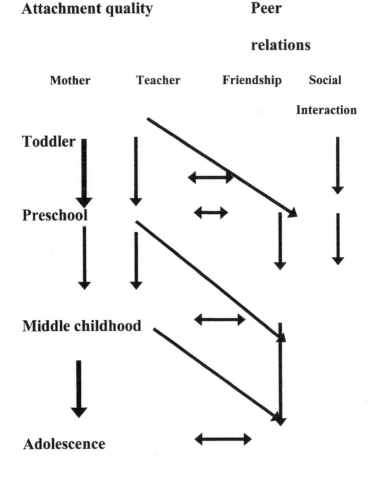

14.7 months). Full-time child care was defined as the child spending more than 20 hours per week in child care. Fifteen percent of the sample began full-time care before their first birthdays, 8 percent as toddlers or preschoolers, and the remaining 77 percent were only in part-time care. Only 25 percent of the sample had two or more changes in child-care teacher between the time they entered child care and the time they went on to kindergarten. Another 25 percent had no teacher changes and the remaining children had one teacher change. Child-care quality was assessed when the children were 4 years old using the Early Childhood Environmental Rating Scale (ECERS; Harms & Clifford, 1980). ECERS scores can range from 1 to 7 with a score of 3 or above indicating acceptable care and scores of 5 or above indicating good care. The average ECERS score was 3.96 (*SD* = .54). Five percent of the children were in child-care centers with unacceptable scores and 7 percent were in child-care centers with good scores. There were no significant associations between social interaction or friendship with peers in middle childhood and adolescence and any measure of child-care history (age entered care, hours in care, changes in teacher, child-care quality).

In the longitudinal study from which this sample was drawn, 94 children participated at 12 months of age, 84 children as 4-year-olds, and 55 children as 9-year-olds. Sixty-five families were located when the children were either age 9 or 12. Forty-eight children were located at both sampling periods. Between 4 and 12 years of age, 15 children moved and could not be located. Five families that could be located declined to participate. The children lost to attrition and to nonparticipation and the children assessed at ages 12 were not significantly different in terms of demographics (family structure, ethnicity, maternal education, and parental occupation), child-care history (age entered care, type of arrangement, and quality of care), maternal attachment category, and teacher attachment security scores collected at ages 12 months and 4 years. There were no significant differences between children who participated at age 9 or 12 and children who did not participate at age 4 when social interaction was measured.

Procedures and Measures

Procedures and measures of the toddler, preschool, and middle childhood portion of the longitudinal study have been elaborated elsewhere (Howes & Hamilton, 1992a; 1992b; Howes et al., 1998; Howes, Matheson, & Hamilton, 1994; Howes & Phillipsen, 1998; Howes et al., 1988). Table 4.1 summarizes the measures and the informant (placed in parentheses) over the longitudinal study.

Attachment Relationship Quality with Mother and Teacher

Toddler and Preschool

Children were seen with their mothers in the strange situation at 12 months. Attachment categories (ABC—avoidant, secure, resistant) were derived by standard procedures (Ainsworth et al., 1978). At age 4, all children participated in a play group session with unfamiliar peers (Howes, Matheson, & Hamilton, 1994). At the conclusion of the play group, mother–child reunions were scored for attachment category using the Cassidy and Marvin (1988) procedure. In this analysis, we used only the secure and insecure categories as assessed at both time points.

Within 6 months of first entering child care, children were observed in-

Table 4.1
Measures Used in the Longitudinal Study

| | Attachment quality | | Peer relations | |
	Mother-child	Teacher-child	Friendship	Social Interaction
Early Adolescence (12 years)				
SAT	-		Bukowski	-
(rated)			(child)	
Middle childhood (9 years)				
Rudolph	Rudolph		Bukowski	Rudolph
(child)	(child)		(child)	(child)
	Pianta			Asher
	(teacher)			(teacher)
Preschool (4 years)				
Separation	AQS		Block & Block	Aggression
(rated)	(observed)		(teacher)	Withdraw
				Play
				(observed)
Toddler (12 -30 months)				
Strange	AQS		-	Aggression
Situation	(observed)			Withdraw
(rated)				Play
				(observed)

teracting with their provider in their child-care arrangement. Attachment security between the child and child-care caregiver was assessed using the Waters Attachment Q-Set (Waters, 1990). Security scores were calculated from the Q-Set. Following procedures derived from a cluster analysis of Q-Set items, each child was classified into an attachment category (Howes & Hamilton, 1992a; Howes & Smith, 1995a; 1995b). Children in the secure category were low in avoiding, high in secure base and high in comfort seeking. Children in the insecure category were either low in avoiding, high in difficult negotiations, and low in positive negotiations or high in avoiding, low in secure base and low in comfort seeking.

Middle Childhood

Children's perceptions of their relationships with their mothers and teachers were assessed with the Children's Expectations of Social Behavior Questionnaire (Rudolph et al., 1995). The measure requires that children encode typical interpersonal transactions, formulate an understanding of the situations and generate predictions about likely outcomes. It is based on theoretical assumptions about the importance of interpersonal expectations in the formation of relationships (Bowlby, 1982). Children are provided with 20 hypothetical vignettes describing interpersonal situations (e.g., "You ask your mom to take you to a movie," "You are having trouble learning how to do a math problem"). Ten vignettes are tied to each social partner—mother and teacher. Three possible responses are provided: a supportive, comforting, or accepting response; an indifferent, avoidant, or withdrawing response; and a hostile, critical, or rejecting response, coded as 1, -1, and -2, respectively. The child is asked to select the most likely response to each vignette. Scores are summed to form a single score for each partner. The Rudolph et al. (1995) measure originally was developed for mothers and peers. For this study, we adapted some of the vignettes designed for mothers so that structure and, wherever possible, content were parallel. For example, both the mother and teacher forms have a vignette based on giving the adult a gift, asking for help, and responding to sad feelings. The adaptations were piloted with children not in the sample. Interviews with the pilot children indicated that the teacher vignettes were plausible situations.

Rudolph et al. (1995) reported Cronbach alphas of .74 for mother, 1-month test-retest reliabilities of $r = .86$ and 5-month test-retest reliabilities of .82. In the current study, Cronbach alphas were .78 for mother and .83 for teacher. Rudolph et al. (1995) reported that interpersonal schema scores for mothers are significantly associated with other measures of cognitive representations of interpersonal relations and with dysfunctional social behavior and less positive status in the peer group.

To create categories of secure and insecure mother-child and teacher-child attachment relationships, the Rudolph scores for mother and for teacher were also coded as secure or insecure based on an analysis of the score distributions, assuming that approximately two thirds of the sample would be secure.

Teachers completed the Pianta Student–Teacher Relationship Scale (Pianta & Steinberg, 1992). This measure contains 30 questions rated on a 5-point scale (e.g., "It is easy to be in tune with what this child is feeling"; "When this child arrives in a bad mood I know we are in for a long and difficult day"). Pianta suggested three subscales to capture negative and positive teacher representations of the teacher–child relationship. These subscale scores are associated with children's classroom and home behaviors (Pianta & Steinberg, 1992). In this study, we used two of the subscales—close ($\alpha = .75$) and conflictual ($\alpha = .81$) teacher perceptions of the teacher-child relationship.

Early Adolescence

At age 12, participating children were interviewed using the Separation Anxiety Test (SAT) for adolescents (automated version, Main, Kaplan & Cassidy, 1985; Resnick, 1991). The SAT asks children to respond to a series of standardized questions concerning six separation pictures (e.g., parents leave for 2 weeks; the teenager runs away from home). Interviews were digitally recorded and coded by Resnick. For the purposes of this analysis, the transcripts were coded as secure or insecure. Scores on the SAT in previous research have correlated with earlier attachment quality in the strange situation (Main et al., 1985); and concurrently with emotional openness (Shouldice & Stevenson-Hinde, 1992). Security ratings on the SAT are considered measures of the child's internal representation of attachment relationships rather than the child's perception of the mother-child relationship (Howes & Rosenblatt, 1999). Teacher-child relationship measures were not collected in early adolescence because the children no longer had primary teachers in self-contained classrooms.

Peer Social Interaction and Friendship Quality

Toddler and Preschool

Between 2 and 6 months after the children first began child care, we observed their peer interactions. Independent observers used the Howes Peer Play scale (Howes & Matheson, 1992) and the Baumrind Preschool Behavior Q-Set (Baumrind, 1968) to assess complexity and content of peer interaction in both toddler and preschool periods. As toddlers and again as preschoolers, children were observed with their familiar peers on two separate days. Each child-care observation lasted 1 hour. Visits were scheduled during times when the child was free to interact with both adults and peers. During each visit, the observer coded three 5-minute samples of social behaviors, six per child. The samples were evenly spaced throughout the observation. During the 5-minute coding period, the complexity and content of the child's play with peers were coded at 20-second intervals. As preschoolers, each child also was seen in a 2-hour long play group. The play groups were composed of four unfamiliar children all within 1 month of their fourth birthdays. Preschool child-care teachers completed the California Child Q-Set (Block & Block, 1980). Each child in the sample had a different teacher.

All observers were blind to the hypotheses of the study. Different observers collected the toddler, preschool, and play group data. Interobserver reliability was established to an 85 percent exact agreement criterion prior to data collection. Interobserver reliability was reestablished at the midpoint of each data collection period. Interobserver reliabilities on individual behaviors ranged from .89 to .93 ($M = .91$) in the toddler period, from .91 to .97 ($M = .96$) in preschool child care, and from .90 to .92 ($M = .91$) in the play group.

Three measures represented toddler social behavior with peers: complex play, aggressive, and withdrawn (Howes, Phillipsen, & Hamilton, 1993). Complex play was the percent of the observation period spent in complementary or cooperative pretend play. The other two measures, aggressive and withdrawn, were composite variables derived from the Peer Play scale and the Q-Set. These composite scores were formed by first converting them to standard scores and then summing them. We used alpha values to evaluate the reliability of the composite variables. Aggressive ($\alpha = .85$) was composed of the percentage of the observation period spent in physical or verbal hostile initiations, the percentage of the observation period spent in fights, the percentage of observed peer initiations met with hostile acts, and four items from the Q-Set: destructively impetuous and impulsive, requires a great deal of adult supervision when playing with peers, cannot be trusted, and bullies other children. Withdrawn ($\alpha = .73$) was the percentage of the observation period in solitary play and two items from the Q-Set: timid with other children and apprehensive.

Three measures represented social interaction with peers as preschool-age children: complex play, aggressive, and withdrawn. Complex play ($\alpha = .66$) was a composite formed by summing two standard scores: the percentage of time engaged in cooperative or complex pretend play with familiar peers and with unfamiliar peers. Aggressive ($\alpha = .79$) was a composite variable formed by summing standard scores from the Peer Play scale (three scores all from observations of familiar peers: percentage of observation period spent in physical or verbal hostile initiations, percentage of observation period in fights, percentage of peer initiations met with hostile acts); the Baumrind Preschool Q-Set (four items, identical to the toddler period); and one item from California Child Q-Set (acts in an aggressive manner). Withdrawn ($\alpha = .84$) was a composite variable formed by summing standard scores from the Peer Play scale (two items, percentage of observation in solitary play with familiar peers and with unfamiliar peers); two items from Preschool Q-Set (timid with other children and apprehensive); and one item from California Child Q-Set (withdraws from peer interaction). One item from the California Child Q-Set (asking about close friendships) was used in the current analysis as the measure of preschool friendship quality.

Middle Childhood

Measures of social interaction with peers were derived from teacher reports using the Cassidy and Asher (1992) teacher assessment of social behavior questionnaire. Each child in the sample had a different teacher. The teacher was asked to rate on 5-point scales the social behavior of the target child in relation to the other children in his or her class (e.g., this child is mean to other children). Cassidy and Asher derived four subscales of which we used three in the current study. The subscales were prosocial ($\alpha = .73$; e.g., "This child is nice and friendly to other children," "This child is cooperative with other children," "This child is helpful to other children"), shy ($\alpha = .68$; e.g., "This child is shy with other children," "This child seems afraid of other children," "This child does not play with other children"), and aggressive ($\alpha = .67$; e.g., "This child is mean to other children," "This child starts fights," "This child hurts other children").

Table 4.2
Children's Relationships with Mothers and Teachers for Participants at 9 and/or 12 Years of Age

	Children	
	n	percent secure
Toddler		
Mother	65	65
Teacher	45	46
Preschool		
Mother	65	71
Teacher	64	65
Middle childhood		
Mother	55	59
Teacher	55	62
Early adolescence		
Mother	54	48

In addition, 10 hypothetical vignettes describing interpersonal situations from the Children's Expectations of Social Behavior Questionnaire (Rudolph et al., 1995) were used to assess the child's perception of his or her social interaction with peers. These vignettes were scored as previously described for the child's perceptions of mother and teacher.

The Friendship Quality Scale (Bukowski, Hoza, & Boivin, 1994) was used at age 9 and again at age 12 to assess the child's perception of his or her best friendship. This measure was completed with reference to a specific child, in this case named by the mother and the child as a best friend. The measure includes 23 questions rated on a 5 point scale (e.g., "I think about my friend when my friend is not around"). Bukowski et al. (1994) derived five subscales from this measure with alphas ranging from .71 to .86 for each subscale. In this study, we found acceptable alpha levels for a single composite score. This was positive (subscales of closeness, help, and security) with a Cronbach alphas of .78.

RESULTS

Children's Relationships with Adults: Mothers and Teachers

The distribution of secure and insecure mother-child attachment relationships over time is displayed in Table 4.2. The distribution of secure relationships is similar to other samples of middle-class, White children raised in two-parent families (Ainsworth et al., 1978). The smallest percentage of children had secure maternal-child attachment relationships in the early adolescent period. This decrease is consistent with other literature on SAT attachment security in older children (Resnick, 1997). In the toddler and preschool periods (Howes & Hamilton, 1992a, 1992b) and again in middle childhood (Howes et al., 1998) children's security with mothers was independent of their security with teachers.

Overall attachment relationship quality with mothers and teachers was stable and continuous between toddler and early adolescent developmental periods (Howes et al., 1998; Howes & Rosenblatt, 1999). That is, children who were secure in one developmental periods tended to be secure in the subsequent period. This relation is represented in Figure 4.2 by the vertical solid arrows between mother-child relationships and between teacher-child relationships at different developmental periods.

Children's Social Interaction and Friendships with Peers across Development

Descriptive statistics for all measures of children's social competence and friendships with peers across the four developmental periods are shown in Table 4.3. Overall, the children in this sample tended to be competent with peers and to have positive friendships. However, there is a considerable range for each measure.

Previously published work on this sample found that children who were more competent with peers as toddlers and preschoolers were more competent with peers in middle childhood (Howes & Phillipsen, 1998). Children who were rated by teachers as having close friendships in preschool rated themselves as having a more positive friendship in middle childhood (Howes et al., 1998). Children who rated themselves as having a more positive friendship in middle childhood rated themselves as having a more positive friendship in adolescence [r (52) = .40; $p < .05$]. Returning to Figure 4.2, these links are represented by the solid vertical arrows between social interaction with peers and between friendships with peers at different developmental periods.

Associations between Friendship Quality and Social Interaction with Peers

Friendship quality and social interaction with peers are viewed as related but semi-independent constructs (Asher et al., 1996). In order to examine the relations between friendship quality and social interaction with peers in this longitudinal sample we computed correlations between measures of friendship quality in preschool and middle childhood and social interaction with peers in preschool and middle childhood. These relations are in Table

Figure 4.2
Links between Family and Peer Relationships across Developmental Periods:
Results

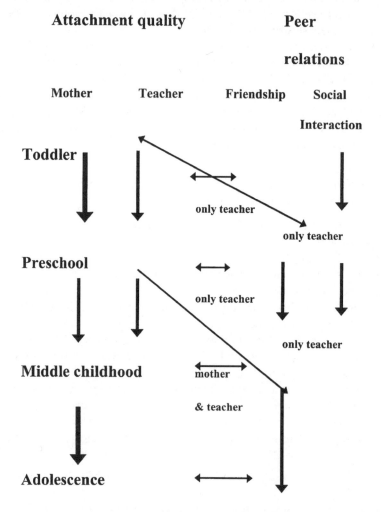

4.4. Children rated by their teachers as having closer friendships in preschool were observed to be less withdrawn in preschool, and rated by their teachers as less aggressive in middle childhood. There were no significant associations between friendship quality and social interaction in middle childhood.

Table 4.3
Social Interaction and Friendships with Peers across Development

Measures	Mean	SD	Range
Toddler			
Observed/rated			
Play	-.09	.76	-.84 to 3.22
Withdrawal	-.02	1.00	-1.32 to 2.74
Aggressive	-.13	2.22	-2.07 to 8.31
Preschool			
Observed/rated			
Play	-.05	1.49	-3.46 to 4.34
Withdrawal	-.03	2.81	-6.00 to 8.36
Aggression	.05	1.87	-1.08 to 8.31
Teacher rated			
Friendship	5.53	2.48	1.00 to 9.00
Middle childhood			
Teacher rated			
Prosocial	4.12	.83	1.67 to 5.00
Shy	1.42	.56	1.00 to 3.33
Aggressive	1.33	.51	1.00 to 3.00
Child perceived			
Social competence	4.90	3.17	-9.00 to 7.00
Friendship quality	3.92	.51	2.81 to 5.18
Adolescent			
Friendship quality	3.87	.52	2.63 to 4.75

Links between Adult-Child Attachment Relationships and Peer Social Interaction and Friendship

Mother-Child Attachments

Table 4.5 depicts associations between mother-child attachment relationships and peer social interaction and friendship across all four developmental periods. In the toddler, preschool, and adolescent periods, attachment relationship quality is a categorical variable. Attachment relationships are either secure or insecure. In the middle childhood period, attachment relationship quality is a continuous variable. Therefore, correlations were computed between attachment quality in middle childhood and measures of peer social interaction and friendship. *T* tests were used to test the association between attachment quality in middle childhood and measures of peer social interaction and friendship in the other three developmental periods. For ease of presentation only significant associations are fully tabled.

Previous published work with this sample found that variations in the quality of mother-child attachment relationships in the toddler and preschool developmental periods were not concurrently or predictably associ-

Table 4.4
Relations between Friendship and Social Interaction with Peers over Development

| | *Friendship* | |
	Preschool	Middle childhood
Social competence		
Preschool		
Observed/rated		
Aggression	-.25	-
Withdrawal	-.35**	-
Play	.04	-
Middle childhood		
Teacher		
Aggression	-.29*	.05
Withdraw	.06	.06
Social competence	.24	.05
Child perception		
Social competence	.03	.08

*$p < .05$; **$p < .01$.

ated with variations in children's social interaction and friendships with peers (Howes, Matheson, & Hamilton, 1994). As can be seen in Table 4.5, mother-child attachment quality when the children were toddlers or when they were preschoolers did not predict social interaction or friendships with peers in middle childhood or adolescence.

In contrast, contemporary mother-child attachment relationship quality was linked to peer relations in the middle childhood and adolescent periods. Again referring to Table 4.5, children who perceived their mother-child relationships more positively in middle childhood also were rated by teachers as more prosocial with peers and rated themselves as more socially competent with peers. Children who were rated as secure in their attachment representations as adolescents were more positive about their friendships. Figure 4.2 represents these links by horizontal lines between attachment quality and peer relations within the middle childhood and adolescent periods.

Teacher-Child Attachments

Table 4.6 depicts associations between teacher-child attachment relationships and peer social interaction and friendship across all four developmental periods. Security scores were used for toddler and preschool teacher-child attachment quality. Therefore, correlations were used to test the association between teacher-child relationship quality in the toddler, preschool, and middle childhood periods and social interaction and friendships with peers across all four developmental periods. As the associations within and across

Table 4.5

Associations between Mother-Child Attachment Relationships and Peer Social Interaction and Friendship

	Toddler	Preschool	Middle Childhood	Adolescence
		Mother-child attachment		
Toddler	NS			
Preschool	NS	NS		
Middle Childhood				
Teacher rated				
Prosocial	NS	NS	$r = .33$*	
Shy	NS	NS	NS	
Aggressive	NS	NS	NS	
Child perceived				
Social competence				
	NS	NS	$r = .41$**	
Friendship quality				
	NS	NS	NS	
Adolescent				
Friendship quality				
	NS	NS	NS	M (S) = 4.06
				M (I) = 3.71
				$t = 3.07$**

*$p < .05$; **$p < .01$.

the toddler and preschool periods are previously published (Howes, Matheson, & Hamilton, 1994), these relationships are only represented as significant. In all other cases the correlation coefficient is tabled.

In previously published work, strong links were found between early teacher-child attachment relationship quality and social interaction and friendships with peers through preschool (Howes, Matheson, & Hamilton, 1994). Figure 4.2 represents these links by the horizontal line between attachment quality and peer relations within the preschool period. Consistent with these earlier findings, children who had more secure teacher-child attachment relationships in preschool were more positive about their friendships in middle childhood. Turning again to Fig. 4.2, this linkage is represented by the diagonal line between attachment quality in preschool and peer relations in middle childhood.

During middle childhood, children whose teachers rated their teacher-child relationships as more positive and less conflictual were rated as less aggressive and more socially competent. Furthermore, children in this period who were rated by teachers as having more positive teacher–child relationships rated themselves as more competent and as having more positive

Family and Peers

Table 4.6
Associations between Teacher-Child Attachment Relationships and Peer Social Interaction and Friendship

	Toddler	Preschool	Teacher Positive	Conflict	Child
		Teacher-child attachment			
			Middle childhood		
Toddler	Sign.				
Preschool	Sign.	Sign.			
Middle Childhood					
Teacher rated					
Aggression	-.17	-.13	-.29*	.76**	-.12
Withdraw	-.10	-.20	-.10	.20	-.04
Social competence	.02	.11	.45**	-.59**	.11
Child perceived					
Social competence	.11	.15	.33**	-.14	.25
Friendship quality	.12	.31*	.36*	-.02	.29*
Adolescent					
Friendship quality	.09	.15	.19	.12	.04

$*p < .05; **p < .01.$

friendships. Children who rated themselves as more socially competent rated their friendships as more positive. These links appear in Fig. 4.2 in the horizontal line between attachment quality and peer relations within the middle childhood period.

Teacher-child relationship quality in any developmental period did not predict perception of friendship quality in adolescence. We did not measure teacher–child relationship quality in early adolescence, so these contemporary links cannot be examined.

Prediction of Relations with Peers in Middle Childhood and Early Adolescence

Friendship Quality

We used the links represented in Fig. 4.2 in a series of hierarchical linear regressions to predict friendship quality in early adolescence. In the first regression, we simultaneously entered as predictors friendship quality in middle childhood, mother-child attachment relationship quality in early adolescence, mother-child attachment relationship quality in middle childhood, and teacher perceptions of teacher-child relationship quality in middle childhood. Early adolescent friendship quality could be predicted [R (44) = .50,

Figure 4.3
Prediction of Friendship Quality

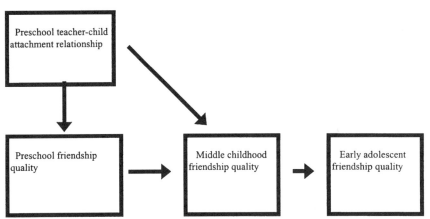

$r^2 = .25; p = .04$]. The only significant beta ($\beta = .49, t = 2.88; p = .01$) was friendship quality in middle childhood. We then computed a second regression equation entering friendship quality in the first step and as a second step mother-child attachment relationship quality in early adolescence, mother-child attachment relationship quality in middle childhood, and teacher perceptions of teacher-child relationship quality in middle childhood. Friendship quality in middle childhood predicted friendship quality in early adolescence [R (44) $= .47, r^2 = .23; p = .002$]. The second step predictors only explained 2 percent in additional variance. This suggests friendship relationship quality in early adolescence can be best predicted by earlier friendship relationship quality rather than from previous attachment relationships. Finally, we recomputed the regressions using preschool teacher-child attachment quality as an additional predictor. Friendship quality in middle childhood remained the only significant predictor of early adolescent friendship quality.

We then completed a series of regressions to predict friendship quality in middle childhood by simultaneously entering as predictors friendship quality in preschool, mother-child attachment relationship quality in middle childhood, teacher perceptions of teacher-child relationship quality in middle childhood, and teacher-child attachment relationship quality in preschool. Middle childhood friendship quality could be predicted [R (51) $= .52, r^2 = .27; p = .03$]. Two predictors had significant beta values: friendship quality in preschool ($\beta = .36, t = 2.67; p = .05$) and teacher-child attachment quality in preschool ($\beta = .37, t = 3.83; p = .04$).

The results of these analyses are represented in Figure 4.3. Children with more secure teacher-child relationships and more close friendship relationships in preschool are likely to have positive friendships in middle childhood. Children with positive friendships in middle childhood are likely to have positive friendships in early adolescence.

Social Interaction

Social interaction in middle childhood was predicted in previously published work with this sample by social interaction with peers as preschoolers and toddlers. We recomputed these regression equations adding teacher-child and mother-child relationship quality as additional predictors. Adding teacher-child or mother-child relationship quality in either middle childhood or preschool did not improve predictability.

DISCUSSION

In this chapter we examined links between adult attachment and peer relations across development: from children's first experiences within a peer group through early adolescence. To understand these links it is important to note the context of development for these children. These children have grown up in relatively privileged family circumstances. They first encountered peers within organized and stable groups. Although most children experienced one change in primary child-care teacher during their time in child care, very few children had more than one child-care teacher change.

Given these life circumstances, the remarkable stability of individual variations in relationship quality and in social interaction is perhaps not surprising. However, it is noteworthy that the strongest links in this sample are within social partner—within mother-child relationships, teacher-child relationships, friendship relationships, and peers in general. Once established, individual differences in relationship quality and in social interaction remained relatively stable.

The stability of early individual differences in peer relations and the strong links between teacher-child attachment quality and peer relations during early developmental periods highlights the importance of the teacher in child care for children constructing their peer relations. The findings also provide support for the proposition that once engaged with peers, children develop social interaction within the peer group rather than relying on current adult-child relationships as templates. Attachment quality with teacher or with mother failed to predict social interaction with peers across the developmental period. As well, contemporary attachment quality only was associated with social interaction in middle childhood when teachers rated both their relationships with the children and the social interaction of the children.

In contrast, friendship quality was more closely linked to adult attachment relationship quality, particularly to attachment quality with early teachers. This is consistent with the proposition that there will be stronger links between adult-child attachment quality and friendship than between attachment quality and social interaction (Park & Waters, 1989). Early teacher-child attachment quality was linked contemporarily to friendship quality and predicted friendship quality in middle childhood. Although children with more positive attachment representations rated their friendships as more positive in adolescence, the regression analysis suggested that earlier teacher-child attachment quality was the more powerful predictor.

When links between mother-child and teacher-child attachment relationships and peer relations are compared across development, maternal attachment quality appears to be more influential in later periods than in earlier ones. Mother-child attachment was only associated with peer relations in middle childhood and early adolescence. Furthermore, although early teacher-child attachment relationship quality predicted later peer relations, there were no predictive links for mother-child attachment quality. All links between mother-child attachment quality and peer relations were contemporary.

Mothers of children who construct their relations with peers in child care appear to have a different function than do traditional mothers. These mothers may spend less time actually supervising their children's peer contacts than do mothers of children whose primary peer encounters are within the family. Therefore, the influence of these mothers on their children's peer relations cannot be explained using the secure base mechanism suggested by attachment theory. Children who are enrolled in child care do form attachment relationships with their mothers and presumably have access to an internal representation of their mother-child relationship. This representation of mother is one of several internalized representations available to children who also have attachment relationships with their child-care teacher. Our data suggests that the maternal representation is not dominant within this network of relationships.

REFERENCES

Ainsworth, M. S., Blehar, M., Waters, E., & Wall, S. (1978). *Patterns of attachment.* Hillsdale, NJ: Erlbaum.

Asher, S. R., Parker, J. G. & Walker, D. L. (1996). Distinguishing friendship from acceptance: Implications for intervention and assessment. In Bukowski, W. M. Newcomb, A. F., & Hartup, W. W. (Eds.), *The company they keep: Friendships during childhood and adolescence* (pp. 366–405). New York: Cambridge University Press.

Baumrind, D. (1968). *Manual for the Preschool Behavior Q-Sort.* Berkeley: University of California.

Birch, S. H., & Ladd, G. W. (1997). The teacher-child relationship and children's early school adjustment. *Journal of School Psychology, 35,* 61–79.

Block, J., & Block, J.-H. (1980). *The California Child Q-Set.* Palo Alto, CA: Consulting Psychologist Press.

Booth, C., Rose-Krasnor, L., MacKinnon, J., & Rubin, K. (1994). Predicting social adjustment in middle childhood: The role of preschool attachment security and maternal style. *Social Development, 3,* 189–204.

Booth, C., Rose-Krasnor, L., & Rubin, K. (1991). Relating preschoolers' social competence and their mothers' parenting behaviors to early attachment security and high risk status. *Journal of Social and Personal Relationships, 8,* 363–382.

Bost, K., Vaughn, B. E., Washington, W. N., Cielinski, K., & Bradbard, M. R. (1998). Social competence, social support, and attachment: Demarcation of construct domains, measurement, and paths of influence for preschool children attending Head Start. *Child Development, 69,* 192–218.

Bowlby, J. (1982). *Attachment and loss: Loss, sadness and depression.* New York: Basic.

Bretherton, I. (1985). Attachment theory: Retrospect and prospect. In Bretherton, I., & Waters, E. (Eds.), Growing points of attachment: Theory and research (pp. 3–38). Chicago: University of Chicago Press.

Bukowski, W. M., Hoza, B., & Boivin, M. (1994). Measuring friendship quality during pre- and early adolescence: The development and psychometric properties of the friendship quality scale. *Journal of Social and Personal Relationships, 11,* 471–484.

Cassidy, J. (1988). The self as related to child-mother attachment at age six. *Child Development, 59,* 121–134.

Cassidy, J., & Asher, S. (1992). Loneliness and peer relations in young children. *Child Development, 63,* 350–365.

Cassidy, J., & Marvin, R. S. (1988, April). *A system for coding the organization of attachment behavior in three- and four-year-old children.* Paper presented at the International Conference on Infant Studies, Washington, DC.

Cohn, D. (1990). Child-mother attachment of six-year-olds and social competence at school. *Child Development, 61,* 152–162.

Coie, J. D. (1990) Towards a theory of peer rejection. In Asher, S. R., & Coie, J. D. (Eds.), *Peer rejection in childhood* (pp. 365–401). New York: Cambridge University Press.

Elicker, J., Egland, M., & Sroufe, L. A. (1992). Predicting peer competence and peer relationships in childhood from early parent-child relationships. In Parke, R. D., & Ladd, G. W. (Eds.), *Family–peer relationships: Modes of linkage* (pp. 77–106). Hillsdale, NJ: Erlbaum.

Egeland, B., & Hiester, M. (1995). The long-term consequences of infant day-care and mother-infant attachment. *Child Development, 66,* 474–485.

Gossen, F. A., & van Ijzendoorn, M. H. (1990). Quality of infant's attachment to professional caregivers: Relation to infant-parent attachment and daycare characteristics. *Child Development, 51,* 832–837.

Harms, T., & Clifford, R. M. (1980). *Early childhood environmental rating scale.* New York: Teacher's College Press.

Hay, D. (1985). Learning to form relationships in infancy: Parallel attainments with parents and peers. *Developmental Review, 5,* 122–161.

Howes, C. (1983). Patterns of friendship. *Child Development, 54,* 1041–1053.

Howes, C. (1988). Peer interaction of young children. *Monographs of the Society for Research in Child Development, 53* (1, serial no. 217).

Howes, C. (1992). *The collaborative construction of pretend: Social pretend play functions.* New York: State University of New York Press.

Howes, C. (1996). The earliest friendships. In Bukowski, W. M., Newcomb, W. F., & Hartup, W. W. (Eds.), *The company they keep: Friendships in childhood and adolescence* (pp. 66–86). New York: Cambridge.

Howes, C. (1997). Teacher sensitivity, children's attachment, and play with peers. *Early Education and Development, 8,* 41–49.

Howes, C. (in press). Attachment relationships in the context of multiple caregivers. In Cassidy, J. & Shaver, P. R. (Eds.), *Handbook of attachment theory and research.* New York: Guilford.

Howes, C., & Hamilton, C. E. (1992a). Children's relationships with caregivers: Mothers and child care teachers. *Child Development, 53,* 859–878.

Howes, C., & Hamilton, C. E. (1992b). Children's relationships with child care teachers: Stability and concordance with maternal attachment. *Child Development, 53,* 879–892.

Howes, C., Hamilton, C. E., & Althusen, V. (in press). Using the attachment Q-Set to describe non-familial attachments. In Vaughn, B., & Waters, E. (Eds.), *Attachment.* Hillsdale, NJ: Erlbaum.

Howes, C., Hamilton, C., & Matheson, C. (1994). Children's relationships with peers: Differential associations with aspects of the teacher-child relationship, *65,* 253–263.

Howes, C., Hamilton, C., & Phillipsen, L. C. (1998). Stability and continuity of child-caregiver and child-peer relationships. *Child Development, 69,* 418–426.

Howes, C., & Matheson, C. (1992). Sequences in the development of competent play with peers: Social and social pretend play. *Developmental Psychology, 28,* 961–974.

Howes, C., Matheson, C., & Hamilton, C. E. (1994). Maternal, teacher and child care history correlates of children's relationships with peers. *Child Development, 55,* 257–273.

Howes, C., Phillips, D. A., & Whitebook, M. (1992). Thresholds of quality: Implications for the social development of children in center-based care. *Child Development, 63,* 449–460.

Howes, C., & Phillipsen, L. C. (1998). Continuity in children's relations with peers. *Social Development, 1,* 230–242.

Howes, C., Phillipsen, L. C., & Hamilton, C. E. (1993). Constructing social communication with peers: Domains and sequences. In Nadel, J., & Camaioni, L. (Eds.), *New perspectives in early communicative development* (pp. 215–232). New York: Routledge.

Howes, C., Phillipsen, L. C., & Piesner-Feinberg, E. (1997). *The consistency and predictability of teacher-child relationships during the transition to kindergarten.* Manuscript submitted for review.

Howes, C., Rodning, C., Galluzzo, D. C., & Myers, L. (1988). Attachment and child care: Relationships with mother and caregiver. *Early Childhood Research Quarterly, 3,* 703–715.

Howes, C., & Rosenblatt, S. (1999). *Stability of adult-child attachment relationships.* unpublished manuscript.

Howes, C., & Smith, E. W. (1995a). Children and their child care caregivers: Profiles of relationships. *Social Development, 4,* 44–61.

Howes, C., & Smith, E. W. (1995b). Relations among child care quality, teacher behavior, children's play activities, emotional security, and cognitive activity in child care. *Early Childhood Research Quarterly, 10,* 381–707.

LaFreniere, P., & Sroufe, L. A. (1985). Profiles of peer competence in preschool: Interrelations between measures, influence of social ecology, and relation to attachment theory. *Developmental Psychology, 21,* 56–69.

Main, M., Kaplan, N., & Cassidy, J. (1985). Security in infancy, childhood and adulthood: A move to the level of representation. In Bretherton, I., & Waters, E. (Eds.), Growing points of attachment: Theory and research (pp. 55–107). Chicago, IL: University of Chicago Press.

Park, K., & Waters, E. (1989). Security of attachment and preschool friendships. *Child Development, 60,* 1076–1081.

Pianta, R. C., & Sternberg, M. (1992). Teacher–child relationships and adjusting to school. In R. C. Pianta (Ed.), *Beyond the parent: The role of other adults in children's lives. New Directions for Child Development, 57,* 51–80.

Pianta, R. C., Sternberg, M., & Rollins, K. B. (1995). The first two years of school: Teacher–child relationships and deflections in children's classroom adjustment. *Development and Psychopathology, 7,* 295–312.

Pianta, R. C., & Walsh, D. J. (1996). *High risk children in schools.* New York: Routledge.

Pierrehumbert, B., Ramstein, T., Karmaniola, A., & Halfon, O. (1994). *Child care in the preschool years, behavior problems and cognitive development.* Unpublished paper, Service Universitaire de Psychiatrie l'Enfant et de l'Adolescent, Lausanne, Switzerland.

Resnick, G. (1991, April). *Attachment and self-representation during early adolescence.* Paper presented at the biennial meeting of the Society for Research in Child Development, Seattle, WA.

Resnick, G. (1997, April). *The correspondence between the Strange Situation at 12 months and the Separation Anxiety Test at 11 years in an Israeli Kibbutz sample.* Paper presented at the biennial meeting of the Society for Research in Child Development, Washington, DC.

Rudolph, K., Hammen, C., & Burge, D. (1995). Cognitive representations of self, family, and peers in school age children: Links with social competence and sociometric status. *Child Development, 66,* 1385–1402.

Sagi, A., Lamb, M., Lewkowicz, K., Shoham, R., Dvir, R., & Estes, D. (1985). Security of infant-mother, infant-father, infant-metapelet attachments among kibbutz reared Israeli children. In Bretherton, I., & Waters, E. (Eds.), Growing points of attachment: Theory and research (pp. 257–275). Chicago: University of Chicago Press.

Shouldice, A., & Stevenson-Hinde, J. (1992). Coping with separation distress: The separation anxiety test and attachment classifications at 4.5 years. *Journal of Child Psychology and Psychiatry, 33,* 331–348.

Turner, P. J. (1991). Relations between attachment, gender, and behavior with peers in preschool. *Child Development, 62,* 1475–1488.

Waters, E. (1990). *The Attachment-Q-Set.* Stony Brook: State University of New York.

Waters, E., & Sroufe, L. A. (1983). Social competence as a developmental construct. *Developmental Review, 3,* 79–97.

Waters, E., Wippman, J., & Sroufe, L. A. (1979). Attachment, positive affect, and competence in the peer group: Two studies in construct validation. *Child Development, 50,* 821–829.

5

Living in a Hostile World: Toward an Integrated Model of Family, Peer, and Physiological Processes in Aggressive Preschoolers

Lynn Fainsilber Katz

Childhood antisocial behavior is a significant mental health problem. Children who have conduct problems (CP) show a range of concurrent developmental difficulties, including poor academic achievement, impaired peer relationships, and anxiety and depressive disturbances (e.g., Patterson, DeBaryshe, & Ramsey, 1989). Moreover, the long-term outlook for children with CPs is also poor. They are at increased risk for school dropout, alcoholism, drug abuse, suicide, and criminality in adolescence and adulthood (e.g., Loeber & Dishion, 1983; Robins, 1978; West & Farrington, 1973).

Children who begin the developmental trajectory early are at greatest risk for the most severe developmental outcomes (Moffitt, 1993). However, most of what is known about these "early starters" and the identification of factors that predict continued antisocial behavior is largely based on research with children during the middle childhood years. Yet, a significant number of children with CPs show difficulties as early as the preschool period. Identification of the child as disruptive during the preschool years appears to have strong predictive significance for subsequent adjustment. Disruptive behavior significantly predicts peer relationships, self-esteem, academic achievement, as well as both externalizing and internalizing problems in the elementary school period (Campbell, Breaux, Ewing, & Szumoski, 1986; Chamberlain & Nader, 1971). Furthermore, a substantial proportion of preschool children identified as disruptive continue to show behavior problems from ages 3 to 9 (Campbell et al., 1986; Campbell & Ewing, 1990). Given evidence that children showing early signs of disruptive behavior are at greatest risk for the most severe forms of CPs at later ages (Loeber, 1982),

Figure 5.1
Family-based Emotion Regulation Model of Childhood Antisocial Behavior

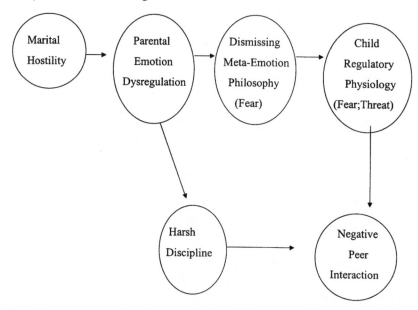

preschool-aged early starters may be those children who are on a life course toward persistent and severe CPs. Early identification of risk factors related to the continuity of disruptive behavior from the preschool period to middle childhood is essential for the prevention of more chronic CPs. It not only leads to the early detection of children at greatest risk, but is also important for building successful intervention and prevention programs for young CP children.

Toward this end, this chapter reviews current understanding of risk factors associated with childhood antisocial behavior. Familial, peer, and physiological processes associated with childhood antisocial behavior are reviewed. A family-based emotion regulation model of childhood antisocial behavior that integrates key risk factors is proposed. Although several risk factors have been identified as contributing to the development of antisocial behavior, there is little understanding of the relation among them, and no systematic theory that articulates how these factors interact. In the proposed model, marital hostility, individual parental emotion regulation abilities, parenting skill deficits, parental "meta-emotion philosophy," and children's physiological regulatory ability are the key constructs in theory building. The theoretical model is depicted in Figure 5.1. Each key theoretical construct is reviewed in turn.

MARITAL HOSTILITY AND ABUSE

Substantial research has pointed to a powerful relation between marital discord and externalizing difficulties in both clinic and nonclinic populations (for reviews, see E. Cummings & Davies, 1994; Emery, 1988; Grych & Fincham, 1990). Children growing up in homes characterized by marital distress exhibit a variety of externalizing difficulties, including higher levels of hostility, negativity toward peers, and delinquency (e.g., E. Cummings & Davies, 1994). Demonstrations of aggression and noncompliance in children appear to be related to specific processes in the marriage. Katz and Gottman (1993) found that when couples were hostile toward each other during attempts to resolve marital conflict, their children were rated by teachers 3 years later as showing higher levels of externalizing difficulties.

The presence of physical marital violence is perhaps one of the strongest correlates of children's externalizing difficulties (e.g., Emery & Laumann, 1998; Jouriles, Norwood, McDonald, Vincent, & Mahoney, 1996; Wolfe, Jaffe, Wilson, & Zak, 1985). For example, Jouriles, Murphy, and O'Leary (1989) reported that the physical aggression subscale of the Conflict Tactics scale predicted parental ratings of conduct disorder and clinical levels of child behavior problems, even after controlling for level of marital satisfaction. Similarly, Johnson and O'Leary (1987) found that parents of girls rated as high on the Conduct Disorder subscale of the CBCL (Conduct Behavior Checklist) reported more interparental hostility and aggression than did parents of girls not viewed as exhibiting conduct disorder, even though the two groups of parents did not differ in marital satisfaction.

Although the link between physical marital violence and children's conduct-related difficulties has been well established, there is little understanding of the mechanisms by which these effects occur. One prominent hypothesis is that physical marital violence may indirectly affect children's behavior through its spillover effects on parenting. It is well known that marital violence increases the risk of parental aggression toward children, particularly boys (Jouriles et al., 1989; McCloskey, Figueredo, & Koss, 1995). Physical marital violence may also affect children's aggression because of children's emotional processing of and reactions to interparental violence. There is some suggestion that exposure to physical marital violence may heighten children's sensitivity and reactivity to conflict (E. Cummings & Davies, 1994; Grych & Fincham, 1990). Children who report a history of physical conflict between their parents exhibit greater distress when observing angry interactions between unfamiliar adults (E. Cummings, Vogel, Cummings, & El-Sheikh, 1989). They are also more distressed than others by conflicts involving their mother, show increased preoccupation, concern, and support seeking, and take more responsibility for their mothers' feelings and behavior (J. Cummings, Pellegrini, Notarius, & Cummings, 1989).

Thus, conflict involving physical aggression is upsetting to children and may be closely linked to a hypersensitivity to conflict.

Although these data are suggestive, there is a need to develop a process-oriented theoretical model that explains how marital violence is associated with childhood antisocial behavior. Descriptions of maritally violent homes paint a picture of couples who are emotionally volatile and out of control. Yet there has been little attention paid to how emotion dysregulation within the family leads to negative outcomes in children living in maritally violent homes (Emery, 1989). Emotion dysregulation may occur in several different subsystems within the family. An understanding is needed of how marital violence affects parents' emotion regulation abilities, and how these intra-individual and marital regulatory deficits impact parenting skills and parents' awareness of children's emotions. It is also necessary to understand children's emotional reactions to living in maritally violent homes. Do children in maritally violent homes show heightened fear and hypervigilance to threatening cues of impending conflict between parents or do they habituate to threat over time? These emotional reactions may be seen both at the behavioral and physiological levels, with children from domestically violent homes showing increased hypervigilance and fear as well as increased autonomic nervous system reactivity. As a first step in exploring these multiple levels of analysis within the family, evidence of links between marital violence and individual emotion dysregulation is reviewed. Individual psychopathology in parents with CP children is also discussed to determine whether a conceptual basis exists for theorizing that similar emotion-related processes within the family may lead to CPs in children.

PARENTAL PSYCHOPATHOLOGY AND EMOTION DYSREGULATION

Although no one personality type is reflective of an abusive or abused spouse, many common personality types and disorders appear to be associated with interspousal aggression. In general, battered women show worse psychological adjustment on a variety of mental health indices than nonbattered women (e.g., McCloskey et al., 1995). Male batterers have been found to be more dysphoric than nonbatterers, and tend to have greater elevations on test scales reflecting personality disorders and nonconformity (Hamberger & Hastings, 1986; 1988). Anecdotal data from clinical case reports describe abusers as having difficulty with control issues and coping with the stress of intimate relationships (Gondolf, 1985).

Parental psychopathology and emotion dysregulation have also been associated with CPs in children. There is an increased prevalence of antisocial personality disorder (APD), criminal behavior, and substance abuse in fathers of CP children, and an increased prevalence of depression, antisocial personality, and antisocial behavior in mothers of CP children (Capaldi & Patterson, 1991). Thus, parents of CP children appear to have difficulties regulating intense feelings of anger and sadness.

Parental psychopathology and emotion dysregulation may be indirectly related to children's CPs through marital or parenting processes. Lahey and colleagues proposed that the link between marital processes (i.e., marital satisfaction, divorce) and child CPs can be explained by their common relation with maternal APD (Frick, Lahey, Hartdagen, & Hynd, 1989; Lahey et al., 1988). This suggests that linkages between marital physical aggression and child CPs may be mediated by parental APD or other emotion regulatory difficulties. Parental antisocial behavior may also affect parenting skills in families with CP children (Bank, Forgatch, Patterson, & Fetrow, 1993; Patterson, Reed, & Dishion, 1994). As is seen here, parents who have difficulty regulating anger may engage in more harsh and punitive parenting practices, and may be unaware of their children's feelings.

PARENTING SKILL DEFICITS

Child Management and Discipline

It has been well established that parents of CP children show parenting skill deficits. For example, parents of oppositional children exhibit high rates of aversive interchanges, provide inconsistent and ineffective discipline, exhibit fewer positive behaviors, and often fail to monitor their children's behaviors (Patterson, 1982). Using structural equation modeling with five different school-age samples, Patterson (1982) demonstrated that ineffective discipline and poor monitoring each accounted for significant variance in children's antisocial behavior. Negative maternal control has also been related to aggression in preschool-aged disruptive children (Campbell, 1994; Campbell et al., 1986; Campbell, March, Pierce, Ewing, & Szumonowski, 1991). Recent evidence suggests that harsh discipline may play a more important role than poor monitoring in the development or maintenance of child antisocial behavior during the preschool period. Bank et al. (1993) reported that parental monitoring does not contribute to children's antisocial behavior until third grade.

Parental Meta-Emotion Philosophy

Parenting deficits in families with CP children may not only lie with ineffective discipline practices and associated difficulties in gaining child compliance, but may also be related to the nature of the emotional connection between parent and child. There is increasing evidence that the parent's awareness of the child's feelings and parental ability to coach the child during emotionally upsetting moments is related to positive child adjustment. The importance of the day-to-day emotional world of the child was emphasized in the clinical work of Ginott (1965). In Gottman, Katz, and Hooven (1996), we built on Ginott's notions and introduced a new concept of parenting referred to as parental *meta-emotion philosophy*. With normally developing children and, most recently, with children with antisocial behavior problems, studies have examined the executive functions of emotion and its regulation in longitudinal research on meta-emotion (Gottman, Katz, & Hooven, 1997; Katz, 1997; Katz, Gottman, & Hooven, 1996). Meta-emotion refers to parents' and children's feelings, metaphors, and other cognitive structures about basic emotions (particularly anger, sadness, and fear).

This interest in parents' awareness of their children's emotional lives and their attempts to make an emotional connection with their children led to the development of the meta-emotion interview (Katz & Gottman, 1986). Each parent was separately interviewed about his or her own experience of sadness and anger, philosophy of emotional expression and control, and attitudes and behavior about their children's anger and sadness. Parents displayed great variety in the emotions, experiences, philosophies, and attitudes that they had about their own emotions and the emotions of their children. For example, one pair of parents said that they viewed anger as being "from the devil," and that they would not permit themselves or their children to express anger. Other parents were not disapproving of anger but instead ignored anger in their children. Still other parents encouraged the expression and exploration of anger. There was similar variation with respect to sadness. Some parents minimized sadness in themselves and in their children, whereas other parents thought that emotions like sadness in their children were opportunities for intimacy or were important sources of information about one's life.

The active dimension in this research was a parental attitude and activity we called *emotion coaching* versus an attitude of *emotion dismissing*. This dimension concerned the way parents interact with their children when the children display negative affect, particularly anger and sadness. This dimension was orthogonal to parental warmth. Parents who held an emotion coaching philosophy of emotion did five things with their children:

1. They noticed lower intensity negative affects in their children.

2. They used these moments as opportunities for intimacy or teaching.

3. They communicated understanding of and empathy for their children's negative affect (even if it underlay misbehavior).

4. They helped their children verbally label their affect.

5. They set limits on their children's behaviors (but not on feelings or wishes) and coached their children in child-directed problem solving if misbehavior was involved.

Parents who were emotionally dismissive did not notice negative affects in their children until these were considerably escalated, believed that talking about these affects was unprofitable and even harmful, tried to cajole or distract their children into more cheerful moods, and tried to avoid discussing their children's moods or emotions. The data do not claim that emotion dismissing is never appropriate as a coping mechanism, but instead describe characteristic approaches of parents toward these child emotions.

With normally developing children, we discovered that at age 5, the parental meta-emotion system was strongly related to parenting during a laboratory teaching interaction, and to the child's autonomic regulatory physiology (vagal tone and the suppression of vagal tone). In a path-analytic model, these variables at age 5 were, in turn, related to observations of the child's peer social competence at age 5 and predictive of a wide range of child outcomes at age 8, including the child's greater ability to inhibit automatic responses (Stroop Word–Color Association test), enhanced peer social competence, lower levels of child behavior problems, greater emotional regulatory ability, higher levels of academic achievement in reading and mathematics (even controlling for age 5 IQ), and better physical health with respect to infectious illness.

Furthermore, we discovered that emotion coaching was related to higher levels of marital satisfaction, greater marital stability, and less hostile marital interaction. Hence, it was the case that the concept of meta-emotion provided a central theoretical link between marital, parent-child, and child-peer systems. Also, these linkages were mediated by the physiological regulatory system of the child, as well as his or her emotion regulation abilities.

This research also revealed a connection between parental views about the basic emotions of sadness and anger, parents' actual behavior during a teaching task, and the child's regulatory physiology. Children who were "emotion coached" by their parents and whose parents used scaffolding or praising methods of teaching had higher vagal tone and greater ability to suppress vagal tone when engaging in tasks that demand impulse control and mental effort. This regulatory physiology was a strong index of the ability to self-soothe when upset and to inhibit impulsive behavior. Regulatory physiology at age 5 predicted the children's ability to down regulate their own negative affect at age 8, and both abilities, in turn, predicted a host of child outcomes. Thus, an emotion dismissing approach with normally functioning children produced many emotion regulatory problems reminiscent of the behavior of the aggressive child. This has led to the present hypothesis that these patterns of family interaction around meta-emotion are related to the emotional regulatory deficits in aggressive children. These regulatory deficits may be seen in both behavioral and physiological domains. The nature of the physiological regulatory difficulties in CP children is reviewed next.

THE PSYCHOPHYSIOLOGY OF ANTISOCIAL BEHAVIOR

There is little research on the psychophysiological correlates of antisocial behavior in preschool children. In the adolescent and adult literature, one prominent physiological hypothesis proposes that antisocial behavior is associated with physiological *underarousal*. In support of this hypothesis, lower resting heart rate (HR) has been found in a subgroup of undersocialized, aggressive children with conduct disorder (Raine & Jones, 1987). CP children also show lower resting skin conductance levels and decreased responsivity to stimulus events (Schmidt, Solanto, & Bridger, 1985). This underarousal has been theoretically linked to the relative lack of ability to appreciate fear-provoking cues and lack of avoidance conditioning in antisocial populations (Hare, 1970; Mednick, 1977).

From a developmental perspective, it is yet unclear whether underarousal is also characteristic of very young children (i.e., toddlers or preschoolers), or whether it emerges at a particular point in development. Findings to date are conflicting, with some data supporting the externalizing behavior-low HR link in preschool-aged children (El-Shiekh, Ballard, & Cummings, 1994), and other data reporting no differences in HR between externalizing and normally developing toddlers and preschoolers (Calkins, personal communication, August 18, 1998; Katz, 1998).

Even if underarousal does emerge to be characteristic of young children with high levels of externalizing behavior, the physiological mechanisms responsible for their low HR have yet to be described. Heart rate is affected both by sympathetic nervous system (SNS) and parasympathetic nervous system activation (PNS). The SNS is a"fight-or-flight" system that is responsible for the body's mobilization of resources; it functions to increase HR. The PNS is the branch of the autonomic nervous system (ANS) most related to soothing and the restoration of calm in the body; it functions to decrease HR. Thus, it is unclear from these data whether low HR observed in CP children is due to low SNS drive or high PNS activation. Advances in statistical methodology and understanding of basic biological processes can now enable the separation of effects of PNS activation on cardiovascular functioning of CP children (Porges, 1984).

The clinical picture of CP children, however, is more consistent with a physiological model of low PNS activation. Descriptions of CP children suggest that they may show deficits in the ability to attend and in the ability to regulate negative emotions. If these deficits are valid, they may have a physiological basis in the functioning of the PNS. Porges (1984) suggested that vagal tone, which is the tonus of the vagus nerve (the main nerve of the parasympathetic branch of the ANS), provides a theoretical basis for the child's ability to focus attentional processes and inhibit inappropriate action. Vagal tone assesses the functioning of the parasympathetic branch of the ANS and can be indexed by spontaneous HR variability, particularly in the respiratory range. Vagal tone is measured by the rhythmic fluctuations in HR that accompany respiration.

The vagal contribution to attentional processes has been established in both adult and child populations (Porges, 1980; 1994). Vagal tone has also been related to emotional reactivity and the ability to regulate emotion in infants (Fox, 1989). Thus, if high vagal tone reflects the organism's ability to focus attention and regulate emotion, then psychophysiological thinking can provide a theoretical tie that unites diverse findings regarding skill deficits in CP children. Poor anger regulation skills and attentional deficits often characteristic of CP children may have a physiological basis in the functioning of the PNS, which can best be tapped through measurement of vagal tone. This would suggest that CP children have low basal vagal tone.

There is another dimension of vagal tone that needs to be considered, namely, the ability to suppress vagal tone. In general, vagal tone is suppressed during states that require focused or sustained attention, mental effort, focusing on relevant information, and organized responses to stress. Low vagal suppression has been associated with behavior problems in children. In comparing hyperactive to retarded children, Porges, Walter, Korb, and Sprague (1975) found that retarded children did not suppress vagal tone and had a lower baseline HR variability, whereas hyperactive children were more likely to have normal levels of baseline HR variability but a deficit in suppression during task demands. Porges, Doussard-Roosevelt, Portales, and Greenspan (1996) found that 9-month-old infants who had lower baseline vagal tone and less vagal suppression during the Bayley examination had the greatest behavioral problems at age 3.

It would be consistent with Dodge's work (Crick & Dodge, 1994) to propose that CP children are unable to suppress vagal tone because they are hypervigilant to cues of threat and vagal tone is related to the focusing of attention. Dodge reported that it is in ambiguous peer provocation situations that aggressive children show a bias toward seeing hostile intent in peers and that these hostile attributional biases are exacerbated under conditions of threat. Thus, a model of poor vagal suppression under conditions of interpersonal threat may differentiate CP from control children. This would be consistent with Venables' (1988) suggestion that CP children are "vagotonic," or high vagal reactors.

Difficulties in vagal suppression may partly be a function of living in a maritally violent home. Indirect support for this possibility can be found in research on adult male batterers. Gottman et al. (1995) found evidence of two types of male batterers who showed different patterns of physiological activity during marital conflict. Type 1 batterers lowered their HRs below baseline levels, whereas Type 2 batterers increased their HRs above baseline levels during marital conflict. Comparisons of the two groups of batterers indicated that Type 1 batterers were more exposed to bidirectional violence between parents as children than Type 2 batterers. Interestingly, Type 1

batterers were vagal reactors; their tendency to decrease their HR was associated with high vagal tone during marital conflict (Jacobson, Gottman, &
Shortt, 1995). Given the high level of bidirectional violence between parents
in the families of Type 1 batterers, one possible interpretation is that these
men may have learned that the best way to cope with a violent family environment is to reduce their physiological activation and monitor their environment for cues of threat. To the extent that this is true, children exposed
to physical marital aggression may show a similar pattern of increased vagal
tone in response to interpersonal threat.

One important interpersonal context in which to examine children's reactions to threat is the peer context. Aggressive acts by CP children are often
displayed in the peer context, and the peer situation carries cues of threat
that may function to elicit such aggression.

PEER RELATIONSHIPS IN CONDUCT-DISORDERED POPULATIONS

Aggressive children have been found to display a variety of social skill
deficits (K. Dodge & Frame, 1982; K. Dodge, Murphy, & Buchsbaum, 1984;
Pettit, Harrist, Bates, & Dodge, 1991). Children who are aggressive and
disruptive with peers also quickly become rejected (Ladd, Price, & Hart,
1990) and early rejection has been found to predict school maladjustment
and conduct disorder in later childhood (Coie, Lochman, & Terry, 1990)
and delinquency and school dropout in adolescence (Kupersmidt & Coie,
1990). Evidence of a link between peer relationships and family experience
in studies of antisocial children is beginning to emerge (Cohn, Patterson, &
Christopoulos, 1991; Dishion, 1990; Dishion, Duncan, Eddy, & Fagot,
1994). In general, parents who are inconsistent, affectively negative, controlling, and punitive with their children are more likely to have children
who are actively disliked and rejected by peers (Dishion, 1990; Dishion et
al., 1994; Kolvin et al., 1977). However, it remains unclear how these negative parenting behaviors result in peer rejection in aggressive children.

In normally developing children, family linkages to child peer social competence have now been reliably identified, and these linkages seem to concern the way parents assist the child in the regulation of negative emotion
(Katz & Gottman, 1993). Children unable to regulate negative affect are
more likely to be hostile, boisterous, and intrusive in peer play, qualities that
have been attributed to the CP child. Thus, one possibility is that parents
of antisocial children may not teach their children how to regulate negative
affect.

Understanding the emotion regulation deficits of aggressive children may
also explain why they have difficulty with peer relationships during the transition from preschool to middle childhood. Major changes occur in peer
relationships in middle childhood. Children become aware of a much wider

social network than the dyad, increasingly become aware of peer norms for social acceptance, and teasing and avoiding embarrassment suddenly emerge as important social processes (see Gottman & Parker, 1986). The correlates of peer acceptance and rejection change dramatically, particularly with respect to the expression of emotion. One of the most interesting changes is that the socially competent response to a number of salient social situations such as peer entry and teasing is to be a good observer, somewhat wary, "cool," and emotionally unflappable (see Gottman & Parker, 1986). These skills are very difficult for CP children, who tend to be emotionally volatile, confrontational, and physically aggressive.

TOWARD AN INTEGRATED MODEL OF FAMILIAL, PEER, AND PHYSIOLOGICAL PROCESSES IN THE DEVELOPMENT OF CHILDHOOD AGGRESSION

As this review suggests, there is clear evidence that familial, peer, and physiological factors each independently contribute to risk for childhood antisocial behavior. However, there is little understanding of the relation among them, and no systematic theory that articulates how these factors may interact in predicting problem behaviors. Figure 5.1 presents a family-based emotion regulation model of childhood antisocial behavior that integrates key risk factors for childhood aggression. Marital hostility, individual parental emotion regulation abilities, parenting skill deficits, parental meta-emotion philosophy, and children's physiological regulatory ability are proposed as constructs that attempt to explain the processes by which interactions within the family lead to aggressive behavior in children.

The model proposes that the central deficit of aggressive children lies with difficulty regulating emotion, and places this deficit within the context of dysregulation within the entire family system. It is proposed that hostility within the marital relationship is a key component in families with aggressive children. This hostility may take the form of physical marital aggression, but may also include verbal aggression that is power-assertive and emotionally abusive, such as expressions of contempt and belligerence and attempts to dominate. The model therefore is restricted to families in which the marriage has deteriorated to the point where physical or verbal aggression are commonly used when dealing with marital conflict.

It is further proposed that marital hostility leads to individual difficulties with emotion regulation in spouses. Although the direction of effects may be reversed, with individual dysregulation leading to marital hostility, there is increasing evidence that marital distress may be a lead indicator of individual emotional distress. For example, male withdrawal appears to be a response to high levels of negative affect in a marriage rather than a personality attribute that husbands bring to the marriage (Komarovsky, 1962; Rubin, 1976). Withdrawn husbands had not always been withdrawn; rather, the origins of the withdrawal appear to have more to do with the development of an ailing marriage than with the spouse's a priori personality characteristics. Similarly, there is evidence that depression in women is not only an antecedent but can also be a consequence of marital conflict and distress, and that the relation between marital distress and depression may best be described as cyclical (Assh & Byers, 1996; Davila, Bradbury, Cohan, & Tochluk, 1997; Gotlib & Beach, 1995).

According to the model, marital hostility and its associated impact on parental ability to self-regulate emotion creates a dual deficit in parenting. Parents in abusive marital relationships are both more harsh and punitive toward their children, and are also unaware of and unable to help their children manage their emotions. Although these parents may be cognizant of their aggressive children's anger, they may be unaware of and unable to coach their children when they are experiencing more internal and subtle emotions, such as fear and sadness. There are many possible reasons why parents are unable to coach their children around these more subtle emotions. These parents may be aware of their children's fear but given their own difficulty regulating emotion may not have well-developed strategies of handling fear that they can teach to their children. In families with boys, a dismissive attitude toward fear may be rooted in the feeling that boys should be strong and not scared, and therefore these parents may be unwilling to attend to displays of fear in their children. Although this theorizing is consistent with the idea that parents of aggressive children are generally less sensitive to their children, the concept of parental emotion coaching goes beyond the traditional notion of parental sensitivity. With the concept of parental emotion coaching, there is a description of the specific ways in which parents neglect their children's emotional lives, an articulation of the specific emotions that parents may have trouble with, and the introduction of the notion that a parenting deficit includes parent's inability to teach their children how to problem solve when their children are upset.

Given that these children are living in a home in which parents are physically aggressive toward one another, emotionally dysregulated, punitive toward them, and not teaching them how to regulate their emotions, these children are likely to show difficulty regulating emotional arousal. To the extent that parents in maritally violent families are unaware of subtle and less observable emotions in their children (such as fear and sadness), these children may have particular difficulty managing emotions like fear. Yet, living in a hostile and threatening environment in which interactions between their caregivers can be dangerous, they are likely to repeatedly feel threatened and experience high levels of fear. Such fear reactivity is consistent with findings by Hennessy, Rabideau, Cicchetti, and Cummings (1994) that abused children reported greater fear in response to all forms of interadult anger and were more sensitive to whether anger between adults was resolved than nonabused children. Thus, although they are regularly exposed to fear-inducing social interaction between their caretakers, these children may not have well-developed cognitive or behavioral coping strategies for managing their fear.

The salience of cues of threat and fear in the social environment may also lead them to process social interaction between their caregivers and between themselves and their caregivers in distorted ways (Rossman, 1998). Substantial evidence on the sociocognitive skills of aggressive and CP children suggest that they are biased toward presuming hostile intent in others. Aggressive children also inaccurately interpret peers' intentions (K. Dodge et al., 1984) and fail to attend to relevant social cues (D. Dodge, Bates, & Pettit, 1990). Furthermore, these sociocognitive deficits and biases are exacerbated under conditions of threat (K. Dodge & Somberg, 1987). Given the high level of threat and sense of insecurity in maritally aggressive families (Cummings & Davies, 1994), these children may develop an expectation that disagreement and anger are threatening and unpredictable, and that they need to prepare for danger by mobilizing aggressive coping strategies.

The sense of unpredictability sustained over long periods of time may also lead to hypervigilance toward threat. Research on posttraumatic stress disorder (PTSD) is replete with descriptions of the hypervigilance experienced by children and adults exposed to trauma and abuse. This hypervigilance involves cognitive monitoring of the environment for cues of threat. It may also be expressed in a pattern of physiological functioning that supports the attentional demands needed for continuous scanning of the environment. In adult PTSD victims, prolonged stress response has been linked to changes in the functioning of the hypothalamic-pituitary-adrenocortical axis and increased ANS arousal (Griffin, Nishith, Resick, & Yehuda, 1997; Shalev, 1997; van der Kolk, 1996). The family-based emotion regulation model proposes that children from maritally hostile homes may exhibit increased vagal reactivity during threat (i.e., failure to suppress vagal tone). Heightened vagal tone in response to threat may help with attention deployment and threat detection so the child is readily prepared for action. Increased vagal reactivity would be consistent with findings that adult male batterers who as children experienced a high level of bidirectional violence between their parents show high vagal reactivity during interpersonal threat (Gottman et al., 1995).

It is also proposed that increased vagal reactivity, in turn, relates to negative peer interaction and antisocial behavior. Low vagal suppression has been associated with behavior problems in children (Porges et al., 1996; Porges et al., 1975), and low vagal tone has been associated with children's negative interaction with peers and poor prosocial behavior (Eisenberg et al., 1996; Eisenberg et al., 1995; Gottman et al., 1997).

Harsh and ineffective parenting also provides another pathway to poor peer relations in CP children (Dishion, 1990; Dishion et al., 1994). Although the current model proposes a direct link between parenting practices and poor peer relations, several intervening mechanisms may account for these effects. Parents function not only as interactive partners but also as providers of opportunities for social contact with extrafamilial social partners (Hartup, 1979; Ladd, Profilet, & Hart, 1992; Parke, MacDonald, Beitel, & Bhavnagri, 1988; Parke et al., 1989). Harsh parents in the midst of high levels of marital conflict may be too preoccupied with marital concerns to facilitate opportunities for social contact, thereby limiting their young child's possibilities for successful social exchanges. The model does not propose a link between parenting practices and physiological regulatory abilities given previous evidence that parental meta-emotion philosophy rather than specific parenting practices drives children's regulatory physiology (Gottman et al., 1996).

IMPLICATIONS AND FUTURE DIRECTIONS

One proposition of the model presented here is that children's difficulty regulating emotion can best be seen when the fear system is activated. Much remains to be done to test this hypothesis. One avenue for future research is to examine children's physiological reactions to interpersonal threat. However, the understanding of the physiological correlates of antisocial behavior in children has been limited by the contexts in which physiological processes have been examined. Physiological responding has largely been examined under baseline conditions or during relatively benign task instructions (e.g., listening to tones) or stressors (e.g., instructions to perform a task quickly; prior to a medical examination). Physiological reactivity to an interpersonal stressor has not been examined, despite the fact that the interpersonal domain is usually the context in which deviant antisocial behavior occurs. There is a need to understand how CP children respond physiologically to emotionally laden situations, particularly because those contexts present difficulty for them. Because CP children's physiological underarousal has been theoretically linked to a relative lack of responsiveness to fear provocation (Hare, 1970; Mednick, 1977), it may be particularly important to understand how CP children respond to fear-eliciting situations. Changes over time in their reactivity to and processing of fear-eliciting events may be linked to their difficulty in interpersonal situations.

If the fear system needs to be activated to detect possible aberrant physiological responses, observing CP children's physiological reactions to discrete interpersonal threat may enable a better understanding of the interpersonal situations in which emotion regulation deficits of aggressive children occur. To the extent that children's emotional reactions have generalized beyond the initial reaction to interparental hostility and violence, any emotion-eliciting circumstances may lead to these physiological responses. Research in my laboratory with preschool-aged antisocial children and their families is currently under way to examine these issues in relation to hostility within the family.

The family-based emotion regulation model also makes predictions about coping responses that CP children may use to regulate arousal. If maritally violent parents are emotionally dismissive, children may also learn that emotions are dangerous and come to use avoidant coping responses to handle strong affect. If this coping strategy is successful at decreasing fear associated with marital violence, these techniques may over time be generalized to circumstances beyond those of the initial threat, and dismissive coping responses may preempt constructive problem solving in situations that are less unpredictable and uncontrollable. The suggestion that children exposed to marital hostility use avoidant coping strategies is consistent with Rossman's (1998) findings that children exposed to domestic violence show difficulties taking in and using new information as an avoidant protective strategy. Additional research on children's own meta-emotion philosophy and coping strategies is needed to address these issues.

The proposed model focuses the discussion of family relationships and processes to the marital and parent-child subsystems. Other relationship dynamics within the family may also be operative in maritally dysregulated homes. Because children are most adversely affected by child-related marital conflict (Grych & Fincham, 1990), understanding how parents work together in coparenting their child may be an important dynamic to examine in relation to marital violence. *Coparenting processes* refer to the ways in which partners support one another in their joint role as leaders of the family. From the child's perspective, observing the quality of the coparenting relationship provides rich information about relationship skills, such as the exchange and expression of affect, and conflict resolution strategies. The heart of coparenting involves mutual support and commitment to coordinated parenting of the child, processes that may be difficult to achieve in a domestically violent home.

Another important familial relationship dynamic occurs at the level of the whole family. Emphasis on whole-family processes is rooted in family systems thinking that psychopathology in individual family members is a manifestation of global family dysfunction (Haley, 1967; Minuchin, Rosman, & Baker, 1978). According to this systems framework, family-level processes affect children's development over and above any individual subsystem, and interactions at the family level are a unique social force that goes beyond the sum of its parts (Minuchin, 1974). This theorizing is supported by research showing that parent and child behavior changes between the dyadic and triadic (mother-father-child) contexts (Buhrmester, Comparo, Christensen, Gonzalez, & Hinshaw, 1992; Gjerde, 1986).

More importantly, coparenting and family-level processes appear to be related to both the quality of the marriage (Katz & Gottman, 1996; McHale, 1996) and to children's socioemotional development (Belsky, Putnam, & Crnic, 1996; McHale & Rasmussen, 1998). Thus, further articulation of these larger interactive contexts may provide a broader understanding of the large set of interactions that children experience on a daily basis.

Several caveats are in order. The model does not address the issue of reciprocal influences between parents and child or discuss whether child characteristics such as temperament may influence parent–child and marital interaction. A closer examination of the contribution of child characteristics and of the reciprocal influences between parents and child is clearly warranted. The stress placed on parents of children with negative behavioral characteristics may well diminish their ability to be effective parents (Anderson, Lytton, & Romney, 1986; Crnic & Acevedo, 1995). When the child is irritable and noncompliant, the coordination among all family members may deteriorate and even attempts at positive and playful parent-child interactions may turn into stressful situations. The potential for a two-way interaction between marital conflict and child maladjustment over time has also been overlooked. For most marital relationships, the presence of children in the home leads to a decrease in marital satisfaction and an increase in marital conflict (Belsky & Pensky, 1988; Belsky, Spanier, & Rovine, 1983). Consistent with these findings, Finkel and Hansen (1992) found that retrospective accounts of marital satisfaction were lower for parents who encountered problems during the childrearing stage. In the context of maritally hostile homes, it is plausible that a child with behavioral disturbances may add stress to an already strained marriage.

Additionally, the model does not capture all variables that may explain how marital hostility may be linked to child outcomes. Intraindividual child processes such as the child's perception of marital conflict (Grych & Fincham, 1990) and the child's emotional security (Cummings & Davies, 1994) may also moderate the child's regulatory physiology and in so doing impact the child's socioemotional adjustment in the face of marital hostility.

CONCLUSION

The family-based emotion regulation model provides an integration of diverse risk factors facing CP children. It is only through the systematic testing of each pathway that a clearer understanding of linkages between individual difficulties in emotion regulation in parents and children and emotion regulation deficits in family subsystems can be articulated.

REFERENCES

Anderson, K. E., Lytton, H., & Romney, D. M. (1986). Mothers' interactions with normal and conduct-disordered boys: Who affects whom? *Developmental Psychology, 22*, 604–609.

Assh, D. S., & Byers, S. E. (1996). Understanding the co-occurrence of marital distress and depression in women. *Journal of Social and Personal Relationships, 13*, 537–552.

Bank, L., Forgatch, M. S., Patterson, G. R., & Fetrow, R. A. (1993). Parenting practices of single mothers: mediators of negative contextual factors. *Journal of Marriage and the Family, 55*(2), 371–384.

Belsky, J., & Pensky, E. (1988). Marital change across the transition to parenthood. *Marriage and Family Review, 12,* 133–156.

Belsky, J., Putnam, S., & Crnic, K. (1996). Coparenting, parenting, and early emotional development. In McHale, J. P., & Cowan, P. A. (Eds.), *Understanding how family-level dynamics affect children's development: Studies of two-parent families. New Directions for Child Development, 74,* 45–55.

Belsky, J., Spanier, G. B., & Rovine, M. (1983). Stability and change in marriage across the transition to parenthood. *Journal of Marriage and the Family, 45,* 567–577.

Buhrmester, D., Camparo, L., Christensen, A., Gonzalez, L. S., & Hinshaw, S. (1992). Mothers and fathers interacting in dyads and triads with normal and hyperactive sons. *Developmental Psychology, 28,* 500–509.

Campbell, S. B. (1994). Hard-to-manage preschool boys: Externalizing behavior, social competence, and family context at two-year follow-up. *Journal of Abnormal Child Psychology, 22,* 147–166.

Campbell, S. B., Breaux, A. M., Ewing, L. J., & Szumowski, E. K. (1986). Correlates and predictors of hyperactivity and aggression: A longitudinal study of parent referred problem preschoolers. *Journal of Abnormal Child Psychology, 14*(2), 217–234.

Campbell, S. B., & Ewing, L. J. (1990). Follow-up of hard-to-manage preschoolers: Adjustment at age 9 and predictors of continuing symptoms. *Journal of Child Psychology & Psychiatry & Allied Disciplines, 31*(6), 871–889.

Campbell, S. B., March, C. L., Pierce, E., Ewing, L. J., & Szumowski, E. K. (1991). Hard-to-manage preschool boys: Family context and the stability of externalizing behavior. *Journal of Abnormal Child Psychology, 19,* 301–318.

Capaldi, D., & Patterson, G. R. (1991). Relation of parental transitions to boys' adjustment problems: I. A linear hypothesis. II. Mothers at risk for transitions and unskilled parenting. *Developmental Psychology, 27,* 489–504.

Chamberlain, R. W., & Nader, P. R. (1971). Relationship between nursery school behavior patterns and later school functioning. *American Journal of Orthopsychiatry, 41*(2), 597–601.

Cohn, D. A., Patterson, C. J., & Christopoulos, C. (1991). The family and children's peer relations. *Journal of Personal and Social Relationships, 8,* 315–346.

Coie, J. D., Lochman, J. E., & Terry, R. (1990, January). *Child peer rejection and aggression as predictors of multiple forms of disorder in early adolescence.* Paper presented at the annual meeting of the Society for Research in Child and Adolescent Psychopathology, Miami, FL.

Crick, N. R., & Dodge, K. A. (1994). A review and reformulation of social information-processing mechanisms in children's social adjustment. *Psychological Bulletin, 115,* 74–101.

Crnic, K., & Acevedo, M. (1995). Everyday stresses and parenting. In Bornstein, M. H. (Ed.), *Handbook of parenting, Vol. 4: Applied and practical parenting* (pp. 277–298). Hillsdale, NJ: Lawrence Erlbaum Associates.

Cummings, E. M., & Davies, P. T. (1994). Maternal depression and child development. *Journal of Child Psychology & Psychiatry & Allied Disciplines, 35,* 73–112.

Cummings, E. M., Vogel, D., Cummings, J. S., & El-Sheikh, M. (1989). Children's responses to different forms of expression of anger between adults. *Child Development, 60,* 1392–1404.

Cummings, J. S., Pellegrini, D. S., Notarius, C. I., & Cummings, E. M. (1989). Children's responses to angry adult behavior as a function of marital distress and history of interparent hostility. *Child Development, 60,* 1035–1043.

Davila, J., Bradbury, T. N., Cohan, C. L., & Tochluk, S. (1997). Marital functioning and depressive symptoms: Evidence for a stress generation model. *Journal of Personality and Social Psychology, 73,* 849–861.

Dishion, T. J. (1990). The family ecology of boys' peer relations in middle childhood. *Child Development, 61,* 874–892.

Dishion, T. J., Duncan, T. E., Eddy, E. J., & Fagot, B. I. (1994). The world of parents and peers: Coercive exchanges and children's social adaptation. *Social Development, 3,* 255–268.

Dodge, D. A., Bates, J. E., & Pettit, G. S. (1990). Mechanisms in the cycle of violence. *Science, 250,* 1678–1683.

Dodge, K. A., & Frame, C. L. (1982). Social cognitive biases and deficits in aggressive boys. *Child Development, 53,* 620–635.

Dodge, K. A., Murphy, R. R., & Buchsbaum, K. (1984). The assessment of intention-cue detection skills in children: Implications for developmental psychopathology. *Child Development, 55,* 163–173.

Dodge, K. A., & Somberg, D. R. (1987). Hostile attributional biases among aggressive boys are exacerbated under conditions of threats to the self. *Child Development, 58,* 213–224.

Eisenberg, N., Fabes, R. A., Karbon, M., Murphy, B. C., Smith, S., & Maszk, P. (1996). The relations of children's dispositional prosocial behavior to emotionality, regulation, and social functioning. *Child Development, 67,* 974–992.

Eisenberg, N., Fabes, R. A., Murphy, B. C., Maszk, P., Smith, S., & Karbon, M. (1995). The role of emotionality and regulation in children's social functioning: A longitudinal study. *Child Development, 66,* 1360–1384.

El-Sheikh, M., Ballard, M., & Cummings, E. M. (1994). Individual difference in preschoolers' physiological and verbal responses to videotaped angry reactions. *Journal of Abnormal Child Psychology, 22,* 303–320.

Emery, R. E. (1988). *Marriage, divorce, and children's adjustment.* Newbury Park, CA: Sage.

Emery, R. E. (1989). Family violence. Special Issue: Children and their development: knowledge base, research agenda, and social policy application. *American Psychologist, 44,* 321–328.

Emery, R. E., & Laumann, L. B. (1998). An overview of the nature, causes, and consequences of abusive family relationships: Toward differentiating maltreatment and violence. *American Psychologist, 53,* 121–135.

Finkel, J. S., & Hansen, F. J. (1992). Correlates of retrospective marital satisfaction in long-lived marriages: A social constructivist perspective. *Family Therapy, 19,* 1–16.

Fox, N. (1989). The psychophysiological correlates of emotional reactivity during the first year of life. *Developmental Psychology, 25,* 364–372.

Frick, P. J., Lahey, B. B., Hartdagen, S, & Hynd, G. W. (1989). Conduct problems in boys: Relations to maternal personality, marital satisfaction and socioeconomic status. *Journal of Child Clinical Psychology, 18*(2), 114–120.

Ginott, H. (1965). *Between parent and child*. New York: Avon Books.

Gjerde, P. (1986). The interpersonal structure of family interactional settings: Parent-adolescent relations in dyads and triads. *Developmental Psychology, 48*, 711–717.

Gondolf, E. W. (1985). Fighting for control: A clinical assessment of men who batter. *Social Casework, 66*, 48–54.

Gotlib, I. H., & Beach, S. R. H. (1995). A marital/family discord model of depression: Implications for therapeutic intervention. In Jacobson, N. S., & Gurman, A. S. (Eds.), *Clinical handbook of couple therapy* (pp. 411–436). New York: Guilford Press.

Gottman, J. M., Jacobson, N. S., Rushe, R. H., Short, J. W., Babcock, J., LaTaillade J. J., & Waltz, J. (1995). The relationship between heart rate reactivity, emotionally aggressive behavior, and general violence in batterers. *Journal of Family Psychology, 9*, 227–248.

Gottman, J. M., Katz, L. F., & Hooven, C. (1996). Parental meta-emotion philosophy and the emotional life of families: Theoretical models and preliminary analysis. *Journal of Family Psychology, 10*, 243–268.

Gottman, J. M., Katz, L. F., & Hooven, C. (1997). *Meta-emotion: How families communicate emotionally*. Mahwah, NJ: Lawrence Erlbaum.

Gottman, J. M., & Parker, J. (1986). *Conversations of friends: Speculations on affective development*. New York: Cambridge University Press.

Griffin, M. G., Nishith, P., Resick, P. A., & Yehuda, R. (1997). Integrating objective indicators of treatment outcome in posttraumatic stress disorder. In Yehuda, R., & Alexander, A. C. (Eds.), *Psychobiology of posttraumatic stress disorder. Annals of the New York Academy of Sciences* (Vol. 821, pp. 388–409). New York: New York Academy of Sciences.

Grych, J. H., & Fincham, F. D. (1990). Marital conflict and children's adjustment: A cognitive contextual framework. *Psychological Bulletin, 108*, 267–290.

Haley, J. (1967). Towards a theory of pathological systems. In Zuk, G., & Nagy, I. (Eds.), *Family therapy and disturbed families*. Palo Alto, CA: Science & Behavior Books.

Hamberger, L. K., & Hastings, J. E. (1986). Personality correlates of men who abuse their partners: A cross-validation study. *Journal of Family Violence, 1*, 323–341.

Hamberger, L. K., & Hastings, J. E. (1988). Characteristics of male spouse abusers consistent with personality disorders. *Hospital and Community Psychiatry, 39*, 763–770.

Hare, R. D. (1970). *Psychopathy: Theory and research*. New York: Wiley.

Hartup, W. W. (1979). The social worlds of childhood. *American Psychologist, 34*, 944–950.

Hennessy, K. D., Rabideau, G. J., Cicchetti, D., & Cummings, M. E. (1994). Responses of physically abused and nonabused children to different forms of interadult anger. *Child Development, 65*(3), 815–828.

Jacobson, N. S., Gottman, J. M., & Shortt, J. W. (1995). The distinction between type 1 and type 2 batterers—further considerations: Reply to Ornduff et al. (1995), Margolin et al. (1995), and Walker (1995). *Journal of Family Psychology, 9*, 272–279.

Jouriles, E. N., Murphy, C. M., & O'Leary, K. D. (1989). Interspousal aggression,

134 Family and Peers

marital discord, and child problems. *Journal of Consulting and Clinical Psychology, 57,* 453–455.

Jouriles, E. N., Norwood, W. D., McDonald, R., Vincent, J. P., & Mahoney, A. (1996). Physical violence and other forms of marital aggression: Links with children's behavior problems. *Journal of Family Psychology, 10,* 223–234.

Katz, L. F. (1997, April). *Regulatory physiology and parenting as buffers from marital conflict and dissolution.* Paper presented at the biennial meeting of the Society for Research in Child Development. Washington, DC.

Katz, L. F. (1998, May). *Living in a hostile world: Toward an integrated model of family, peer and physiological processes in childhood aggression.* Paper presented at the meeting of the Kent Forum, Kent State University, Kent, OH.

Katz, L. F., & Gottman, J. M. (1986). *The Meta-Emotion Interview.* Unpublished manual, University of Washington, Seattle, WA.

Katz, L. F., & Gottman, J. M. (1993). Patterns of marital conflict predicts children's internalizing and externalizing behaviors. *Developmental Psychology, 29,* 940–950.

Katz, L. F., & Gottman, J. M. (1996). Spillover effects of marital conflict: In search of parenting and coparenting mechanisms. In McHale J. P., & Cowan, P. A. (Eds.), Understanding how family-level dynamics affect children's development: Studies of two-parent families. *New Directions for Child Development, 74,* 57–76.

Katz, L. F., Gottman, J. M., & Hooven, C. (1996). Meta-emotion philosophy and family functioning: A reply to Cowan and Eisenberg. *Journal of Family Psychology, 10,* 284–291.

Kolvin, I., Garside, R., Nicol, A., MacMillan, A., Wolstenholme, F., & Leitch, I. (1977). Familial and sociological correlates of behavioral and sociological deviance in 8-year old children. In Graham, P. (Ed.), *Epidemiology of childhood disorders* (pp. 195–222). New York: Academic Press.

Komarovsky, M. (1962). *Blue collar marriage.* New York: Random House.

Kupersmidt, J. B., & Coie, J. D. (1990). Preadolescent peer status and aggression as predictors of externalizing problems in adolescence. *Child Development, 61,* 1350–1362.

Ladd, G. S., Price, J. M., & Hart, C. H. (1990). Preschooler's behavioral orientations and patterns of peer control: Predictive of peer status? In Asher, S. R., & Coie, J. D. (Eds.), *Peer rejection in childhood* (pp. 90–115). Cambridge, UK: Cambridge University Press.

Ladd, G. W., Profilet, S. M., & Hart, C. H. (1992). Parents' management of children's peer relations: Facilitating and supervising children's activities in the peer culture. In Parke, R. D., & Ladd, G. W. (Eds.), *Family–peer relationships: Modes of linkage* (pp. 215–253). Hillsdale, NJ: Lawrence Erlbaum.

Lahey, B. B., Hartdagen, S., Frick, P. J., McBurnett, K., Connor, R., & Hynd, G. W. (1988). Conduct disorder: Parsing the confounded relation to parental divorce and antisocial personality. *Journal of Abnormal Psychology, 97*(3), 334–337.

Loeber, R. (1982). The stability of antisocial and delinquent child behavior: A review. *Child Development, 53,* 1431–1446.

Loeber, R., & Dishion, T. J. (1983). Early predictors of male adolescent delinquency: A review. *Psychological Bulletin, 94,* 68–99.

McCloskey, L. A., Figueredo, A. J., & Koss, M. P. (1995). The effect of systematic family violence on children's mental health. *Child Development, 66,* 1239–1261.

McHale, J. P. (1996). Coparenting and triadic interactions during infancy: The role of marital distress and child gender. *Developmental Psychology, 31,* 985–996.

McHale, J. P., & Rasmussen, J. L. (1998). Coparental and family group-level dynamics during infancy: Early family precursors of child and family functioning during preschool. *Development & Psychopathology, 10,* 39–59.

Mednick, S. (1977). A bio-social theory of the learning of law-abiding behavior. In S. A. Mednick & K. O. Christiansen (Eds.), *Biosocial bases of criminal behavior* (pp. 1–8). New York: Gardner Press.

Minuchin, S. (1974). *Families and family therapy.* Cambridge, MA: Harvard University Press.

Minuchin, S., Rosman, B. L., & Baker, L. (1978). *Psychosomatic families: Anorexia nervosa in context.* Cambridge, MA: Harvard University Press.

Moffitt, T. E. (1993). Adolescent-limited and life-course-persistent antisocial behavior: A developmental taxonomy. *Psychological Review, 100,* 674–701.

Parke, R. D., MacDonald, K. B., Beitel, A., & Bhavnagri, N. (1988). The role of family in the development of peer relationships. In Peters, R. D., & McMahon, R. J. (Eds.), *Social learning and systems approaches to marriage and the family* (pp. 17–44). New York: Brunner/Mazel.

Parke, R. D., MacDonald, K. B., Burks, V. M., Carson, J., Bhavnagri, N. P., Barth, J. M. & Beitel, A. (1989). Family and peer systems: In search of the linkages. In Kreppner, K., & Lerner, R. A. (Eds.), *Family systems and life-span development* (pp. 65–92). Hillsdale, NJ: Lawrence Erlbaum.

Patterson, G. R. (1982). *Coercive family process.* Eugene, OR: Castalia.

Patterson, G. R., DeBaryshe, B. D., & Ramsey, E. (1989). A developmental perspective on antisocial behavior. Special Issue: Children and their development: Knowledge base, research agenda, and social policy application. *American Psychologist, 44,* 329–335.

Patterson, G. R., Reed, J. B., & Dishion, T. J. (1994). *A social learning approach. IV: Antisocial boys.* Eugene, OR: Castalia.

Pettit, G. S., Harrist, A. W., Bates, J. E., & Dodge, K. A. (1991). Family interaction, social cognition, and children's subsequent relations with peers at kindergarten. Special issue: Family–peer relationships. *Journal of Personal and Social Relationships, 8*(3), 383–402.

Porges, S. W. (1980). Individual differences in attention: A possible physiological substrate. In Keogh, B. K. (Ed.), *Advances in special education* (Vol. 2, pp. 111–134). Greenwich, CT: JAI.

Porges, S. W. (1984). Heart rate oscillation: An index of neural mediation. In Coles, M. G. H., Jennings, J. R., & Stern, J. A. (Eds.), *Psychophysiological perspectives: Festschrift for Beatrice and John Lacey* (pp. 229–241). New York: Van Norstrand Reinhold.

Porges, S. W. (1994, October). Orienting in a defensive world: A poly-vagal theory of our evolutionary heritage. Presidential Address, Society for Psychophysiological Research.

Porges, S. W., Doussard-Roosevelt, J. A., Portales, A. L., & Greenspan, S. I. (1996). Infant regulation of the vagal "brake" predicts child behavior problems: A psychobiological model of social behavior. *Developmental Psychobiology, 29,* 697–712.

Porges, S. W., Walter, G. F., Korb, R. J., & Sprague, R. L. (1975). The influences of methylphenidate on heart rate and behavioral measures of attention in hyperactive children. *Child Development, 46,* 727–733.

Raine, A., & Jones, F. (1987). Attention, autonomic arousal, and personality in behaviorally disordered children. *Journal of Abnormal Child Psychology, 15,* 583–599.

Robins, L. N. (1978). Sturdy childhood predictors of adult antisocial behaviour: Replications from longitudinal studies. *Psychological Medicine, 8,* 611–622.

Rossman, R. (1998). Descartes' error and posttraumatic stress disorder: Cognition and emotion in children who are exposed to parental violence. In Holden, G. W., Geffner, R., & Jouriles, E. N. (Eds.), *Children exposed to marital violence* (pp. 223–256). Washington, DC: American Psychological Association.

Rubin, L. B. (1976). *Worlds of pain: Life in the working class family.* New York: Basic Books.

Schmidt, K., Solanto, M. V., & Bridger, W. H. (1985). Electrodermal activity of undersocialized aggressive children. *Journal of Child Psychology and Psychiatry, 26,* 653–660.

Shalev, A. Y. (1997). Acute to chronic: Etiology and pathophysiology of PTSD: A biopsychosocial approach. In Fullerton, C. S., & Ursano, R. J. (Eds.), *Posttraumatic stress disorder: Acute and long-term responses to trauma and disaster* (Vol. 51, pp. 209–240). Washington, DC: American Psychiatric Press.

van der Kolk, B. A. (1996). The body keeps score: Approaches to the psychobiology of posttraumatic stress disorder. In van der Kolk, B. A., & McFarlane, A. C. (Eds.), *Traumatic stress: The effects of overwhelming experience on mind, body, and society* (pp. 214–241). New York: Guilford Press.

Venables, P. H. (1988). Psychophysiology and crime: Theory and data. In Moffitt, T. E., & Mednick, S. A. (Eds.), *Biological contributions to crime causation* (pp. 3–13). Dordrecht: Martinus Nijhoff Publishers.

West, D. J., & Farrington, D. P. (1973). *Who becomes delinquent? Second report of the Cambridge Study in Delinquent Development.* New York: Crane, Russak.

Wolfe, D. A., Jaffe, P., Wilson, S. K., & Zak, L. (1985). Children of battered women: The relation of child behavior to family violence and maternal stress. *Journal of Consulting and Clinical Psychology, 53,* 657–665.

6

Explaining the Link between Parenting Behavior and Children's Peer Competence: A Critical Examination of the "Mediating-Process" Hypothesis

Jacquelyn Mize, Gregory S. Pettit, and Darrell Meece

Research linking parenting attributes and children's social competence in peer relationships dates back several decades (e.g., Baldwin, 1949), but only fairly recently have investigators begun to focus specifically on the mechanisms that may account for these links. Within this subspecialty in the socialization literature have been rich theoretical speculations about how, or through what sociocognitive mediators, parenting affects children's social behavior. The Bowlby–Ainsworth attachment perspective is one such theoretical tradition; the Bandura social learning perspective is another. Although these (and other) well-worked theoretical explanations have provided a fairly solid conceptual basis for understanding the processes through which parenting behavior may influence children's peer relations, the empirical evidence in support of the various mediating-processes explanations is, to date, somewhat less than compelling. In fact, there is as yet no clear-cut support for one kind of process over another, or, for that matter, whether intervening processes are even necessary for explaining links between parenting and children's social–behavioral competence.

This chapter provides a critical appraisal of the mediating-process (M-P) hypothesis and offers a set of reasonable guidelines for evaluating and conducting research seeking to explain connections between parenting and children's peer competence. We are particularly well positioned to offer a critique of past work and a blueprint for future research because we have devoted considerable effort to understanding the sociocognitive and emotional underpinnings of young children's social behavior (e.g., Mize & Ladd, 1988), because we have in the past several years explored differing pathways through which children may acquire social competencies (e.g., Mize & Pettit, 1997; Pettit & Mize, 1993), and because we have been active contributors to the literature on sociocognitive mediators of links between early family experience and later child behavior and competence (e.g., Dodge, Bates, & Pettit, 1990; Pettit, Harrist, Bates, & Dodge, 1991). Our critique and appraisal seems timely, given that it has been more than a decade since the publication of what many would consider to be the first systematic examination of the M-P hypothesis (Pettit, Dodge, & Brown, 1988) in the family-peer relations literature.

We have found it useful to cluster the proposed mediating processes into one of five groups. The first and largest group is concerned with acquired social information-processing (SIP) styles, such as hostile attributional biases (e.g., Dodge et al., 1990). The second, related group focuses on sociocognitive and social learning (SL) processes not typically thought of as indexes of SIP, including self-efficacy and social outcome expectancies (e.g., Bandura, 1986). The remaining three groups or clusters of M-P explanations more explicitly address the emotional underpinnings of social experience. Drawing on the Bowlby-Ainsworth-Bretherton attachment formulations, several recent investigations have sought to examine family-peer connections in terms of acquired internal working models (IWM) and related attachment-oriented phenomena (Belsky, Spritz, & Crnic, 1996; Cassidy, Kirsh, Scolton, & Parke, 1996). Another emerging research focus has been concerned with emotion understanding (EU) and the motivational role of emotions (e.g., empathy) in guiding behavior (Eisenberg & Fabes, 1998). A fifth group of M-P explanations centers on emotion regulation (ER) and dysregulation and associated processes, including underlying psychophysiological mechanisms, that may accompany emotional experience (e.g., Gottman, Katz, & Hooven, 1996). These five general clusters of presumed process are not, of course, mutually exclusive, and some investigators have examined combinations of them (e.g., Rogosch, Cicchetti, & Aber, 1995).

The chapter is laid out in three main parts. First, we briefly survey literature pertaining to each of the five types of M-P explanation and highlight key patterns of empirical support and nonsupport for mediation. To foreshadow our main conclusion, we believe that the research literature has yet to provide a solid foundation for the notion that intervening processes mediate links between family experience and peer relationships. Next, we detail several plausible reasons for these less than compelling patterns of findings. In particular, we consider the following possibilities:

1. The M-P hypothesis is untenable.

2. Accurate estimates of mediation effects are difficult to obtain, partly due to measurement error.

3. Family experience predictors are less specific than reflected in theory and analyses.

4. Mediational links are more specific than reflected in theory and analyses.

5. The effects of parenting on mediators and peer outcomes are moderated by parenting, child, or ecological factors.

6. The key mediating variables have not been studied, and mediators may be moderated by other sociocognitive or affective processes.

We conclude the chapter by offering a set of conceptual and empirical guidelines for the next generation of studies seeking to evaluate the efficacy and utility of the various M-P hypotheses.

It may be useful at this point to revisit the criteria for establishing a mediated relationship as outlined by Baron and Kenny (1986) and others (e.g., MacKinnon, 1994). First, the independent variable (IV) and the dependent variable (DV) must be correlated significantly; otherwise, there is no relation for the mediator to explain.[1] Second, the mediator variable should be correlated significantly with the IV and with the DV. Finally and importantly, the effects of the IV on the DV must be less when the effects of the mediator are controlled; although the mediated, or indirect, path need not be 0, some statisticians (e.g., MacKinnon, 1994) add the condition that the mediated path must be significant. The model must also be specified correctly in that the DV is not the cause of the mediator (Baron & Kenny, 1986) and the shared variance between the mediator and the DV is not due to an omitted variable that influences both the mediator and the DV (Kenny, Kashy, & Bolger, 1998). Baron and Kenny also stipulated that the mediator must be measured without error; although the reliability bar is set impossibly high, measurement limitations do place significant constraints on the power to detect mediated relations. Each of these criteria has implications for interpreting and guiding research seeking to examine sociocognitive or affective factors as mediators of the link between family experiences and children's peer relationships.

WHAT DOES EXISTING RESEARCH TELL US ABOUT POSSIBLE MEDIATING PROCESSES?

Table 6.1 contains a summary of 18 studies of family-peer relationship linkages in which the M-P hypothesis was explicitly tested. We have restricted the review here to studies that examine peer-relationship or peer-relationship-relevant outcomes (e.g., peer acceptance, delinquency); mediational studies that focus on nonsocial outcomes such as academic achievement (e.g., Grolnick & Slowiaczek, 1994) were not included. A subset of studies also was excluded even though they assessed one or more of the relevant mediational constructs and their associations with family predictors, peer-relevant outcomes, or both. However, because no attempt was made to evaluate mediation in the statistical sense, these studies are not

Table 6.1
Published Articles Examining Mediational Links between Family and Peer Relationships

Authors and [theoretical perspective]	Participants	IV	Mediator(s)	DV(s)	Method to test for mediation	Evidence of mediation?
Cassidy et al., 1996 (Study 2) [IMW]	33 kindergarten and first grader children and mothers	Attachment classification (assessed within 2 weeks of IV and DV)	Peer representations (composite of 5 responses to hypothetical stories [attributions, strategies, etc.])	Number of reciprocated friendships	Hierarchical regression	When entered in Step 1, both IV and mediator reduced beta for the other equally
Cassidy et al., 1992 [EU]	61 kindergarten and first grader children and both parents	Family emotion expression at home and lab	Understanding of emotion (composite of responses to probes about hypothetical stories, e.g., how is kid feeling? If your mom saw you feeling this way, what would she do?)	Sociometric ratings	Hierarchical regression with mediator entered in second step	1 of 92 correlations between 12 family expression variables and 6 child understanding variables was significant; correlation of composites not reported; beta for mom home emotion expression reduced from .29* to .20 (ns), and beta for dad lab emotion expression reduced from .30* to .21 (ns) controlling for EU
Davies & Cummings, 1998 [ER]	56 6- to 9-year olds and mothers	Marital functioning (seven questionnaire indicators)	Emotional insecurity (three latent constructs; emotional reactivity, regulation of exposure to parent affect, internal representations of marital relations; multiple indicators via observed response to simulated conflict and interview following audiotaped argument)	Externalizing and internalizing measured via multiple indicators from mother and child questionnaires	SEM with LVPLS with mediators as 3 latent constructs and 2 DVs in single mediational model	3 of 6 possible indirect paths significant (through internal representations to internalizing; through emotional reactivity to internalizing & externalizing); significant direct path to internalizing; mediational model fit better than nonmediated model

140

Study	Participants	Status measures	SIP/SL measures	Outcome	Analysis	Results
Dodge et al., 1990 [SIP] [SL]	44 abused, 255 nonabused kindergarten children	Abuse status (assessed via interviews prior to kindergarten)	5 SIP measures (encoding, hostile attributions, proportion aggressive responses, proportion competent responses, number of responses); 2 SL measures (evaluation of aggressive and competent responses)	Teacher-rated, peer-rated, observed aggression	MANCOVA (sex by abuse status) on 3 aggression measures controlling for all SIP measures as block	4 of 21 specific links meet B & K criteria; different SIP measures correlated with different measures of aggression; the block of social-cognitive measures reduced F from 4.10** to 2.16 (ns) for aggression composite
Dodge et al., 1995 [SIP] [SL]	69 abused, 515 nonabused kindergarten, followed to grade 4	Abuse status (assessed via interviews prior to kindergarten)	3 SIP constructs (encoding, hostile attributions, aggressive strategies); 1 SL construct (evaluation of aggressive responses) each with multiple indicators, assessed over 4 years	conduct problems (CBCL-TRF) in third and fourth grades	1 SEM using each SIP step as a separate latent construct	Mediated model has significant x^2, but is a significantly better fit than direct model, reducing direct path from .24* to .16*; 2 of 4 mediational paths significant (encoding, aggressive strategies)
Downey & Walker, 1989 [SIP]	9- and 10-year-olds; 19 with psychiatric parent, 25 maltreated, 11 maltreated with psychiatric parent; 28 comparison	Status (see participants)	6: 4 Interpersonal problem solving (IPS) strategies, adequate strategies, relevant consequences, plus hostile attributions and aggressive responses to ambiguous stories	2: Mother-rated aggression and peer rejection	Mediators entered individually in series of regression analyses predicting aggression	none of the 36 potential paths met Baron & Kinney criteria for testing mediation; none of the mediators reduced the beta for maltreatment
Feldman & Weinberger, 1994 [ER]	108 grade 6 boys (Time 1), 81 were followed to 10th grade (Time 2)	Mother & son reports effective parenting (rejection, power assertion, inconsistency); observations of family at Time 1 and 2	Sons', mothers', and teachers' ratings of boys' self-restraint (e.g., "I lose my temper...") assessed at Time 1 and 2	Sons' and parents' ratings of frequency of delinquent behaviors (Time 2)	Simultaneous regression; self-restraint at Times 1 and 2 as mediators of 3 sets of IVS (mother, father, & combined family functioning at Time 1)	3 possible paths from parenting (mother, father, composite) to delinquency become ns with self-restraint at Times 1 and 2 in equation (e.g., beta reduced from -.22* to .05 for composite parenting); family functioning retains significant or near significant direct links also

Garner et al., 1994 (Study 1) [EU]	46 4- and 5-year olds	Mother reports of anger and hostility in family, maternal suppression of negative affect	Emotion expression and situation knowledge for each of 4 emotions (happy, angry, sad, afraid)	Composite of mutual friendship nominations and sociometric ratings)	Hierarchical regression entering in four steps: age, the 3 mother variables, a composite expression knowledge, and a composite situation knowledge	3 of 24 correlations between IV and DV variables significant; in regression, situation knowledge only significant predictor; appear to conclude that because mediator is correlated with both IV and DV, but IV not correlated with DV, this is evidence of an indirect effect of IV on DV
Gottman et al., 1996 [ER]	56 families with 4- to 5-year-olds (Time 1); 53 followed up at age 7 to 8 (Time 2)	Meta-emotion awareness and coaching assessed via parent interview at Time 1	At Time 1: 2 measures of child's regulatory physiology (delta and basal vagal tone); at Time 2: mother reports of need to "down regulate" child	At Time 2: child illness, achievement test, teacher ratings of aggressive and antisocial behavior	SEM with EQS; separate models run with parental derogation and parental scaffolding for each outcome	For 2 peer-outcome models significant paths through vagal tone measures and down regulation; for model with derogation also significant direct path not mediated by child measures; do not contrast mediated and nonmediated models
Hart et al., 1992 [SL]	136 preschoolers and mothers	Inductive versus power-assertive discipline by mothers (assessed via interview)	Outcome expectations for friendly assertive and unfriendly assertive strategies to hypothetical vignettes	Observed prosocial, withdrawn, and antisocial playground behavior	6 MANCOVAs (sex x age x mother discipline) with mediators as covariate	No evidence of mediation in any analyses
Hart et al., 1990 [SL]	144 first and fourth graders and mothers	Ratings of mothers' interview responses on power assertive to inductive scale	8 measures of outcome expectations (instrumental and relational expectations of friendly and unfriendly assertive and unassertive strategies)	Sociometric peer preference	Regression with age, grade, SES, and unfriendly strategies before discipline and discipline interaction terms	1 of 8 possible paths tested for mediation (based on patterns of correlation); no evidence of mediation found
Krevans & Gibbs, 1996 [EU]	78 middle-school and junior high children and mothers	Mother and child reports of discipline yielded 7 indexes	3 measures of empathy (composited to form total empathy); 2 measures of guilt	Composite of 5 measures of prosocial behavior (ratings, observations)	Simultaneous regression analysis including sex, net discipline, and child total empathy	Empathy (but not guilt) correlated with IV and DV; beta for net discipline reduced from .31* to .16 (ns) with empathy in equation

Peiser & Heaven, 1996 [SL]	105 15- to 16-year-olds	Teens' perceptions of parents' punitiveness, love-withdrawal, induction, positive and negative family relations	Teens' self-esteem and locus of control	Self-reported delinquency	SEM with PROC CALIS	No evidence of mediation even though several variable sets met B and K criteria for testing for mediation
Pettit et al., 1988 [SIP]	46 low-income preschoolers	6 from mother interview: exposure to aggressive models, peer experience, preventive teaching, endorsement of aggression, biased expectations, restrictive discipline	5 SIP measures to hypothetical stories (2 measures of aggressive strategies, number of solutions, relevant solutions, prosocial solutions)	Sociometric social preference, teacher ratings of social skill and aggression	Hierarchical regression controlling for block of 5 SIP measures, 6 family experience measures entered second step	7 of 90 specific paths met B and K correlational criteria; R^2 for family block reduced from .34 * to .12 (ns) controlling for SIP (a reduction of 65%)
Pettit et al., 1991 [SL]	30 5-year-olds (10 high CBCL aggression, 10 low aggression, 10 average)	Parental responsiveness, proactive involvement, coerciveness and intrusiveness from home observations	Hypothetical vignette interviews yielding effectance and outcome expectations for competent and aggressive responses	Teacher ratings of aggression, social competence, and social disengagement	3 hierarchical regression equations	3 of 48 possible mediational paths met B and K criteria; beta for family interaction in all equations became nonsignificant in all equations when social cognition controlled
Rogosch et al., 1995 [SIP] [EU]	46 abused, 43 nonabused children assessed at three times: (at $\underline{M}$ ages 5.9, 6.6, and 8.2)	Abuse status	6 mediators: Time 1: understanding of 4 emotions; Time 2: 2 Leveling/Sharpening (L/S) assessments to a nonaggressive and to an aggressive stimulus (L/S assesses awareness of subtle changes in visual stimuli)	Time 3: Teacher and peer ratings yielded measures of social effectiveness and behavioral dysregulation	Hierarchical regression, controlling for age and PPVT scores	1 of 4 possible SIP paths and 2 of 8 EU paths met or nearly met B and K criteria; direct paths slightly reduced (e.g., from .28* to .23*), but still significant in both that were originally significant; authors conclude L/S mediates IV →social effectiveness but negative affect understanding mediates IV → behavioral dysregulation

Study	Sample	Predictor	Mediator measures	Outcome measures	Analysis	Results
Shields, et al., 1994 [ER]	81 maltreated, 48 nonmaltreated 8- to 12-year olds	Abuse status	7 measures of self regulation: observer rating of emotional regulation (ER); 6 observer or counselor ratings of behavioral regulation (acting out, aggression, TRF-Externalizing withdrawal, TRF-Internalizing withdrawal, prosocial behavior)	2 social competence: camp counselors' q-sort and observers' ratings of highest level of Parten's play	IV predicted q-sort DV but not Parten's play; hierarchical regression with block of internalizing + externalizing + composites + ER	ER alone did not reduce beta for maltreatment; 3 measures as a block reduced maltreatment beta from -.19* to -.09 (ns); authors conclude self-regulation mediates effects of maltreatment on social competence
Weiss, et al. 1992 [SIP] [SL]	562 kindergarten children in two cohorts	Mother interviews yielded measures of harsh discipline for 2 eras (early childhood, recent)	3 SIP variables from interviews (encoding, hostile attributions, generation of aggressive strategies); 1 SL (positive evaluation of aggressive strategies)	3 used in main mediational analyses: teacher, peer, & observer judgments of aggression	SEM with 4 SIP measures as a single latent construct	2 of 48 specific paths met B & K criteria; many SIP measures correlated with discipline and aggression, but specifics varied by cohort; latent SIP reduced direct path from discipline → aggression from .33* to ns in cohort 1; from .34* to .29* in cohort 2

Theoretical perspectives guiding mediational analysis: [IWM] = Internal working models; [SIP] = Social information processing; [EU] = Emotion understanding, empathy, etc.; [ER] = emotion regulation, including physiological processes; [SL] = Social learning (efficacy for performing social strategies, self esteem, etc.).

B & K criteria (correlational criteria for mediation according to Baron & Kenny, 1986): independent variable, dependent variable, and proposed mediator must be significantly intercorrelated to establish potential for mediation.

* the value was reported as statistically significant in the published study.

considered in this section, although they do inform the discussion of issues raised in subsequent portions of this chapter. The majority of investigations considered here use either structural equation modeling (SEM) or hierarchical or simultaneous regression to evaluate the mediational hypothesis, with a smaller number using analysis of covariance (ANCOVA), in which the mediator serves as the covariate. In the following section, we distinguish between analyses that test specific mediational links (i.e., those in which conceptually distinct measures are treated as separate mediators), and omnibus analyses (i.e., those in which measures of conceptually distinct constructs are treated as a single mediator).

Studies Conducted within a Social Information-Processing Perspective

Six of the 18 studies in Table 6.1 were conducted within (or partially within) an SIP theoretical perspective (Dodge et al., 1990; Dodge et al., 1995; Downey & Walker, 1989; Pettit et al., 1988; Rogosch et al., 1995; Weiss et al., 1992. It should be noted that the Dodge et al., 1990; Dodge et al., 1995; Weiss et al., 1992, studies make use of varying portions of the same data set.) SIP describes the cognitive processes involved in an individual's response to a specific social situation (Dodge, Pettit, McClaskey, & Brown, 1986), with special reference to how individuals perceive social cues (encoding), make attributions and inferences about those cues, generate possible solutions, and make behavioral decisions about how to respond. The SIP mediators considered here derive, at least in part, from Dodge's formulation (with the exception of Rogosch et al., 1995). Children typically are presented with hypothetical stories depicting peer conflict and then are asked to describe the events, to explain why peers acted as they did, and to suggest possible responses. We have placed the Rogosch et al. (1995) study in this category because it assessed a construct—Leveling/Sharpening (L/S)—that seems conceptually similar to the SIP notion of encoding. The L/S measure assesses children's awareness of subtle changes in drawings of aggressive and nonaggressive stimuli; children who perform well on this task are described as being skilled at detecting nuances in perceptual stimuli. Each of the SIP studies discussed in this section examines harsh or abusive parenting as a predictor variable. Dependent variables were aggression or conduct problems, although other outcomes were considered as well (e.g., peer rejection in Downey & Walker, 1989; see Table 6.1).

For many of these studies, the number of potentially testable predictor-mediator-outcome relationships could be quite large (e.g., with 3 predictors, 4 mediators, and 3 outcomes there are 36 possible tests). Typically, however, only a small proportion of specific links met Baron and Kenny's (1986) correlational criteria for testing for mediation. (Some studies do not report correlations among all variables, and so cannot be evaluated in terms of

Baron and Kenny criteria.) These criteria appear to have been met by 4 of the 21 possible linkages in Dodge et al. (1990), by 1 of the 4 SIP links in Rogosch et al. (1995), by none of the 36 links in Downey and Walker (1989), by 7 of the 90 links in Pettit et al. (1988), and by 2 of the 48 links in Weiss et al. (1992). In terms of pervasiveness of effects, then, at the specific variable level, evidence of mediation is not strong.

Linkage specificity (i.e., the mediating role of individual SIP indexes vs. global aggregates) was not assessed in three studies. Rather, an omnibus mediational test was employed whereby all potential mediators (encoding, attributions, strategy generation, and so on) were entered as a block in multiple regression or ANCOVA, or treated as a single latent construct in SEM. This approach may be justified if investigators are interested only in aggregated effects because they conceptualize sociocognitive processes as working in concert rather than in isolation (Dodge et al., 1986). However, others might argue that findings stemming from the use of an omnibus approach shed little light on specific processes that may be responsible for links between family experience and children's social competence. Complicating the interpretation of the omnibus test results is the fact that putative mediators sometimes are included that may be related to the predictor only, to the outcome only, or to neither (e.g., in Pettit et al., 1988, aggressive responding was not correlated with any measure of classroom competence or with any measure of family experience, but was included in omnibus regression analyses). Use of this technique resulted in an attenuated direct effect of the IV in Dodge et al. (1990), Pettit et al. (1988), and Weiss et al. (1992, Cohort 1 only; see Table 6.1).

Three SIP studies evaluated specific processing steps (as opposed to a block or set of steps) in their mediational analyses. Dodge et al. (1995) reported that a mediated SEM model provided a better fit than an unmediated model, and the direct path coefficient linking abuse with conduct problems was reduced, but still significant, in the mediated model. Significant paths were found from early maltreatment to encoding and generation of aggressive strategies, and from these two mediators to later conduct problems; the paths through hostile attributions and evaluation of aggressive responses were not significant. Rogosch et al. (1995) found that the direct path from abuse to social effectiveness was reduced, but still significant, when the non-aggressive L/S measure was controlled (the aggressive L/S measure was not correlated with the outcome variables), and that the paths from maltreatment to L/S and from L/S to social effectiveness (i.e., the two legs of the indirect path) were significant. Downey and Walker (1989), as previously noted, found that no specific paths met the Baron and Kenny (1986) correlational criteria; not surprisingly, then, none of the regression analyses controlling for the seven SIP measures individually resulted in a reduction of the effects of abuse on aggression.

Thus, within the set of studies attempting to establish aspects of SIP as mediational links between family experience and children's peer relationships, only a small proportion of specific linkages met minimal correlational criteria even for testing for mediation, let alone establishing that mediation was present. Researchers have had more success when several SIP measures are treated as a block or single latent construct. Although this approach is consistent with some theoretical construals, it might be argued that the practice of combining variables that reflect potentially different mediating mechanisms obfuscates, rather than illuminates, family-to-peer socialization processes. To our knowledge, there have been no replications of specific mediational links in this body of research. Moreover, despite the fact that most SIP measures heavily rely on children's ability to understand verbal instructions and on their ability to describe verbally events and strategies, only one of these studies (Rogosch et al., 1995) controlled for children's verbal ability.

Studies Conducted within a Social Learning Perspective

The second category of M-P study is concerned with mediators derived loosely from SL theory, such as outcome expectations of friendly or aggressive social strategies (i.e., Dodge et al., 1995; Hart et al., 1992; Hart et al., 1990; Pettit et al., 1991), and self-esteem and locus of control (Peiser & Heaven, 1996). Various qualities of parenting (e.g., discipline, responsiveness, proactive involvement) served as the predictor variable(s) in each study. Outcomes were preschoolers' observed playground behavior (Hart et al., 1992), teacher ratings of 5-year-olds' peer behaviors (Pettit et al., 1991), elementary school children's peer preferences (Hart et al., 1990), and adolescents' self-reported delinquency (Peiser & Heaven, 1996).

As with the SIP studies, many specific mediating links were possible and omnibus tests often were the analytic strategy of choice. Only one of the SL studies found any evidence of mediation (Pettit et al., 1991). Even in this study, however, the data are not strongly supportive because the number of possible mediational paths that met correlational prerequisites do not exceed what one would expect on a chance basis (e.g., 3 of the 48 specific paths met the Baron and Kenny, 1986, criteria), and some of the apparent paths are counterintuitive (e.g., effectance for aggression mediating the link between family responsiveness and social competence). Our reading of this set of studies, therefore, is that they have produced no convincing evidence that evaluation of strategies or self-efficacy mediates the relationship between parenting and children's social competence.

Studies in Which Internal Working Models Are Mediators

Only one published paper could be located that explicitly attempted to assess the viability of IWM-type measures as mediators of the link between family experiences and children's peer relationships (Cassidy et al., 1996, Study 2). This is surprising given that IWMs are so central to the formulation of the presumed link between attachment quality and subsequent peer relationships (e.g., Bretherton, 1985), but understandable given the difficulty in measuring IWMs. Cassidy et al. assessed representations of peer relationships (rather than of caregiver relationships) as the mediating link between attachment classification (assessed in kindergarten-aged children) and children's reciprocated friendships. Representations of peer relationships were measured by asking children a series of questions about stories depicting hypothetical peer conflicts. About half the derived indexes were nearly identical to those typically used to assess SIP processes (i.e., attributions for peer behavior and behavioral response strategies). The remaining indexes focused on feelings about the event and the peer (e.g., "Do you think the boy/girl liked you?"). There was a significant effect for attachment status on three of the six questions (attributions, strategies, "How do you think the boy/girl feels after . . ."), and the entire set was subsequently composited and used in mediational analysis. When entered first in a regression equation, the peer representation composite attenuated the direct effect of attachment on number of reciprocated friendships.

Studies in Which Emotion Understanding Serves As Mediator

The fourth category of mediational study reflects the growing interest in emotion as a motivation for appropriate or inappropriate behavior. Within mediational studies of children's understanding of emotions, EU has been operationalized as children's ability to label emotions (Garner et al., 1994, Study 1), accuracy in identifying emotions in hypothetical situations (Garner et al., 1994; Rogosch et al., 1995), empathy in response to affect-eliciting video clips (Krevans & Gibbs, 1996), and a composite of children's ability to identify an emotion expression, describe situations that would elicit the emotion, and describe what they and others (e.g., their mother) would do and feel should the child express the emotion (Cassidy et al., 1992). The family-experience predictors used in these studies were family emotional expression (Cassidy et al., 1992; Garner et al., 1994), abuse status (Rogosch et al., 1995), and parental discipline (Krevans & Gibbs, 1996). Peer-relevant outcomes were peer acceptance and friendship (Cassidy et al., 1992; Garner et al., 1994), prosocial behavior (Krevans & Gibbs, 1996), and teacher and peer ratings of social effectiveness and behavioral dysregulation (Rogosch et al., 1995).

Cassidy et al. (1992) found only 1 significant correlation between the 12 family emotional expression variables and the 6 EU variables (the correlation between a composite index of family emotion expression and the mediator is not reported), and Garner et al. (1994) reported a nonsignificant correlation between mother negative emotion expression and children's peer competence. Rogosch et al. (1995) had a somewhat higher success rate: Even after controlling for child age and PPVT (Peabody Picture Vocabulary Test) scores, two of eight possible EU mediational paths met or nearly met Baron and Kenny correlational criteria, and the direct paths were reduced slightly when the mediator was controlled. Thus, the Rogosch et al. study provides modest evidence that negative affect understanding may partially mediate the relation between maltreatment and social behavior.

Krevans and Gibbs (1995) provided perhaps the most persuasive demonstration of mediation of any study in this category because the authors proposed a small number of theoretically derived potential mediational links (two) and found strong evidence for one of the two. These investigators composited multiple measures of each of the constructs eventually used in mediational analyses (parent discipline, child empathy, child prosocial behavior) and all composites were moderately interrelated. Including empathy in a simultaneous regression equation reduced the beta for discipline, whereas the beta for empathy was significant. Measures of guilt, also initially proposed as potential mediators, were not correlated with parenting.

Studies Examining Emotion Regulation As a Mediating Mechanism

Studies in this final category are concerned with aspects of ER as mediators of the link between family experiences and children's peer relationships. Although optimal ER may require an understanding of one's own and others' emotions, this set of studies focuses on the ability to modulate arousal rather than on skills in interpreting emotional expression and in understanding the causes and motivational functions of emotion.

The studies in this category operationalized ER in a variety of ways. Davies and Cummings (1998) measured three regulatory constructs: emotional reactivity to adult conflict, efforts to intervene in or to avoid adult-adult conflict, and internal representations of marital relations. Each construct had multiple indicators derived from observations of children as they watched simulated conflict, children's reports of their feelings during the conflict, and children's views (representations) of their parents' relationship. Mother, teacher, and adolescent boys' ratings of the boys' self-restraint (measured prior to and concurrent with the DV) served as mediating links in a study by Feldman and Weinberger (1994). Although these investigators did not explicitly refer to self-restraint as ER, sample items from their instruments (e.g., "I lose my temper . . .") would seem to index ER abilities. In Gottman et al. (1996), ER was assessed via mother reports of the need to calm down, or "down regulate," the child and with a physiological measure of vagal tone. Vagal tone is a measure of heart rate variability that presumably indexes the parasympathetic nervous system's ability to modulate arousal, and thus calm emotion and direct attention. Shields et al. (1994) operationalized ER (which served as one of two proposed mediators) as observer ratings of appropriate and inappropriate expressions of emotions during social interaction. A second proposed mediator in the Shields et al. study was behavioral regulation, the constituents of which (e.g., teacher-rated internalizing and externalizing problems, social withdrawal, aggressive and prosocial behavior) closely resemble the peer-relevant outcomes (vs. mediators) in this and other studies.

Family-experience predictors in this set of studies were marital functioning (Davies & Cummings, 1998), mother and son reports of family functioning (Feldman & Weinberger, 1994), abuse status (Shields et al., 1994), and parents' awareness of and coaching about emotions (Gottman et al., 1996). Peer-relevant outcomes were mother and child reports of internalizing and externalizing behaviors (Davies & Cummings, 1998), sons' and parents' ratings of delinquent behavior (Feldman & Weinberger, 1994), counselors' and observers' judgments of children's social competence (Shields et al., 1994), and teacher ratings of children's aggressive and antisocial behavior (Gottman et al., 1996).

Davies and Cummings (1998) used the three mediators and the two dependent measures, externalizing and internalizing, as separate latent constructs (each with multiple indicators) in contrasting a mediational model with a direct effects model. Three of six possible mediated paths (through internal representations and emotional reactivity) were significant, and the mediated model fit the data significantly better than a direct effects model. In Feldman and Weinberger (1994), the effects of parenting on delinquency were reduced to nonsignificant when both measures of self-restraint were controlled, but observed family functioning continued to contribute directly to delinquency. The meaning of the statistical mediation in this study is difficult to interpret, however, given shared method variance among the IV, the mediator, and the DV (i.e., all were based largely on parent and child reports of conceptually similar behaviors).

In the only study of which we are aware that uses a physiological measure of ER in statistical mediation analyses, Gottman and colleagues (1996) found significant paths from parent emotion coaching through children's ER (vagal tone and down regulation). Gottman et al. did not contrast the fit of mediated and nonmediated models, nor did they report path coefficients for a nonmediated model. Analyses by Shield et al. (1994) showed that after controlling for the effects of gender, maltreatment status predicted only one of the two dependent measures (camp counselor q-sorts of children's social competence). ER alone did not reduce the direct effects of maltreatment on social competence, but by including ER, internalizing, and externalizing as mediators, the direct path from maltreatment was reduced to nonsignificant. Although Shield et al. concluded that self-regulation mediates the effects of abuse on children's social competence, as in Feldman and Weinberger (1994), the meaningfulness of this claim is difficult to evaluate given the conceptual and measurement overlap between the dependent variable (ratings of social behavior) and the mediators (derived from behavioral ratings in the same setting).

Conclusions Regarding Current Evidence for Mediation

In many of the studies summarized in this section, researchers examined many (occasionally dozens of) specific possible paths to find only a few that potentially could provide such evidence (e.g., Cassidy et al., 1992; Hart et al., 1990; Pettit et al., 1988; Pettit et al., 1991; Rogosch et al., 1995; Weiss et al., 1992). This technique sometimes appears to capitalize on chance associations, especially when the links that do meet minimal criteria (intercorrelation among IV, mediator, and DV) do not appear to have theoretical priority over those that do not meet criteria. In several studies with evidence for mediation, researchers composite, or use in a single-step or latent construct, measures that seem conceptually dissimilar, and purportedly (often by the authors' own accounts) reflect different socialization processes (e.g., Dodge et al., 1990; Pettit et al., 1988; Weiss et al., 1992).

Studies reporting data that are consistent with models of specific sociocognitive or emotional process linkages between family experiences and children's relationships with peers reflect a variety of theoretical perspectives. The most substantial support for mediation, in our view, can be found in Davies and Cummings (1998; ER, specifically emotion reactivity, and internal representations of marital relationships partially mediated a link between marital discord and externalizing and internalizing), Dodge et al. (1995; encoding and generation of aggressive strategies partially mediated the link between abuse and conduct problems), Gottman et al. (1996; ER partially mediated the link between parent emotion awareness/coaching and quality of peer relationships), and Krevans and Gibbs (1996; EU, specifically empathy, partially mediated the link between discipline and prosocial behavior).

That a relatively small proportion of studies just reviewed provide persuasive evidence of specific mediational links is surprising given the fact that many of the family predictors and child sociocognitive processes examined in this literature have shown significant associations with one another and with peer relationship outcomes. In the next section, we consider possible reasons (some plausible, some probably less so) as to why convincing specific mediational links have not been easier to document.

WHY HAVE PAST RESEARCH FINDINGS PROVIDED LIMITED SUPPORT FOR THE MEDIATING-PROCESSES HYPOTHESIS?

Possibility 1: The Mediational Hypothesis Is Wrong

The first possibility is that the premise on which the prototypical mediational study is based is flawed. One version of the "model-is-wrong" hypothesis is that although parenting affects children's social relationships with peers, the effect is not mediated by sociocognitive or affective processes (Patterson, 1997). Although such a black box explanation of behavioral transfer is difficult for many cognitively oriented developmentalists to consider seriously, behaviorally oriented psychologists offer persuasive descriptions of how such a process might operate. One model suggests that interactional synchrony is originally orchestrated by parents but becomes transactional (e.g., Wahler & Meginnis, 1997). If parents respond to children in ways that are appropriate (not specifically or necessarily with positive reinforcement), children act to sustain the reciprocity and cooperation (Wahler & Meginnis, 1997). Conversely, if parental responses are noncontingent, inconsistent, or irrelevant, turn-taking and positive reciprocity are disrupted, and in this setting chaos or negative reciprocity patterns of coercion and aggressive behavior thrive (Wahler, 1996). It is not hard to envision how such well-learned behavior patterns, if generalized to peer relationships, would yield quite different responses and relationship styles. Even researchers who propose sociocognitive mediators linking family experiences and children's peer relationships acknowledge the possibility that some behavioral styles practiced with parents (e.g., mutually responsive style) may be reproduced in interactions with peers in the absence of sociocognitive mediation (Lindsey, Mize, & Pettit, 1997; Russell, Pettit, & Mize, in press).

Another extreme version of the mediation-is-wrong idea is that the family has relatively little effect on children's relationships with peers or on sociocognitive processes related to peers, especially in comparison to the effects of experiences in the peer group. Correlations between behavior and social cognitive measures, in this case, would not indicate a causal role for social cognition, but instead would reflect consequences of the child's behavior and experiences with peers (Patterson, 1997). For instance, hostile attributional "biases" may not cause a child to act aggressively, but instead may accurately mirror peers' reactions to a child's aversive style (Trachtenberg & Viken, 1994). To extend the causal arrow further, experiences with peers may influence relationships and interactions with family members (Repetti, 1996). If the primary direction of effect is from (not to) peer experiences, correlations among family experiences, social cognition, and peer competence would not be evidence of M-P hypothesis because the association would violate Baron and Kenny's (1986) criterion that the DV not cause the mediator.

Possibility 2: Accurate Estimates of Mediation Are Difficult to Obtain, Even When Proposed Processes Are "Real"

Mediation, even when it is "real" and all relevant theoretical constructs are identified, is difficult to detect because of low statistical power (particularly for regression models). According to Judd and Kenny (1981) and Kenny et al. (1998), low power for detecting mediation results from co-linearity between the IV and the mediator, and from measurement error in the dependent variables. Because in mediational analyses there are, in effect, at least two dependent variables in any causal chain, attenuation of mediated effects due to measurement error is magnified. When multiple indicators are available, it is possible to reduce or eliminate problems associated with mea-surement error by the use of SEM (Baron & Kenny, 1986). It is worth noting that of the four studies that we concluded had provided convincing evidence of mediation, three used multiple indicators of constructs (Davies & Cum-mings, 1998; Dodge et al., 1995; Krevans & Gibbs, 1996).

Possibility 3: Family Experience Predictors Are Less Specific Than Reflected in Theory and Analyses

A less severe version of the mediational-hypothesis-is-wrong idea is that family experiences do influence sociocognitive links, but that specific socio-cognitive processes and outcomes can be affected by a wide range of different experiences (the principle of equifinality; Cicchetti & Rogosch, 1996), or by an accumulation of experiences rather than by any particular experience (e.g., the cumulative risk hypothesis; Sameroff, Seifer, Baldwin, & Baldwin, 1993). If family-peer linkages are consistent with the principle of equifinality, any of a variety of family risk and protective factors could result in similar pro-cesses and outcomes (Dealer-Deckard, Dodge, Bates, & Pettit, in press). Similarly, if an accumulation of beneficial or adverse experiences is the crit-ical factor, then the number, not the specific types, of positive and negative family experiences should predict sociocognitive processes and outcomes.

Within the attachment perspective, the network or integrative model of how children form IWMs from attachments with multiple caregivers is con-sistent with the "less specific links" possibility. The integrative model does not give priority to any relationship and does not assume that attachment relationships necessarily will be concordant in quality. Rather, the integrative model posits that developmental outcome is a function of the quality of all attachment relationships in the child's network (Howes, in press). If family and peer relationships are connected only in such general or global ways, restricting analyses to specific links (e.g., mother-child relationship quality) would make it very difficult indeed to locate evidence of specific mediation.

Possibility 4: Links Are More Specific Than Theory and Analyses Reflect

Another possibility (the converse of the previous) is that linkages are more circumscribed or specific than typically have been allowed for in measure-ment and analyses. Recently, several researchers have called for more precise specification of linking process, for instance, through identification of constituents of internal working models (e.g., Dunn, 1996). A detailed specific-processes model is proposed by Dodge and colleagues (Dodge et al., 1997). These researchers suggest, and have found some support for, a model in which a family history of maltreatment and rejection results in poorer attention to and encoding of relevant social cues, interpretation of peers' intentions as hostile, and a tendency to frequently access aggressive strategies, which, in turn, are expected to predict patterns of angry-reactive aggression. Proactive, or instrumental aggression, in contrast, should be more strongly correlated with exposure to aggressive models; moreover, positive evaluation of aggression as a problem-solving strategy, but not encoding or attributional problems, should act as a mediator of this link. These speculations are consistent with a differentiated socialization model whereby certain kinds of early experience lead to certain kinds of outcome, with specific and unique intervening social-cognitive processes. If, as proposed by Dodge et al., parental rejection is associated with hostile bias and hostile bias is associated with angry-reactive aggression but not proactive aggression, the indirect link could be expected to be attenuated if the dependent measure tapped all forms of aggression rather than angry-reactive aggression only.

Compelling support for a specific-process model would require evidence that a particular aspect of family experience contributes to some aspect of children's sociocognitive-affective processes (but not to others) and to an associated peer relationship outcome (and, depending on the theory, perhaps not to other outcomes), while ruling out the possibility that the link can be equally well explained by joint correlations with other factors (Judd & Kenny, 1981). Thus, for instance, an unambiguous demonstration that emotion understanding specifically mediates the link between parents' emotion talk and peer competence would require evidence that the link cannot be as readily accounted for by verbal ability, or positive orientation to others (among other possibilities), and that parents' emotion talk uniquely predicts emotion understanding and peer competence controlling for other relevant family experience variables, such as parents' responsiveness. We are not aware of any mediational studies that have controlled both for alternative independent variables and potentially confounding third variables. Realistically, attempting to do so may entail measurement problems so pronounced as to make it exceedingly difficult, if not impossible, to detect mediation under such circumstances.

Possibility 5: The Effects of Family Experiences Are Moderated

The principle of multifinality suggests that the effects of any factor vary as a function of other conditions in the system (Cicchetti & Rogosch, 1996).

Applying this principle to the M-P hypothesis would imply that the effects of family experiences are moderated by—dependent on—other factors. Because correlations between a given family experience factor and a sociocognitive mediator would vary depending on the level of the moderator(s), averaging overall levels of the moderator would tend to attenuate linkages. Evidence is abundant that the effects of parenting on children's social competence often are moderated by other factors. There are few studies in which moderators of the effects of parenting on mediators and outcomes have been considered, even though it has been suggested that parenting should influence sociocognitive processes differently as a function of a variety of contextual factors (Grusec & Goodnow, 1994). An exception is the study by Weiss et al. (1992); using SEM, these researchers found that neither child gender, socioeconomic status, or family structure moderated the mediated links between abuse and aggression.

There are at least three classes of variable that may moderate the influence of parenting on children's sociocognitive and affective processing: The focal aspect of parenting may interact with other qualities of parents or parenting, with characteristics of the child, or with ecological factors, such as culture or the family's social support. Each of these possibilities is considered in turn.

The Focal Aspect of Parenting May Interact with Other Qualities of the Parent or Parenting

An accumulating body of evidence suggests that the same parenting behavior may have different effects depending on characteristics of the parent, such as whether the parent is the mother or the father (Grusec & Goodnow, 1994), and, particularly, the parents' child rearing style and qualities of the parent-child relationship (Deater-Deckard & Dodge, 1997). Recent attention has focused on how general parenting style—overall responsiveness or authoritativeness, for instance—and the immediate style in which a particular parenting practice is delivered moderates the effects of a given practice on the child. It probably is reasonable to assume (if we accept the M-P hypothesis in general) that if the effects of parenting on an outcome are moderated, the effects on mediating processes also may be moderated. Parents' style may make particular practices more (or less) effective (Darling & Steinberg, 1993; Mize & Pettit, 1997; Pettit & Mize, 1993) by making the child more (or less) receptive to the parents' message (Darling & Steinberg, 1993; Pettit & Mize, 1993), or by creating in the child an optimal (or insufficient or too high) level of arousal (Bugental & Goodnow, 1998; Hoffman, 1994; Kochanska, 1993).

Consistent with the model of the moderating role of parenting style, Zahn-Waxler, Radke-Yarrow, and King (1979) found that maternal use of affectively charged moralizing explanations to toddlers was related to pro-

social behavior, whereas explanations delivered without affect were less effective; the authors suggest that toddlers were unlikely to attend to and to
internalize their mothers' message during low-affect inductions.

The Focal Aspect of Parenting May Interact with Child Characteristics

The same or similar family experiences may have differential effects as a
function of characteristics of the child, as well. Child gender, age, and temperament perhaps are the child characteristics most often proposed and studied as moderators of the relation between parenting and children's behavior.
A recent study by Pettit, Brown, Mize, and Lindsey (1998) illustrates that
the same parenting behavior may have different effects on boys and girls.
Although there were no mean differences in mothers' and fathers' play or
in the amount or quality of coaching with their boys and girls, constructive
coaching (relevant discussions of the situation, encouraging positive peer
strategies), especially mothers' coaching, was strongly associated with girls',
but not with boys', social competence. In contrast, fathers', but not mothers',
involvement in their children's peer play was associated with boys' social
competence, but this was less true for girls. These differences in patterns of
association may reflect different mediational processes linking boys' and
girls' experiences in the family with their peer relationships.

Given that how children attend to and process information changes with
age, that children's motivations regarding social relationships change with
age, and that similar experiences have different effects on developing as contrasted with more mature brains (Perry et al., 1995), it seems reasonable to
assume that similar family experiences would have different effects on both
children's peer relationships and putative mediating processes as a function
of child age. Although little systematic attention has focused on age-related
changes in family-peer linkages, it has been suggested that more global,
diffuse processes, such as IWMs, may dominate in the early years, with more
precise, situation-specific processes coming into play later in development
(e.g., Pettit, 1997). There is some evidence that among preschool-age children attributions of intent are not strongly associated with behavioral adjustment, perhaps because young children do not easily hold in memory and
weigh several bits of information, such as both intention and consequences
(Pettit, Polaha, & Mize, in press). In contrast, generation of social problem-
solving strategies seems to be a robust predictor of social competence among
young children (Mize & Ladd, 1988; Pettit et al., 1988).

Temperament also has received theoretical and empirical attention as a
factor that may moderate the effects of parenting (Kochanska, 1993; Rothbart & Bates, 1998). In a recent study reporting data from two separate
samples, Bates, Pettit, Dodge, and Ridge (in press) found that firm, restrictive control protected children who were temperamentally resistant to control from risk of later conduct problems; restrictive control was not beneficial

for children who were temperamentally less resistant, however. Although there is not a body of research focusing on how a temperament × parenting interaction may affect sociocognitive processes, the results of the studies summarized in this section clearly have implications for the evolution of such processes.

The Focal Aspect of Parenting May Interact with Ecological Factors

Considerable debate over the past few years has focused on whether socialization processes are universal across different ethnic and socioeconomic groups (Rowe, Vazsonyi, & Flannery, 1994) or whether there are group differences in associations between family experiences and children's development (Deater-Deckard, Dodge, Bates, & Pettit, 1996). In our view, there is sufficient evidence consistent with the differential-processes hypothesis to warrant consideration of whether or how mediational links may operate differently across varying racial, ethnic, or cultural groups. As a case in point, the Deater-Deckard et al. findings that physical discipline predicts externalizing problems in Euro-American children, but not in African-American children, has obvious implications for processes that might mediate links between discipline and peer behavior. One might wonder whether physical discipline engenders hostile attributional biases in Euro-American children, but is less likely to do so among African-American children. Other ecological factors also may constrain or magnify the effects of parenting on sociocognitive processes. Perhaps harsh or disengaged parenting is especially likely to yield negative views of self and others and consequent relationship problems in the absence of other supportive relationships. For each of the classes of potential interactions suggested here, aggregating over groups (African Americans and Euro-Americans, boys and girls, for instance) would, if the parenting → socioaffective processes → peer-outcome linkage differs across groups, attenuate the chances of identifying mediational links.

Possibility 6: The Most Salient Mediators Have Not Been Studied and Mediators May Be Moderated by Other Sociocognitive Processes

Two related points are made in this section. The first is that perhaps researchers studying family-peer links have not identified, or at least rarely measured, processes that are most responsible for associations between family experiences and children's peer relationships. The second, related point is that mediational processes may themselves be moderated (Baron & Kenny, 1986) by other, unmeasured processes. When a mediated relation fails to account for all the variance in a DV associated with the IV, the left-over variance typically is referred to as the *direct effects* of the predictor on the outcome. Unless we accept Possibility 1 (effects of parenting are not mediated), however, the left-over effect is not really direct; rather, it is mediated by unmeasured processes (Hansen & McNeal, 1996). It must be assumed (again, unless one accepts a true direct effect) that had all the appropriate mediators been measured, direct effects would not be observed.

What processes internal to the child might account for the effects that are not explained by the mediators typically assessed in studies of family-peer links? The research literature is replete with potential candidates. A number of sociocognitive or affective processes have been studied as corre-lates of family experiences (e.g., Belsky et al., 1996), or as correlates of chil-dren's peer relationships (e.g., Graham & Hudley, 1994), but have not been explored specifically as mediational links between family and peer relations. In this section, we focus on ER processes because these seem to hold promise as mechanisms that directly link family experiences and peer relationships and also may interact with other processes (e.g., SIP). It is worth noting that two of the four studies reviewed earlier in this chapter that, in our estima-tion, provided persuasive evidence of mediation focused on aspects of ER (Davies & Cummings, 1998; Gottman et al., 1996). Due to increasing re-search on ways that early social relationships may hard-wire emotional reg-ulatory styles (e.g., Dawson, Hessl, & Frey, 1994; Perry et al., 1995), greater focus on the importance of ER for competent social interaction (Coie & Dodge, 1998; Thompson, 1998), and the development of techniques for assessing psychophysiological aspects of emotion and arousal (e.g., Porges, Doussard-Roosevelt, & Maiti, 1994), there are abundant opportunities for exploring ER processes as correlates and mediators of family and peer re-lationships. We particularly want to focus on how ER processes and emotion-relevant cognitions might interact with other sociocognitive processes.

We previously alluded to ways in which emotional arousal may interfere with children's information processing in socialization encounters. A state-ment made by Martin Hoffman (1986) calls attention to the fact that emo-tional arousal also is fundamental in directing, propelling, or impeding information processing during children's interactions with peers.

Affect may initiate, terminate, accelerate, or disrupt information-processing; it may determine which sector of the environment is processed and which processing modes operate; it may organize recall and influence category accessibility; it may contribute to the formation of emotionally charged schemata and categories, it may provide input for social cognition; and it may influence decision making. (pp. 245–246)

In the peer relationship literature, however, only a few studies have examined emotion, arousal, or emotion-relevant cognitions as moderators of the so-ciocognitive processes under scrutiny. Dodge and Somberg (1987) demon-strated that aggressive boys were especially likely to make attributions of hostile intent when they felt threatened; Dorsch and Keane (1994) found that children were more likely to attribute hostile intent to peers when they had just had a failure experience; and Graham and Hudley (1994) reported that nonaggressive boys made more hostile attributions after the construct of blame had been primed, but that aggressive boys were likely to infer hostile intent even in the absence of priming. As a set, these studies show that children are more likely to make hostile attributions under some cognitive-affective conditions (negative arousal, recent priming of a congruent construct) than others, and furthermore, that the effects of the moderating process are not necessarily equivalent for all children. It is possible that findings in these studies reflect emotion's tendency to make constructs (Higgins & Bargh, 1987) congruent with the felt emotion more accessible. For instance, a child may be more likely to access blame- or hostility-related explanations when he or she is experiencing emotions that in past experience often were associated with the construct of blame.

Emotion influences not only how a social event is interpreted, but also what is perceived, and what strategies are accessed (among perhaps many other aspects of information processing; Bugental & Goodnow, 1998; Hoffman, 1986), and so many other potential emotion × processing interactions remain unexplored. A critical point is that mediational paths may be more detectable when presumed mediators are assessed under conditions of emotional arousal (or cognitive appraisal) that are salient in children's real-world interactions with peers.

RECOMMENDATIONS

Based on our reading of the research literature exploring sociocognitive and affective processes as mediators of links between parenting and children's peer relationships, we would like to propose some directions for future research. These suggestions follow from our analysis of the possible reasons why evidence supporting the various M-P hypotheses so often appears inconclusive.

A serious measurement concern is shared method variance among variables in a mediational chain. Shared method variance between a mediator and other variables is likely to inflate estimates of mediated effects, and we raised this concern regarding some of the studies reviewed earlier. Kenny et al. (1998) discuss method variance as a special case of an omitted variable. Specifically, shared method variance (e.g., self-reports from one person) may be the true cause of the associations among variables in the IV-mediator-DV chain. Thus, confidence in the meaningfulness of mediated effects is compromised when correlations among variables can be attributed to common method variance. Future research should avoid stacking the deck in favor of finding apparent evidence of mediation by using multiple methods or multiple informants as data sources for each step in the mediational chain.

Earlier, we suggested that perhaps researchers have had only modest success demonstrating mediational links between family experiences and children's peer relationships due to the low statistical power to detect such mediated relations. Statisticians identify two sources of low power; one, paradoxically, is that the higher the collinearity between the IV and the mediator, the lower the power, and the larger the sample size needed to detect mediation (see Kenny et al., 1998). Another source of low power (one that is at least potentially controllable) is measurement error. Generally, measurement error attenuates the magnitude of measures of association; given the multiple links in a mediational chain, measurement problems are doubled (at least). According to Kenny et al. (1998), if the mediator is measured with less than perfect reliability, estimates of mediation are likely to be biased. As discussed previously, one solution is to use SEM with multiple indicators of each construct. (A description of SEM for testing mediation is beyond the scope of this chapter, but reader-friendly introductions can be found in Tabachnick & Fidell, 1996.) However, the time and resources required to assess many hypothesized mediating processes in the study of family-peer linkages often results in small sample sizes that limit applicability of SEM. When use of SEM is not feasible (and even when it is), researchers should be cognizant of constraints placed on the ability to detect mediation by less-than-perfect measures and should, therefore, commit sufficient initial resources to ensure the best possible measurement of each construct.

Because of small sample sizes, multiple regression is often the method of choice for testing mediated effects in the family-peer relations literature. Unfortunately, the results from many studies using the regression approach are difficult to interpret. The most common source of interpretational difficulties is that if a significant association between the IV and DV is not reduced to 0 by controlling for the mediator (as it rarely is), the reader is left wondering whether or not the reduction in the direct effect is sufficient to claim mediation. In none of the studies reviewed earlier in which a regression approach was used did the researchers report tests for significance for the mediated path. Results of future studies using the regression approach can be clarified by testing the significance of the mediated path (see the appendix).

To complicate the matter further, researchers sometimes find that data meet some, but not all, of the correlational prerequisites for testing for mediation. What does one make of a situation in which the IV predicts the mediator, and the mediator predicts the DV, but the IV and the DV are not significantly correlated? Usually there are several possible causes for failure to fulfill any of the requisites for demonstrating mediation, ranging from inadequate measurement or sample size to flawed theory. MacKinnon (1994) identified the range of results possible from regression analyses of mediation in prevention and intervention studies and describes several interpretations of each. Even more interpretations (such as errors in specifying direction of effects) are available for researchers engaged in nonexperimental studies, however.

Even when statistical evidence consistent with the mediational hypothesis is obtained, caution nonetheless is warranted because this evidence does not rule out the possibilities that the causal chain runs in the direction opposite that specified and that other, unmeasured variables influence associations among those in the hypothesized chain (Davis, 1985; Kenny et al., 1998). Overestimation of the mediated effect can occur when the DV is the true cause of the mediator (Baron & Kenny, 1986) or when a third variable that is associated with both the mediator and the DV is not measured (Davis, 1985; Judd & Kenny, 1981). Statistically, omitted variables that are related to a predictor and its criterion can increase, decrease, or completely change the sign of the association (Davis, 1985). It is important, therefore, to measure and control for such variables to the extent possible: Does exposure to cultural images of emotion expression (e.g., in books for preschoolers) explain links between parenting and children's emotion understanding as well as does family emotional expressiveness? Although longitudinal designs, in which assessments of family predictors, sociocognitive mediators, and peer group outcomes are assessed in the presumed temporal sequence of influence, are assumed to give greater confidence to causal claims, the designs typically are imperfect because co-occurring peer relationships (and mediators) are not controlled. By the age at which family and mediating processes typically are measured, most children have had years of experience with peers (Howes, 1988), and so peer relationships would have had ample opportunity to influence sociocognitive and regulatory processes. It also is possible that the socialization process operates in ways that are not reflected in variations among sociocognitive, affective, or psychophysiological measurements (e.g., Wahler & Megginis, 1997). The strongest and most compelling test of the M-P hypothesis would be an experimental study in which associations between mediating processes and outcomes are examined as a function of family intervention (see Mize & Ladd, 1990, for an example of changes in children's sociocognition mediating behavioral improvements during social skills intervention). In the absence of such designs, however, researchers should rule out if possible, but certainly consider and acknowledge, alternative explanations than the one favored.

Our next recommendation is that investigators adhere to the dictates of the guiding theoretical perspective in deciding whether individual mediators or sets of mediators should be examined. Some of the research in this area has been explicitly theory driven and the proposed mediators follow logically from the conceptual framework guiding the research. Other times, however, the research seems to be driven by a strong confirmation bias to find some evidence of mediation, even if it means using constructs that are, at best, tangentially related to the proposed socialization process (e.g., Pettit et al.,

1991). Progress in understanding processes responsible for family-peer linkages might proceed more rapidly if reliably measured, clearly differentiated constructs (Dunn, 1996) could be rejected or accepted as potential mediators.

For theory about family-peer linkages to advance, it also seems important to cast our explanatory frameworks in developmental terms (Pettit et al., in press). Although scholars for years have called for a developmental focus in studies of sociocognitive processes, hypothesis-driven examination of age differences has yet to be incorporated into tests of the M-P hypothesis. We should begin to examine more carefully age-related changes in how family experiences influence processing and how processing influences children's relationships with peers at different ages. Do some types of processes differentiate among young children who have good relationships with peers and those who do not, with other processes becoming important later? Do particular aspects of parenting affect some aspects of processing more at some ages than at others? Answers to these questions await systematic comparisons of family-peer relationship linkages at different ages.

Progress in understanding how early relationships with caregivers affect children's ER and advancements in assessing ER provide unprecedented opportunities for refining conceptualizations of family-peer pathways. The recent focus on emotion also underscores the importance of considering the context, particularly the child's emotional state, when sociocognitive processes are assessed. It is likely that children's sociocognitive processing during real-life, emotionally charged peer interactions is very different than it is in laboratory assessments. Thus, assessments that elicit approximations of the emotional arousal that occurs during social interaction are likely to yield measures that are more strongly related to children's actual behavior than are measures gathered in emotionally sterile contexts (see Mize & Ladd, 1988).

Methodological contextualists recommend an approach toward theory testing that involves a continuing search for conditions under which the predicted relationship maintains contrasted with those in which it does not (Greenwald, Pratkanis, Leippe, & Baumgardner, 1986). What is considered error variance at the population level may, under critical examination, reveal understandable diversity in process-outcome linkages. The meaning for a given child of a particular family experience may vary as a function of (at least) the child's age, gender, culture, and other relationships. It seems important to begin to examine and explain such diversity. Theory-driven investigations of differential M-P links might increase the likelihood of finding strong evidence of mediation and shed brighter light on socialization processes. Moreover, specifying conditions under which a mediational process appears to operate may help clarify the socialization and sociocognitive-affective processes that are responsible for observed associations between family experiences and peer relationships.

Although a clear picture has not yet emerged of the processes that link children's experiences in the family and their relationships with peers, the M-P hypothesis has spawned a body of enormously creative research and thinking about how such links might operate. As theory and measurement of complex hypothetical constructs move forward over the next few years, the field holds rich promise for shedding light on how experiences in the family are linked to children's lives with peers.

APPENDIX

Baron and Kenny (1986) presented the standard error for a test of significance of mediated effects (originally given by Sobel, 1982), but a fuller discussion of the approach, including interpretational cautions, can be found in Kenny et al. (1998). This approach to testing the significance of the mediated path requires the calculation of three regression equations. For equation 1, use the IV to predict the DV (this regression coefficient is path c, the direct effect in an unmediated model); a significant coefficient demonstrates that there is a path to be mediated.[1] For equation 2, use the IV to predict the mediator (this regression coefficient is path a). Finally, for equation 3, predict the DV from the IV and the mediator using simultaneous regression (the regression coefficient for the mediator is used as path b, the mediator-DV link, and the coefficient for the IV becomes path c, or the direct path in the mediated model). The formula, which is distributed as z, is (approximately):

$$\frac{ab}{[(se_a^2 b^2) + (se_b^2 a^2)]}$$

where se_a is the standard error of the regression coefficient for the a path (from equation 2), se_b is the standard error of the b path (from equation 3), a is the unstandardized regression coefficient for the a path (from equation 2), and b is the unstandardized regression coefficient from the b path (from the third equation. Note that mathematically, $ab = c - c'$.) If $z > 1.96$, there is a significant ($p < .05$) mediated effect. However, studies by MacKinnon indicate that this is a conservative test (MacKinnon & Lockwood, under review), and so, given this and the low power to detect mediation, interpretation of marginally significant effects probably is warranted (Baron & Kenny, 1986).

Note: The formula for the denominator given here (which is the standard error of the ab path) is that originally given by Sobel (1982). The formula for the standard error given by Baron and Kenny (1986) adds the term $(se_a^2 se_b^2)$ in the denominator, but other versions of the formula subtract this term (MacKinnon, Warsi, & Dwyer, 1995). In any case, this term usually is trivially small.

NOTES

Preparation of this chapter was supported by grants from the National Institute of Mental Health (MH 49869), the National Institute of Child Health and Human Development (HD 30572), and the Alabama Agricultural Experiment Station (10–004). We are grateful to David P. MacKinnon for his guidance regarding statistical

164 Family and Peers

issues in mediational analyses. Special thanks to Robert Laird for his helpful comments on an earlier draft. Correspondence should be sent to Jacquelyn Mize at the Department of Human Development and Family Studies, Auburn University, AL 36849; mizejac@mail.auburn.edu

1. It is possible, though, probably rare in most research (MacKinnon & Krull, 1997), to have a mediated relationship in the absence of a significant correlation between the IV and the DV if the ab path (mediated path) is opposite in sign to the c path (direct effects path; Kenny, Kashy, & Bolger, 1998). Such instances are referred to as inconsistent or suppressor models (Davis, 1985; MacKinnon, 1994). A discussion and examples of suppressor systems can be found in Davis (1985).

REFERENCES

Baldwin, A. L. (1949). The effect of home environment on nursery school behavior. *Child Development, 20*, 49–62.

Bandura, A. (1986). *Social foundations of thought and action: A social cognitive theory.* Englewood Cliffs, NJ: Prentice-Hall.

Baron, R. M., & Kenny, D. A. (1986). The moderator-mediator variable distinction in social psychological research: Conceptual, strategic, and statistical considerations. *Journal of Personality and Social Psychology, 51*, 1173–1182.

Bates, J. E., Pettit, G. S., Dodge, K. A., & Ridge, B. (in press). The interaction of temperamental resistance to control and restrictive parental discipline in the development of externalizing problems. *Developmental Psychology.*

Belsky, J., Spritz, B., & Crnic, K. (1996). Infant attachment security and affective-cognitive information processing at age 3. *Psychological Science, 7*, 111–114.

Bretherton, I. (1985). Attachment theory: Retrospect and prospect. In Bretherton, I., & Waters, E. (Eds.), Growing points of attachment theory and research (pp. 3–35). *Monographs of the Society for Research in Child Development, 50* (1–2, Serial No. 209).

Bugental, D. B., & Goodnow, J. J. (1998). Socialization processes. In Damon, W. (Series Ed.), Eisenberg, N. (Vol. Ed.), *Handbook of child psychology, Vol. 4. Social, emotional, and personality development* (pp. 389–462). New York: Wiley.

Cassidy, J., Kirsh, S. J., Scolton, K. L., & Parke, R. D. (1996). Attachment and representations of peer relationships. *Developmental Psychology, 32*, 892–904.

Cassidy, J., Parke, R. D., Butkovsky, L., & Braungart, J. M. (1992). Family–peer connections: The roles of emotional expressiveness within the family and children's understanding of emotions. *Child Development, 63*, 603–618.

Cicchetti, D., & Rogosch, F. A. (1996). Equifinality and multifinality in developmental psychopathology. *Development and Psychopathology, 8*, 597–600.

Coie, J. D., & Dodge, K. A. (1998). Aggression and antisocial behavior. In Damon, W. (Series Ed.), Eisenberg, N. (Vol. Ed.), *Handbook of child psychology, Vol. 4. Social, emotional, and personality development* (pp. 779–862). New York: Wiley.

Darling, N., & Steinberg, L. (1993). Parenting style as context: An integrative model. *Psychological Bulletin, 113*, 489–496.

Davies, P. T., & Cummings, E. M. (1998). Exploring children's emotional security as a mediator of the link between marital relations and child adjustment. *Child Development, 69*, 124–139.

Davis, J. A. (1985). *The logic of causal order*. Newbury Park, CA: Sage.

Dawson, G., Hessl, D., & Frey, K. (1994). Social influences on early developing biological and behavioral systems related to risk for affective disorder. *Development and Psychopathology, 6,* 759–779.

Deater-Deckard, K., & Dodge, K. A. (1997). Externalizing behavior problems and discipline revisited: Nonlinear effects and variation by culture, context, and gender. *Psychological Inquiry, 8,* 161–175.

Deater-Deckard, K., Dodge, K. A., Bates, J. E., & Pettit, G. S. (1996). Discipline among African-American and European-American mothers: Links to children's externalizing behaviors. *Developmental Psychology, 32,* 1065–1072.

Deater-Deckard, K., Dodge, K. A., Bates, J. E., & Pettit, G. S. (in press). Multiple risk factors in the development of externalizing behavior problems: Group and individual differences. *Development and Psychopathology.*

Dodge, K. A., Bates, J. E., & Pettit, G. S. (1990). Mechanisms in the cycle of violence, *Science, 250,* 1678–1683.

Dodge, K. A., Lochman, J. E., Harnish, J. D., Bates, J. E., & Pettit, G. S. (1997). Reactive and proactive aggression in school children and psychiatrically impaired chronically assaultive youth. *Journal of Abnormal Psychology, 106,* 37–51.

Dodge, K. A., Pettit, G. S., Bates, J. E., & Valente, E. (1995). Social information processing patterns partially mediate the effect of early physical abuse on later conduct problems. *Journal of Abnormal Psychology, 104,* 632–643.

Dodge, K. A., Pettit, G. S., McClaskey, C. L., & Brown, M. (1986). Social competence in children. *Monographs of the Society for Research in Child Development, 51* (1, Serial No. 213).

Dodge, K. A., & Somberg, D. R. (1987). Hostile attributional biases among aggressive boys are exacerbated under conditions of threat to the self. *Child Development, 58,* 213–224.

Dorsch, A., & Keane, S. P. (1994). Contextual factors in children's social information processing. *Developmental Psychology, 30,* 611–616.

Downey, G., & Walker, E. (1989). Social cognition and adjustment in children at risk for psychopathology. *Developmental Psychology, 25,* 835–845.

Dunn, J. (1996). The Emanuel Miller Memorial Lecture 1995: Children's relationships: Bridging the divide between cognitive and social development. *Journal of Child Psychology and Psychiatry, 37,* 507–518.

Eisenberg, N., & Fabes, R. A. (1998). Prosocial development. In Damon, W. (Series Ed.), Eisenberg N. (Vol. Ed.), *Handbook of child psychology, Vol. 4. Social, emotional, and personality development* (pp. 701–778). New York: Wiley.

Feldman, S. S., & Weinberger, D. A. (1994). Self-restraint as a mediator of family influences on boys' delinquent behavior: A longitudinal study. *Child Development, 65,* 195–211.

Garner, D. C., & Miner, J. L. (1994). Social competence among low-income preschoolers: Emotion socialization practices and social cognitive correlates. *Child Development, 65,* 622–637.

Garner, P. W., Jones, D. C., & Miner, J. L. (1994). Social competence among low-income preschoolers: Emotion socialization practices and social cognitive correlates. *Child Development, 65,* 622–637.

Gottman, J. M., Katz, L. F., & Hooven, C. (1996). Parental meta-emotion philosophy and the emotional life of families: Theoretical models and preliminary data. *Journal of Family Psychology, 10,* 243–268.

Graham, S., & Hudley, C. (1994). Attributions of aggressive and nonaggressive African-American male early adolescents: A study of construct accessibility. *Developmental Psychology, 28,* 731–740.

Greenwald, A. G., Pratkanis, A. R., Leippe, M. R., & Baumgardner, M. H. (1986). Under what conditions does theory obstruct research progress? *Psychological Review, 93,* 216–229.

Grolnick, W. S., & Slowiaczek, M. L. (1994). Parents involvement in children's schooling: A multidimensional conceptualization and motivational model. *Child Development, 65,* 237–252.

Grusec, J. E., & Goodnow, J. J. (1994). Impact of parental discipline methods on the child's internalization of values: A reconceptualization of current points of view. *Developmental Psychology, 30,* 4–19.

Hansen, W. B., & McNeal, R. B. (1996). The law of maximum expected potential effect: Constraints placed on program effectiveness by mediator relationships. *Health Education Research, 11,* 501–507.

Hart, C. H., DeWolf, D. M., & Burts, D. C. (1992). Linkages among preschoolers' playground behavior, outcome expectations, and parental disciplinary strategies. *Early Education and Development, 3,* 265–283.

Hart, C. H., Ladd, G. W., & Burleson, B. R. (1990). Children's expectations of the outcomes of social strategies: Relations with sociometric status and maternal disciplinary styles. *Child Development, 61,* 127–137.

Higgins, E. T., & Bargh, J. A. (1987). Social cognition and social perception. *Annual Review of Psychology, 38,* 369–425.

Hoffman, M. L. (1986). Affect, cognition, and motivation. In Sorrentino, R. M., & Higgins, E. T. (Eds.), *Handbook of motivation and cognition: Foundations of social behavior* (pp. 244–280). New York: Guilford Press.

Hoffman, M. L. (1994). Discipline and internalization. *Developmental Psychology, 30,* 26–28.

Howes, C. (1988). Peer interaction of young children. *Monographs of the Society for Research in Child Development, 53* (217).

Howes, C. (in press). Attachment relationships in the context of multiple caregivers. In Cassidy, J., & Shaver, P. R. (Eds.), *Handbook of attachment theory and research.* New York: Guilford.

Judd, C. M., & Kenny, D. A. (1981). Process analysis: Estimating mediation in treatment evaluations. *Evaluation Review, 5,* 602–619.

Kenny, D. A., Kashy, D. A., & Bolger, N. (1998). Data analysis in social psychology. In Gilbert, D. T., Fiske, S. T., & Lindzey G. (Eds.), *The handbook of social psychology* (Vol. 1, pp. 233–265). Boston: McGraw-Hill.

Kochanska, G. (1993). Toward a synthesis of parental socialization and child temperament in the early development of conscience. *Child Development, 64,* 325–347.

Krevens, J., & Gibbs, J. C. (1996). Parents' use of inductive discipline: Relations to children's empathy and prosocial behavior. *Child Development, 67,* 3263–3277.

Lindsey, E. W., Mize, J., & Pettit, G. S. (1997). Mutuality in parent-child play: Consequences for children's peer competence. *Journal of Social and Personal Relationships, 1,* 523–538.

MacKinnon, D. P. (1994). Analysis of mediating variables in prevention and intervention research. In Beatty, L. A., & Cezares, A. (Eds.), *Scientific methods in prevention research* (National Institute on Drug Abuse, Monograph #139, DHHS Publication No. 94–3631, pp. 127–153). Washington, DC: U.S. Government Printing Office.

MacKinnon, D. P., & Krull, J. L. (1997, August). *Inconsistent mediation models.* Paper presented at the Annual Convention of the American Psychological Association, New York, NY.

MacKinnon, D. P., & Lockwood, C. M. (manuscript under review). *Distribution of the products tests for the medicated effect Power and Type 1 error rates.*

MacKinnon, D. P., Warsi, G., & Dwyer, J. H. (1995). A simulation study of mediated effect measures. *Multivariate Behavioral Research, 30,* 41–62.

Mize, J., & Ladd, G. W. (1988). Predicting preschoolers' peer behavior and status from their interpersonal strategies: A comparison of verbal and enactive responses to hypothetical social dilemmas, *Developmental Psychology, 24,* 782–788.

Mize, J., & Ladd, G. W. (1990). A cognitive-social learning approach to social skill training with low-status preschool children. *Developmental Psychology, 26,* 388–397.

Mize, J., & Pettit, G. (1997). Mothers' social coaching, mother-child relationship style, and children's peer competence: Is the medium the message? *Child Development, 68,* 291–311.

Patterson, G. R. (1997). Performance models for parenting: A social interactional perspective. In Grusec, J. E., & Kuczynski, L. (Eds.), *Parenting and children's internalization of values* (pp. 193–226). New York: Wiley.

Peiser, N. C., & Heaven, P. C. L. (1996). Family influences on self-reported delinquency among high school students. *Journal of Adolescence, 19,* 557–568.

Perry, B. D., Polard, R. A., Blakely, T. L., Baker, W. L., & Vigilante, D. (1995). Childhood trauma, the neurobiology of adaptation, and "use-dependent" development of the brain: How "states" become "traits." *Infant Mental Health Journal, 16,* 271–289.

Pettit, G. S. (1997). The developmental course of violence and aggression: Mechanisms of family and peer influence. *Psychiatric Clinics of North America, 20,* 283–299.

Pettit, G. S., Brown, E. G., Mize, J., & Lindsey, E. (1998). Mothers' and fathers' socializing behaviors in three contexts: Links with children's peer competence. *Merrill-Palmer Quarterly, 44,* 173–193.

Pettit, G. S., Dodge, K. A., & Brown, M. (1988). Early family experience, social problem solving patterns, and children's social competence. *Child Development, 59,* 107–120.

Pettit, G. S., Harrist, A. W., Bates, J. E., & Dodge, K. A. (1991). Family interaction, social cognition and children's subsequent relations with peers at kindergarten. *Journal of Social and Personal Relationships, 8,* 383–402.

Pettit, G. S., & Mize, J. (1993). Substance and style: Understanding the roles that parents play in teaching children about social relationships. In Duck, S. (Ed.), *Understanding relationship processes. Vol. 2: Learning about relationships* (pp. 118–151). Newbury Park, CA: Sage.

Pettit, G. S., Polaha, J. A., & Mize, J. (in press). Perceptual and attributional processes in aggression and conduct problems. In Hill, J., & Maughan, B. (Eds.),

Conduct disorders in childhood. Cambridge, UK: Cambridge University Press.

Porges, S. W., Doussard-Roosevelt, J. A., & Maiti, A. K. (1994). Vagal tone and the physiological regulation of emotion. In Fox, N. A. (Ed.), The development of emotion regulation: Biological and behavioral considerations. *Monographs of the Society for Research in Child Development, 59* (Serial No. 240), 167–186.

Repetti, R. L. (1996). The effects of perceived daily social and academic failure on school-age children's subsequent interactions with parents. *Child Development, 67,* 1467–1482.

Rogosch, F. A., Cicchetti, D., & Aber, J. L. (1995). The role of child maltreatment in early deviations in cognitive and affective processing abilities and later peer relationship problems. Special Issue: Developmental processes in peer relations and psychopathology. *Development and Psychopathology, 7,* 591–609.

Rothbart, M., & Bates, J. E. (1998). Temperament. In Damon, W. (Series Ed.), Eisenberg, N. (Vol. Ed.), *Handbook of child psychology, Vol. 4. Social, emotional, and personality development* (pp. 105–176). New York: Wiley.

Rowe, D. C., Vazsonyi, A. T., & Flannery, D. J. (1994). No more than skin deep: Ethnic and racial similarity in developmental process. *Psychological Review, 101,* 396–413.

Russell, A., Pettit, G. S., & Mize, J. (in press). Horizontal qualities in parent-child relationships: Parallels with and possible consequences for children's peer relationships. *Developmental Review.*

Sameroff, A. J., Seifer, R., Baldwin, A., & Baldwin, C. (1993). Stability of intelligence from preschool to adolescence: The influence of social and family risk factors. *Child Development, 64,* 80–97.

Shields, A. M., Cicchetti, D., & Ryan, R. M. (1994). The development of emotional and behavioral self-regulation and social competence among maltreated school-age children. *Development and Psychopathology, 6,* 57–75.

Sobel, M. E. (1982). Asymptotic confidence intervals for indirect effects in structural equation models. In Leinhart, S. (Ed.), *Sociological methodology* (pp. 290–312). San Francisco: Jossey-Bass.

Tabachick, B. G. & Fidell, L. S. (1996). *Using multivariate statistics* (3rd ed.). New York: HarperCollins.

Thompson, R. A. (1998). Early sociopersonality development. In Damon, W. (Series Ed.), Eisenberg, N. (Vol. Ed.), *Handbook of child psychology, Vol. 4. Social, emotional, and personality development* (pp. 25–104). New York: Wiley.

Trachtenberg, S., & Viken, R. J. (1994). Aggressive boys in the classroom: Biased attributions or shared perceptions? *Child Development, 65,* 829–835.

Wahler, R. G. (1996). Chaos and order in the parenting of aggressive children: Personal narratives as guidelines. In Ferris, C. F., & Girsso, T. (Eds.), *Understanding aggressive behavior of children: Annals of the New York Academy of Sciences* (Vol. 794, pp. 153–167). New York: Academy of Sciences.

Wahler, R. G., & Meginnis, K. L. (1997). Strengthening child compliance through positive parenting practices: What works? *Journal of Clinical Child Psychology, 26,* 433–440.

Weiss, B., Dodge, K. A., Bates, J. E., & Pettit, G. S. (1992). Some consequences of early physical harm: Child aggression and a maladaptive social information processing style. *Child Development, 63,* 1321–1335.

Zahn-Waxler, C., Radke-Yarrow, M., & King, R. A. (1979). Child rearing and children's prosocial initiations toward victims in distress. *Child Development, 50,* 319–330.

7

Parental Management of Adolescent Peer Relationships: What Are Its Effects on Friend Selection?

Nina S. Mounts

Since the 1980s there has been growing interest in understanding the effects of parenting on peer relationships. Despite this interest, there are some aspects of these linkages that have not received much research attention. In particular, researchers have devoted little attention to the ways in which parents directly and consciously affect peer relationships during adolescence. This chapter explores the effects of direct parental management of peer relationships on friend selection during adolescence. In particular, I examine whether particular parenting practices increase the likelihood that adolescents will select friends who have high levels of academic achievement and low levels of delinquency, using a short-term longitudinal design.

CONCEPTUALIZING LINKAGES BETWEEN PARENTAL AND PEER CONTEXTS

Indirect Parenting Influences on Peer Relationships

Parke and Bhavnagri (1989) proposed that researchers think of parents as affecting children's peer relationships through direct or indirect means. Indirect influences are those things that are done by parents that are not explicitly intended to affect peer relationships, yet do so. Parenting style (Putallaz & Heflin, 1990) and attachment (Cohn, Patterson, & Christopoulos, 1991) are examples of indirect influences on peer relationships. Much of the literature that explores how parent and peer contexts are linked during adolescence focuses on indirect modes of influence (Brown & Huang, 1995;

Brown, Mounts, Lamborn, & Steinberg, 1993; Fuligni & Eccles, 1993; Kandel & Andrews, 1987; Mounts & Steinberg, 1995).

Direct Parenting Influences on Peer Relationships

Direct influences are those things that parents do that are specifically intended to affect peer relationships. Although only a few of these methods have been investigated empirically, parents use a number of strategies to directly influence their children's peer relationships (see Ladd, 1992, for a discussion of these methods). A number of studies have examined direct parental involvement in young children's peer relationships (see Ladd, Profilet, & Hart, 1992, for review). For example, Ladd and Golter (1988) reported that young children whose parents arranged peer contacts for them had larger social networks than those whose parents did not. Hart and his colleagues (in press) explored several direct strategies that parents from China, Russia, and the United States use to affect preschoolers' peer competence. Medrich, Roizen, Rubin, and Buckley (1982) found that when parents choose to live in neighborhoods with sidewalks and playgrounds, children have more opportunities to interact with peers.

Despite the progress in understanding direct linkages between parent and peer relationships for young children, a paucity of research exists on parents' direct involvement in adolescents' peer relationships. Parke and Ladd's (1992) informative book on parents–peer linkages devotes an entire section to direct parental influences on peer relationships, yet there are very few references describing how the parents of adolescents manage peer relationships. This is most likely attributable to the fact that there is no clear body of literature that examines this issue. An exception is work by Vernberg, Beery, Ewell, and Abwender (1993) that explored parental friendship facilitation strategies with early adolescents who had recently moved to new communities. They found that when parents used friendship-facilitation strategies, adolescents reported greater intimacy and companionship in their new friendships. That researchers have left these direct linkages, for the most part, unexplored might indicate that many still view parental and peer contexts as operating in isolation from and in opposition to one another during adolescence. This notion, introduced by Coleman (1961) and espoused by psychoanalysts as well (Blos, 1979; Freud, 1958), persists despite a number of researchers' findings to the contrary (Brown & Huang, 1995; Brown et al., 1993; Fuligni & Eccles, 1993; Kandel & Andrews, 1987; Mounts & Steinberg, 1995; Patterson & Dishion, 1985).

Developmental Issues in Understanding Direct Parental Influence of Peer Relationships

At first thought, it may seem that direct parent influences become minimal as children get older. However, it is more likely that direct influences change in form as children age (Parke & Bhavnagri, 1989). During adolescence, parents often report concerns about their children's choice of friends, worry about the effects of negative peer pressure on their adolescents, and worry about children's involvement in deviant activities (Gecas & Seff, 1990; Olson et al., 1983; Pasley & Gecas, 1984; Small, Eastman, & Cornelius, 1988; Steinberg, 1990). Because of these concerns, many parents may be motivated to be directly involved in their adolescent's peer relationships. Susceptibility to peer influence peaks at about age 14 (Berndt, 1979) and there also is a decline in susceptibility to parental influence during this time period (Steinberg & Silverberg, 1986). Peer influence has also been identified in the literature as a strong predictor of adolescent substance use (Glynn, 1981; Hawkins, Catalano, & Miller, 1992; Kandel & Andrews, 1987; Kandel, Kessler, & Margulies, 1978; Newcomb & Bentler, 1989; Patterson & Dishion, 1985), premarital sexual activity (Billy & Udry, 1985a; 1985b), and delinquency (Magnusson, Stattin, & Allen, 1986). There is also evidence in the literature that academic achievement may be affected by peer relationships (Epstein, 1983; Ide, Parkerson, Haertel, & Walberg, 1981; Mounts & Steinberg, 1995). Therefore, there are good reasons for direct parental management of peer relationships during adolescence.

One important developmental issue in considering direct parental influence on adolescents' peer relationships is susceptibility to peer influence. The development of autonomy, especially autonomy from parents, is an issue that becomes increasingly important during adolescence (Steinberg & Silverberg, 1986). This move toward autonomy from parents is often obvious when adolescents turn for advice to peers or other adults, rather than to their parents. In conjunction with this increasing need for autonomy from parents, adolescents are often more oriented toward the peer group during this period (Brown, Clasen, & Eicher, 1986). Increasing reliance on the peer group during this push toward autonomy may create a bridge for adolescents between being reliant on parents and engaging in truly autonomous behavior (Steinberg & Silverberg, 1986). Because of this growing need for autonomy, during early and middle adolescence there is an increase in adolescents' susceptibility to peer influence, particularly in the area of antisocial peer influence (Berndt, 1979; Brown, 1990; Steinberg & Silverberg, 1986). Adolescents who report that they are more susceptible to peer pressure report higher levels of involvement in antisocial activities (Steinberg & Silverberg, 1986). Because of the relation between susceptibility to peer pressure and involvement in antisocial activities, it has been hypothesized that direct parental management might have greater effects on peer selection for adolescents depending on their levels of susceptibility to peer influence. The exact nature of this relation was difficult to specify at the outset of the investigation. Adolescents with high levels of susceptibility to peer pressure might be least influenced by parental management because of their orientation toward the peer group, or alternatively, the susceptibility may be indicative of a more general orientation to be influenced by other people, parent or peers. If this is the case, adolescents with high levels of susceptibility to peer pressure would be most likely to be influenced by parental management techniques.

Another important developmental issue in examining direct parental influences on adolescents' peer relations is the extent to which adolescents believe that parental involvement in their peer relationships is appropriate. Again, because issues of autonomy from parents become important during adolescence (Steinberg, 1990), parental involvement in adolescent peer relationships may be more challenging than parental involvement in the peer relationships of younger children. Indeed, Smetana and Asquith's (1994) work demonstrates that adolescents believe that friendship selection is a personal choice over which their parents should have little authority. Parents, on the other hand, believe that they have legitimate authority over friendships because the effects of adolescent friendships may carry over into other domains of the adolescent's life, such as moral domains.

Because adolescents and their parents have different conceptions concerning authority over the friendship domain, I hypothesized that parents who are successful in their efforts to manage their adolescent's peer relationships would not be overly intrusive in their peer-relationship management practices. Too much parental intrusiveness might cause resentment, causing the adolescent to react by doing exactly what the parent has requested he or she avoid or not having the intended effect. On the other hand, parents who make few management attempts are missing an important opportunity to affect their child's peer relationships, which may increase susceptibility to peer pressure (Steinberg, 1990).

What Do We Know About Direct Influences on Peer Relationships During Adolescence?

There are many ways in which parents could attempt to directly influence peer interactions. Because little research has been conducted in this area, my initial work examined the range of strategies that parents use in an effort to affect adolescents' peer relationships. In the first investigation, I asked parents to disclose the strategies they use to affect their children's peer relationships. Because there is a relatively small research literature on this issue, I went directly to parents with no preexisting responses in mind that might limit their responses. One hundred and three mothers of ninth graders (54 percent male; 46 percent female) were asked to respond to two open-ended questions to assess direct parental management practices. The first question was: "If you try to prevent your child from being influenced by peers, what do you do?" After collecting responses from all of the mothers, responses were grouped into 9 categories. These categories are displayed in Figure 7.1. No significant differences based on adolescent gender were found for responses to either of the two questions. As can be seen in Figure 7.1, 37

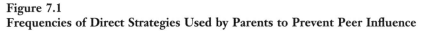

Figure 7.1
Frequencies of Direct Strategies Used by Parents to Prevent Peer Influence

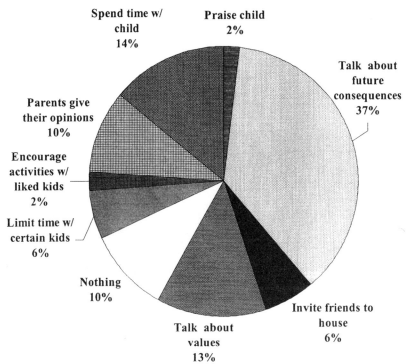

percent of the mothers reported that they try to keep their children from being influenced by peers by talking with them about the future consequences of their behavior. Other strategies included spending time with their child (14 percent), talking about values (13 percent), giving their opinions about the peers (10 percent), and doing nothing in particular (10 percent). Several other responses were reported by parents with less frequency, including having child invite "desirable" friends to the house (6 percent), limiting interaction with particular children who may negatively affect the adolescent (6 percent), encouraging activities with "desirable" peers (2 percent), and praising the child (2 percent).

The second question was, "What things do you do, if any, to influence your child's selection of friends?" Figure 7.2 displays the frequencies of the responses to this question. Similar to the first question, talking about future consequences was the most frequently occurring response (24 percent). However, the percentage was not as large as it was for the first question. Nineteen percent of the parents reported they did nothing to influence their children's selection of friends. These parents reported that they

Figure 7.2
Frequencies of Direct Strategies Used by Parents to Influence Friend Selection

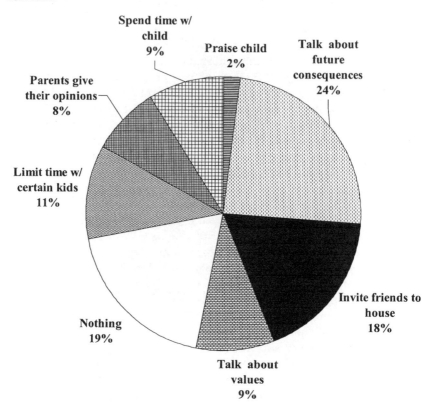

trusted their children to make good decisions about friends or that selecting friends was a personal decision with which parents should not interfere. Eighteen percent of the sample reported that they encouraged their children to invite adolescents that they liked to the house. Prohibiting contact or limiting contact with particular peers was reported by approximately 11 percent of the sample, whereas 8 percent gave their opinions of peers as a method to influence peer selection. Nine percent of the parents reported that they talked about values in an effort to affect peer selection, whereas 9 percent reported spending time with the child. The remaining 2 percent relied on praise to affect peer selection.

These results suggest that parents engage in a wide range of behaviors intended to affect their adolescents' peer relationships. Some of the strategies that parents use for managing peer relationships, such as prohibiting contact with particular friends, appear to be quite intrusive. On the other hand, some parents reported doing nothing at all. That some parents do nothing in the way of peer relationships is interesting. In the future, it would be interesting to examine whether parents adopt this strategy when children are doing well and have appropriate friends or whether there are other reasons for adopting this stance such as general childrearing philosophy. Furthermore, it is of interest to examine the effects of parent nonmanagement on friend selection and friend influence. Another interesting finding was that many parents reported that they talked about values or encouraged adolescents to think about future consequences as ways of influencing adolescents' peer relationships. These strategies are probably less obvious than simply giving adolescents prohibitions. One would expect that they are more effective because parents are encouraging adolescents to actually think for themselves rather than simply dictating rules. This open-ended, pilot investigation provided the groundwork for further examination of direct parental management of adolescents' peer relationships. Drawing from the initial study, I was interested in examining the role that three types of parental management (prohibiting, guiding, and monitoring) played in adolescents' peer relationships.

Prohibiting Peer Relationships. Previously Mounts (1998) examined the role of parental monitoring and parental prohibitions in peer influence. A curvilinear relation was found between parental prohibitions and peer influence on adolescent drug use. Adolescents who reported moderate levels of parental prohibitions of peer relationships were less influenced by peers to use drugs. Similarly, moderate levels of prohibiting were associated with the lowest levels of delinquency. In contrast, high levels of monitoring were associated with lower levels of peer influence to use drugs and toward delinquency. Because prohibitions concerning peers are more intrusive, or could be viewed as more of a threat to the adolescent's growing sense of autonomy than monitoring or other management practices, the curvilinear relation for the prohibiting variable was expected.

Guiding Peer Relationships. Drawing from the open-ended questions that were given to parents, a second type of direct parental influence, guiding, was of interest. Guiding included parental attempts to influence peer relationships, such as talking about future consequences of a particular friendship, talking about values, and giving opinions about peers. These were fairly common responses that parents gave to the initial open-ended questions. In comparison with prohibiting friendships, guiding should be viewed by adolescents as less intrusive. Therefore, I hypothesized a linear relation where high levels of guiding would be associated with selecting friends with high levels of academic achievement and low levels of deviance.

Monitoring Peer Relationships. To my knowledge, monitoring is the only direct influence technique that is consistently attributed to the parents of adolescents (Ladd, 1992). Previous research documents the importance of parental monitoring during adolescence (Patterson & Stouthamer-Loeber, 1984; Snyder, Dishion, & Patterson, 1986; Steinberg, Lamborn, Darling,

Mounts, & Dornbusch, 1994). Although not all parental monitoring is focused specifically on peer interactions, some clearly is. Some researchers might argue that monitoring is actually an indirect parent influence on peer relationships. However, parents also may monitor in an attempt to intervene in social relationships. For purposes of this investigation, monitoring is considered a direct parental influence.

There is strong support in the literature for the relation between parental monitoring and involvement with delinquent peers during adolescence. Patterson and Stouthamer-Loeber (1984) and Snyder et al. (1986) found a significant relation between low levels of parental monitoring and delinquent behavior. Similarly, Steinberg (1986) found that adolescents in self-care after school who were monitored distally by their parents, through telephone calls, were less susceptible to antisocial peer pressure than adolescents whose parents did not monitor. Other researchers have found similar relations between monitoring and involvement in deviant activities (Dornbusch et al., 1985; Mounts, 1998; Steinberg et al., 1994). Given that delinquent activities frequently occur in the presence of peers (Dishion, Patterson, Stoolmiller, & Skinner, 1991), monitoring can be an effective direct method of affecting adolescent peer relationships.

This chapter presents research that examined three aspects of direct parental management in peer relationships: monitoring, prohibiting, and guiding peer relationships. In considering the effects of direct parental management of adolescent peer relationships, parents may affect peer relationships by affecting whom an adolescent selects as a friend, or by affecting peer influence processes once friendships have formed. Previous research suggests that parents can affect peer influence processes using direct peer management techniques (Mounts, 1998). However, it is unknown whether direct parental management affects the process of friend selection. This chapter focuses on the effects of direct parent management in peer relationships on peer selection. Parents may manage because of concerns about adolescent's selection of friends, particularly concern that adolescents are involved with delinquent or deviant friends (Gecas & Seff, 1990; Olson et al., 1983; Pasley & Gecas, 1984; Small et al., 1988; Steinberg, 1990).

The focus of this investigation was on whether direct peer management practices (prohibiting, guiding, and monitoring) would be associated with selecting friends who are better adjusted (low levels of deviant behavior and high levels of academic achievement). I hypothesized that parents who used moderate levels (curvilinear relation) of prohibiting would have a more positive effect on the types of friends that adolescents select. Based on previous research, I hypothesized that the relation between parental monitoring and selection of antisocial friends would be negative, whereas the relation between parental monitoring and selection of well-adjusted peers would be positive. That is, the more parents monitor the more likely that adolescents would choose friends with low levels of deviance and high levels of academic achievement. A similar relation between guiding and peer selection was also hypothesized with higher levels of guiding being associated with selecting friends with lower levels of deviance and higher levels of academic achievement. Although most research that examines peer relationships focuses on antisocial activities, in the current investigation I was interested in examining the effects of parental management on selecting friends with negative as well as positive measures of adjustment. As such, two measures of negative adjustment were used: drug use and delinquency. Two measures of positive adjustment were used: grade point average (GPA) and attitudes toward school.

METHOD

Sample

The data from this study are from a 1-year longitudinal study of parent influences on the peer relationships of ninth graders. Three waves of questionnaire data (beginning of the school year, midyear, and the end of the school year) were collected from adolescents and their friends. Only the data from Time 1 and Time 3 were used in the current analyses. The sample size varied somewhat across the three waves of data collection. For Time 1 (the first wave) 249 adolescents completed the questionnaire and 202 completed the questionnaire at Time 3. Eighty-one percent of the adolescents completed questionnaires at Time 1 and Time 3. The data from friends were matched with target ninth graders' data and used in the analyses.

Approximately 40 percent of the sample was male and 60 percent was female. The family structure of the adolescents was as follows: intact (54.4 percent), single parent (18.2 percent), stepfamily (19.3 percent), and other (8.1 percent). The majority of the sample was White (85.4 percent) with African Americans (7.5 percent), Asians (2.8 percent), Hispanic (1.6 percent), Native American (1.2 percent), and other (1.5 percent). Father's education was used as a proxy for socioeconomic status and was represented by less than a high school education (18 percent), high school graduate (33.9 percent), trade school or some college (26.2 percent), college graduate (14.8 percent), and graduate degree (7.1 percent).

Measures

Parenting Practices

Monitoring was assessed using a five-item scale in which adolescents were asked to indicate on a scale ranging from 1 (*know a little*) to 3 (*know a lot*) (Dishion, 1990; Dornbusch et al., 1985). Items were phrased as: "How much do your parents really know?" concerning several different activities. Alpha for this scale at Time 1 was .82.

Parental management of peer relationships was assessed using items derived from a 28-item measure of parental management. These items were generated from the open-ended responses to pilot questions to parents that were described earlier in this chapter. A sample of 315 adolescents then completed the measure. Subsequently, items were grouped theoretically to describe different aspects of parental management of peer relationships and were refined using correlational and factor analyses. Alpha for prohibiting at Time 1 was .78. A sample item for the prohibiting measure was, "My parents tell me if they don't want me to hang around with certain kids." The alpha for guiding at Time 1 was .76. A sample item for the guiding measure was, "My parents tell me that who I have for friends will affect my future." The Time 1 correlations between guiding and monitoring was .12 ($p < .05$), guiding and prohibiting was .52 ($p < .001$), and prohibiting and monitoring was $-.11$.

Susceptibility to Peer Pressure

The susceptibility to peer pressure measure was used to examine whether parental involvement effects vary as a function of adolescents' actual susceptibility to peer pressure. Adolescents' susceptibility to antisocial peer pressure was assessed using Berndt's (1979) measure. Adolescents read hypothetical situations describing scenarios involving antisocial situations and were asked to indicate how likely they were to engage in various antisocial activities. Alpha for this scale at Time 1 was .79.

Friendship Nominations

Following Kandel (1978), subjects were asked to name their three best same-school friends at Time 1 and Time 3. This information was used to match subjects and their friends to obtain measures of friend adjustment at Time 1 and Time 3. Prior research using this methodology demonstrates that this is an effective way of documenting peer relationships and adolescents are compliant in completing this measure (Mounts & Steinberg, 1995).

Adolescent and Friend Adjustment

The focus of this investigation was on two types of adjustment: antisocial behavior and academic achievement. Antisocial behavior was assessed using two scales (drug use and delinquency), whereas two aspects of academic achievement (GPA and attitudes toward school) were assessed. Adjustment of friends was derived by first calculating individual friend's adjustment scores. Then, the adjustment scores of the friends were averaged. At least two friends had to complete adjustment measures in order for them to be included in the analyses. These scores were entered as the best friends' adjustment scores in all analyses.

On all antisocial behavior items, subjects and their friends were asked to report "How often in the last 3 months have you . . . ?" McCord (1990) suggested that although self-reports of antisocial behavior are subject to under- and overreporting, they appear to be a more valid method of assessing problem behaviors in adolescence than police records. Furthermore, they are more valid than observational methods since many antisocial behaviors are not readily observable. Drug use is a five-item scale that assesses students' use of alcohol, marijuana, and other drugs (Greenberger, Steinberg, & Vaux, 1981). Alphas for this scale at Time 1 and Time 3 were, respectively, .92 and .93. Delinquency is a nine-item scale that assesses the extent of adolescent involvement in deviant activities (Gold, 1970). Time 1 and Time 3 alphas for this scale were both .89.

GPA was assessed by asking adolescents to indicate the statement that best describes their school grades. Dornbusch, Ritter, Leiderman, Roberts, and Fraleigh (1987) reported a correlation of .76 between self-reported grades and actual GPA. Attitudes toward school were assessed using a six-item measure in which students indicate the value of education (Lamborn, Mounts, Steinberg, & Dornbusch, 1991). Alphas for the scale at Time 1 and Time 3 were, respectively, .61 and .59.

RESULTS

Plan of Analysis

The first set of analyses examines the effect of direct parental management of peer relationships on the selection of friends. I was interested in ascertaining whether parental involvement in peer relationships would be associated with the selection of better adjusted friends. Analyses were conducted using multiple regression analyses. All analyses were conducted separately for the four outcome variables. Because some of these processes may vary based on adolescent gender, it was included in all analyses. In these hierarchical regression analyses, the friends' level of adjustment was regressed on adolescent adjustment, susceptibility to peer pressure, and the parenting variables. Gender was entered first into the regression, followed by adolescents' Time 1 adjustment and susceptibility to peer pressure. The adolescents' Time 1 adjustment was entered in the equation to control for effects that would draw adolescents of similar adjustment levels together. By entering the adolescent's level of adjustment into the regression equation first, one can then assess the extent to which parents have an effect on friend selection over and above the effects of similarity in adjustment that often brings two people together. Similarly, susceptibility to peer pressure might work to bring particular peers together so this was included in the regression equation. The three parenting variables (guide, monitor, and prohibit) were entered in the next step. To examine whether there was a curvilinear relation between prohibit and the selection of friends, the prohibiting term was squared and then entered into the regression analyses (Jaccard, Turrisi, & Wan, 1990; Pedhazur, 1982). Finally, because the effects of parental management on peer relationships may vary according to the adolescent's susceptibility to peer pressure, the interactions between susceptibility to peer pressure and the parenting terms were entered.

Direct Parental Influence Effects on Peer Association at Time 1

Results of these analyses for all four of the adjustment variables are presented in Table 7.1. As can be seen in Table 7.1, the effects of monitoring on selection of friends are small as are the curvilinear effects of prohibiting. High levels of prohibitions are associated with selecting friends with high levels of drug use and delinquency, whereas high levels of prohibitions are associated with selecting friends with lower GPAs. Both of these findings suggest that parents, through the use of prohibiting peer contact, may be driving adolescents to select more deviant friends or, alternatively, parents are prohibiting contact with peers that they believe may have a negative influence on their children. Longitudinal analyses can be used to ascertain the nature of this relationship.

High levels of guiding were associated with selecting friends with lower levels of antisocial behavior, higher GPAs, and more positive attitudes toward school. There were very few significant interactions between susceptibility to peer pressure and the parenting variables. Those that were significant were only at the trend level. For that reason, further analyses to describe the nature of the interactions were not conducted. This suggests that the effects of parental management practices on friend selection do not vary according to the level of the adolescent's susceptibility to peer pressure.

Direct Parental Influence Effects and Longitudinal Patterns of Peer Selection

The second set of analyses examined the effects of direct parenting practices on long-term patterns of friendship selection. These analyses reveal whether parents are leading adolescents to select better adjusted friends because of their management practices or whether management behaviors are occurring largely in response to association with peers that parents believe are negative influences on their children. Such issues cannot be addressed using a cross-sectional design. Whether the relation between parenting and peer adjustment was significant for the first set of analyses, but not for the second, would indicate that parents may be using management in response to particular peer selections rather than the management practices actually having an effect on peer selection. A significant relation for both the first

Table 7.1
Parental Effects on Peer Selection at Time 1 Controlling for Adolescents' Adjustment at Time 1

Variables	Delinquency (Friend)		Drug Use (Friend)		GPA(Friend)		Attitudes(Friend)	
	B	Beta	B	Beta	B	Beta	B	Beta
Gender	-.24	-.26***	.13	.10	.02	.01	.27	.28
Susceptibility	.13	.21***	.18	.19**	-.45	-.24***	-.12	-.18**
Adjustment	.09	.12	.32	.40***	.01	.02	.12	.14*
Guide	-.18	-.20**	-.30	-.22***	.57	.20**	.22	.23***
Prohibit	.10	.14*	.16	.15*	-.26	-.12+	-.07	-.10
Monitor	-.03	-.03	-.03	-.02	.27	.10	.10	.11+
Prohibit squared	.02	.10	.01	.05	-.11	-.26	-.04	-.02
Guide * Susc	.11	.48	.08	.23	-.24	-.35	.14	.59+
Prohibit * Susc	.11	.06	.10	.35	-.14	-.27	-.13	-.67+
Monitor * Susc	.08	.30	.04	.09	-.51	-.60+	-.05	-.18
Total $\underline{R}^2$	.20		.34		.14		.22	

+$p < .10$; *$p < .05$; **$p < .01$; ***$p < .001$.

set of analyses as well as the second set would indicate that management practices are actually affecting the peer selection of adolescents. Likewise, a significant effect on only the second set of analyses would suggest that the management practices were having an effect on friend selection.

Hierarchical regression analyses were conducted using the same procedure described in the previous set of analyses except the dependent variable was peer adjustment at Time 3. Results are presented in Table 7.2. There were no significant relations between monitoring or prohibiting for any of the adjustment variables. Guiding had a significant negative relation with association with delinquency and drug use. When parents used high levels of guiding, adolescents were less likely to select friends at Time 3 who were engaging in antisocial activities. Moreover, when parents used high levels of guiding, adolescents were more likely to select friends with higher GPAs. There was only one significant interaction term in the analyses that was significant only at the trend level. For that reason, further analyses to examine the nature of the interaction were not conducted. Again, this would indicate that the effects of parenting practices on adolescents' friend selection do not vary according to susceptibility to peer pressure.

DISCUSSION

The results suggest that the role of direct parental management of peer relationships varies according to the friend adjustment variable of interest as well as the type of management that is used. Monitoring appears to play very little role in the selection of friends. This may be puzzling to many researchers, given the strong and consistent association between monitoring and involvement in antisocial activities (Mounts, 1998; Patterson & Stouthamer-Loeber, 1984; Snyder et al., 1986; Steinberg et al., 1994). However, this investigation only focuses on the relation between monitoring and peer selection. Indeed, in a previous investigation (Mounts, 1998), I reported a strong negative relation between monitoring and antisocial peer influence. This effect occurred even when controlling for the adjustment level of the best friends. This would suggest that even in the presence of peers whom parents believe to be a positive influence, if adolescents are not monitored they may become involved in antisocial behavior. This study, in conjunction with the findings of the previous investigation, demonstrates that monitoring probably plays little role in peer selection but plays a stronger role in peer influence processes.

Parental prohibitions were associated with peer selection at Time 1 but not at Time 3. These results suggest that prohibiting probably occurred in response to adolescents' association with antisocial behavior or antisocial friends. It does not appear that parental prohibiting plays a significant role in determining the types of people that adolescents select as friends. This demonstrates a different type of linkage between parenting and peer rela-

Table 7.2
Parental Effects on Peer Selection at Time 3 Controlling for Adolescents' Adjustment at Time 1

Variables	Delinquency (Friend)		Drug Use (Friend)		GPA(Friend)		Attitudes(Friend)	
	B	Beta	B	Beta	B	Beta	B	Beta
Gender	-.20	-.23***	-.06	-.04	.06	.04	.17	.21***
Susceptibility	.03	-.01	-.08	-.08	-.11	-.11	-.05	-.10
Adjustment	.22	.31***	.50	.62***	.05	.13+	.11	.16*
Guide	-.17	-.19*	-.20	-.14*	.22	.14+	.05	.07
Prohibit	-.02	-.02	-.06	-.05	.34	.29	-.01	-.02
Monitor	.01	.01	-.06	-.05	.14	.10	-.07	-.10
Prohibit squared	-.07	-.05	-.03	-.13	-.09	-.37	.03	.25
Guide*Susc	.14	.63	.17	.47	.13	.34	-.05	-.27
Prohibit*Susc	-.05	-.31	.02	.08	-.06	-.19	-.06	-.40
Monitor*Susc	-.11	-.42	-.18	-.42	-.28	-.61+	-.04	-.16
Total R^2	.19		.36		.08		.12	

$^+p < .10$; $^*p < .05$; $^{**}p < .01$; $^{***}p < .001$.

tionships. In this case, however, the directionality probably stems from prior antisocial behavior by the adolescent or involvement with antisocial peers. Once parents become aware of the situation they then react by prohibiting involvement with the undesirable peers. The cross-sectional analyses presented here are suggestive of this relation. However, the longitudinal analyses demonstrated that prohibiting does not have the desired effect on adolescents because there is no relation between it and future peer selections. It appears that prohibiting is not a very effective means of managing the peer relationships of adolescents and parents should be aware of its limitations.

Finally, in contrast to the other two types of direct parental management, guiding of peer relationships had an effect on the selection of friends. Adolescents whose parents used high levels of guiding selected friends who had low levels of antisocial behavior and high levels of academic achievement. Even controlling for prior levels of adjustment (which would rule out peer selection that could be explained by adolescents being drawn to peers who are similar to themselves in adjustment levels) guiding still emerged as a significant predictor of friend adjustment. Moreover, this effect occured over a period of 9 months, indicating that parents are not guiding simply in response to particular behaviors on the part of their children but are having an affect on their children's selection of friends.

The interaction analyses were, for the most part, not significant. These results suggest that susceptibility to antisocial peer pressure does not moderate the relation between the parental management variables and selection of friends. That is, the parenting variables have the same effect on friend selection, regardless of adolescents' levels of susceptibility to antisocial peer pressure. Instead, susceptibility to peer pressure was strongly related to friend adjustment at Time 1 but not at Time 3. This suggests that adolescents who are susceptible to peer pressure are most likely to select peers who are engaged in antisocial behavior and who have lower levels of academic achievement.

In summary, these results demonstrate quite clearly the need to examine the processes underlying linkages between parent and peer relationships. The mechanisms explaining the relation between these three parenting variables and peer selection are all very different from one another. Additionally, the current investigation points to the need for more studies that examine direct parental influences on peer relationships during adolescence in general. Aside from the research on monitoring, there is little research that examines how parents attempt to directly affect the peer relationships of adolescents. The current investigation demonstrates quite clearly how different aspects of management may differentially affect peer relationships. Research of this nature has important practical implications as well. Parents often voice concern over peer relationships during adolescence and seek information on managing these relationships. Patterson's (1986) work suggests that parents who learn more effective child management techniques can affect adolescents' peer relationships using these indirect and direct methods. Information derived from the research on direct parental management of peer relationships might also be used in similar way to create intervention programs for the families of adolescents.

There are several limitations of the current investigation. First, all of the adolescents in the sample were ninth graders. This limits the generalizability of the findings to other age groups. One would expect that as children proceed through adolescence, more intrusive types of management would be less acceptable to them. One would expect that the amount of management should decline over the period of adolescence. Future investigations should examine direct parental management practices and the processes by which they affect peer relationships from middle childhood through adolescence. In particular, researchers should focus on adolescents' growing need for autonomy and how this affects processes related to parental management of peers.

A second limitation with the investigation is that the sample was primarily comprised of white adolescents from lower middle- and middle-class backgrounds. It is not clear how well these direct parental management techniques apply to adolescents in other ethnic or socioeconomic status groups, although some researchers are beginning to address this issue (Brown, Hamm, & Myerson, 1996; Hart et al., in press). Hart et al.'s work with preschoolers from China, Russia, and the United States demonstrates similarities as well as differences in the ways in which parents attempt to directly affect the peer relationships of preschoolers. Such work is indicative of the need for studying parental management of adolescents' peer relationships within different ethnic or cultural contexts. Wilson (1997) reported that parents of African-American adolescents in inner cities traveled out of their neighborhood to church in order for their children to meet friends who they believed would have a positive influence on their children. These studies at least suggest some of the ways that parents actively engage in management within other ethnic and socioeconomic contexts.

A second area of interest within different ethnic or cultural contexts would be adolescents' responses to parental management. For example, Chao's (1994) work suggests that in Chinese families, Confucian tradition requires respect from subordinate members of the family (children) toward the senior members (parents) of the family. One would expect that direct parental management of peer relationships within this context would operate in a different fashion from that of White, middle-class adolescents where respect for elders is less strongly enforced. That is, in Chinese families, adolescents would probably view direct parental involvement as falling well within the realm of parental authority and, therefore, it would be less likely that adolescents would have difficulty with this parenting practice. Further research is necessary to examine the nature of parental management of peer relationships in other contexts and its effects on peer selection and peer influence.

Finally, in creating a sample where friends report on their own behavior, a substantial portion of the sample is often lost because data from the friends are not available. Because of these criteria, the adolescents in the final sample are probably better adjusted and more conforming than their peers. Because friends are reporting on their own behavior, rather than having adolescents report on their friend's behavior, we believe this is a more valid means of assessing peer relationships. Future investigations might ask adolescents to recruit their friends into the study in an effort to get a more complete set of adolescent-friend dyads (Buhrmester & Yin, 1997).

Future Directions

Given the relative infancy of this area of research, a number of issues need to be examined in future investigations.

Creating a Framework for Conceptualizing Direct Parental Influences

Using Ladd's (1992) work as a base, researchers might explore whether his framework can be used to guide research on parental management of adolescents' peer relationships. Ladd suggested that parents of young children play four roles in directly managing their children's peer relationships. Parents of adolescents might also play these roles in directly managing peer relationships.

As *designers* of the social environment of young children, parents may choose particular neighborhoods in which to live with an eye on prospective play partners for their children (Ladd, 1992). Parents of adolescents in all likelihood maintain this role even though the environment for adolescents is much wider ranging, and harder to control, than it is for younger children. Parents may buy houses in certain neighborhoods to ensure that their adolescents attend the best public high schools, enroll their children in private schools with the goal of exposing them to other adolescents who have high academic aspirations, or travel to other neighborhood churches to expose their children to peers who might have a positive influence on them (Wilson, 1997). Much research is needed to examine whether parents are engaging in these practices because they are consciously trying to define the parameters around which their adolescents' potential friendships will be based, and whether this practice does have an effect on the types of friends that adolescents select.

As *mediators* of peer relationships, parents of young children arrange peer contacts and regulate their children's choice of peer partners (Ladd, 1992). Although the parents of adolescents do not typically arrange peer contacts for their children, they may attempt to regulate children's choice of peer partners. This may arise in response to concerns about negative peer influence or because parents want adolescents to meet peers who will have a positive influence on them. For example, parents might believe that membership in a church or synagogue youth group will expose their children to adolescents who will protect them from negative influence. The prohibiting and directing constructs used in the current investigation explore parents' roles as mediators.

Parents function as *supervisors* by monitoring peer interactions. Parents of adolescents may monitor peer interactions, although in a less proximal or intrusive fashion than for younger children. As suggested earlier, there is a considerable amount of research that documents the effects of parental monitoring during adolescence (Mounts, 1998; Patterson & Stouthamer-Loeber, 1984; Steinberg et al., 1994). Some of the effects of monitoring might accrue because monitoring limits opportunities to be influenced by peers who are engaging in deviant activities.

As children grow older the parent may function as a *consultant* on peer interactions (Ladd, 1992). In this capacity they might assist children with problem solving in peer relationships when they are having some type of difficulty, or they might help adolescents think through a variety of issues related to peer relationships. As peer relationships become more complex and more important during adolescence, this role may also increase in importance. Furthermore, as adolescents acquire new cognitive skills, parents may be better able to support peer relationships through a consultant role. Because adolescents have a greater capacity to consider the workings of social relationships, researchers might explore whether parents of adolescents function as a consultant more frequently than do parents of younger children. To summarize, Ladd's (1992) framework of the four roles parents play in managing the peer relationships of younger children is useful in suggesting how research efforts on direct parental influences on adolescent peer relationships might proceed.

Parental Versus Adolescent Reports of Management

This investigation only discussed adolescent reports of parental management. Because parents and adolescents might differ in their perceptions of how management occurs, an important component of any research on direct parental management of adolescent peer relationships would be to examine multiple informants' perceptions of management. As suggested by Steinberg (1996), it is important to consider how informants differ in their perceptions of a particular construct. In the case of the parental management construct one informant is not more accurate or valid than the other, but each provides unique information regarding the construct in question. As the literature on parental management of peer relationships develops, there is a need for data from both parents' and adolescents' perspectives.

Bidirectionality of Effects

Parke (1992) suggested that research on parent-peer linkages needs to consider bidirectional effects. Particularly as children reach adolescence, peers may affect children, which may subsequently affect parenting practices. Parents may institute certain direct management techniques in response to the type of friends the adolescent has selected or the type of behavior in which the adolescent has been engaging. Longitudinal studies across the adolescent years can be employed to document whether certain management techniques precede particular friendships or behaviors or whether the reverse is true. The analyses reported here illustrated some of the bidirectional relations. That is, the results suggest that parents resort to prohibiting interactions with friends after their children are already involved with antisocial peers. Analyses that ask about management at a microlevel might also shed more light on this issue. For example, researchers might use Ladd and Golter's (1988) methodology of telephoning parents and adolescents about management techniques on a weekly basis. This would lend itself to a more detailed analysis of whether management is being done in response to a particular incident or friend or whether the management is simply being used to facilitate peer relationships in general.

Goals of Parental Management of Peer Relationships

Research in this area should also be directed toward discovering what the intended effect is of parental management of adolescents' peer relationships on the adolescent in relation to the actual effect on peer relationships. Although parents may have particular goals in mind as they engage in direct management of peer relationships, it is not known whether these goals are being met. These goals may also be critical in determining which direct parenting practices are used (Darling & Steinberg, 1993). The underlying motivations for parental management of peer relationships is largely unexplored, even within the literature on young children (see Ladd et al., 1992, for review). Unlike parents of younger children, who may have concerns with social competence and supporting the formation of healthy friendships, parents of adolescents may be more concerned with keeping their children away from potentially bad influences. Indeed, in the current investigation, the findings on prohibiting suggests that parents are probably engaging in this behavior in response to their children becoming involved with antisocial peers or activities but it has little effect on future peer selection. Other parents may believe that contact with the right group of peers will help their children continue on a trajectory toward success. That is, the peer group will support the goals that parents have for their children. Research is needed to explore the relation between parental goals and their selection of particular management techniques. It is also of interest to examine whether parental goals concerning management change as children enter adolescence.

That is, during adolescence do parents become more focused on keeping their children away from potentially negative influences as opposed to supporting healthy friendships?

In summary, this chapter provides some insight into the nature of direct parental management of adolescents' peer relationships. Because this research has strong practical implications, continuing research efforts in this area should be very worthwhile. The open-ended responses by parents present a range of practices that warrant further investigation. Furthermore, exploring these issues with different age groups is desirable because some of these practices may vary according to the age of the child, and the child's view or acceptance of parental management may vary with age. Finally, expanding this work to other cultural or ethnic contexts is clearly of interest both practically and theoretically.

NOTE

Support for data collection and manuscript preparation was provided by a B/START grant from the National Institute of Mental Health (MH57232–01) and a grant from the Research Board of the University of Illinois at Urbana-Champaign. I gratefully acknowledge the assistance of Benjamin Perry for his help with the data collection and coordination of the study. Penny Brucker, Jennifer Marchand, and Steven Toefl provided assistance with the data collection. I am especially grateful to the children, parents, and schools for their participation in this project. Address correspondence to the author at the Department of Psychology, Northern Illinois University, DeKalb, IL 60115–2892.

REFERENCES

Berndt, T. (1979). Developmental changes in conformity to peers and parents. *Developmental Psychology, 15*, 608–616.

Billy, J., & Udry, J. (1985a). The influence of male and female best friends on adolescent sexual behavior. *Adolescence, 20*, 21–32.

Billy, J., & Udry, J. (1985b). Patterns of adolescents' friendship and effects on sexual behavior. *Social Psychology Quarterly, 48*, 27–41.

Blos, P. (1979). *The adolescent passage.* New York: International Universities Press.

Brown, B. (1990). Peer groups and peer cultures. In Feldman, S. S. & Elliott, G. R. (1990). *At the threshold: The developing adolescent* (pp. 171–196). Cambridge, MA: Harvard University Press.

Brown, B. B., Clasen, D. R., & Eicher, S. A. (1986). Perceptions of peer pressure, peer conformity dispositions, and self-reported behavior among adolescents. *Developmental Psychology, 22*, 521–530.

Brown, B. B., Hamm, J. V., & Myerson, P. (1996). Encouragement, empowerment, detachment: Ethnic differences in approaches to parental involvement with peer relationships. In Brown, B. B. (Chair), *Buzz off or butt in?: Parental involvement in adolescent peer relations.* Symposium conducted at the biennial meeting of the Society for Research on Adolescence, Boston, MA.

Brown, B. B., & Huang, B. (1995). Examining parenting practices in different peer contexts: Implications for adolescent trajectories. In Crockett, L. J. & Crouter, A. C. (Eds.), *Pathways through adolescence* (pp. 2–37). Hillsdale, NJ: Erlbaum.

Brown, B. B., Mounts, N. S., Lamborn, S. D., & Steinberg, L. (1993). Parenting practices and peer group affiliation in adolescence. *Child Development, 64,* 467–482.

Buhrmester, D., & Yin, J. (1997, April). *A longitudinal study of friends' influence on adolescents' adjustment.* Poster presented at the biennial meeting of the Society for Research in Child Development, Washington, DC.

Chao, R. (1994). Beyond parental control and authoritarian parenting style: Understanding Chinese parenting through the cultural notion of training. *Child Development, 65,* 1111–1119.

Cohn, D., Patterson, C., & Christopoulos, C. (1991). The family and children's peer relationships. *Journal of Social and Personal Relationships, 8,* 315–346.

Coleman, J. (1961). *The adolescent society.* Glencoe, IL: The Free Press.

Darling, N., & Steinberg, L. (1993). Parenting style as context: An integrative model. *Psychological Bulletin, 113,* 487–496.

Dishion, T. (1990). The peer context of troublesome child and adolescent behavior. In Leone, P.E. (Ed.), *Understanding troubled and troubling youth* (pp. 128–153). Newbury Park, CA: Sage.

Dishion, T., Patterson, G., Stoolmiller, M., & Skinner, M. (1991). Family, school, and behavioral antecedents to early adolescent involvement with antisocial peers. *Developmental Psychology, 27,* 172–180.

Dornbusch, S., Carlsmith, J. M., Bushwall, P. L., Ritter, P., Leiderman, P. H., Hastorf, A. H., & Gross, R. T. (1985). Single parents, extended households, and the control of adolescents. *Child Development, 56,* 326–341.

Dornbusch, S., Ritter, P., Leiderman, H., Roberts, D., & Fraleigh, M. (1987). The relation of parenting style to adolescent school performance. *Child Development, 58,* 1244–1257.

Epstein, J. (1983). The influence of friends on achievement and affective outcomes. In Epstein, J. L., & Karweit, N. (Eds.), *Friends in school* (pp. 177–200). New York: Academic Press.

Freud, A. (1958). Adolescence. *Psychoanalytic Study of the Child, 13,* 255–278.

Fuligni, A. J., & Eccles, J. S. (1993). Perceived parent-child relationships and early adolescents' orientation towards peers. *Developmental Psychology, 29,* 622–632.

Gecas, V., & Seff, M. A. (1990). Families and adolescents: A review of the 1980s. *Journal of Marriage and the Family, 52,* 941–958.

Glynn, T. J. (1981). From family to peer: A review of transitions of influence among drug-using youth. *Journal of Youth and Adolescence, 10,* 363–383.

Gold, M. (1970). *Delinquent behavior in an American city.* Belmont, CA: Brooks/Cole.

Greenberger, E., Steinberg, L., & Vaux, A. (1981). Adolescents who work: Health and behavioral consequences of job stress. *Developmental Psychology, 17,* 691–703.

Hart, C. H., Yang, C., Nelson, D., Jin, S., Bazarskaya, N., & Nelson, L. (in press). Peer contact patterns, parenting practices, and preschoolers' social competence in China, Russia, and the United States. In Slee, P., & Rigby, K. (Eds.), *Peer relations amongst children: Current issues and future directions.* London: Routledge.

Hawkins, J. D., Catalano, R. F., & Miller, J. Y. (1992). Risk and protective factors for alcohol and other drug problems in adolescence and early adulthood: Implications for substance abuse prevention. *Psychological Bulletin, 112*, 64–105.

Ide, J. K., Parkerson, J., Haertel, G., & Walberg, H. (1981). Peer group influence on educational outcomes: A quantitative synthesis. *Journal of Educational Psychology, 73*, 472–484.

Jaccard, J., Turrisi, R., & Wan, C. (1990). *Interaction effects in multiple regression.* Newbury Park, CA: Sage.

Kandel, D. (1978). Homophily, selection, and socialization in adolescent friendships. *American Journal of Sociology, 84*, 427–436.

Kandel, D., & Andrews, K. (1987). Processes of adolescent socialization by parents and peers. *The International Journal of the Addictions, 22*, 319–342.

Kandel, D. B., Kessler, R. C., & Margulies, R. Z. (1978). Antecedents of adolescent initiation into stages of drug use: A developmental analyses. In Kandel, D. B. (Ed.), *Longitudinal research and drug use: Empirical findings and methodological issues* (pp. 73–98). Washington, DC: Hemisphere.

Ladd, G. (1992). Themes and theories: Perspectives on processes in family-peer relationships. In Parke, R., & Ladd, G. (Eds.), *Family-peer relationships: Modes of linkage* (pp. 3–34). Hillsdale, NJ: Erlbaum.

Ladd, G., & Golter, B. (1988). Parents' management of preschooler's peer relations: Is it related to children's social competence? *Developmental Psychology, 24*, 109–117.

Ladd, G. W., Profilet, S., & Hart, C. (1992). Parents' management of children's peer relations: Facilitating and supervising children's activities in the peer culture. In Parke, R., & Ladd, G. (Eds.), *Family-peer relationships: Modes of linkage* (pp. 215–253). Hillsdale, NJ: Erlbaum.

Lamborn, S., Mounts, N. S., Steinberg, L., & Dornbusch, S. (1991). Patterns of competence and adjustment among adolescents from authoritative, authoritarian, indulgent, and neglectful families. *Child Development, 62*, 1049–1065.

Magnusson, D., Stattin, H., & Allen, V. (1986). Differential maturation among girls and its relation to social adjustment: A longitudinal perspective. In Baltes, P., Featherman, D., & Lerner, R. (Eds.), *Life-span development and behavior* (Vol. 7, pp. 135–172). Hillsdale, NJ: Erlbaum.

McCord, J. (1990). Problem behaviors. In S. Feldman & G. T. Ellio (Eds.), *At the threshold: The developing adolescent* (pp. 414–430). Cambridge, MA: Harvard University Press.

Medrich, E. A., Roizen, J. A., Rubin, V., & Buckley, S. (1982). *The serious business of growing up: A study of children's lives outside school.* Berkeley: University of California Press.

Mounts, N. S. (1998). *Parental management of adolescents' friendships: Is it related to academic achievement and antisocial behavior?* Manuscript submitted for publication.

Mounts, N., & Steinberg, L. (1995). An ecological analysis of peer influence on adolescent grade-point-average and drug use. *Developmental Psychology, 31*, 915–922.

Newcomb, M. D., & Bentler, P. M. (1989). Substance use and abuse among children and teenagers. *American Psychologist, 44*, 242–248.

Olson, D. H., McCubbin, H., Barnes, H. L., Larson, A. S., Muxen, M. J., & Wilson, M. A. (1983). *Families: What makes them work*. Beverly Hills, CA: Sage.

Parke, R. D. (1992) Epilogue: Remaining issues and future trends in the study of family-peer relationships. In Parke, R., & Ladd, G. (Eds.) *Family-peer relationships: Modes of linkage* (pp. 425–438). Hillsdale, NJ: Erlbaum.

Parke, R., & Bhavnargi, N. (1989). Parents as managers of children's peer relationships. In Belle, D. (Ed.), *Children's social networks and social supports* (pp. 241–259). New York: Wiley.

Parke, R., & Ladd, G. (Eds.) (1992). *Family-peer relationships: Modes of linkage*. Hillsdale, NJ: Erlbaum.

Pasley, K., & Gecas, V. (1984). Stresses and satisfactions of the parental role. *The Personnel and Guidance Journal*, 400–404.

Patterson, G. R. (1986). Performance models for antisocial boys. *American Psychologist, 41*, 432–444.

Patterson, G. R., & Dishion, T. J. (1985). Contributions of families and peers to delinquency. *Criminology, 23*, 63–79.

Patterson, G. R., & Stouthamer-Loeber, M. (1984). The correlation of family management practices and delinquency. *Child Development, 55*, 1299–1307.

Pedhazur, E. (1982). *Multiple regression in behavioral research*. New York: Holt, Rinehart & Winston.

Putallaz, M., & Heflin, A. H. (1990). Parent-child interaction. In Asher, S. R., & Coie, J. D. (Eds.), *Peer rejection in childhood* (pp. 189–216). New York: Cambridge University Press.

Small, S., Eastman, G., & Cornelius, S. (1988). Adolescent autonomy and parental stress. *Journal of Youth and Adolescence, 17*, 377–392.

Smetana, J., & Asquith, P. (1994). Adolescents' and parents' conceptions of parental authority and personal autonomy. *Child Development, 65*, 1147–1162.

Snyder, J., Dishion, T., & Patterson, G. (1986). Determinants and consequences of associating with deviant peers during preadolescence and adolescence. *Journal of Early Adolescence, 6*, 29–43.

Steinberg, L. (1986). Latchkey children and susceptibility to peer pressure: An ecological analysis. *Developmental Psychology, 22*, 433–439.

Steinberg, L. (1990). Autonomy, conflict, and harmony in the family relationship. In Feldman, S. S., & Elliott, G. R. (Eds.), *At the threshold: The developing adolescent* (pp. 255–276). Cambridge, MA: Harvard University Press.

Steinberg, L. (1996, March). *The assessment of parent-child relationships in adolescence: Some conceptual and methodological suggestions*. Paper presented at the biennial meetings of the Society for Research on Adolescence, Boston.

Steinberg, L., Lamborn, S., Darling, N., Mounts, N., & Dornbusch, S. (1994). Over-time changes in adjustment and competence among adolescents from authoritative, authoritarian, indulgent, and neglectful families. *Child Development, 65*, 754–770.

Steinberg, L., & Silverberg, S. (1986). The vicissitudes of autonomy in early adolescence. *Child Development, 57*, 841–851.

Vernberg, E., Beery, S., Ewell, K., & Abwender, D. (1993). Parents' use of friendship facilitation strategies and the formation of friendships in early adolescence: A prospective study. *Journal of Family Psychology, 3,* 356–369.

Wilson, W. J. (1997, April). *When work disappears: The new challenge facing families and children in America's inner cities.* Invited address at the biennial meetings for the Society for Research in Child Development, Washington, DC.

8

Family-Peer Relationships: The Role of Emotion Regulation, Cognitive Understanding, and Attentional Processes as Mediating Processes

Robin O'Neil and Ross D. Parke

The acquisition of social skills in childhood appears to be a key developmental task that is linked to successful adjustment over the life span. Research on links between peer relationships in childhood and later competence and social functioning in adolescence and adulthood has established a range of negative consequences of poor peer relationships in childhood for adaptation and competence in later life including delinquency, poor academic achievement, and high school drop out, as well as criminality and other forms of social and emotional disorder in adulthood (Cowen, Pederson, Babijian, Izzo, & Trost, 1973; Parker & Asher, 1987). Recently, scholars have begun to identify the developmental pathways through which children acquire social skills and behavioral styles that promote interpersonal competence with peers during the early school years (Hartup, 1979; Parke & Ladd, 1992) and a growing body of literature identifies a number of modes by which children's early socialization experiences are linked to peer competence in early and middle childhood.

In this chapter, we briefly review literature concerning three ways in which families are hypothesized to influence social adaptation in childhood and adolescence. In doing so, we emphasize recent work from a longitudinal study of familial influences on children's social development currently being conducted in our laboratory. Specifically, we examine the role that parents play as interaction partners, advisers and instructors, and co-regulators and sources of opportunities for social contact with peers. We also review research on the processes that account for relations between experiences with familial social partners and social competence in childhood: emotion regulatory processes, social cognitive models of relationships, and attention regulatory processes. We illustrate each mediational process with data we collected.

The University of California, Riverside (UCR) Social Development Project is a longitudinal study initiated in 1990 with the goal of understanding links between children's experiences in their families during early and middle childhood and their developing social competence with peers. The study sample was generated using a two-stage procedure. In the first stage, approximately 800 kindergartners from nine elementary schools in two southern California communities were interviewed in order to determine level of social acceptance by peers. In the second phase of sampling, this sociometric information was used to select children of varying degrees of social acceptance. The parents of these children were invited to participate in the laboratory assessment phase of the project. In 1990–1991, 116 families with a kindergartner participated in the study. In 1994–1995, an additional 84 families with a fourth grader joined the study. The ethnic distribution of the resulting sample was approximately 55 percent Euro-American, 35 percent Latino, and 10 percent other ethnicities including Asian and African American. The yearly assessments in kindergarten through Grade 2 included questionnaires and interviews as well as dyadic interaction tasks between children and parents. In Grades 3 through 6, the interaction tasks were augmented to include triadic tasks that involved children, mothers, and fathers as well as a set of interaction tasks between children and a self-selected friend and an unacquainted peer.

A TRIPARTITE MODEL OF FAMILY-PEER RELATIONSHIPS

Work on the UCR Social Development Project has been guided by a model that hypothesizes three modes by which parents influence their children's peer relationships (Parke, Burks, Carson, Neville, & Boyum, 1994; Parke, Cassidy, Burks, Carson, & Boyum, 1992). First, parents are viewed as influencing their children's peer relationships through their childrearing practices and styles of interaction. This is often viewed as a nondirect or implicit source of influence because the parent's goal is not explicitly to modify or enhance children's social competence with peers. Second, this model suggests that parents explicitly influence the quality of children's peer relationships in their role as instructor or educator. Parental strategies such as advising or consulting with children about appropriate social behavior and supervising or intervening in children's early interactions with peers are examples of techniques that parents adopt to educate or train children concerning appropriate behavioral strategies for interacting with peers. A third mode of familial influence is the management of children's social lives. In this role, parents provide opportunities for children to interact with peers and other social partners. Access to peers is thought to provide a social arena to practice relationship skills that develop in the context of the family.

Pathway 1: The Parent-Child Relationship

The best researched way in which parents indirectly socialize children's peer competence is through the quality of their relationship with their children. Two research traditions illustrate this approach. First, in the parent-child attachment tradition, the focus has been on the impact of early infant-mother attachment on social adaptation to the peer group (Sroufe & Fleeson, 1986). The second tradition is illustrated by studies of the effect of particular childrearing styles (Baumrind, 1973) or parent-child interaction patterns on children's social competence with peers (MacDonald & Parke, 1984; Puttalaz & Heflin, 1989). Together, studies of parent-child relationships and children's peer competence in early childhood suggest that parents who are responsive, warm, and synchronous have children who are more accepted by their peers (Harrist, Pettit, Dodge, & Bates, 1994; Puttalaz, 1987). In contrast, parents of children who are low in peer acceptance can be characterized as more directive and demanding, expressing more negative affect, eliciting more negative affect in their children, exhibiting less ability to engage and sustain play interaction with their children, and displaying less ability to modulate their level of playful stimulation with their children (Barth & Parke, 1993; Harrist et al., 1994; Parke et al., 1992; Parke, Mac-Donald, Beitel, & Bhavnagri, 1988; Parke et al., 1989). Family interaction patterns relate not only to concurrent peer relationships, but also predict children's competence with peers over time.

Findings from the UCR Social Development Project add further evidence to a growing body of literature that suggests that the affective quality of parents' relationship with their children is an important correlate of children's success in developing relationships with others. Among kindergarten-aged children in the study, expressions of positive and negative affect by both mothers and fathers during physical play were linked to children's social competence in both kindergarten and 1 year later (Isley, O'Neil, & Parke, 1996). In same-gender dyads, the strongest predictor of peer- and teacher-rated social competence in Grade 1 was parental expression of negative affect.

A major goal of work on this project also has been to understand the extent to which parental affect has a *direct* (statistically unmediated) versus an *indirect* (mediated) impact on the development of children's level of social competence. As may be seen in Figures 8.1 and 8.2, latent variable path analyses (Isley, O'Neil, Clatfelter, & Parke, in press) suggest both unmediated and mediated influences of parental affect on children's affect expression and social competence. Considerable evidence exists for the mediating role of children's affect expression. Specifically, exposure to varying

Figure 8.1
Direct and Indirect Influences of Fathers' Affect on Children's Kindergarten and First-Grade Social Competence

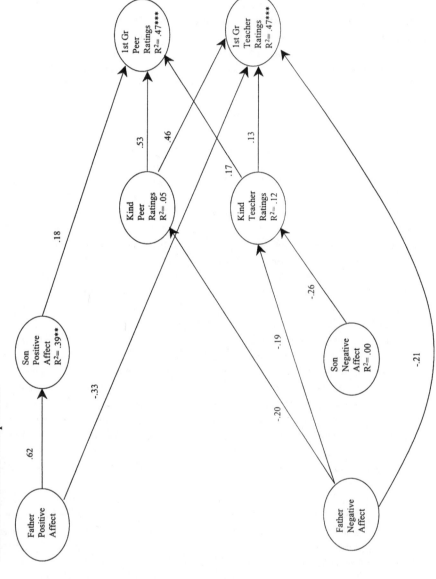

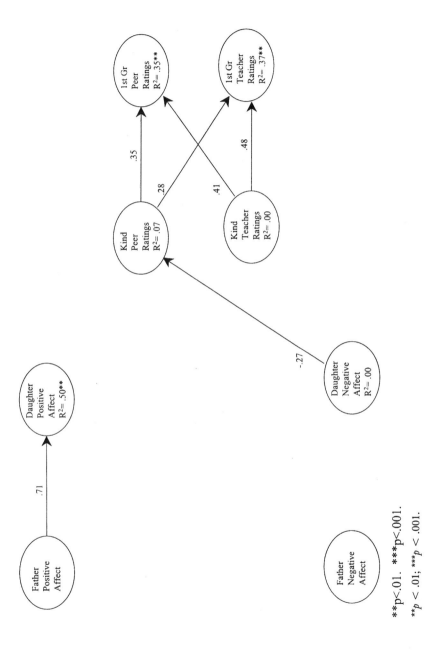

Father Positive Affect → .71 → Daughter Positive Affect R²= .50**

Kind Peer Ratings R²= .07 → .35 → 1st Gr Peer Ratings R²= .35**

Kind Peer Ratings R²= .07 → .28 → 1st Gr Teacher Ratings R²= .37**

Kind Teacher Ratings R²= .00 → .41 → 1st Gr Peer Ratings R²= .35**

Kind Teacher Ratings R²= .00 → .48 → 1st Gr Teacher Ratings R²= .37**

Daughter Negative Affect R²= .00 → -.27 → Kind Peer Ratings R²= .07

Father Negative Affect

**p<.01. ***p<.001.

**p < .01; ***p < .001.

199

Figure 8.2
Direct and Indirect Influences of Mothers' Affect on Children's Kindergarten and First-Grade Social Competence

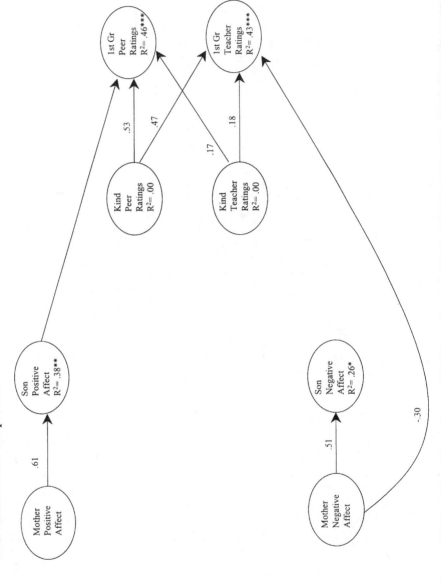

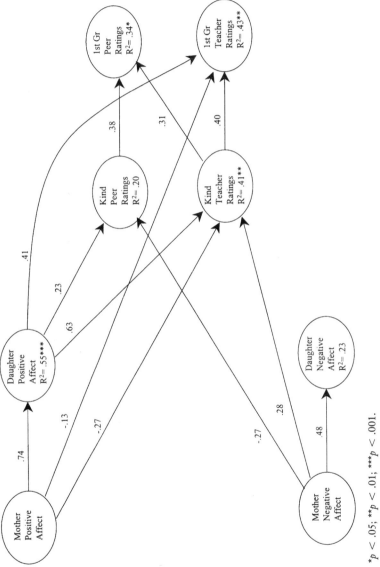

*p < .05; **p < .01; ***p < .001.

degrees of positive and negative parental affect appear to indirectly influence children's social competence by providing a model for the child's own emotional expressions, which over time might influence the quality of relationships with others outside the family. These relationships vary, however, by parent and child gender. Additionally, the models also suggest the existence of unmediated or "direct" links of positive and negative affect expressed by parents that influence children's social competence independent of their influence on children's affect expression, perhaps by enhancing or disrupting key developmental processes that lead to competence with peers. For example, although the expression of negative affect by parents is not related to the expression of negative affect in mother-son and father-daughter dyads, it appears to be linked directly to social acceptance and social competence outcomes in kindergarten and first grade. The data suggest that although young children may not reciprocate negative affect in play interactions with their same gender parents, they may be modeling negative affect in other social contexts or developing patterns of emotional dysregulation that interfere with positive peer relationships.

Pathway 2: Parental Advice and Social Guidance

Socialization agents can influence youngsters' adjustment not only through their patterns of interaction but also through their influence on the quality of children's peer experiences. Thus, in contrast to the implicit socializing influence of parental style on children's social competence, parenting activities such as instructing, advising, and coaching may be more explicit methods of educating children concerning the appropriate manner of initiating and maintaining social relationships. The role that parents play as managers or regulators of children's social experiences has received a modest amount of attention in recent years. These studies indicate that young children benefit from parents' direct involvement in the supervision and management of their interactions with peers (Bhavnagri & Parke, 1991; Finnie & Russell, 1988; Ladd & LeSieur, 1995; Ladd, Profilet, & Hart, 1992; Russell & Finnie, 1990). In general, these studies indicate that when mothers facilitate preschool-aged children's interactions with peers by giving assistance to "help them play together" and by monitoring their play activities in a nonintrusive manner, children are rated as more socially competent.

As children move through early childhood, however, the influence that parents have on their developing social relationships is likely to shift from active supervising and regulation of peer interactions to coaching, consulting, and advice giving (Ladd, LeSieur, & Profilet, 1993). Recent literature has shown that the quality of maternal advice is related to children's competence with peers. For example, mothers of socially accepted children have been found to suggest positive and assertive strategies when dealing with hypothetical social situations, whereas mothers of less well-accepted children tend to suggest avoidant strategies (Finnie & Russell, 1988). Similarly, Mize and Pettit (1997) found that when mothers suggested more positive strategies and framed social dilemmas in nonhostile, optimistic terms, children were rated as better liked, less aggressive, and more socially skilled. Their findings also indicated that a synchronous, warm style of imparting parental advice remains a unique predictor of social acceptance even after controlling for the content of social coaching, particularly among boys. To date, however, these studies have continued to focus on relatively young children, typically preschoolers. (Mounts, Chapter 7, this volume, is a recent and notable exception.) Little is known about the role that parental advice giving or coaching plays in facilitating older children's relationships with peers. Additionally, previous studies have focused almost exclusively on mothers, leaving relatively unexplored the role that fathers' advice giving plays in the development of competent peer interaction styles.

Findings from this project offer support for the role of both mothers' and fathers' advice giving and the development of children's social acceptance and competence with peers. In one phase of the study (O'Neil, Garcia, Zavala, & Wang, 1995), parents were asked to read to their third-grade children short stories that described common social themes (e.g., group entry, ambiguous provocation, relational aggression) and to advise the children about the best way to handle each situation. High-quality advice was considered to promote a positive, outgoing, social orientation on the part of the children rather than avoidance or aggressive responses. The findings tended to vary as a function of parent-child gender. Among father-son dyads and mother-daughter dyads, parental advice that was more appropriate and more structured was associated with less loneliness and greater social competence among children. For example, more appropriate advice from fathers to sons about how to handle conflict with a peer was associated with less self-reported loneliness. Similarly, more appropriate advice from mothers to daughters was associated with lower levels of depressed mood. Interestingly, when father-daughter dyads and mother-son dyads were the focus of analysis, higher quality advice about how to handle social conflict was associated with poorer teacher-rated social competence. However, in contrast to the gender-specific findings for the content of parental advice, the quality of parent-child interactions during the advice-giving session was positively related to a number of indicators of children's social competence, less loneliness in mother-son and mother-daughter dyads and lower levels of depressed mood in father-son dyads. These findings suggest that parental interaction style may make important contributions to children's social adjustment, irrespective of parent or child gender. In contrast, the impact of the "message" that parental advice conveys to children may be more strongly influenced by parent and child gender.

Interestingly, other results from the study based on a triadic advice-giving session in which mothers, fathers, and their third graders discussed how to handle problems that the children had when interacting with peers indicated that parental style of interaction appeared to be a better predictor of children's social competence than the actual solution quality generated in the advice-giving session (Wang & McDowell, 1996). Specifically, the controlling nature of fathers' style and the warmth and support expressed by mothers during the advice-giving task were significant predictors of both teacher and peer ratings of children's social competence. When fathers were more controlling during the advice-giving sessions, children were described by teachers and peers as more disliked. The direction of effects in each of these studies is difficult to determine and future models that explain links between parental management strategies and children's social development need to incorporate bidirectional processes. Under some circumstances, parents may be making proactive efforts to provide assistance to their children's social efforts, whereas under other circumstances, parents may be providing advice in response to children's social difficulties (see also Ladd & Golter, 1988; Mize, Pettit, & Brown, 1995). Overly involved or extremely specific parents, for example, may be attempting to remediate their children's poor social abilities. Alternatively, high levels of control may inhibit children's efforts to develop their own strategies for dealing with peer relations (Cohen, 1989). Comparison of data from kindergarten, third grade, and fifth grade suggests gender-based shifts in parental advising and consulting. In early childhood, both mothers and fathers appear to use advice giving as a mode of social skills training. However, by middle childhood, mothers appear to do more remediation of poor social skills, whereas fathers appear to be involved in advising and consulting with their children about social relationships once the children have acquired good social skills (Wang, 1998).

Most investigations of the role of parental guidance and advice to children regarding peer relationships has been based on structured opportunities to provide advice in a laboratory context. However, in one recent study, the nature of naturally occurring advice was assessed in a sample of preschoolers and their mothers (Laird, Pettit, Mize, Brown, & Lindsey, 1994). These investigators found that about half the mothers of the preschoolers in the study reported that they frequently engage in conversations with their children about peer relationships. Rates of conversation about peers were related to both peer- and teacher-rated measures of social competence. Advice giving was a unique predictor of peer-rated competence even after controlling for the amount of conversation. Finally, the extent to which the child initiated the conversation was a further positive predictor of peer-rated competence. Although based on self-reports, this work extends prior work by demonstrating the impact of maternal advice giving in ecologically valid contexts.

Pathway 3: Parents As Sources of Social Opportunities

Parents also play an important role in the facilitation of their children's peer relationships by initiating informal contact between their own children and potential play partners especially among younger children (Bhavnagri, 1987). A series of studies by Ladd and his colleagues suggests that parents' role as social activity arranger may play a facilitory part in the development of their children's friendships. Ladd and Golter (1988) found that children of parents who tended to arrange peer contacts had a larger range of play-mates and more frequent play companions outside of school than children of parents who were less active in initiating peer contacts. When children entered kindergarten, boys, but not girls, with parents who initiated peer contacts were better liked and less rejected by their classmates than were boys with noninitiating parents. Other evidence (Ladd, Hart, Wadsworth, & Golter, 1988) suggests that parents' peer management (initiating peer contacts; purchasing toys for social applications) of younger preschool children prior to enrollment in preschool was, in turn, linked to the time that children spent in peers' homes. Work by Ladd and Hart (1992) also provides evidence of the importance of parental initiating and arranging of activities. Parents who frequently initiated informal peer-play opportunities tended to have children who were more presocial toward peers and spent less time in onlooking and unoccupied behaviors. Children's own initiation activity has been linked with measures of social competence. Children who initiated a larger number of peer contacts outside of school had larger playmate networks and tended to be better liked by their peers in preschool settings. This work serves as a corrective to the view that initiation activity is only a parental activity and reminds us that variations in how active a role children play in organizing their own social contacts is an important correlate of their social competence. Of interest for future research is to plot in more detail how parental and child-initiating activities shift over the course of development. It is clear that parental initiating is important, but over time it decreases and the factors that govern this decrease are important issues to explore.

Parents' own social networks also may enhance children's social development and adjustment. Cochran and Niego (1995) suggested several ways that parents' own networks may influence children's social competence. First, the structure of parents' networks influence the exposure children have to possible social interactive partners (e.g., the offspring of adult network members). Second, the extent to which children observe the social interactions of parents with members of their networks may influence the children's own styles of social interaction. Third, parents in supportive social networks may have enhanced well-being that, in turn, may improve parents' relationships with their children. Research suggests that larger, more supportive social networks are associated with greater parental competence, particularly among mothers (Jennings, Stagg, & Connor, 1991; Melson, Ladd, & Hsu, 1993; Roberts, 1989), and evidence has begun to emerge that suggests that structural characteristics of parents' networks such as network size are associated with social adjustment in young children. Homel, Burns, and Goodnow (1987), for example, found that the number of friends in parents' social networks was related to social skill and social adjustment in 9- to 11-year-olds.

Recently, this work was extended by showing relationships among characteristics of parents' networks, parents' relationship attitudes, and children's social competence in kindergarten and first grade (O'Neil, Lee, Parke, & Wang, 1998). When mothers reported more closeness and enjoyment from their networks, they reported greater efficacy in managing their own relationships and felt more efficacious in assisting their children in forming social relationships. Similarly, when mothers had larger non-kin networks and when they reported that non-kin networks were a source of more agemates for their child, they reported greater efficacy in managing relationships. In contrast, fathers' network relationships were unrelated to relationship efficacy and the ease with which they could assist their children in developing relationships. However, paralleling the finding for mothers, fathers whose networks contained more non-kin members and were a source of more agemates for their children reported feeling more efficacious in their personal relationships. When mothers viewed their social networks as sources of closeness and enjoyment, teachers and peers described children as better accepted by classmates. Similarly, when fathers described their network relationships in a more positive light, children were rated by teachers as better accepted and less aggressive. When mothers' non-kin network provided the study child with more agemates, children were rated by peers as better accepted. Similarly, when fathers reported a larger network of kin members and when fathers' network of non-kin afforded their children more agemates, children tended to be rated by peers as better accepted. Although the specific mechanisms that account for these relationships remain to be determined, these findings suggest that parents' social networks may provide children with both better models of social relationships as well as more opportunities to interact with same-aged peers and refine developing social skills.

The role that parents' own social network plays as a source of opportunities for children to develop relationships and practice social skills with peers is likely to diminish over the course of children's development as youngsters become more active arrangers of their own social lives. Older children, however, may continue to learn styles of interaction with peers by observing their parents' attitudes toward and behavioral styles with network members. Thus, some positive associations can be expected between the indices of relationship quality between parents' and youngsters' social networks. Steinberg, Darling, and Fletcher (1995) suggested that children also benefit from the increased exchange of resources and vigilance that is associated with parents' social integration. Accordingly, parents who report higher levels of social support would be expected to have children who exhibit better social adjustment. Although a growing body of literature offers descriptive information about the structure and qualities of children's and adolescents' networks, few studies have examined the links between children's network characteristics and social functioning.

MECHANISMS THAT LINK CHILDREN'S INTERACTIONS WITH FAMILIAL SOCIAL PARTNERS AND SOCIAL FUNCTIONING

As outlined in Figure 8.3, there are three sets of processes that may, in part, mediate the relations that have been proposed: (a) emotional regulatory skills; (b) social cognitive processes concerning intentionality, goals, strategies, and sense of efficacy associated with children's styles of social interaction; and (c) attention regulatory processes. Although conceptualized as distinct processes, these three sets of processes represent different aspects of a complex set of intervening processes that are necessary for the successful enactment of social behavior. The social information-processing (SIP) model (Crick & Dodge, 1994; Dodge, 1986) is consistent with the assumption of the multiply determined nature of social interaction. Although this model has been applied primarily to peer-peer relationships, it can be applied in a parallel manner to other relationships. It is assumed that these skills, which are important for social competence and adjustment, are learned in the context of youngsters' experiences with multiple social partners. Ongoing research that assesses these skills has begun to yield clues concerning the family-based origins of emotional regulatory skills, sociocognitive models of relationships, and attentional processes as mediating links.

Emotion Regulatory Processes as Mediating Links

Several sets of emotional processes are assumed to be important for successful social interaction, including encoding and decoding skills, understanding the causes and consequences of emotions, understanding and utilizing display rules, and the regulation of emotional expression. Our view is that competence in emotional understanding (EU) and emotional regulation (ER) are acquired over the course of children's development. The rudiments of these processes are acquired in infancy and childhood whereas more sophisticated understanding of complex emotions and social rules for emotional expression develops over middle childhood and adolescence. For example, according to Parker and Gottman (1989), the emotional tasks of early and middle childhood differ from the tasks of adolescence. In early childhood, the major affective goal is "management of arousal in interac-

Figure 8.3
Emotional, Attentional, and Cognitive Mediators of the Family-Peer Interface

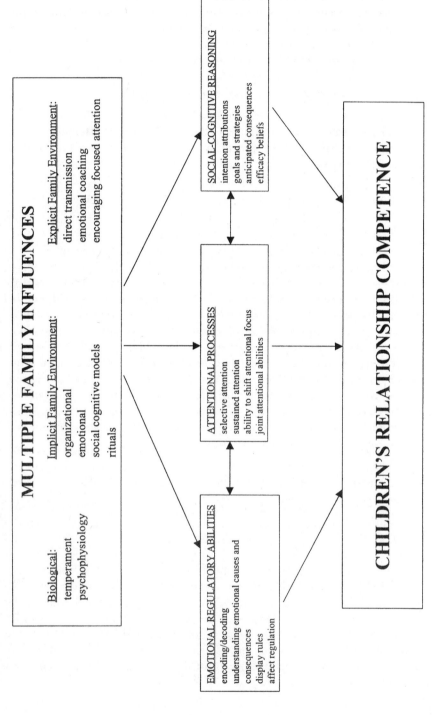

tion," in middle childhood, the affective task is to acquire "display and feeling rules," and in adolescence the affective task is the management and regulation of self-disclosure and intimacy.

Emotion Encoding and Decoding

One set of skills relevant to successful peer interaction is the ability to encode emotional signals and to decode the emotional signals of others. Arousing physical play is thought to be a particularly important context for the development of encoding and decoding skills. Through physically playful interaction with their parents, especially fathers, children may learn how to use emotional signals to regulate social behavior of others. They may also learn how to decode the social and emotional signals of other social partners. Recent work has found that variations in parent–child interaction are related to emotional encoding and decoding skills (Camaras et al., 1988; Parke et al., 1989), and these skills, in turn, are related to children's sociometric status (Cassidy, Parke, Butovsky, & Braungart, 1992; Field & Walden, 1982; Parke et al., 1992). Together, these two sets of evidence suggest that emotion production and recognition skills may serve as mediating mechanisms between early experiences with parents and the quality of interaction with peers. Other recent work (Carson & Parke, 1999) suggests that the families of peer-rejected children may use idiosyncratic or "familycentric" affect cues that are recognized within the context of the family, but are not as well recognized outside the family. To date, however, this work has focused principally on the early childhood period and on production and recognition skills among family members.

Emotional Understanding

Evidence also suggests that successful peer functioning requires an understanding of the causes, consequences, and meaning of emotional experiences. Cassidy and colleagues (1992) found that higher levels of social competence among 5- and 6- year-olds were associated with the ability to identify emotions, the ability to describe appropriate causes of emotions, the acknowledgment of experiencing emotion, and the expectation that they and their parents would respond appropriately to the display of emotions. Similarly, Denham, McKinley, Couchard, and Holt (1990) found that children's understanding of the type of emotion that would be elicited by different situations was positively related to peer likability. These findings confirm the findings of other research that suggest connections between other components of social understanding and peer relations (Asher & Renshaw, 1981; Dodge, Pettit, McClaskey, & Brown, 1986; Hart, Ladd, & Burlson, 1990). However, the early familial antecedents of emotional understanding are unclear and need closer scrutiny (Saarni, 1990).

Emotional Expressiveness

A growing body of research indicates that parental patterns of emotional expressiveness are associated with children's own expressiveness styles, social behavior, and acceptance by peers (Boyum & Parke, 1995; Cassidy et al., 1992). However, studies typically have assessed emotional expressiveness with self-report measures and have tended to focus on maternal expressiveness (see Halberstadt, Crisp, & Eaton, in press, for a recent review of this literature). Our lab has extended this work using observational assessments of mothers' and fathers' affect expression, and evidence in support of the role of emotional expression in regulating social interaction comes from these recent studies (Carson & Parke, 1996; Isley, 1996). Carson and Parke found that patterns of reciprocated negative affect between children and their fathers, but not their mothers, was linked to verbal and physical aggression. Other work (Isley, 1996) has extended this work to older children (7- to 9-year-olds) and found that negative paternal affect was correlated with lower peer social acceptance and social competence. These data underscore the importance of examining fathers as well as mothers.

Emotional Regulatory Abilities

Children's skill in regulating emotions also may be important to successful development of peer relationships (Eisenberg et al., 1995; O'Neil, Parke, Isley, & Sosa, 1997). Based on responses of fourth graders to a series of vignettes representing situations that might generate anger, frustration, or excitement, our data indicate that the ability to control the level of emotional arousal and the strategies selected for coping with high levels of emotional arousal are related to a number of indicators of children's social competence with peers. Children who report better control over their levels of emotional arousal are described by peers and teachers as more socially skilled. In contrast, peers and teachers view children who report less control over their emotions as more aggressive and disruptive. Children's strategies for handling emotional arousal appear to be linked to their social competence in a similar fashion. Children who report using temper tantrums or other displays of negative emotion in the face of emotional upset are viewed as less socially competent by peers and viewed by teachers as more aggressive and disruptive. In contrast, children who indicate that they would use a nonemotional method, such as reasoning, to cope with emotional upset are described as more prosocial.

Recent investigations indicate that the extent to which parents tolerate the expression of negative emotions and assist their children with the resolution of emotional upset are associated with children's emotional regulatory abilities as well as their social competence. Eisenberg and Fabes (1992), for example, found that when mothers expressed less tolerance for children's expression of anger, 4- and 6-year-olds expressed higher levels of negative affect and a greater tendency to escape rather than to vent when angered. Furthermore, in a rare examination of the role that fathers play in the socialization of children's emotional regulatory abilities, Gottman Katz, and Hooven (1996) found that fathers' acceptance and assistance with children's sadness and anger when children were 5 years old was related to children's social competence with peers at 8 years of age.

Findings from the UCR Social Development Project also suggest that the strategies parents employ to manage children's negative emotion are associated with children's emotional reactivity, coping, and social competence (O'Neil et al., 1997). Several findings underscore this link. When mothers reported that they encouraged the expression of negative affect when their child was upset, children indicated that they would be less likely to use social withdrawal as a strategy to deal with emotional upset. Similarly, mothers who reported that they would help the child find solutions to deal with emotional distress had children who reported that they would be more likely to use reasoning to cope with emotional upset. Mothers who expressed more awareness and sensitivity to their child's emotional state in a family problem-solving task had children who expressed their emotions more clearly. In contrast, mothers who made more attempts to regulate their child's emotional expressiveness in the problem-solving task had children who expressed less positive affect and more negative affect in the problem-solving task. When mothers modeled problem-solving approaches to handling disagreement and upset, children were less likely to report becoming angry when faced with an upsetting event, less likely to express negative affect during the parent-child discussion task, were clearer in their emotional expressions, and more likely to adopt problem-solving strategies in the discussion task.

Fathers' regulation of children's emotions were only modestly related to social competence. Fathers who reported being more distressed by their child's expressions of negative affect had children who were more likely to report using anger and other negative emotions to cope with distressing events. When fathers reported using strategies to minimize distressing circumstances, children were more likely to report using reasoning to cope with a distressing situation. Fathers who reported emotion and problem focused reactions to the expression of negative emotions had children who were described by teachers as less aggressive and disruptive.

Display Rules for Emotion Expression

During early and middle childhood, children acquire and use rules for the socially appropriate expression of emotion. Most work in this area has focused either on the developmental course of display rule acquisition (Gnepp & Hess, 1986; Saarni, 1984) or on individual differences in display rule knowledge within the preschool and elementary school years (Cole, Zahn-Waxler, & Smith, 1994; Garner, 1996). A few studies have examined links between display rule knowledge and social competence. Underwood, Coie, and Herbsman (1992), for example, found that aggressive children have more difficulty understanding display rules.

Other work on our project examines the relations between children's use of socially appropriate rules for displaying negative emotions and social competence with peers (McDowell, O'Neil, & Parke, in press). We have employed Saarni's (1984) "disappointing gift paradigm," which enables the assessment of children's ability to mask negative emotions in the face of disappointment. Although Saarni's work suggests that this ability improves with age and may be a critical component of successful ER, to date, researchers have not examined the links between individual differences in the ability to mask or control negative emotions and children's competence with peers. Our data indicate that among fourth graders, children who display negative affect or behavior following the presentation of a disappointing gift (thus, not using display rules) are rated by teachers as more socially withdrawn. Girls who are able to maintain levels of positive affect after receiving a disappointing gift are viewed as more socially competent by teachers and peers. Similarly, children who express more tension and anxiety in response to a disappointing gift are described by peers as more socially avoidant and rated as more aggressive or disruptive by teachers. Recent evidence (Hubbard & Coie, 1994; Underwood et al., 1992) also suggests that display-rule utilization may vary across social contexts (e.g., peers vs. adults). Underwood and colleagues, for example, found the likelihood of masking anger toward teachers increased with age. However, among girls, the likelihood of expressing anger toward peers increased as they became adolescents. Studies only recently have begun to examine links between children's experiences with parents and their ability to use display rules. Garner and Power (1996), studying a preschool sample, found that children's negative emotional displays in a disappointment situation were inversely related to observed maternal positive emotion. However, much remains to be understood in this domain regarding the intergenerational continuity between parents' and children's display-rule use.

Together, these studies suggest that various aspects of emotional development—encoding, decoding, EU and ER—continue to play an important role in accounting for variations in peer competence into the late middle childhood period. However, it has been customary to examine the contributions of each of these emotional processes to children's social competence separately. In turn, most studies report modest contributions of any single process to children's social outcomes. However, these predictors are best viewed as a family of emotional processes that operate in concert in real-life contexts. Progress in this area is likely to come from this multivariate view of emotional processes and the incorporation of multiple emotional indices into single-study designs.

Cognitive Representations as Mediating Links between Family and Peer Systems

Cognitive representations about social relationships represent a second linking mechanism between family and extrafamilial social contexts. The SIP model proposed by Dodge (1986) provides a convenient framework for organizing sociocognitive factors that are relevant to youngsters' reasoning and decision making in social contexts (see Crick & Dodge, 1994). According to this five-step model, the way in which children handle each decision point will determine how appropriately and competently children will react to a social stimulus or event. Considerable evidence supports links between competence in these steps and children's early social acceptance or rejection by peers (e.g., Asher & Renshaw, 1981; Crick & Dodge, 1994; Dodge, 1986). However, little is known concerning the origins of these cognitive representational factors. Similarly, a major challenge to researchers has been to understand how children and adolescents transfer social strategies that are acquired during interactions in one social domain, for example, the family, to interactions in other social domains, such as with peers. Sociocognitive mediators may be acquired in the context of the familial and extrafamilial experiences. We also expect that over the course of development these cognitive representational models increase in complexity and are reflected in an increasing ability to take into account multiple and/or conflicting goals in social relationships and to utilize planning strategies.

Research in a social interactional tradition reveals links between parent and child cognitive representations of social relationships. Burks and Parke (1996), in a study based on responses to hypothetical social dilemmas, have shown substantial correspondence in mothers' and children's cognitive representations (attributions, goals, and anticipated social consequences). Similarly, MacKinnon-Lewis et al. (1994) found links between mothers' and sons' hostile attributions, which suggest some family-based similarities across generations. However, no relations were found between these attributions and their classroom behavior. Recently, we also have explored the links between parent and child cognitive representations of social relationships (Spitzer & Parke, 1994). In our study, parents and their children responded to a series of vignettes reflecting interpersonal dilemmas by indicating how they might react in each situation, and these open-ended responses were coded for goals, causes, strategies and advice. Paralleling earlier work, we find that the cognitive representations of social behavior of both fathers and mothers are related to their children's representations. This confirms earlier work that showed that maternal and child representations are linked (Burks & Parke, 1996), and provides the first evidence that fathers' representational models are linked to children's models of social relationships. Although our study and the work of Burks and Parke (1996) point to links between mothers' and children's cognitive representational schemes that may develop over the course of children's experiences with family members, the precise mechanisms through which these schema are acquired is not yet specified.

In an extension of the work described earlier (Spitzer & Howe, 1995; Spitzer & Parke, 1994) based on parents' and children's open-ended responses to social dilemmas, it is apparent that in addition to there being links between parents' and children's cognitive models of relationships, the quality of both mothers' and fathers' goals and strategies for handling social conflict are linked to children's social acceptance. Mothers who are high in their use of confrontational strategies have children with high levels of teacher-nominated physical and verbal aggression. Similarly, mothers who provide specific and socially skilled advice have more popular children. Fathers' strategies that are rated high on confrontation and instrumental qualities are associated with low teacher ratings of children's prosocial behavior and high teacher ratings of physical aggression and dislike. Fathers with relational goals have children who are less often nominated as aggressive by their peers and rated by teachers as more liked and less disliked. These findings begin to offer evidence that children may learn cognitive representational schemas through their family relationships which, in turn, serve as guides for their subsequent relationships with peers.

Attentional Regulation as a Third Potential Mediating Mechanism

In concert with ER and sociocognitive representations, attentional regulatory processes have come to be viewed as an additional mechanism through which familial socialization experiences might influence the development of children's social competence. These processes include the ability to attend to relevant cues, to sustain attention, to refocus attention through such processes as cognitive distraction and cognitive restructuring, and other efforts to purposefully reduce the level of emotional arousal in a situation that is appraised as stressful (Lazarus & Folkman, 1984). Attentional processes are thought to organize experience and to play a central role in cognitive and social development beginning early in infancy (Rothbart & Bates, in press; Rothbart & Derryberry, 1981). Thus, Wilson and Gottman (1994) aptly considered attention regulatory processes as a "shuttle" linking ER and sociocognitive processes because attentional processes organize both cognitions and emotional responses, and thus, influence the socialization of relationship competence. Although studies are only beginning to emerge, evidence suggests that attentional regulation may have direct effects on children's social functioning (Eisenberg et al., 1997; Wilson & Gottman, 1994) and, in some circumstances, attentional control may function in interaction with dimensions of emotionality and SIP. In support of direct influences,

Eisenberg and colleagues (1993) found that children who were low in attention regulation were also low in social competence. Other recent work suggests that attentional control and emotional negativity may interact when predicting social competence. Attention regulatory skills appear to be more critical among children who experience higher levels of emotional negativity. Eisenberg et al. argued that when children are not prone to experience intense negative emotions, attention regulatory processes may be less essential to positive social functioning. In contrast, the social functioning of children who experience anger and other negative emotions may only be undermined when these children do not have the ability to use attention regulatory processes such as cognitive restructuring and other forms of emotion-focused coping.

Work emanating from the UCR Social Development Project also suggests that attentional processes may work in tandem with emotional regulatory abilities to enhance social functioning. Furthermore, as indicated in Figure 8.4, parenting style may be an important antecedent of children's abilities to refocus attention away from emotionally distressing events. Data from fifth graders in our study indicated that when mothers adopted a negative, controlling parenting style in a problem-solving discussion, children were less likely to use cognitive decision making as a coping strategy. Additionally, children were more likely to report greater difficulty in controlling negative affect when distressed. Lower levels of cognitive decision making and higher levels of negative affect, in turn, were associated with more problem behaviors and higher levels of negative interactions with classmates (as reported by teachers). Similarly, when fathers adopted a negative, controlling style, children were more likely to use avoidance as a mechanism for managing negative affect. Additionally, fathers who reported expressing more negative dominant emotions such as anger and criticism in everyday interactions had children who reported greater difficulty controlling negative emotions. Avoidant coping and negative emotionality, in turn, were related to higher levels of parent-reported problem behaviors.

CONCLUSIONS AND FUTURE DIRECTIONS

This chapter uses data from a longitudinal study of children's social development to illustrate the multiple pathways and processes through which children acquire skills to interact competently with peers. Clearly, however, a number of issues remain to be addressed in future research. Of critical importance is the specification of how socialization processes described here are modified by development, particularly the transition to adolescence. Models of familial socialization such as the tripartite model typically address development in social competence in early and middle childhood. As youngsters approach adolescence, a number of critical developmental changes are

Figure 8.4
Links between Parenting, Attentional and Emotional Regulatory Processes, and Children's Social Competence

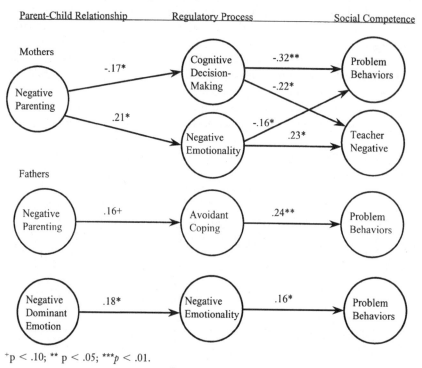

$^+$p < .10; ** p < .05; ***p < .01.

likely to modify the processes that are associated with competence in peer relationships. First, puberty alters parent-child relationships (Paikoff & Brooks-Gunn, 1991). Increased conflict and emotional distance between adolescents and their parents, especially mothers, accompanies pubertal change (Holmbeck, 1996; Papini, Farmer, Clark, & Snell, 1988). Pubertal development is also linked to changes in peer relationships. Early pubertal onset associated with a smaller network of close friends and greater likelihood of engaging in certain "adultlike" behaviors (e.g., smoking, drinking, sex) at a younger age than for later maturing girls (Gustafson & Magnusson, 1991; Stattin & Magnusson, 1990).

Second, as children enter adolescence, they spend increasing time with peers and establish more intimate, enduring relationships with friends. Additionally, in early adolescence, youngsters begin to differentiate more sharply between "best friends" and other peer relationships on the basis of characteristics such as level of intimacy and sharing, reciprocity, companionship, and conflict (Berndt, 1996). Supportive friendships have been shown to be important to adolescents' self-esteem, coping abilities, and adjustment (Berndt & Savin-Williams, 1993; Renshaw & Brown, 1993). Recent work (Collins, 1997) suggests that family and friends make differential contributions to adolescent social adjustment and underscores the importance of examining the relative importance of family and friends in adolescent social outcomes.

Third, adolescents' expanding social worlds begin to incorporate relationships with nonparental adults. In contrast to parent and peer influences, very little attention has been devoted to the role of nonparental adults on adolescent adjustment (Greenberger, Chen, & Beam, in press). Several lines of prior work underscore the importance of relationships with nonparental adults who serve as support agents or mentors (Rhodes, Ebert, & Fischer, 1992; Rutter, 1990; Werner & Smith, 1982). Although prior research has examined the frequency and nature of these "mentors," little work has documented their impact on adolescent social functioning.

Fourth, throughout middle childhood, parents and children are thought to become "co-regulators" of peer relationships (Maccoby, 1984), with the balance of the management role gradually shifting to the child over time. A shift from active parental supervision to more distal monitoring of children's activities is associated with middle childhood and early adolescence. Monitoring refers to the parents' awareness and knowledge about children's locations, companions, and activities. Although clear relations have been established between parental monitoring and delinquent behavior among preadolescent and adolescent samples, especially boys (Crouter, McDermid, McHale, & Perry-Jenkins, 1990; Dishion, 1990; Patterson & Stouthamer-Loeber, 1984), there is little information on the stability of monitoring and the predictive value of early patterns of monitoring for social adjustment in early adolescence. With the gradual shift of the management role out of parents' domain, other social agents such as peers and other significant adults (e.g., coaches) may play a growing role as co-managers or influencers of adolescents' social experiences. Adolescence is associated with increases in friendship intimacy as indexed by confiding and self-disclosure. Studies suggest that adolescents increasingly turn to friends to discuss and resolve peer issues (Parker & Gottman, 1989; Raffaelli & Duckett, 1989). Both the susceptibility to negative peer influence as well as the supportive influence of friends appear to peak in middle adolescence (Buhrmester, 1990; Steinberg & Silverberg, 1986; Urberg, Cheng, & Shyu, 1991). Thus, early adolescence appears to be a point at which parents' more distal monitoring and regulating of youngsters' lives may be accompanied by increases in the proximal influences of peers and other nonparental adults.

In summary, the literature to date suggests that the transition to adolescence is associated with qualitative changes in youngsters' relationships with parents as well as in a broadening of their social worlds. Clearly, the broadening social worlds of adolescents generate an expanded source of socializing influences. However, we have yet to determine whether youngsters' growing experiences with peers and important nonparental adults may be associated with the development of EU and ER in adolescence. Research is beginning to emerge that suggests that family emotional expressiveness continues to be relevant to adolescent functioning (Julian, McKenry, & McKelvey, 1991) and recent longitudinal studies indicate that positive emotional expressiveness in the family during childhood is related to better psychosocial functioning in adolescence (Bronstein, Briones, Brooks, & Cowan, 1996; Bronstein, Fitzgerald, Briones, Pieniadz, & D'Ari, 1993). These findings suggest that when adolescents experience positively expressive family environments in childhood, they may feel more freedom in adolescence to express emotions. Another recent study (Capaldi, Forgatch, & Crosby, 1994) found that fathers' expression of hostility during discussion of "hot" topics was negatively related to eighth-grade boys' self-esteem. However, to date, the links between parental expressed negative affect and adolescent outcomes appears less well understood.

Similarly, although research on adolescents' working models of attachment are linked with adjustment to peers during adolescence (Greenberger & McLaughlin, in press; Kobak & Sceery, 1988), less attention has been devoted to adolescents' current representations of their social relationships of families and peers. The role of sociocognitive representations in achieving these behavioral and attitudinal changes are less well understood. Moreover, in early and middle adolescence the issue is not simply the choice of a single appropriate social goal (i.e., relational vs. instrumental) during the course of interactions with peers and family members, the task becomes one of goal coordination and interpersonal negotiation (Rabiner & Gordon, 1992; Selman & Schultz, 1989). Little is known, however, regarding the role that the family plays in the development of such complex interpersonal negotiating skills during adolescence. Similarly, few studies have examined the similarities between the types of cognitive representations of children and their parents, particularly in the early adolescence period, and links between the cognitive representations of youngsters and nonfamilial significant others remains virtually unexplored. Nonparental very important persons may be especially valuable sources of influence on adolescents' cognitive models of relationships as they frequently provide advice and support to adolescents (Greenberger, Chen, & Beam, 1998). More work is needed to better understand the role of cognitive representations as mediators of relations between familial and nonfamilial interaction and social adaptation in adolescence.

Clearly, developmental change is likely to be a potent influence on the socialization of children's peer relationship skills. As we extend our examination of models that link parent-child and peer relationships to older youngsters, it also is important to develop a better understanding of the direction of influence between parents and children, the extent to which short- and long-term stressors moderate socialization influences, and the extent to which the processes described generalize to various ethnic and cultural groups. Finally, it remains to be understood how each of these factors changes as a function of children's and adolescents' development.

REFERENCES

Asher, S. R., & Renshaw, P. D. (1981). Children without friends: Social knowledge and social skill training. In Asher, S. R., & Gottman J. M. (Eds.), *The development of children's friendships* (pp. 273–296). New York: Cambridge University Press.

Barth, J. M., & Parke, R. D. (1993). Parent-child relationship influences on children's transition to school. *Merrill-Palmer Quarterly, 39*, 173–195.

Baumrind, D. (1973). The development of instrumental competence through socialization. In Pick, A. D. (Ed.), *Minnesota symposium on child psychology* (Vol. 17, pp. 3–46). Minneapolis: University of Minnesota Press.

Berndt, T. J. (1996). Transitions in friendship and friends' influence. In Graber, J. A., Brooks-Gunn, J., & Petersen, A. C. (Eds.), *Transitions through adolescence: Interpersonal domains and context* (pp. 57–84). Mahwah, NJ: Erlbaum.

Berndt, T. J., & Savin-Williams, R. C. (1993). Variations in friendships and peer-group relationships in adolescence. In Tolan, P., & Cohler, B. (Eds.), *Handbook of clinical research and practice with adolescents* (pp. 203–219). New York: Wiley.

Bhavnagri, N. P. (1987). *Parents as facilitators of preschool children's peer relationships.* Unpublished doctoral dissertation.

Bhavnagri, N., & Parke, R. D. (1991). Parents as direct facilitators of children's peer relationships: Effects of age of child and sex of parent. *Journal of Social and Personal Relationships, 8*, 423–440.

Boyum, L., & Parke, R. D. (1995). Family and emotional expressiveness and children's social competence. *Journal of Marriage and the Family, 57*, 593–608.

Bronstein, P., Briones, M., Brooks, T., & Cowan, B. (1996). Gender and family factors as predictors of late adolescent emotional expressiveness and adjustment: A longitudinal study. *Sex Roles, 34*, 739–765.

Bronstein, P., Fitzgerald, M., Briones, M., Pieniadz, J., & D'Ari, A. (1993). Family emotional expressiveness as a predictor of early adolescent social and psychological adjustment. *Journal of Early Adolescence, 13*, 448–471.

Buhrmester, D. (1990). Intimacy of friendship, interpersonal competence, and adjustment during preadolescence and adolescence. *Child Development, 61*, 1101–1111.

Burks, V., & Parke, R. D. (1996). Parent and child representations of social relationships: Linkages between families and peers. *Merrill-Palmer Quarterly, 42*, 358–378.

Camaras, L. A., Ribordy, S., Hill, J., Martino, S., Spaccarelli, S., & Stefani, R. (1988). Recognition and posing of emotional expressions by abused children and their mothers. *Developmental Psychology, 24*, 776–781.

Capaldi, D. M., Forgatch, M. S., Crosby, L. (1994). Affective expression in family problem-solving discussions with adolescent boys. *Journal of Adolescent Research, 9,* 29–49.

Carson, J. L., & Parke, R. D. (1996). Reciprocity of parent-child negative affect and children's social competence. *Child Development, 67,* 2217–2226.

Carson, J. L., & Parke, R. D. (Last draft, 1999). *Family-peer linkages: The role of affective exchanges between children of varying degrees of social acceptance and their parents.*

Cassidy, J., Parke, R. D., Butovsky, L., & Braungart, J. (1992). Family-peer connections: The roles of emotional expressiveness within the family and children's understanding of emotions. *Child Development, 63,* 603–618.

Cochran, M. M., & Niego, S. (1995). Parenting and social networks. In Bornstein, M. H. (Ed.), *Handbook of Parenting: Vol. 3: Status and social conditions of parenting* (pp. 393–418). Hillsdale, NJ: Erlbaum.

Cohen, J. S. (1989). *Maternal involvement in children's peer relationships during middle childhood.* Unpublished doctoral dissertation, University of Waterloo, Waterloo, Ontario, Canada.

Cole, P. M., Zahn-Waxler, C., & Smith, K. D. (1994). Expressive control during a disappointment: Variations related to preschoolers' behavior problems. *Developmental Psychology, 30,* 835–846.

Collins, W. A. (1997). Relationships and development during adolescence: Interpersonal adaptation to individual change. *Personal Relationships,* 1–14.

Cowen, E. L., Pederson, A., Babijian, H., Izzo, L. D., & Trost, M. A. (1973). Long-term follow-up of early detected vulnerable children. *Journal of Consulting and Clinical Psychology, 41,* 438–446.

Crick, N. R., & Dodge, K. A. (1994). A review and reformulation of social information-processing mechanisms in children's social adjustment. *Psychological Bulletin, 115,* 74–101.

Crouter, A., McDermid, S., McHale, S., & Perry-Jenkins, M. (1990). Parental monitoring and perceptions of children's school performance and conduct in dual and single-earner families. *Developmental Psychology, 26,* 649–652.

Denham, S. A., McKinley, M., Couchard, E., & Holt, R. (1990). Emotional and behavioral predictors of preschool peer ratings. *Child Development, 61,* 1145–1152.

Dishion, T. J. (1990). The family ecology of boys' peer relations in middle childhood. *Child Development, 61,* 1145–1152.

Dodge, K. A. (1986). A social information processing model of social competence in children. In Perlmutter, M. (Ed.), *Minnesota symposium on child psychology* (Vol. 18, pp. 77–125). Hillsdale, NJ: Erlbaum.

Dodge, K. A., Pettit, G. S., McClaskey, C. I., & Brown, M. (1986). Social competence in children. *Monographs of the Society for Research in Child Development, 51* (2, Serial No. 213).

Eisenberg, N., & Fabes, R. A. (1992). Young children's coping with interpersonal anger. *Child Development, 63,* 116–128.

Eisenberg, N., Fabes, R. A., Bernzweig, J., Karbon, M., Poulin, R., & Hanish, L. (1993). The relations of emotionality and regulation to preschoolers' social skills and sociometric status. *Child Development, 64,* 1418–1438.

Eisenberg, N., Fabes, R. A., Murphy, B., Maszk, P., Smith, M., & Karbon, M. (1995).

The role of emotionality and regulation in children's social functioning: A longitudinal study. *Child Development, 66,* 1239–1261.

Eisenberg, N., Guthrie, I. K., Fabes, R. A., Reiser, M., Murphy, B. C., Holgren, R., Mask, R., & Losoya, S. (1997). The relations of regulation and emotionality to resiliency and competent social functioning in elementary school children. *Child Development, 68,* 295–311.

Field, T. M., & Walden, T. A. (1982). Production and discrimination of facial expressions by preschool children. *Child Development, 53,* 1299–1311.

Finnie, V., & Russell, A. (1988). Preschool children's social status and their mother's behavior and knowledge in the supervisory role. *Developmental Psychology, 24,* 789–801.

Garner, P. W. (1996). The relations of emotional role-taking, affective/moral attributions, and emotional display rule knowledge to low-income children's social competence. *Journal of Applied Developmental Psychology, 17,* 19–36.

Garner, P. W., & Power, T. G. (1996). Preschoolers' emotional control in the disappointment paradigm and its relation to temperament, emotional knowledge, and family expressiveness. *Child Development, 67,* 1406–1419.

Gnepp, J., & Hess, D. L. R. (1986). Children's understanding of verbal and facial display rules. *Developmental Psychology, 22,* 103–108.

Gottman, J. M., Katz, L. F., & Hooven, C. (1996). Parental meta-emotion philosophy and the emotional life of families: Theoretical models and preliminary data. *Journal of Family Psychology, 10,* 243–268.

Greenberger, E., Chen, C., & Beam, M. R. (1998; Unpublished data). Department of Psychology and Social Behavior, University of California, Irvine.

Greenberger, E., Chen, C., & Beam, M. R. (in press). The role of "very important" nonparental adults in adolescent development. *Journal of Youth and Adolescence.*

Greenberger, E., & McLaughlin, C. S. (in press). Attachment, coping and explanatory style in late adolescence. *Journal of Youth and Adolescence.*

Gustafson, S. B., & Magnusson, D. (1991). *Female life careers: A pattern approach.* Hillsdale, NJ: Erlbaum.

Halberstadt, A. G., Crisp, V. W., & Eaton, K. L. (in press). Family expressiveness: A retrospective and new directions for research. In Philippot, P., Feldman, R. S., & Coats, E. (Eds.), *The social context of nonverbal behavior.* New York: Cambridge University Press.

Harrist, A. W., Pettit, G. S., Dodge, K. A., & Bates, J. E. (1994). Dyadic synchrony in mother-child interaction: Relation with children's subsequent kindergarten adjustment. *Family Relations, 43,* 417–424.

Hart, C. H., Ladd, G. W., & Burlson, B. R. (1990). Children's expectations of the outcomes of social strategies: Relations with sociometric status and maternal disciplinary styles. *Child Development, 61,* 127–137.

Hartup, W. W. (1979). The social worlds of childhood. *American psychologist, 34,* 944–950.

Holmbeck, G. N. (1996). A model of relational transformations during the transition to adolescence: Parent–adolescent conflict and adaptation. In Graber, J. A., Brooks-Gunn, J., & Petersen, A. C. (Eds.), *Transitions through adolescence: Interpersonal domains and context* (pp. 167–199). Mahwah, NJ: Erlbaum.

Homel, R., Burns, A., & Goodnow, J. (1987). Parental social networks and child development. *Journal of Social and Personal Relationships, 4,* 159–177.

Hubbard, J. A., & Coie, J. D. (1994). Emotional determinants of social competence in children's peer relationships. *Merrill-Palmer Quarterly, 40,* 1–21.

Isley, S. (1996). *Affect expressions and reciprocity in parent–child dyads: Links with children's social acceptance and competence.* Unpublished doctoral dissertation, University of California, Riverside.

Isley, S., O'Neil, R., Clatfelter, D., & Parke, R. D. (in press) Parent and child expressed affect and children's social acceptance and competence: Modeling direct and indirect pathways. *Developmental Psychology.*

Isley, S., O'Neil, R., & Parke, R. D. (1996). The relation of parental affect and control behavior to children's classroom acceptance: A concurrent and predictive analysis. *Early Education and Development, 7,* 7–23.

Jennings, K. D., Stagg, V., & Conners, R. E. (1991). Social networks and mothers' interactions with their preschool children. *Child Development, 62,* 966–978.

Julian, T. W., McKenry, P. C., & McKelvey, M. W. (1991). Mediators of relationship stress between middle-aged fathers and their adolescent children. *The Journal of Genetic Psychology, 152,* 381–386.

Kobak, R. R., & Sceery, A. (1988). Attachment in late adolescence: Working models, affect regulation and representations of self and others. *Child Development, 59,* 135–146.

Ladd, G., & Golter, B. S. (1988). Parent's management of preschoolers' peer relations: Is it related to children's social competence? *Developmental Psychology, 24,* 109–117.

Ladd, G. W., & Hart, C. H. (1992). Creating informal play opportunities: Are parents' and preschoolers' initiations related to children's competence with peers? *Developmental Psychology, 28,* 1179–1187.

Ladd, G. W., Hart, C. H., Wadsworth, E. M., & Golter, B. S. (1988). Preschoolers' peer network in nonschool settings: Relationship to family characteristics and school adjustment. In Salzinger, S., Antrobus, J., & Hammer, M. (Eds.), *Social networks of children, adolescents, and college students* (pp. 61–92). Hillsdale, NJ: Erlbaum.

Ladd, G. W., & LeSieur, K. D. (1995). Parents and children's peer relationships. In Bornstein M. H. (Ed.), *Handbook of parenting, Vol. 4: Applied and practical parenting* (pp. 377–409). Hillsdale, NJ: Erlbaum.

Ladd, G. W., LeSieur, K., & Profilet, S. M. (1993). Direct parental influences on young children's peer relations. In Duck, S. (Ed.), *Learning about relationships* (Vol. 2, pp. 152–183). London: Sage.

Ladd, G. W., Profilet, S. M., & Hart, C. H. (1992). Parents' management of children's peer relations: Facilitating and supervising children's activities in the peer culture. In Parke, R. D., & Ladd, G. W. (Eds.), *Family–peer relationships: Modes of linkage.* Hillsdale, NJ: Erlbaum.

Laird, R. D., Pettit, G. S., Mize, J., Brown, E. G., & Lindsey, E. (1994). Mother-child conversations about peers: Contributions to competence. *Family Relations, 43,* 425–432.

Lazarus, R. S., & Folkman, S. (1984). *Stress, appraisal, and coping.* New York: Springer.

MacDonald, K. B., & Parke, R. D. (1984). Bridging the gap: Parent-child play interaction and peer interactive competence. *Child Development, 55,* 1265–1277.

Maccoby, E. (1984). Middle childhood in context of the family. In Collins, W. A.

(Ed.), *Development during middle childhood: The years from six to twelve*. Washington, DC: National Academy Press.

MacKinnon-Lewis, C., Volling, B. L., Lamb, M. E., Dechman, K., Rabiner, D., & Curtner, M. E. (1994). A cross-contextual analysis of boys' social competence: From family to school. *Developmental Psychology, 30,* 325–333.

McDowell, D., O'Neil, R., & Parke, R. D. (In press). *The relation of children's use of display rules during a disappointing situation and social competence.*

Melson, G. F., Ladd, G. W., & Hsu, H. (1993). Maternal support networks material cognitions and young children's social and cognitive development. *Child Development, 64,* 1401–1417.

Mize, J., & Pettit, G. S. (1997). Mothers' social coaching, mother-child relationship style, and children's peer competence: Is the medium the message? *Child Development, 68,* 312–332.

Mize, J., Pettit, G. S., & Brown, E. G. (1995). Mothers' supervision of their children's peer playa: Relations with beliefs, perceptions, and knowledge. *Developmental Psychology, 31,* 311–321.

O'Neil, R., Garcia, J., Zavala, A., & Wang, S. (1995, April). *Parental advice giving and children's competence with peers: A content and stylistic analysis.* Paper presented at the biennial meetings of the Society for Research in Child Development.

O'Neil, R., Lee, J., Parke, R. D., & Wang, S. (1998). Parents' and children's social networks: Relations to parental regulatory strategies and children's social competence. Manuscript submitted for review.

O'Neil, R., Parke, R. D., Isley, S., & Sosa, R. (1997, April). *Parental influences on children's emotion regulation in middle childhood.* Paper presented at the biennial meetings of the Society for Research in Child Development, Washington, DC.

Paikoff, R. L., & Brooks-Gunn, J. (1991). Do parent-child relationships change during puberty? *Psychological Bulletin, 110,* 47–66.

Papini, D. R., Farmer, F. L., Clark, S. M., & Snell, W. E. (1988). An evaluation of adolescent patterns of sexual self-disclosure to parents and friends. Special Issue: Adolescent sexual behavior. *Journal of Adolescent Research, 3,* 387–401.

Parke, R. D., Burks, V., Carson, J., Neville, B., & Boyum, L. (1994). Family-peer relationships: A tripartite model. In Parke, R. D., & Kellam, S. (Eds.), *Advances in family research Vol. 4: Family relationships with other social systems* (pp. 115–145). Hillsdale, NJ: Erlbaum.

Parke, R. D., Cassidy, J., Burks, V., Carson, J., & Boyum, L. (1992). Familial contribution to peer competence among young children: The role of interactive and affective processes. In Parke, R., & Ladd, G. (Eds.), *Family-peer relationships: Modes of linkage* (pp. 107–134). Hillsdale, NJ: Erlbaum.

Parke, R. D., & Ladd, G. W. (Eds.). (1992). *Family-peer relationships: Modes of linkage.* Hillsdale, NJ: Erlbaum.

Parke, R. D., MacDonald, K. B., Beitel, A., & Bhavnagri, N. (1988). The role of the family in the development of peer relationships. In Peters, R., & McMahon, R. J. (Eds.), *Social learning systems approaches to marriage and the family* (pp. 17–44). New York: Brunner-Mazel.

Parke, R. D., MacDonald, K. B., Burks, V. M., Carson, J. L., Bhavnagri, N., Barth, J. M., & Beitel, A. (1989). Family and peer systems: In search of the linkage.

In Kreppner, K., & Lerner, R. M. (Eds.), *Family systems and life span development* (pp. 65–92). Hillsdale, NJ: Erlbaum.

Parker, J. G., & Asher, S. R. (1987). Peer relationships and later personal adjustment: Are low-accepted children at risk? *Psychological Bulletin, 102*, 357–389.

Parker, J. G., & Gottman, J. (1989). Social and emotional development in a relational context. In Berdt, T. J., & Ladd, G. W. (Eds.), *Peer relationships in child development*. New York: Wiley.

Patterson, G. R., & Stouthamer-Loeber, M. (1984). The correlation of family management and delinquency. *Child Development, 55*, 1299–1307.

Puttalaz, M. (1987). Maternal behavior and children's sociometric status. *Child Development, 58*, 324–340.

Puttalaz, M., & Heflin, A. H. (1989). Parent-child interaction. In Asher, S. R., & Coie, J. D. (Eds.), *Peer rejection during childhood: Origins, maintenance and intervention* (pp. 189–216). New York: Cambridge University Press.

Rabiner, D. L., & Gordon, L. V. (1992). The coordination of conflicting social goals: Differences between rejected and nonrejected boys. *Child Development, 63*, 1344–1350.

Raffaelli, M., & Duckett, E. (1989). "We were just talking . . .": Conversations in early adolescence. *Journal of Youth and Adolescence, 18*, 567–582.

Renshaw, P. D., & Brown, P. J. (1993). Loneliness in middle childhood: Concurrent and longitudinal predictors. *Child Development, 64*, 1271–1284.

Rhodes, J. E., Ebert, L., & Fischer, K. (1992). Natural mentors: An overlooked resource in the social networks of young, African American mothers. *American Journal of Community Psychology, 20*, 445–461.

Roberts, W. L. (1989). Parents' stressful life events and social networks: Relations with parenting and children's competence. *Canadian Journal of Behavioral Science, 21*, 132–146.

Rothbart, M. K., & Bates, J. E. (in press). Temperament. In Damon, W. (Ed.), *Handbook of child psychology* (Vol. 3). New York: Wiley.

Rothbart, M. K., & Derryberry, D. (1981). Development of individual differences in temperament. In Lamb, M. E., & Brown, A. L. (Eds.), *Advances in developmental psychology* (Vol. 1, pp. 37–86). Hillsdale, NJ: Erlbaum.

Russell, G., & Finnie, V. (1990). Preschool children's social status and maternal instructions to assist group entry. *Developmental Psychology, 26*, 603–611.

Rutter, M. (1990). Psychosocial resilience and protective mechanisms. In Rolf, J., Masten, A. S., Cicchetti, D., Neuchterlein, K., & Weintraub, S. (Eds.), *Risk and protective factors in the development of psychopathology* (pp. 181–214). New York: Cambridge University Press.

Saarni, C. (1984). An observational study of children's attempts to monitor their expressive behavior. *Child Development, 55*, 1504–1513.

Saarni, C. (1990). Emotional competence: How emotions and relationships become integrated. In Thompson, R. A. (Ed.), *Socioemotional development* (pp. 115–182). Lincoln: University of Nebraska Press.

Selman, R. L., & Schultz, L. H. (1989). Children's strategies for interpersonal negotiation with peers: An interpretive/empirical approach to the study of social development. In Berndt, T. J., & Ladd, G. W. (Eds.), *Peer relationships in child development* (pp. 371–406). New York: Wiley.

Spitzer, S., & Howe, T. (1995). *The social information processing of fathers and mothers and their children's social acceptance.* Paper presented at the biennial meetings of the Society for Research in Child Development, Indianapolis, Indiana.

Spitzer, S., & Parke, R. D. (1994). *Family cognitive representations of social behavior and children's social competence.* Paper presented at the biennial meetings of the Society for Research in Child Development, Indianapolis, Indiana.

Sroufe, L. A., & Fleeson, J. (1986). Attachment and the construction of relationships. In Hartup, W. W., & Rubin, Z. (Eds.), *Relationships and development* (pp. 51–72). Hillsdale, NJ: Erlbaum.

Stattin, H., & Magnusson, D. (1990). *Pubertal maturation in female development* (Vol. 2). Hillsdale, NJ: Erlbaum.

Steinberg, L. D., Darling, N. E., & Fletcher, A. C. (1995). Authoritative parenting and adolescent adjustment: An ecological journey. In Moen, P., Elder, G. H., & Luescher, K. (Eds.), *Examining lives in context: Perspectives on the ecology of human development* (pp. 423–466). Washington, DC: American Psychological Association.

Steinberg, L., & Silverberg, S. (1986). The vicissitudes of autonomy in early adolescence. *Child Development, 57,* 841–851.

Underwood, M. K., Coie, J. D., & Herbsman, C. R. (1992). Display rules for anger and aggression in school-age children. *Child Development, 63,* 366–380.

Urberg, K., Chen, C., & Shyu, S. (1991). Grade changes in peer influences on adolescent smoking: A comparison of two measures. *Addictive Behaviors, 16,* 21–28.

Wang, S. (1998). *Child social competence: Relations with parent social cognitive skills, parent advice-giving, and child social cognitive skills.* Unpublished doctoral dissertation, University of California, Riverside.

Wang, S., & McDowell, D. (1996). *Parental advice-giving: Relations to child social competence and psychosocial functioning.* Poster presented at the annual meetings of the Western Psychological Association, San Jose, CA.

Werner, E. E., & Smith, S. (1982). *Vulnerable but not invincible: A study of resilient children.* New York: McGraw-Hill.

Wilson, B. J., & Gottman, J. M. (1994). Attention: The shuttle between emotion and cognition: Risk, resiliency, and physiological bases. In Hetherington, E. M., & Blechman, E. A. (Eds.), *Stress, coping, and resiliency in children and families. Family research consortium: Advances in family research.* Hillsdale, NJ: Erlbaum.

9

Intimacy in Preadolescence and Adolescence: Issues in Linking Parents and Peers, Theory, Culture, and Findings

Ruth Sharabany

Relationships with peers are a very significant aspect of the social environment for school-aged children and adolescents. Peers are the ones with whom children identify, learn, fight, discover new enterprises, and learn about themselves. Through the years, the peer group becomes more significant in children's social and emotional development. One type of peer relationship is with a close friend, often named best friend, in which intimacy is the central feature (Newcomb & Begwell, 1995). During infancy and early childhood, parents are the main providers of closeness and intimacy (Furman & Buhrmester, 1985, 1992). The issue investigated here is how intimacy with parents is related to intimacy with peers, namely relationships between two sets of groups. I examine under which conditions the parallel is enhanced and reduced.

The bioecological perspective (Bronfenbrenner, 1986; Bronfenbrenner, McClelland, Wethingtan, & Moen, 1996) provides a broad model of the link between parents and peers. This perspective lends importance to different levels of influence: biosocial developmental level, overall culture, living setting, relationships outside and within the family, and finally all possible inter-relationships of these elements (Parke & Tinsley, 1984). The bioecological model tries to put in order variables that may have impact on the behavior of the individual, from the most indirect, residing within the macrosystem, to the most immediate, defined as belonging to the direct microsystem. The parent-child dyad sets the basis for a secure emotional and social development. Practicing reciprocal interactions with the parent on a regular basis helps shape a strong mutual attachment, which may affect the child's behavior in future social contexts. Bronfenbrenner defined the interaction between two or more microsystems (e.g., parent-child, child-peers) as a mesosystem. Within this ecological system, parent-child relationships contribute in some manner to the child's behavior within the peer group, and vice versa. A third ecological system, the exosystem, involves relationships between two or more macrosystems, from which at least one excludes direct participation of the child. For example, problematic relationships between the father and the mother, which may lead to a divorce, may influence the way the child behaves with his or her peers. The child may try to have a relationships with a best friend, which is quite different from the one with one or both parents. The presentation here is limited to an examination of how parent–child intimacy is related to the child-best friend intimacy, under various ecological conditions.

First, I compare children in two developmental stages: preadolescents and adolescents. Second, I examine intimacy in a special ecological condition, the Israeli kibbutz, where children do not sleep at their parents' house. Third, I examine the parallel between intimacy with a friend and intimacy with parents among delinquents and adolescents at risk. Fourth, I examine the degree of similarity between intimacy with parents and intimacy with a friend in families of divorce. Finally, I discuss findings from the Israeli studies in relation to U.S. studies, thus pointing to possible cross-cultural differences.

I use a broad definition of *intimacy* to check the aspects of closeness that exist concurrently in the home with the parent and with a best friend outside the home. The domain of peer relationships examined here is intimate friendships with a best friend, defined by several qualitative dimensions, rather than focusing on social aspects of relationships with peers that are related to interaction with a number of peers (e.g., acceptance–rejections, popularity, etc.). This chapter deals with dimensions of intimacy that are defined as a core of close, one-to-one relationships that are likely to be common in interactions with both peers and parents.

INTIMACY: THE CORE OF CLOSE RELATIONSHIPS

I use a broad definition of *intimate friendship* (Sharabany, 1974, 1994). This definition of *intimacy* is similar to the intimacy component in the definition of *love* by Sternberg (1986). My definition differs from some other studies that have defined *intimacy* as a synonym for self-disclosure or as an element of closeness (e.g., Lempers & Clarks-Lempers, 1992; Prager, 1995).

Intimate friendship is a configuration of the following eight diverse but coherently related dimensions:

1. *Frankness and spontaneity*. This is a form of self-disclosure about both positive and negative aspects of oneself ("I feel free to talk with him/her about almost anything/everything") as well as honest feedback about deeds ("If he does something that I do not like, I can talk with him about it.").

2. *Sensitivity and knowing*. This is a sense of empathy or understanding that is not necessarily achieved by talking. This dimension is very important as a counter-balance to frankness; intimacy may be indicated by sensitivity to and knowing about another person, and not only by self-disclosure. This dimension may be an indicator of accurate sensitivity or inaccurate assumptions ("I can tell when he is worried. . . . I know how he feels about things without telling me. . . . I know which activities he likes."). This dimension was intended to include groups who prefer not to talk, but may still be intimate (e.g., males).

3. *Attachment*. This dimension involves attachment to the friend (e.g., liking friend, feeling close) and missing that person when absent ("When my friend is not around I miss him/her."). In this dimension exists a feeling of connection and importance attached to the friend.

4. *Exclusiveness*. This dimension identifies unique qualities not present in other relationships, and preference for this relationship over other relationships (e.g., "The most exciting things happen when I am with him/her and nobody else is around.").

5. *Giving and sharing*. This dimension includes spending time listening to the friend and sharing material goods ("I let him/her use my things; I listen whenever necessary.").

6. *Imposition*. This is the degree to which the friend can be taken from and imposed on. This indicates some degree of openness and readiness to require and accept the friend's help ("I can always count on his/her help whenever I ask for it.").

7. *Common activities*. This is the extent of joint activities. Often the basic feature of friendship is enjoyment of time spent together ("I like to do things with him/her."). Just being together is a form of intimacy within the context of other features of the relationship, and is often found among less verbal and less self-disclosing people.

8. *Trust and loyalty*. This is the degree to which a friend can be counted on to keep secrets, be supportive, and not to betray ("I speak up to defend him/her when other kids say bad things about him/her.").

These dimensions may vary in quality and quantity, allowing for diverse configurations of closeness. For example, males can be low on Dimension 1, self-disclosure (Reis, Senchack, & Solomon, 1985), and high on Dimension 7, common activities; Dimension 2, sensitivity and knowing; and Dimension 3, attachment, thus creating a unique pattern of intimacy. Also, it is possible that each element has its own course of development and is interesting in its own right. It is the overall presence of these elements in various weights that is important for the definition and assessment of intimate friendship.

The Structure of the Intimacy Scale

The intimate friendship scale consists of eight dimensions corresponding to those definitions just described. Each dimension contains four items (N = 32 items; see Table 9.1). In early studies, the scale consisted of 64 items; 32 expressed how the respondent behaves toward the friend ("self" items), and 32 expressed how the respondent describes the friend's behavior toward him or her ("other" items). For example, "I know which kinds of books, games, and activities he likes. He/She knows which kinds of books, games, and activities I like" (see Table 9.1).

There were different forms for girls and boys. The response format contained six choices, three of agreement (Choices 4–6) and three of disagreement (Choices 1–3). In some studies, a middle point of "no decision" was added, creating a 7-point agreement scale. For each of the eight dimensions, a mean of the four items was tallied. These eight mean scores were then averaged to compute a total intimacy score.

Reliability of the Intimacy Scale

Internal consistency among the four items for each of the eight dimensions was estimated using alpha coefficients based on Guilford (1965). In the initial study (Sharabany, 1974), the alpha coefficients within each dimension ranged from .72 to .77.

Validity of the Scale

Research conducted since the 1970s suggests that the scale has construct validity (reviewed in Sharabany, 1994). There were developmental studies that included comparisons of best friend versus another friend, comparing popularity to intimate friendship, gender differences, and comparisons under various ecological conditions. With very slight adaptations it has been used in a wide range of age levels: children (Sharabany 1994); adolescents (Mayseless, Wiseman & Hai, 1998); and adults (Mayseless, Sharabany, & Sagi, 1997). The scale is not correlated with social desirability.

THEORETICAL PERSPECTIVES: INTIMACY WITH PARENTS AND PEERS

There are various theories that are relevant to the linking of intimacy with parents and peers. A contribution by each theory is highlighted here and its relevance to the overall picture is demonstrated. First, psychoanalytic theories dealt mainly with one-way influence of parents to peers. The root of social development, particularly close relationships, has been placed mainly with children's experience with parents and in within-family relationships.

Table 9.1
Intimacy Scale: Dimensions and Items (Male-Male Format)

1. Frankness and spontaneity

   I feel free to talk with him about almost everything.

   If he does something that I do not like, I can always talk with him about it.

   I talk with him about my hopes and plans for the future.

   I tell him when I have done something that other people would not approve of.

2. Sensitivity and knowing

   I know how he feels about things without his telling me.

   I know which kinds of books, games, and activities he likes.

   I know how he feels about the girl he likes.

   I can tell when he is worried about something.

3. Attachment

   I feel close to him.

   I like him.

   I miss him when he is not around.

   When he is not around I keep wondering where he is and what he is doing.

4. Exclusiveness

   The most exciting things happen when I am with him and nobody else is around.

   I do things with him that are quite different from what other kids do.

   It bothers me to have other kids come around and join in when the two of us are doing something together.

   I stay with him when he wants to do something that other children do not want to do.

5. Giving and sharing

   When something nice happens to me, I share the experience with him.

   Whenever he wants to tell me about a problem, I stop what I am doing and listen for as long as he wants.

   I offer him the use of my things (like clothes, toys, food, or books).

   If he wants something, I let him have it even if I want it, too.

6. Imposition

   I can be sure he'll help me whenever I ask for it.

   I can plan how we'll spend our time without having to check with him.

   If I want him to do something for me all I have to do is ask.

   I can use his things without asking permission.

7. Common activities

   Whenever you see me you can be pretty sure that he is also around.

   I like to do things with him.

Table 9.1 (*continued*)

    I work with him on some of his hobbies.

    I work with him on some of his school work.

8. Trust and loyalty

    I know that whatever I tell him is kept secret between us.

    I will not go along with others to do anything against him.

    I speak up to defend him when other kids say bad things about him.

    I tell people nice things about him.

The importance of parents and within-family relationships, particularly at an early age, were thought to be a major influence on later psychological development of the individual. The similarity and continuity between intimacy with parents and intimacy with peers is reviewed in a concurrent way. The comparison of two age groups examines the prediction that the parallel between intimacy with parents and peers will be greater in the younger cohort than in the older one.

A research paradigm that investigated experimentally the bi-directionality of influence of parental and peer interactions to social adaptation was carried out with primates. The research program by Harlow and Harlow (1996) examined the development of mature social behavior of rhesus monkeys. Their studies were forerunners of the attachment theory, which has been the basis for studies of attachment to parents and peer friendships in recent years (e.g., Kerns, 1996; Kerns, Klepac, & Cole, 1996; Park & Waters, 1989). The normal developmental sequence is that primates are raised with great contact with their mothers first, and then gradually are exposed to a peers. The Harlows attempted to compare and weigh the relative impact of the "parental system" and the "peer system" on social development. They especially focused on the degree of compensation that can be provided by one system to the other, when one of the systems is not available. They created conditions of raising monkeys only with mothers, thus providing only a parental system to the growing rhesus monkeys. Also, they deprived their subjects of mothers and exposed them only to a peer system. They employed various sequences and combinations of these two systems. They examined the outcome—the normal social adjustment and functioning of the monkeys as adults. They attempted to learn the degree of compensation that one system can provide for the other, as well as the unique aspects of each system—mothers versus peers. They found that rhesus mothers could compensate to some extent for the lack of contact with peers by providing playful interactions, which normally are provided by peers. Likewise, they found that rhesus peers compensated for lack of mothering in early development by furnishing some attachment needs to each other. According to these researchers, certain behaviors are imported from the peer interactions into the parents' interactions. Nevertheless, the concluded that there are degrees of overlap from one system to the other, with additional unique contributions from each system (maternal and peer).

This chapter takes advantage of a natural experiment that occurred in Israel, in which there was an ecological-structural shift in the balance between exposure to parents and peers. Some of the children studied were raised on a kibbutz. Beginning at 3 months of age, children were placed in special collective houses in the kibbutzim where they spent most of the day and every night with peers and a nonparental caregiver. Thus, from infancy, they spent much more time with peers than with their parents. The possibility can be explored that a reduced parallel exists in degree of intimacy with parents and peers in the communal sleeping in the kibbutz, because the common familiar developmental sequence that places the initial intimacy arena with the parent-child system is changed. Thus, one can question how special ecological variations are manifested in the questions previously asked.

The importance of peer relationships was further explicated by Sullivan's (1953) theory of social-personal development, which identifies at each stage a unique dimension of social development. Sullivan contributed a developmental mark that identified the emergence of social needs in different developmental periods. The series of basic needs, which are normatively met by certain significant others, are tenderness, companionship, acceptance, intimacy, and sexuality. Sullivan placed the emergence of intimacy with a peer, named a "chum," in the juvenile era. Intimacy with a best friend was considered as a need that arises in preadolescence. He wrote: "At this stage—if only because the juvenile has just come from the home situation and his previous experience has been with older and younger siblings, or with really imaginary playmates—there is a truly rather shocking insensitivity to feelings of personal worth in others" (p. 230). Sullivan's theory was the basis for the inclusion here of preadolescence because this is the developmental period he emphasized.

Recent attempts to elaborate and amplify the theory, particularly by Furman and his associates (Buhmester & Furman, 1986; Furman, 1993), and by Youniss and his associates (Youniss, 1980; Youniss & Smollar, 1985) stressed the importance of peer relationships. Although not belittling the contribution of the family, intimacy with a peer during preadolescence has the quality of a "template" for later intimate relationships (Furman & Wehner, 1994). According to Furman (1993), the parent-child relationship helps shape the way children behave in relationships with peers. However, having a secure relationship with a parent does not guarantee secure relationships with peers. Relationships with parents contribute certain aspects, but the specific input of peers is needed. Thus, there may be developmentally several social needs, which the parents fulfill and lead to the emergence of intimacy with peers.

They also agree with Sullivan in placing intimacy as a newly emerging social need fulfilled by peers in childhood. Here, a core of intimacy that is expressed in relation to parents as well as toward peers is defined.

Piaget (1965) identified *reciprocity* as a process unique to peer relationships. He defined it as mutuality between equals who, unlike relationships of a child with the parents, cannot exert authority unilaterally. Reciprocity is possible, by definition, only among peers. The new experience with peers, which emerges in childhood, has a profound impact on cognitive as well as social development, and perhaps on the emergence of new perspectives on the relationship with the parents. This direction is also in line with the integration of the theories of Piaget and Sullivan (Youniss 1980; Youniss & Smollar 1985). Reciprocity, in the symmetrical and equal-status aspect, is learned in the peer milieu and thus potentially can be applied at a later stage of development to the relationships with parents.

The ecological theory has also been applied to the parent–peer link. A distinction between direct and indirect influence of the parent on the development of social behavior of the child was articulated by Parke and Ladd (1992), Ladd and LeSieur (1995), and others. The direct influences of parents on peer relationships include managing relationships with peers, consulting with regard to peer relationships, monitoring them, and so on (Ladd & LeSieur, 1995). The definition of indirect parental influence includes processes such as quality of attachment, which is formed between child and parent, parents' childrearing style, and parental discipline. This chapter examines the parallel aspects of intimacy with parent and peers. Thus, the parental influence that is examined is indirect, in that parents are providing the child with intimacy experience within the home that the child may be able to apply to relationships with peers. It is indirect in the sense that the parents are not involved in actually monitoring the application. The focus here is on one of the indirect elements of intimacy in the one-to-one relationship with each parent. The possibility exists that intimacy exercised with the parents is reflected in the relationships with best friends outside the family.

Several related questions are asked. Considering the most indirect parental influence, to what extent is the marital intimacy, as reported independently by father and mother toward each other, relevant to the way the children describe their intimacy with peers? To what extent and under which circumstances do preadolescents and adolescents perceive concordance in the intimacy of mother and father toward them? To what extent do preadolescents and adolescents report similarity in their intimacy with their best friend and each of the parents?

CONCURRENT SYMMETRY, CONCURRENT INDEPENDENCE, AND CONCURRENT COMPLEMENTARITY

When these relations among relationships are examined, three patterns could emerge: a pattern of similarity and continuity; a pattern of no similarity, indicating independence of each relationship; and a pattern of inverse relations, where there is compensation or shift in moving from one relationship to another. Some ecological conditions may attenuate continuity. One example is a situation where there is obviously emotional discord between the parents, resulting in living with mothers, while fathers are not present at home, such as in the case of children of divorce. A second situation where there may be less continuity is when the social milieu is one of high risk, and families fail to protect children from failing to meet social norms, such as in the case of juvenile delinquents. Several different ecological conditions are explored here.

Presented here are data sets that look at specific components of intimacy and compare the similarity between three relationships: same-gender best friend, mother, and father. One influence of parents on relationships with peers may be that children behave with peers in ways similar to their behavior with parents (Gavin & Furman, 1996). To investigate this, the degree of correspondence in intimacy that adolescents report in their relationships with mother, father, and friend were examined. A comparison was made to the degree to which similar behaviors occur in the two types of relationships. Presenting a concurrent similarity between relationships with parents and peers may present evidence of indirect contribution of the relationships with parents to the parallel relationships with peers. Also, we asked how certain conditions in the family may influence the behaviors of parents toward their adolescent child, and therefore influence the relationships of the child with their friends. By examining the impact of culture, setting, and relationships within the family on intimate friendships with a peer, the impact of these variables on the similarity and parallel between parents and peers can be identified.

INDIVIDUATION WITHOUT SEPARATION: ADOLESCENTS IN ISRAEL

A common assumption in the research literature is that adolescence is a phase of greater independence from parents and greater degree of turning to peers. This movement from inside the home and family toward outside the family is often considered to weaken the closeness to the parents (i.e., Newman, 1989). Thus, there is very little evidence from investigations of the continuity between closeness and intimacy with parents and peers measured concurrently. Most previous studies were carried out in Western

English-speaking countries, where the culture is considered more individualistic and where distancing from the family is expected as part of the individual's development (Triandis, McCusker, & Hui, 1990). Data are presented here from Israeli subjects. One of the features of the Israeli society is "individuation without separation" (Lieblich, 1989). Israel is a modern Western culture, yet it has collectivist values, such as importance of the family (Katriel, 1991; Peres & Katz, 1981). The family orientation in Israel creates the cultural context for expecting continuity in intimacy with parents and same gender close friends. The family world and the peer world are more enmeshed than in the United States because they are part of the more collectivistic orientation in Israel (Hofstede, 1980). Thus, the common finding that the family provides a congruent background for the development of peer relationships (Cohn, Patterson, & Christopoulos, 1991) should be even more obvious in our Israeli samples. Several studies that used the same Intimacy Questionnaire are reviewed, ensuring comparability. The studies are described before examining the pattern of mother/father/same-gender peer correlations.

DEVELOPMENTAL ASPECTS: IS INTIMACY WITH A PARENT RELATED TO INTIMACY WITH A PEER TO THE SAME EXTENT IN ADOLESCENCE AND PREADOLESCENCE?

There are changes in the degree of intimacy with a best friend that occur in the transition from preadolescence to adolescence, such as in degree of self-disclosure (Sharabany, Gershoni, & Hofman, 1981). Is this social-biological change reflected in the similarity of intimacy with parents and peers, so that this similarity is reduced?

The intimate friendship between girls and their girl friends were compared with the girls' intimacy with their parents. The sample consisted of 162 subjects, 54 girls and their 54 pairs of parents. Half the girls were from two fourth-grade classes, each from an elementary school, and half the girls were from two seventh-grade classes, each from a junior high school. The girls completed intimacy questionnaires for their best friend and parents, and the parents were interviewed in their home and completed the intimacy scale for their spouse and daughter.

Findings indicated considerable continuity between relationships to parents and peers, according to the reports of the girls. Thus, intimate friendships with a best friend were significantly correlated with intimacy toward the mother and toward the father for fourth-grade as well as for seventh-grade girls (see Table 9.2). This finding was replicated in the kibbutz sample (Study a), including cases where children do not sleep at their parent's house. Stated differently—in the Israeli sample, continuity exists between one's close within-family relationships and with peers outside the family in preadolescence and in adolescence.

Table 9.2

Pearson Correlations between Parents and Friends: Total Intimacy—Israel

		Grade	N	Gender	Mother-Father	Mother-Friend	Father-Friend
Study a[1]	City	Grade 4	27	Girls	.85***	.66***	.65***
		Grade 7	27	Girls	.56***	.60***	.44**
Study b[2]	Sleeping arrangement in kibbutz						
	Familial	Grade 6	20	Girls	.64**	.57**	.52*
	Transitional 8-9 years		21	Girls	.65**	.49*	.78**
	Transitional 3-4 years		18	Girls	.45*	.50*	.75**
	Communal		19	Girls	.66**	.65*	.82**
Study c[3]	Recidivists delinquent	Grades 9-12	30	Boys	.37*	.16	.23
	First offenders		30	Boys	.46**	.56**	.17
	Risk		30	Boys	.58**	.18	.35*
Study d[4]	Intact Families	Grades 5-6	57	Boys	.76***	.32**	.39**
			79	Girls	.65***	.24*	.29**
	Divorced Families		32	Boys	.20	.43**	.29
			40	Girls	.24	.46**	.31*

$*p < .05; **p < .01; ***p < .001.$

[1]Study a, Sharabany, Kissom, & Katz (1988).
[2]Study b, Sharabany & Yariv (1986).
[3]Study c, Sharabany, Hertz-Lazarowitz, & Gabovitz-Hodis (1986).
[4]Study d, Hertz-Lazarowitz, Rosenberg, & Gotman (1989).

An exception to this continuity was found for the delinquent sample in Study d. For older boys, relationships with peers were separate from those with parents. Was this because of the high-risk home environment and, perhaps, the tendency to turn to peers, or was it because of the age and developmental stage of the older boys who were ready to separate from their parents? A recent study of 9th- and 12th-grade Israeli adolescents documented no difference in closeness and warmth toward parents (Mayseless et al., 1998) among 12th graders compared with 9th graders, thus the family context probably has more importance than the age of the children.

DAILY BALANCE BETWEEN EXPOSURE TO PARENTS AND PEERS; ITS RELEVANCE TO PARENT-PEER INTIMACY

The kibbutz in Israel presents a unique setting in which children sleep in collective houses and have limited contact with their parents, but otherwise live in normal and affluent conditions. It, therefore, provides an experiment in socialization and family structure. How does this reduced contact affect the relevance of the parental system to the peer system?

The kibbutzim are small agricultural communities ranging from 100 to 1,000 members (the average is 400) in which material property and many responsibilities are shared. The most salient shared responsibility is child care. They are tightly knit communities, where most people are known personally by all the others. Moreover, there is a great degree of interdependence in everyday life, which is manifest in a common dining hall, collective decisions about work allocations and careers, shared property, and the provision of services (laundry, cooking, gardening, etc.) on a rotation basis by the members.

Another important feature of the kibbutz is child education, which is ideologically based. There is an emphasis on the children's society being self-governed to a certain extent and the allocation of responsibilities and decisions to the children's group. Thus, the place of the peer group is central in the life of children growing up in the kibbutz.

Within this communal setting, the most distinctive feature in the child's socialization has been the communal sleeping arrangement, where children sleep in a children's house and not in their parents' homes (Devereux et al., 1974). Until the late 1970s, this communal sleeping arrangement was practiced in the majority of kibbutzim. Since the 1970s, the familial arrangement has become the dominant pattern, and in the 1990s, the communal sleeping system practically disappeared.

Both communal and familial sleeping arrangements included the exposition of kibbutz infants to multiple caregivers early in their life (Lavi, 1990) as the children spend most of their daytime hours in special children's houses being cared for by special caregivers (*metapelet*). Although infants raised in the familial setting spend the night at home with their parents, infants raised in the communal sleeping arrangement returned to the children's house and remained there for the night, supervised by the night watch women. With the shared caretaking and the dense social network, children were expected to learn to rely on several significant others and the kibbutz as a community, not only on their parents. All kibbutz children, regardless of nighttime arrangements, spend most of their day with their same-age peers in close proximity, going through the same routine, for most of their formative years.

Do daily contact and physical availability of parents enhance the degree of similarity between intimacy with parent and peer? Findings in this study reveal that regardless of sleeping arrangements, intimacy with parents and intimate friendships with a best friend were highly correlated (see Table 9.2). Studying families under reduced proximity such as in the kibbutz, where children do not sleep in their parents' house, with normal relationships, shows that children report intimacy with a best friend as correlated with intimacy with each one of the parents.

PARENTAL PERSPECTIVE: PARENTS' REPORTS OF
THEIR INTIMACY WITH THEIR DAUGHTER

First we examined two questions. Does parental perspective correlate or predict intimacy of the daughter with a peer? Does the relevance of parental perspective on the relationship with the daughter vary as a function of developmental stage?

Reports were obtained from mother and father regarding intimacy toward their daughters. Data on kibbutz and city girls showed variations. Examining Table 9.4 shows that reports of fathers and mothers about their intimacy with their daughters correlate significantly at grade 4 ($r = .66$) but do not correlate at all at grade 7. In the kibbutz; in the family sleeping arrangement, which is like the city; and when sleeping at home was recent (3 to 4 years prior to the study), there were negative correlations between reports of father and mother intimacy toward their daughters ($-.46$ and $-.54$), perhaps indicating a division in the closeness to their daughters between mothers and fathers. This is quite different for the stable communal sleeping arrangements, where reports by mothers and fathers showed low but positive correlations (see Table 9.4). The discrepancy between the two patterns of parents' intimacy toward their daughter was significant. Thus, both factors of developmental stage of the children, as well as the degree of daily contact, seem to play a role in defining the degree of similarity in the intimacy that parents feel toward their children.

To what extent do the reports of mothers and daughters on their intimacy toward each other converge? It seems that the degree of agreement is mediated by developmental stage. Reports of mothers and their daughters agreed at grade 4 but did not agree at grades 6 and 7. Specifically, in the city there was agreement ($r = .37$) for grade 4, but not for grade 7 ($r = -.02$). For the kibbutz girls at grade 6 the $r = .18$ to .30 also was not significant. It seems that parental perspective on their intimacy with their offsprings matches in young age, but becomes more complex and therefore shows less agreement in adolescence.

SIMILARITY IN INTIMACY WITH PARENT AND BEST
FRIEND AMONG DIVORCED FAMILIES

The case of divorced families, where fathers are out of the home, presents a case of ecological variation—emotional variation as well as setting variation. The question is whether these circumstances reduce the degree of similarity in intimacy with parent versus best friend. In families where there is discord, would adolescents be seeking intimacy in different ways in order to compensate, or would they be trying to structure relationships that will be dissimilar to those that are not working? In either case, the prediction would be that intimacy with parents and peers would be different in divorced than in nondivorced families.

Hertz-Lazarowitz et al. (1989) examined the effect of divorced parents on their children's intimacy with their friends and parents. The sample consisted of 208 children in grades 5 and 6 from 10 schools, all middle and upper middle class. Of these, 70 children (32 boys and 38 girls) were from divorced families, living with a mother who did not remarry. The remaining 138 children were from two-parent families (57 boys and 81 girls). Participants were asked to complete the intimacy scale with regard to their same-gender best friend, mother, and father. They were also asked to complete a short intimacy form consisting of eight single items, each representing a dimension from the intimacy scale. Children were asked to describe their relationships with six additional friends (1 to 6) on this short form of the intimacy scale.

The study of city children of divorced parents (Hertz-Lazarowitz et al., 1989) showed that intimacy with fathers who do not share the same household was less correlated with intimacy with best friend than in the control group of children from intact families. With two parents at home, correlations between intimacy with father and friend were statistically significant. Thus, reduced daily contact per se (as in the Kibbutz setting) does not decrease the parental-peer parallel, but emotional change does change the degree of relevance of the two systems—parents and peers. Indeed, studies show reduced intimacy of children toward the fathers in divorced families (i.e., Gonzalez, Field, Lasko, & Harding, 1995).

RELEVANCE OF INTIMACY WITH PARENTS TO INTIMACY WITH PEERS IN JUVENILE DELINQUENTS AND ADOLESCENTS AT RISK

Among families with delinquent offspring or families in a similar high-risk circumstance, it was predicted that there would be a greater split between the close relationships within the family (with the parents) and the closeness to a peer best friend because the adolescent would turn to peers. The findings indicate a smaller congruence between intimacy with parents and a best friend (see Table 9.2). It is likely that adolescents have a compensatory pattern of relations, where they turn to peers for what they do not receive at home. In a similar pattern identified recently, 5 percent of the adolescents, those who reported having cold and controlling parents, turned to their peers and showed an especially high need for exclusivity in their relationships (Mayseless et al., 1998).

CROSS-CULTURAL COMPARISON: U.S. STUDIES

Rice and Mulkeen (1995) examined the intimacy with parents and friends of a midwestern U.S. town. They used an eight-item intimacy scale, which

Table 9.3

Pearson Correlations of Intimacy Between Parents and Friends: Israel and United States

	grade	N	sex	mother-father	mother-friend	father-friend
City	4th grade	27	girls	.85***	.66***	.65***
	7th grade	27	girls	.56***	.60***	.44**
Sleeping arrangement in kibbutz						
Familial		20	girls	.64**	.57**	.52*
Transitional 8-9 years		21	girls	.65**	.49*	.78**
Transitional 3-4 years	6th grade	18	girls	.45*	.50*	.75**
Communal		19	girls	.66**	.65*	.82**
Divorced Families	5th-6th	40	girls	.24	.46**	.31*
Intact families	Grade	79	girls	.65***	.24*	.29**
City U.S.A[5]	8th grade	57	girls	.60***	.18	.22
	12th grade	57	girls	.57***	.19	.28
City	6th-7th grade	151	girls	.33***	-.48***	-.38***
U.S.A[6]	9th-10th grade	232	girls	.09	-.16**	-.15*

*p < .05; **p < .01; ***p < .001.

[5]Rice & Mulkeen (1995).
[6]Lampers et al. (1992).

is comparable in content to the one used in the Israeli studies. Intimacy toward parents was reported as similar, by both boys and girls in grade 8 as well as in grade 12 (see Table 9.3). The finding that adolescents who do not have exceptional life circumstances (such as divorced parents, delinquency, etc.) tend to describe their intimacy with both parents as similar matches the findings in Israel, which were just reported.

However, Rice and Mulkeen's findings were quite different from the Israeli samples presented here. The relevance of father and mother to peer intimacy was not significant (see Table 9.3 for U.S. samples). Specifically, for girls, both in grades 8 and 12, intimacy with mother and friend was not significantly correlated (.18 and .19, respectively). Likewise, intimacy with father and friend was not significantly correlated at both grade levels (.22 and .28). For boys, intimacy with the mother and with the friend at grades 8 and 12 was .01 and .17, and with father-friend, .07 and −.00. Thus, there is "minimal interdependence of adolescent-parent and adolescent-friend intimacy, insofar as the strength of association between these variables was concerned" (p. 354). Using a longitudinal design and regression analysis, these researchers tried to predict a social self-image variable from "intimacy" with parents and peers. They found that all three relationships (father, mother, and best friend) had independent input in predicting social self-image (with specific findings for gender of adolescent by gender of parent).

In contrast, Lempers and Clark-Lempers (1992) reported negative correlations between intimacy with parents and intimacy with peers. They studied three developmental groups: early adolescents (11 to 13 years old), middle adolescents (14 to 16 years old) and late adolescents (17 to 19 years old) from a midwestern U.S. town. Intimacy was measured with the Network of Relationship Inventory (NRI) developed by Furman and Buhrmester (1985). Seven relational attributes were assessed (admiration, affection, companionship, instrumental aid, intimacy, nurturance/reliable alliance, and satisfaction and conflict). The subjects rated five significant relationships, including those with parents and a same-gender best friend. All dimensions (with the exception of conflict) were positively and significantly correlated when applied to a specific relationship. They found that self-worth, affection, and reliable alliance were more prominent among parents, whereas companionship, intimacy, and nurturing behavior were more prominent in the context of a same-gender friend. They found the same patterns of similarity between mother and father on almost all the functions in their three age levels (except for instrumental aid, and except for older females who showed lack of similarity between mother and father on several functions).

Furthermore, the comparison of relationships with each parent and same-gender friend showed negative correlations on almost all the corresponding aspects. Their interpretation was that relationship with parents and peers in early and late adolescence was not similar, but rather was complementary—each relationship addressing a different segment. Citing Ladd (1989), they attempted to illuminate via the study of children's and adolescents' relationships how various relationships complement, elaborate, extend, or impede each other in their respective contributions to their development. This finding was consistent across their three samples, which one may view as a replication of this pattern of complementary correspondence. We can compare these data to those on fifth- and sixth-grade preadolescents from intact families in Israel.

The most similar Israeli sample is in Study c with adolescents from intact families. The results in the Israeli sample showed a consistent but different pattern (see Table 9.2). Total intimacy was significantly correlated for both father-friend and mother-friend.

Examining data from both parents and daughters (see Table 9.4) in grade 4, in addition to the similarity in reports on intimacy between mother and father ($r = .66$), intimacy of fathers to their daughters is correlated with intimacy of daughters to best friends ($r = .41$). Also, mothers' and their daughters' reports agree in grade 4. Finally, intimacy of mother and father towards their daughters, as reported by them, varies, depending on sleeping arrangements in the kibbutz. When the daughter is at home, parents differ in their intimacy toward her; when she is out of the home, they agree ($r =$ .24).

DISCUSSION AND CONCLUSIONS

The first conclusion is that there is a marked difference between the Israeli sample and the U.S. midwest sample. The pattern of greater tendency toward consistency among one's relationships was evident in the Israeli sample, where a tendency toward greater "specialization" or turning away from parents toward peers is more evident in the sample by Lempers and Clark-Lempers (1992). In the Israeli cultural context, lack of correspondence between parent-child and child-child relationships outside the family reflects problems in the family. The lack of continuity between parental and peer intimacy in the delinquent and the risk samples needs further investigation. However, it attests to incongruity in adolescent life. Possibly, these are adolescents who seek compensation outside the family or at least in nonsimilar relationships.

Generally, there is continuity between intimacy with each parent and peer, although there may be variations in intensity, reflected in correlations between mother, father, and peer based on self-reports. Examining the correlations shows that the highest is .85 for the youngest girls (grade 4). The developmental aspect is that younger girls tend to regard their relationships with mother and father as most similar. This perception changes when the girls are in grade 7 ($r = 56$). The lowest correlation was among divorced families of boys (.20), in contrast to boys from intact families (.76) showing incongruent and lack of similarity in their relationships with divorced parents.

The validity of the children's reports is demonstrated in this reality-based report. In the kibbutz, across different sleeping arrangements, intimacy with mother and father was correlated (.66 to .45, all significant, see Table 9.2). Thus, the daily availability of parents was not a significant modifier of the perception of similarity in degree of intimacy with mother and father, in contrast to the children of divorced parents.

A major assertion of the ecological theory is the bidirectionality of the influence of each participant in the system—parents influence relationships with peers and peers influence relationships with parents. However, this is used as an assumption here, but we are unable to investigate directions of influence.

The evidence accumulated from a series of studies carried out in Israel under several ecological conditions lead to several conclusions. Under normal conditions in Israel, there is a considerable degree of a parallel experience in intimate relationships with parents and with peers. Preadolescents and adolescents may be saying that their parents are, to some degree, also their close friends. In addition, it seems that under normal conditions, adolescents and preadolescents perceive intimacy with father and mother has a component of similarity. General intimacy with parents is reflected also in their relationships with their intimate friends. There are gender differences in the specific features of intimacy with parent and friend, particularly for boys.

Reports by parents about their close relationships with their daughters are relevant to the intimacy of their daughter with her best friend only at the young age of preadolescence (see Table 9.4). At adolescence, how parents perceive their intimacy at home corresponds to the way their daughters see it. Collecting data from the parents' home is expensive. It may be argued that there is no relationship between these two perspectives, or that parental perspective is relevant in childhood but less so in adolescence.

Future studies have the difficult task of documenting the directions of influence from the indirect experience with the parent to intimate friendship with a close friend, as well as the opposite direction of influence—meaningful experiences in intimacy with a peer being imported home. Using observations, we can find examples. When children use curses at home, parents easily identify the source as peer. Also, among immigrants, children very often bring the new local language home and parents can easily acknowledge the source.

A limitation in the study is the reliance on self-report of the adolescent, although this may have had a limited impact on the studies. First, the validity of self-reports of adolescents about their relationships with parents and peers is supported by a study that demonstrated consistency in the reports and behavioral measures recorded by observers (Flannery, Montemayor, Eberly, & Torquati, 1993). Second, in two studies we had parental reports, which is an additional source as well. The convergence of two self-reports attests to their validity.

Another shortcoming of these studies is the concurrent nature of the assessment procedure, using similar measurement. Because we asked how certain conditions in the family may influence the behaviors of parents toward their adolescent child or influence the relations of the son or daughter with his or her friends, the discriminant validity of the results can be pointed out. In cases where the circumstances are of lowered emotional parental involvement, such as divorce, results were accordingly. Thus, for adolescents from divorced families and adolescents who have been identified as delinquent or at risk, intimate friendships with peers do not resemble the parental relationship. In these cases there is a socioemotional breakdown. Thus, the emotional circumstances of divorce weaken the link between father intimacy and peer intimacy. In contrast, in the case of physical distance, which is not part of an emotional problem, as in the communal sleeping arrangement in the kibbutz, the similarity between parent and peer intimacy is not reduced.

Table 9.4
Parents and Daughters Report Intimacy: Pearson Correlations

	Parents' report: Daughters' report:	Father-daughter Daughter-friend	Mother-daughter Daughter-friend	Mother-daughter Daughter-mother	Mother-daughter Father-daughter
City	4th grade	.41*	.29	.37*	.66***
	7th grade	-.14	-.09	-.02	.08
Sleeping arrangement in kibbutz					
Familial		-.01	.19	.18	-.46*
Transitional 8-9 years	6th grade	.22	-.09	.28	-.10
Transitional 3-4 years		.04	.13	.26	-.54**
Communal		.14	.29	.30	.24

*p < .05; **p < .01; ***p < .001.

Thus, the measurement is sensitive to different social and familial circumstances, and is valid.

There are indications that the degree of congruence and similarity found in our studies in Israel are specific to the high family orientation in Israel. Two studies carried out in U.S. midwestern towns documented a pattern of less similarity and instead complementarity or a lack of connection between intimacy with parents and peers. These findings call for a specifically designed cross-cultural study that will enable reconciliation of the differing U.S. reports (both from the midwest) and clarify the cultural component. These findings echo an old discussion in the peer literature. Bronfenbrenner and his associates presented the peer culture as opposing parental values, whereas Youniss and his associates documented the congruency between the relationship with parents and the relationships with peers. In Israel, the peer's culture is perhaps the parents' culture in many ways. Judging from the present series of studies, the discrepancy between close relationships with parents and best friend is an indication of a problematic case.

Perhaps viewing intimacy as a complex multidimensional construct enables us to appreciate a greater degree of overlap in relationships with peers and parents. Perhaps there is an element of symmetrical reciprocity that by definition cannot be present in child-parent relationships, and this is one uniquely contributed by the best friend peer experience. There may be individual differences among families having to do with experiencing reciprocity and mutuality in the Piagetian sense, ones that produce intimacy of parents with their children (such as more communication and more democracy). There may also be ones that do not create intimacy of parents and offspring (authoritarian, less democratic). In the latter type of families, children have to find real reciprocity and intimacy outside the home. One such study has already been done (Mayseless et al., 1998).

NOTES

The help of Yael Kidron and Rivka Amir in preparing this chapter is gratefully acknowledged.

Part of this chapter was presented at the Kent Psychology Forum on "Explaining associations between family and peer relationships," Applied Psychology Center, Kent State University, April 26–29, 1998.

REFERENCES

Bronfenbrenner, U. (1986). Ecology of the family as a context for human development: Research perspectives. *Developmental Psychology, 22,* 723–742.

Bronfenbrenner, U., McClelland, P., Wethington, E., & Moen, P. (1996). *The state of Americans: This generation and the next.* New York The Free Press.

Buhrmester, D., & Furman, W. (1986). The changing functions of friends in childhood: A neo-Sullivanian perspective. In Derlega, V. J., & Winstead, B. A. (Eds.), *Friendship and social interaction.* (pp. 41–62). New York: Springer-Verlag.

Cohn, D. A., Patterson, C. J., & Christopoulos, C. (1991). The family and children's peer relations. *Journal of Social and Personal Relationships 8,* 312–346.

Devereux, E. C. Jr., Bronfenbrenner, U., Rodgers, R. R., Kav-Venaki, S., Keily, E., & Karson, E. (1974). Socialization practices of parents, teachers, and peers in Israel: The kibbutz versus the city. *Child Development, 45,* 269–281.

Flannery, D. J., Montemayor, R., Eberly, M., & Torquati, J. (1993). Unraveling the ties that bind: Affective expression and perceived conflict in parent-adolescent interactions. *Journal of Social and Personal Relationships, 10,* 495–509.

Furman, W. (1993). Theory is not a four letter word: Needed directions in the study of adolescent friendships. In B. Laursen (Ed.), *Close friendships in adolescence* (pp. 89–103). San Francisco: Jossey-Bass.

Furman, W., & Buhrmester, D. (1985). Children's perceptions of the personal relationships in their social network. *Developmental Psychology, 21,* 1016–1024.

Furman, W., & Buhrmester, D. (1992). Age and sex differences in perceptions of network of personal relationships. *Child Development, 61,* 103–115.

Furman, W., & Wehner, E. A. (1994). Romantic views: Toward a theory of adolescent romantic relationships. In Montemayor, R., Adams, G. R., & Guttura, T. P. (Eds.), *Advances in adolescent development: Annual book series no. 6* (pp. 168–195). London: Sage.

Gavin, L. A., & Furman, W. (1996). Adolescent girls' relationships with mothers and best friends. *Child Development, 67,* 375–386.

Guilford, J. P. (1965). *Fundamental statistics in psychology and education.* New York: McGraw-Hill.

Gonzalez, K. P., Field, T. M., Lasko, D., & Harding, J. (1995). Adolescents from divorced and intact families. *Journal of Divorce and Remarriage, 23,* 165–175.

Harlow, H. F., & Harlow, M. (1966). Learning to love. *American Scientist, 54,* 244–272.

Hertz-Lazarowitz, R. L., Rosenberg, M., & Gotman, J. (1989). Children of divorce and their intimate relationships with parents and peers. *Youth and Society, 21,* 85–104.

Hofstede, S. (1980). *Culture's consequences: International differences in work-related values.* Beverly Hills, CA: Sage.

Katriel, T. (1991). *Communal webs: Communication and culture in contemporary Israel.* Albany: State University of New York Press.

Kerns, K. A. (1996). Individual differences in friendship quality: Links to child-mother attachment. In Buchowski, W. M., Newcomb, A. F., & Hartup, W. W. (Eds.), *The company they keep: Friendship in childhood and adolescence.* Cambridge UK: Cambridge University Press.

Kerns, K. A., Klepac, L., & Cole, A. (1996). Peer relationships and preadolescents' perception of security in the child-mother relationship. *Developmental Psychology, 32,* 457–466.

Ladd, G. W. (1989). Toward a further understanding of peer relationships and their contributions to child development. In Berndt, T. J., & Ladd, G. W. (Eds.), *Peer relationships in child development* (pp. 1–11). New York: Wiley.

Ladd, G. W., & LeSieur, K. D. (1995). Parents and children's peer relationship. In

Borenstein, M. H. *Journal of Youth and Adolescence, 21*, 53–96. (Ed), *Handbook of parenting, Vol. 4: Applied and practical parenting* (pp. 377–409). Hillsdale, NJ: Erlbaum.

Lavi, Z. (1990). *Kibbutz members study kibbutz children*. Westport, CT: Greenwood Press.

Lempers, J. D., & Clark-Lempers, D. S. (1992). Young, middle, and late adolescents' comparisons of the functional importance of five significant relationships.

Lieblich, A. (1989). *Transition to adulthood during military service: The Israeli case*. Albany: State University of New York Press.

Mayseless, O., Sharabany, R., & Sagi, A. (1997). Attachment concerns of mothers as manifested in parental, spousal, and friendship relationships. *Personal Relationships, 4*, 255–269.

Mayseless, O., Wiseman, H., & Hai, I. (1998). Adolescents' relationships with father, mother, and same-sex friend. *Journal of Adolescence Research, 13*, 101–123.

Newcomb, A. F., & Begwell, C. L. (1995). Children's friendship relations: A meta-analytic review. *Psychological Bulletin, 117*, 306–347.

Newman, B. M. (1989). The changing nature of the parent/adolescent relationship from early to late adolescence. *Adolescence, 96*, 915–924.

Park, K. A., & Waters, E. (1989). Security of attachment and preschool friendships. *Child Development, 60*, 1076–1081.

Parke, R. D., & Ladd, G. W. (Eds.). (1992). *Family-peer relationships: Models of linkage*. Hillsdale, NJ: Erlbaum.

Parke, R. D., & Tinsley, B. R. (1984). Historical and contemporary perspectives on fathering. In McCluskey K. A., & Reese, H. W. (Eds.), *Life span developmental psychology* (pp. 243–248). New York: Academic Press. Peres, Y., & Katz, R. (1981). Stability and centrality: The nuclear family in modern Israel. *Social Forces, 59*, 687–704.

Piaget, J. (1965). *The moral judgment of the child*. New York: The Free Press.

Prager, K. (1995). *The psychology of intimacy*. New York: Guilford.

Reis, H. T., Senchack, M., & Solomon, B. (1985). Sex differences in the intimacy of social interaction: Further examination of potential explanation. *Journal of Personality and Social Psychology, 48*, 1204–1277.

Rice, K. J., & Mulkeen, P. (1995). Relationships with parents and peers: A longitudinal study of adolescent intimacy. *Journal of Adolescent Research, 10*, 338–357.

Sharabany, R. (1974). Intimate friendship among kibbutz and city children and its measurements. *Dissertation Abstracts International, 35*, 10289B.

Sharabany, R. (1994). Intimate friendship scale: conceptual underpinnings, psychometric properties and construct validity. *Journal of Social and Personal Relationships, 11*, 449–469.

Sharabany, R., Gershoni, R., & Hofman, J. (1981). Girlfriend, boyfriend, age and sex differences in intimate friendship. *Developmental Psychology, 17*, 800–808.

Sharabany, R., Hertz-Lazarowitz, R., & Gabovitzh-Hodis, M. (1986). Juvenile delinquents' empathy and perception of their relations with father, mother and best friend. University of Haifa. Unpublished manuscript.

Sternberg, R. J. (1986). A triangular theory of love. *Psychology Review, 93*, 119–135.

Sullivan, H. S. (1953). *The interpersonal theory of psychiatry*. New York: Norton.

Triandis, H. C., McCusker, C., & Hui, C. H. (1990). Multimethod probes of individualism and collectivism. *Journal of Personality and Social Psychology, 59,* 1006–1020.

Youniss, J. (1980). *Parents and peers in social development: A Piaget-Sullivan perspective.* Chicago: University of Chicago Press.

Youniss, J., & Smollar, J. (1985). *Adolescent relations with mothers, fathers, and friends.* Chicago: University of Chicago Press.

10

Family and Peer Relationships and the Real-World Practitioner: A Commentary

Angela M. Neal-Barnett

Peer and family relationships are important aspects of a child's well-being. Understanding how these important interactions influence children's behavior and emotional health is crucial to developing accurate assessments and appropriate interventions. Too often, practitioners who work with children and families on a daily basis do not receive information on state-of-the-art research. Practitioners who are aware of the research may be skeptical because researchers are "not operating in the real world." In the area of family and peer relationships, these criticisms are intensified because of distinct differences between social developmentalists and practitioners. Traditionally, social developmentalists are trained to be scientists and to write for the scientific community. Practitioners are trained in an applied manner for the delivery of clinical services. Practitioners come from a variety of psychology and nonpsychology backgrounds including counselor education, counseling, counseling psychology, clinical psychology, and social work. Surveys suggest that individuals who, on a day-to-day basis, deliver services to children and families are master-level practitioners with limited research experience (Magrab & Wohlford, 1990).

This chapter focuses on integrating family and peer relationships research into the practice of child and family therapy. The first part of the chapter examines barriers and solutions to the research-practice gap. The second half examines ways to integrate this research into the assessment and treatment of children and families with a specific focus on attachment, parenting, and peer interactions. The issues and ideas discussed here grew out of the community participation portion of the 1998 Kent Psychology Forum. Participants included five practicing therapists, three doctoral-level clinical psychologists, one licensed independent social worker (LISW), and one master's level counselor. Two psychologists and the LISW were involved also in policymaking. The community participants attended the second day of the forum and heard presentations based on the chapters in this volume by Howes and Tonyan, (Chapter 4), Contreras and Kerns (Chapter 1), Dishion, Poulin, and Skaggs (Chapter 2), and Mounts (Chapter 7). At the end of the day, I led community participants in a 1-hour roundtable discussion. The discussion touched on the topics of bridging the gap between researchers and practitioners as well as ways to use the presented research in the practice of child and family therapy.

BARRIERS TO RESEARCH USE

As scientists, peer and family relationships experts are trained to write for a specific audience—the academic community. As practitioners, patient flow and paperwork demands leave little time to read scientific journals. Given these facts, how then does the peer and family relationships researcher increase the likelihood that his or her research reaches the child and family practitioner? One possible solution is by publishing in practice journals.

Practice journals are available in clinical psychology, social work, and all the counseling subdisciplines. The writing style and format of papers published in these journals is markedly different from scientific journals. In practice journals, the how-to approach is emphasized. However, for the most part, family and peer relationship experts are in nonpracticing disciplines and are unlikely to submit manuscripts for publication in a practice journal. A need exists for collaboration between family and peer relationship researchers, clinical researchers, and practitioners. An example of such collaboration can be found in Dishion et al. (Chapter 2, this volume). Dishion et al.'s work is conducted in a research and practice center where a team of clinical and nonclinical researchers and practitioners interact. A collaborative effort may produce a win-win situation (Covey, 1990) for everyone. The practitioner gains knowledge, the knowledge gained enhances the treatment provided to children and families, the researcher gains insight into the practice implications of the work, and both the practice and nonpractice researcher gain an additional publication.

Some research does not lend itself easily to a practice journal format, yet the results have significant practice implications. Often, the clinical significance of studies are buried deep within an article. Given the previously mentioned time constraints on the average practitioner, the forum's community participants suggested changes in the way researchers present their scientific findings. Practitioners need to know in a straightforward manner, is the finding meaningful for the assessment and treatment of children and their families? From a practitioner's point of view, rather than or in addition to reporting traditional statistics (e.g., ANOVAS, MANOVAS, Rs), what may be more helpful is reporting results in terms of ratios. For example, if a researcher has conducted a study on attachment and academic achievement rather than or in addition to reporting that the F for attachment and academic achievement was significant at the .001 level, a statement that children who are securely attached are three times more likely to succeed in school may be more meaningful to the practitioner. Combining a ratio report with a section addressing treatment implications would greatly enhance the practice friendly aspects of family and peer relationship research.

Publishing in practice journals or altering the way information is presented in scientific journals is one way to bridge the research-practice gap. Another, more applied approach, is encouraging family and peer relationship experts to engage in consultation. Consultation may take several forms, one possibility is in-service training. Currently, most state licensing boards require practitioners to complete a minimum number of continuing education units (CEUs) for license renewal. In-service training at one's place of employment is the way many therapists obtain their CEUs. By providing in-service training to child- and family-oriented mental health centers and practice groups, the family and peer relationship expert disseminates information about state-of-the-art research as well as helping practitioners fulfill a mandated requirement.

Consultation services may also be provided via a preventative approach. Most referrals for child and family therapy come from day-care centers, preschools, and schools. The attachment literature indicates that day-care providers and preschool teachers serve as attachment figures because, in the mother's absence, they fulfill many of the same caretaking duties (Howes & Tonyan, Chap. 4, this volume). The peer relationship research indicates that from a very early age, peer socialization is important. Given this evidence, having a family or peer relationship consultant work with preschools, day care centers, and school staff could prevent some problems before they occur and could facilitate the children's learning and emotional growth.

The consultant's role need not be limited to the staff but could extend to the parents. The consultant could be available to answer parents' questions on a host of matters including but not limited to providing socialization opportunities, strengthening the attachment bond, and understanding and identifying appropriate and inappropriate socializing behaviors. Several of the forum's research participants have functioned in this capacity, and found it mutually beneficial for themselves, the parents, the preschool–day-care center–school staff, and, most importantly, the children.

I recognize that nonpractice oriented researchers are often uncomfortable transforming their research for use in an applied setting. Yet, the area of family and peer relationships would appear to lend itself easily to applied consultation. Effective treatment of children and their families requires that the therapist have a working knowledge of these groups' social and developmental aspects. As evidenced in this volume, many facets of peer and family relationships are crucial to a child's healthy emotional adjustment.

Thus far, this chapter has focused on barriers and solutions to incorporating family and peer relationships into the practice setting. The remainder of the chapter focuses on aspects of the research, presented in this volume, that are important for the assessment and treatment of children and their families, specifically attachment, parenting, and peer interactions.

ASSESSMENT AND OUTCOME MEASURES

In the managed care age, practitioners have had to pay closer attention to assessment and outcome measures. For this reason, development of assessment and outcome measures cannot occur in a vacuum. The development and validation of assessment measures in research settings alone may only serve to widen the gap between research and practice. Because researchers are generally interested in within-sample variability and how scores relate to other variables within the sample, they are less likely to develop meaningful clinical cutoff points. Such cutoffs are crucial in the applied setting.

Research-world assessments are often administered by research assistants and are frequently several hours in length. Real-world clients and their parents have neither the time nor the desire to spend several hours answering questions and completing lengthy forms, not to mention the time constraints on the clinician who is responsible for assessment and treatment. A more feasible approach might be to include practitioners in the development of assessment measures. By including practitioners from the beginning of assessment and outcome measure development, many of the postdevelopment issues voiced by the practitioners (too long, too cumbersome, too wordy, irrelevant to the practice setting) could be avoided (Sobell, 1996).

The community practitioners felt much of the forum presented research lent itself easily to the task of developing assessment and outcome measures. For example, the attachment research suggests children can and do form attachment relationships with people other than their parents. These individuals include teachers, grandparents, and caregivers (Howes & Tonyan, Chapter 4, this volume). Transforming this information into assessment questions ensures that the therapist will obtain information about important relationships, both familial and nonfamilial, in the child's life. In turn, procuring this information ensures that all available major attachment figures are considered when attempting further assessment and intervention. Such an approach is particularly important when working with ethnic minority children where the extended family plays an important role, but often is a neglected assessment variable (Neal-Barnett & Smith, 1997).

Ideally, when a child is referred for treatment, information is gathered from all the settings in which the child interacts. In the real world, time demands dictate that only the parent and child are interviewed. Yet the attachment literature underscores the importance of attachment in teacher relationships and in fostering appropriate peer relationships. The attachment data presented at the forum underscores the need to make the teachers' report a mandatory part of real-world assessment.

PARENTING

Parenting plays an important role in how a child grows and develops. Within practice settings, many parents who accompany their children to therapy either lack adequate parenting skills or demonstrate a need for enhancement of their skills. As several authors in this volume have noted, parenting is a developmental process. As a child grows and develops, parenting skills also grow and develop. A significant portion of the child and family practitioner's work involves parent training. The research presented at the forum on parenting, parental monitoring, peer autonomy, and parent involvement in peer selection can be easily incorporated into the practice setting. The definitions as well as the positive and negative aspects of monitoring, directing, and prohibiting of peer contacts could easily be integrated into a parent-training program. Once parents gained understanding of the terms, they could then engage in self-study as to if and how each technique is used in their own family. The self-study's results would enable the practitioner to tailor a parenting program that focused on enhancing and changing a family's strengths and weaknesses.

PEER INTERACTIONS

Children who exhibit both internalizing and externalizing psychopathology experience disruptions in their peer relationships. Conduct-disordered children tend to be rejected by their peers, negative peer relationships appear to place children at risk for depression and suicide, and children who are victimized by their peers tend to be anxious and withdrawn (Olweus, 1993; Rubin, LeMare, & Lollis, 1990). Controversy exists as to whether the presence of psychopathology leads to negative peer relationships or if negative peer relationships lead to psychopathology (Parker & Asher, 1987). Regardless, the child practitioner frequently finds that peer interactions are a concomitant focus of therapy. Therefore, it becomes important that the therapist has a working knowledge of peer relationships and interactions. Simply stated, it is difficult to improve a child's peer interactions, if one does not understand how from a developmental perspective those interactions operate.

The information contained in this volume can serve as a valuable resource for practitioners in understanding children's and early adolescents' peer interactions. The work by Contreras and Kerns (Chapter 1, this volume) assists the practitioner in understanding emotion regulation's (ER) role in the process. As these authors point out, children who are securely attached to a parental figure have less difficulty behaving competently with peers. One reason for this fact is that in the mother-child relationship, secure attachment leads to the learning of appropriate and positive ER, which appears to influence peer interactions. Children tend to respond more positively to children who are effective at ER.

For the practitioner, an understanding of ER and its role in peer interaction, may lead to the teaching and modeling of effective ER in therapy. Clinical research indicates that socially anxious and depressed children tend to misread or misinterpret cues from their peers and react in a negative fashion. In turn, this behavior leads to an unfavorable response from peers. Learning new ways to interpret the cues and rehearsing those new skills can have a significant impact on the child's peer interactions.

CONCLUSION

Based on the forum's dialogue between practitioners and researchers, it is clear that family and peer relationships research can benefit the real-world practitioner. This chapter has briefly addressed ways in which the research can be disseminated to practitioners as well as how practitioners can incorporate the research into their respective practices. It is hoped that researchers and practitioners will combine their efforts to further enhance the quality of services delivered to children and their families.

REFERENCES

Covey, S. R. (1990). *The seven habits of highly effective people.* New York: Simon & Schuster.

Magrab, P. R., & Wohlford, P. (1990). *Improving psychological services for children and adolescents with severe mental disorders: Clinical training in psychology.* Washington, DC: American Psychological Association.

Neal-Barnett, A. M., & Smith, J. Sr. (1997). African Americans. In Friedman, S. (Ed.), *Cultural issues in the treatment of anxiety* (pp. 154–174). New York: Guilford.

Parker, J. G., & Asher, S. R. (1987). Peer relations and later personal adjustment: Are low-accepted children at risk? *Psychological Bulletin, 102,* 289–357.

Olweus, D. (1993). Victimization by peers: Antecedents and long-term outcomes. In Rubin, K. H., & Asendorpf, J. B. (Eds.), *Social withdrawal, inhibition, and shyness in childhood* (pp. 315–341). Hillsdale, NJ: Erlbaum.

Rubin, K. H., LeMare, L., & Lollis, S. (1990). Social withdrawal in childhood: Developmental pathways to rejection. In Asher, S. R., & Coie, J. D. (Eds.), *Peer rejection in childhood* (pp. 217–249). New York: Cambridge University Press.

Sobell, L. C. (1996). Bridging the gap between scientists and practitioners: The challenge before us. *Behavior Therapy 27,* 297–320.

Index

Academic achievement, 176–177, 178–
180, 182; attitudes toward, 178–180.
See also School adaptation

Adolescents, viii-ix, 27, 29–32, 170–177,
186–189, 215–219, 235–237, 239–
244. *See also* Early adolescence

Aggression, ix; bullying, 50; emotional
components, 58–59, 74, 118–119, 124–
128, 158–159; indirect, 51; instrumental, 50–51; and marital hostility,
117–118, 125–128; overt, 51, 52–53,
55–56, 58–59, 70–71, 75–77; and
parenting style, 55–57, 67–72, 119,
124–128, 145–147, 150–151, 155; and
peer relationships, 124–125; proactive, 50–51, 56–58; reactive, 52–54,
56–58; relational, 51, 53–54, 56–57,
58–59, 71–72, 75–77; social cognitive
biases, 52–53, 55–56, 123, 127, 145–
147, 154, 158–159; subtypes, 47–48,
50–51, 64–66, 75–77. *See also* Antisocial behavior

Antisocial behavior: and adjustment,
115–116; and marital relationship,
117–118; and parent psychopathology, 117–118; and parenting, 31–
32, 39–40, 119–121, 145–147; and
peers, 171–172, 178–179, 255; and
psychophysiology, 122–124, 128. *See
also* Aggression

Arousal and physiological activity, 57,
121–124, 126–128, 149–151, 158–
159, 162, 210–211. *See also* Emotions;
Temperament

Assessment of peer relationships, 98–
100, 101–102, 244, 254–256

Attachment, ix; attachment figures, 2,
86, 91–92; attachment quality, 2, 95–
98, 254; and emotion regulation, 3,
10–18, 255–256; father-child attachment, 3–4, 14–18; and friendship, 3–
4, 88, 89–91, 103–109, 147–148;
mother-child attachment, 3–4, 14–18,
87–88, 92–93, 95–98, 100–101, 103–
104, 106–109; parent and peer systems, 232–233; and peer social interaction or competence, 3–4, 14–18, 87–
88, 89–91, 92–93, 103–106, 109, 197,
232–233; secure base and safe haven,
11–12, 87; teacher-child attachment,
86, 87–88, 91–93, 95–97, 100–101,

104–109, 254; working models, 4–5,
74, 88, 89, 138, 147–148, 153, 154
Attention processes, 7, 13–14, 122–123,
214–215. *See also* Temperament
Attributions, 55–56, 127, 145–146, 152,
154, 156, 157, 158–159. *See also* Social cognition; Social information
processing
Autonomy, 29–32, 37–40, 171–172,
185, 215–216, 235–236

Bidirectional family-peer effects, 232–
233, 243
Biological influence on peer relationships, 27–28, 29, 37–40, 216
Bullying, 50

Child psychopathology, 255–256. *See
also* Antisocial behavior
Clinical implications of research on
family and peer relationships, 251–
256
Cognitive models of relationships, 213–
214, 218. *See also* Internal representations of relationships; Social cognition; Working models
Consultation, 253. *See also* Practitioners
Continuity across relationships, 89–93,
227, 230–235, 236–243; compensatory processes, 242
Coping, 7–8, 10–12, 15–18, 128–129,
214–215
Culture, ix; cross cultural comparisons,
55, 71–72, 75, 240–243, 246; influence on parent-child relationship or
parenting style, 18–19, 47–50, 157,
185–186, 235–236, 254; influence on
peer relationships, 246; in Israel, 235–
236, 237–238, 243–244; in Russia, 47–
50, 75

Delinquency, 30, 147, 150, 176–177,
178–180, 182, 237, 240, 243, 244–
245
Developmental stage; and family-peer
links, viii, 156, 162, 236–237, 243;
and family relationships, 31–32, 108–
109, 162, 170–172, 185, 202–203,
206–207, 215–216, 217–218, 239; and

peer relationships, 31–32, 108–109,
207–209, 216–217
Direct effects of family relationships,
127–128, 157–158, 169–177, 180–
184, 186–187, 196, 234
Divorce, 239–240, 243, 244–245
Drug Use, 175, 178–179, 182

Early adolescence, 97–98, 103–108, 215–
219, 235–237, 239–244. *See also* Middle childhood; Preadolescents
Early childhood, 196, 197–202. *See also*
Preschool age
Ecological models, 28–29, 40–42, 162,
227–228, 234, 235, 239–240, 243
Emotions: arousal and reactivitiy, 9, 57,
123, 126–128, 149–151, 158–159,
162, 210–211, 214–215; display rules,
211–212; encoding and decoding
skills, 209; parent socialization of, 7,
10–13, 19, 119–121, 124–128, 148–
149, 197–202, 207–212, 215, 217–218;
regulation and dysregulation, 3–8,
122, 162, 214–215; regulation and
marital relationships, 117–119, 123–
124; regulation and parent-child relationships, 3, 10–18, 197–202, 207–
212, 215, 255–256; regulation and
parent psychopathology, 118–119;
regulation and peer relationships, viii,
9, 13, 14–18, 121, 122–123, 124–128,
138, 149–151, 158–159, 197–202, 210–
211, 214–215, 255–256; understanding, 9, 138, 148–149, 209
Equifinality, 153
Evolutionary theory, 27–28, 31

Family processes: cohesion, 58–59; conflict, 58–59; extended family, 254;
family systems, 129
Father-child relationships: influence on
peer relationships, 3–4, 14–18, 156,
197–202, 203–204, 207–212, 213–
214, 236–237, 238–243; interaction
quality, 197–202, 203–204; socialization of emotions, 197–202, 207–212,
215. *See also* Attachment; Parenting
practices and socialization

Friendship, ix; definition, 86; developmental issues, 216–217; friends' adjustment, 178–179; friendship network, 33, 35, 37–40; friendship nominations, 178; friendship quality, 98–100, 228–230; friendship selection, 29, 172, 173–175, 176–177, 180–184; and parent-child relationships, 3–4, 88, 103–109, 170, 180–184, 236–243, 244–246; and social interaction, 101–102

Gender differences: aggression, 52, 53, 57–58, 71, 155; emotion socialization, 126, 197–202; intimacy, 229, 240–241; parenting, 156, 203–204; peer relationships, 3; school adaptation, 35

Indirect effects of family relationships, 127–128, 169–170, 196, 197–202, 234. *See also* Mediation effects for family-peer links
Internal representations of relationships, 88, 89, 109, 138, 147–148. *See also* Working models
Interventions, 42, 184–185, 253
Intimacy: in friendship, 228–230; parent-peer connections, 234, 236–243; with parents, 239; peer influences on intimacy, 30, 233–234, 244

Kibbutz, 237–238, 243. *See also* Culture, in Israel

Longitudinal studies, viii, 32, 85, 93, 101–109, 161, 177, 180–182, 188, 196

Marital relationships, ix; marital distress or hostility and emotion regulation, 57, 117–119, 123–128, 150–151; marital/family conflict and aggression, 57–58, 67–70, 71, 119; marital violence, 117–118, 125–128; and parenting, 117–119, 121, 126, 129
Mechanisms. *See* Mediation effects for family-peer links
Mediation effects for family-peer links, vii-viii, 137–145, 151–163; deviant

peer clustering, 39–40; emotion regulation, 14–18, 149–151, 197–202, 207–212; emotion understanding, 148–149; parent personality, 119; physiological regulation, 121; social information processing, 74, 145–147, 213–214, 218; social learning, 147; working models, 74, 147–148
Middle childhood, 14–18, 92–93, 96–97, 99–100, 103–108, 196, 217. *See also* Early adolescence; Preadolescents
Moderation effects for family-peer links, 154–157; parenting style as moderator, 155–156
Mother-child relationships: influence on peer relationships, 3–4, 14–18, 85, 87–88, 92–93, 103–104, 106–109, 156, 172–175, 197–204, 207–212, 213–214, 236–237, 238–243; interaction quality, 95–96, 100–101, 197–202, 203–204; socialization of emotions, 197–202, 207–212, 215. *See also* Attachment; Parenting practices and socialization
Multifinality, 154–157

Nonparental adults, 217, 218, 238, 254

Parent affect. *See* Parent emotion regulation
Parent-child interaction: and emotion regulation, 10–13, 19, 197–202; and peer relationships, 196, 197–202, 203–204
Parent emotion regulation, 118–119, 125–128, 197–202, 209
Parent meta-emotion philosophy, 119–121, 126, 150–151
Parent social networks, 205–207
Parental authority: conceptions of, 172, 185–186
Parental management of peer relationships, 170–177, 180–189, 196–197, 202–204, 205–207, 234
Parenting goals, 188–189, 214
Parenting practices and socialization, ix; advising and coaching, 120–121, 126, 150–151, 156, 187, 196, 202–204;

control, 119, 126, 145–147, 156–157, 185–186, 215, 217; coparenting, 129; cultural influence on, 18–19, 47–50, 157, 185–186, 235–236, 254; direct and indirect effects, 127–128, 157–158, 169–177, 180–184, 186–187, 196, 197–202, 234; discipline, 119, 149, 157; effects on peer relationships, 54–56, 127–128, 137–145, 147, 151–157, 180–184, 188, 202–205, 207–212; emotion socialization, 7, 10–13, 19, 119–121, 124–128, 148–149, 197–202, 207–212, 215, 217–218; guiding, 175–177, 178, 180–182, 184, 187; harsh parenting, 145–147, 148; interventions, 255; intrusiveness, 172, 175, 185–186; involvement, 170, 171–172; and marital relationship, 117–118; monitoring and supervision, 30–31, 35, 27–40, 119, 175–176, 177–178, 180–182, 187, 196, 202, 217; parenting skills, 119, 126–128, 255; prohibiting, 175–176, 178, 180–183, 187. *See also* Parenting style

Parenting style, 52–64; and child aggression, 55–57, 67–72, 119, 124–128, 145–147, 150–151, 155; and child social competence, 197; and child victimization, 59, 67–70, 72; and culture, 18–19, 47–50; and emotional security, 74; as moderator, 155–156; psychological control and/or overprotection, 49–50, 56, 71–72; and social cognitive mediators, 55–56, 145–147, 213–214

Peer competence. *See* Peer relationships; Sociometric status/peer acceptance

Peer groups, ix, 29–32, 35, 171–172, 238

Peer influence, 171, 182

Peer problems: assessment, 254–256; prevention, 253; treatment, 184–185, 253–256

Peer relationships: assessment issues, 98–100, 101–102, 244, 254–256; and attachment, 3–4, 14–18, 87–88, 89–93, 103–108, 232–233; and dating, 29–32; deviant peer groups, 29–32, 35, 37–40; and emotion regulation, 9, 13, 14–18, 121, 122–123, 124–128, 138, 149–151, 158–159, 197–202, 207–212, 256; friendships, 3–4, 29, 33, 35, 37–40, 88, 89, 98–100, 101–109, 172, 173–175, 176–177, 228–230, 236–243, 244–246; and father-child relationships, 3–4, 14–18, 67–74, 156, 207–212, 213–214, 236–243; mixed sex interactions, 29–30; and mother-child relationships, 3–4, 14–18, 67–74, 87–88, 103–104, 106–109, 156, 207–212, 213–214, 236–243; and parent-child interaction quality, 197–202, 203–204, 209–210, 215; parent management of, 170–177, 180–189, 196–197, 202–204, 205–207, 234; reciprocity, 234, 246; responses to peer provocation, 52–54, 64–66, 67–70, 72–74; social interaction with peers, ix, 9, 16–18, 86, 89–93, 98–100, 101–106, 108–109, 124–125, 147; sociometric status/peer acceptance, 124, 125, 196, 197; stability, viii, 93, 101, 108; susceptibility to peer pressure, 171–173, 178, 182; and teacher-child relationships, 87–88, 92–93, 104–109

Peer selection, 29

Practitioners, ix, 251–256; assessment, 254–256; research-practice gap, 252–254

Preadolescents, 14, 32, 233–234, 236–237, 238–244

Preschool age, 60, 90–91, 95–96, 98–99, 103–108, 115–116

Problem behavior 29–32. *See also* Aggression; Antisocial Behavior

Psychoanalytic theory, 230–232

Psychophysiology: and antisocial behavior, 121–124, 128; family-peer mediator, 149–151

Puberty, 29–31, 37–40, 215–216

School adaptation, 33–35, 37–40. *See also* Academic Achievement

Sexual activity, 30–32, 35, 37–40

Siblings, ix

Social behavior. *See* Peer relationships; social interaction with peers

Social cognition: and aggression, 52–53, 55–56, 123, 127, 145–147, 154, 158–159; and emotion, 158–159; and peer relationships, 145–147, 153, 213–214, 256; representations of relationships, 213–214, 218

Social information processing, x, 52–53, 55–56, 74, 138, 145–147, 153, 154, 213–214, 218, 256

Social interaction model, 29, 41–42

Social learning, 58–59, 71–72, 138

Sociometric status/peer acceptance, 124, 125, 196, 197

Statistical issues in evaluating family-peer links, 138–139, 152–153, 159–161, 163, 164, 252–253

Teacher-child relationships: as attachment figures, viii, 86, 91–92, 95–97, 100–101, 254; and peer relationships, 87–88, 92–93, 104–109

Temperament, 7, 9, 121, 130, 156–157. *See also* Arousal and Physiological activity; Emotions

Toddler age, 90–91, 98–99, 103–106

Victimization: and adjustment, 51–52, 54; and family relationships, 59, 67–70, 72; subtypes of victims 51–52, 64–66

Working models: as family-peer mediator, 4–5, 74, 88, 89, 109, 138, 147–148, 153, 154, 218. *See also* Internal representations of relationships

About the Editors and Contributors

JEFFERY E. ASPELMEIER received his doctorate in social psychology from Kent State University and is an assistant professor at Radford University. His research interests include social cognition and close relationships.

JOSEFINA M. CONTRERAS is a clinical/developmental psychologist whose research interests include the study of parent-child relationships and the development of socioemotional competence in children. Her research focuses on normative aspects of parent-child relationships as well as on factors influencing parenting in at-risk and minority populations, with special emphasis on Latino families. Dr. Contreras received her doctorate from the University of Illinois at Chicago and is currently an assistant professor at Kent State University.

THOMAS J. DISHION, PhD, is a research scientist at the Oregon Social Learning Center and an associate professor in clinical psychology at the University of Oregon. His interests include research on child and adolescent social development, especially the joint influence of family and peers within an ecological framework. His work integrates developmental and intervention research in the interest of advancing understanding in both fields of inquiry. Dr. Dishion's NIDA-funded intervention research focuses on support in families within a public school context through the adolescent transition, minimizing problem behavior and promoting health and well being.

CRAIG H. HART is a professor and chair of the Marriage, Family, and Human Development Program, School of Family Life, Brigham Young University. He received his doctorate from Purdue University in 1987 and served on the faculty at Louisiana State University for five years. Dr. Hart has authored and co-authored some 40 scientific papers on parenting, peer relations, and early childhood education curriculum, along with two edited volumes on related topics. He is currently an associate editor of *Early Childhood Research Quarterly*.

CAROLLEE HOWES, Ph.D., is a professor whose research interests are based in the area of social development. One line of research is on the development of peer social interaction skills and friendships, particularly as related to networks of adult attachment relationships. Her recent studies concern the formation and maintenance of friendships in children under three years of age and the development of the ability to communicate with friends in pretend play. A second line of research is on the long-term effects of infant and toddler day care.

LYNN FAINSILBER KATZ, PhD, is a research associate professor in the Department of Psychology at the University of Washington. Her research interests focus on understanding linkages among marital, parenting, and peer relationships using a social psychophysiological approach. Her work on how parents feel about their own and their children's emotions culminated in her recent book entitled *Meta-Emotion: How Families Communicate Emotionally*.

KATHRYN A. KERNS is a developmental psychologist with research interests in the area of parent-child and peer relationships. Some of her studies have examined how parent-child attachment is related to the quality of children's peer relationships. In addition, she has investigated age-related changes in friendships and peer groups. Dr. Kerns received her doctorate from SUNY StonyBrook and is currently an associate professor at Kent State University.

TREVOR R. MCKEE is an associate professor of marriage, family, and human development at the School of Family Life, Brigham Young University. He received his doctorate from Brigham Young University in 1973. His specialties include language development and duolingual education. He is president of International Language Programs, which has numerous sites in Russia.

MARY KAY MCNEILLY-CHOQUE is a doctoral student in marriage, family, and human development at the School of Family Life, Brigham Young University. Her specialty includes the study of different forms of aggression in childhood.

DARRELL MEECE, PhD, is assistant professor of family and child ecology at Michigan State University. He received his doctorate in child development from Auburn University. His current research interests include young children's social cognitions and representations of relationships, emotion regulation, and effects of child care history on children's socioemotional development.

JACQUELYN MIZE received her doctorate in child development from Purdue University and is professor of human development and family studies at Auburn University. Her research focuses on preschool children's social competence and children's relationships with peers and parents. She currently serves on the editorial boards of the *Developmental Psychology* journal and *Merrill-Palmer Quarterly*.

NINA S. MOUNTS is a developmental psychologist with research interests in the areas of parent-child relationships, peer relationships, and adolescent development. Some of her studies have examined how parental management of adolescents' peer relationships is related to friend selection, friend influence, and adolescent adjustment. She has also investigated the effects of parenting style on adolescent adjustment. Dr. Mounts received her doctorate from the University of Wisconsin–Madison and is currently an assistant professor at Northern Illinois University.

ANGELA M. NEAL-BARNETT, PhD, is a nationally recognized expert in the area of anxiety disorders among African-American children. Dr. Neal-Barnett's work has focused on fears and social anxiety in African-American children as well as treatment issues within this population. She is the author of numerous journal articles and book chapters on African Americans and anxiety disorders. Currently, she is an associate professor at Kent State University.

DAVID A. NELSON received his doctorate from the Institute of Child Development, University of Minnesota, and is an assistant professor in the School of Family Life, Brigham Young University. His specialties include socialization processes and children's social development.

SUSANNE F. OLSEN is an associate professor of marriage, family, and human development at the School of Family Life, Brigham Young University. She received her doctorate from the University of Georgia in 1992. Her specialties include intergenerational transmission of parenting, childhood socialization practices, and family processes for children with disabilities.

ROBIN O'NEIL is currently a research analyst for Orange County Social Services Agency in Santa Ana, CA, and adjunct lecturer in the Department of Psychology and Social Behavior at the University of California, Irvine. She received her doctorate in social ecology at UC Irvine and held a postdoctoral position at UCLA, where she studied children with ADD. From 1993–1998, O'Neil was research associate and co-director of the Social Development Project at the University of California, Riverside. She has interests in family-work relationships as well as family-peer linkages.

ROSS D. PARKE is a distinguished professor of psychology and director of the Center for Family Studies at the University of California, Riverside. He is past president of the Division 7 (Developmental Psychology) of APA, and in 1995 received the G. Stanley Hall Award from this division. He is currently editor of the *Journal of Family Psychology* and past editor of *Developmental Psychology*. Parke is author of *Fatherhood* (1996) and co-author of *Throwaway Dads* (1999). His research interests include fathers' roles in infancy and early childhood, family–peer linkages, and the impact of economic stress on families of different ethnic backgrounds.

GREGORY S. PETTIT, PhD, is alumni professor of human development and family studies at Auburn University. He received his doctorate in child development from Indiana University. His research focuses on family and peer relationships and children's social behavior and competence. He currently serves as associate editor of *Developmental Psychology*.

CHRISTIN L. PORTER is an assistant professor of marriage, family, and human development at the School of Family Life, Brigham Young University. He received his doctorate from Purdue University in 1996. His specialties include infant development, socialization processes in early childhood, and attachment.

FRANÇOIS POULIN, PhD, a visiting researcher at the Oregon Social Learning Center since January 1996, also holds a courtesy appointment at the University of Oregon Psychology Department. His research interests include the contribution of peers in growth of adolescent problem behavior and the development of intervention strategies targeting the peer environment.

CLYDE C. ROBINSON is an associate professor of marriage, family, and human development at the School of Family Life, Brigham Young University. He received his doctorate from the University of North Carolina at Greensboro in 1982. His specialties include socialization process and children's social development and early childhood education curriculum.

RUTH SHARABANY is an associate professor in the Psychology Department, University of Haifa, Israel. She is the current chairperson of the department's doctoral program and past chair of the clinical program. She is on the editorial board of the *Journal of Personal Relations*, the *International Society for the Study of Personal Relationships*, and *Psychology*, the journal of the Israeli Psychological Association. Her doctorate is from Cornell University. Her current research is on social development, close relationships, and socialization.

NANI MEDICI SKAGGS, PhD, is a researcher at the Oregon Social Learning Center with a background in physiological and developmental psychology. She also holds a courtesy appointment at the University of Oregon, Department of Psychology. Her interest is in learning and substance abuse; she has conducted laboratory research on the effects of cocaine ingestion during pregnancy. She is interested in understanding the basic mechanisms of addiction and applying that to understanding the developmental process underlying the emergence of problem substance use in adolescents and young adults.

PATRICIA L. TOMICH is a doctoral candidate of experimental social psychology in the Department of Psychology at Kent State University. Her research interests include the study of attachment styles and attributional biases.

HOLLI TONYAN is a doctoral candidate whose research interests are based in the area of social development within the context of adult attachment relationships. Recent studies include examinations of peer and caregiver relationships among 2- to 3-year-old children in foster care, and of links between emotion dysregulation, adult relationships, and peer interactions in 4-year-old children.

ISBN 0-275-96506-6

90000>

EAN

9 780275 965068

HARDCOVER BAR CODE